JAMES JOYCE'S ULYSSES

JAMES JOYCE'S ULYSSES

Critical Essays

EDITED BY
CLIVE HART AND
DAVID HAYMAN

UNIVERSITY OF CALIFORNIA PRESS
BERKELEY · LOS ANGELES · LONDON

University of California Press
Berkeley and Los Angeles, California
University of California Press, Ltd.
London, England
Copyright © 1974, by
The Regents of the University of California
First Paperback Printing, 1977
ISBN: 0-520-03275-6
Library of Congress Catalog Card Number: 73-76108
Printed in the United States of America

4   5   6   7   8   9   0

The paper used in this publication meets the minimum
requirements of American National Standard for
Information Sciences—Permanence of Paper for
Printed Library Materials, ANSI Z39.48–1984. ∞

CONTENTS

PREFACE

It is more than fifty years since astonished readers first encountered the blue-and-white covered book of Eccles. If we are no longer astonished, this volume of essays by various hands on the unified diversity of *Ulysses'* eighteen chapters will show in how many ways we can still be intrigued and challenged by a book that endlessly exfoliates, becoming more like itself and its readers every year.

This collection grew out of the assumption that *Ulysses* could best be seen in its multivalence by critics focussing their particular lenses on the subdivisions established by Joyce himself. Treated as unities in the larger context of the novel and scrutinized for all a given critic can discover in them, the chapters should reveal hitherto unsuspected dimensions. The reader, like the original reader of *Ulysses*, jogged by the transitionless shift from critical stance to critical stance should achieve a new awareness of the novel, an awareness surpassing that of any one critic.

Hoping to set up reciprocal reflections, among the novel, the reader, and the critical visions, we approached writers with an abiding interest in Joyce and *Ulysses*, asking each to treat his chosen chapter as an analysable unit, to come upon it as though afresh. The task was difficult, given our writers' experience with this book, the need to detach themselves not only from the legacy of half a century of critical commentary, but, to a degree, even from their own critical prejudices. We were aware from the start that a complete divorce was out of the question, but we were also aware that ignorance of the literature or too slight a knowledge of the book would disable the writer in other, perhaps more serious, ways.

Not all those approached were willing or free to do the job, some were obliged to withdraw, but in the end eighteen critics agreed to engage pragmatically with the subject. Long before we asked them to participate, many of our authors had already become deeply engaged with the special delights and problems of their chosen chapters. Acceptances were uniformly enthusiastic, and the sense of involvement is everywhere evident. The result is a much more 'novelistic' reading than one might expect, a reading that stresses the relationship of form and action to character development and dramatic conflict, relating them only tangentially to matters of symbol, allegory, or theme. No two writers take precisely the same tack and yet, though no attempt was made to correlate positions, there is very little disagreement and almost no redundancy.

It is a tribute to Joyce's craftsmanship that, though the treatments supplement each other nicely and produce a remarkable number of fresh insights, this book is not the last word on *Ulysses*. We hope that it is a fresh word, a pointer that will lead readers back from a concern with particular patterns or themes or 'cruxes' toward an investigation of the novel's unity and the manifold mystery of its texture as a literary event. These rigorous but necessarily partial statements point up the continuing need to 'wipe your glosses with what you know' and the surprise and joy that any aspect of the book can generate, the challenges, the continuing vitality of *Ulysses*.

Certain assumptions were shared at least tacitly by all of our contributors. First, the parallel with the *Odyssey* is not only present but ironic. It is, however, not responsible for the form taken by the book, whatever its role in the shaping of episodes and actions and in the choice of styles. Second, the major themes: paternity, identity, adultery, responsibility, paralysis, exile, creation, guilt, are part of the fabric of the episodes and hence need not be treated as discrete entities. Third, the styles and structures and strategies of the chapters have never been fully explicated. Joyce's own version of what he was doing hardly enables us to understand the problem. Thus the schema for *Ulysses* is an aid but not an answer. Fourth, much of *Ulysses* that can be explained on the naturalistic level has been overlooked by critics intent on symbolic readings. Such readings are effective precisely because they constitute a counter-reality to the day of 16 June 1904. Fifth, there is always more to *Ulysses* than meets the eye of any one observer during any particular reading. Thus statements tend to be not so much tentative as partial, subject to meaningful supplementation or even reversal.

Much new data and many fresh readings have resulted from our tactics, but this book is less a revolutionary approach to *Ulysses* than a carefully modulated reassessment of Joyce's accomplishment.

C. H.
D. H.

ACKNOWLEDGMENTS

The following presses have kindly granted permission to quote from Joyce's works: Jonathan Cape, Ltd., and Columbia University Press, for quotations from *Chamber Music* (copyright 1918 by B. W. Huebsch, Inc., renewed 1946 by Nora Joyce); Jonathan Cape, Ltd., and The Viking Press, Inc., for quotations from *Dubliners*; Jonathan Cape, Ltd., and New Directions Publishing Corp., for quotations from *Stephen Hero*; Jonathan Cape, Ltd., and The Viking Press, Inc., for quotations from *A Portrait of the Artist as a Young Man*; The Bodley Head and Random House, Inc., for quotations from *Ulysses*; Faber and Faber, Ltd., and The Viking Press, Inc., for quotations from *Finnegans Wake* (copyright 1939 by James Joyce), *Letters of James Joyce*, Vol. I, ed. by Stuart Gilbert (copyright © 1957, 1966 by The Viking Press, Inc.; all rights reserved), and *The Critical Writings of James Joyce*, ed. by Ellsworth Mason and Richard Ellmann (copyright © 1959 by Harriet Weaver & F. Lionel Monro as administrators of the Estate of James Joyce).

We are also grateful to W. H. Freeman and Co., for permission to quote from Linus Pauling's *General Chemistry*; to Grove Press, Inc., and Calder and Boyars, Ltd., for permission to quote from Alain Robbe-Grillet's *For a New Novel*; to Grune and Stratton, Inc., for permission to quote from Laurance Sparks's *Self-Hypnosis*; and to Princeton University Press and Routledge and Kegan Paul, for permission to quote from Paul Valéry's *Masters and Friends,* translated by Martin Turnell.

Special thanks are due to Moira Anthony and Dronwen Wolton for their able assistance with the preparation of the typescript.

ABBREVIATIONS
AND CONVENTIONS

Quotations from *Ulysses* are taken from the 'New Edition' published by Random House, New York, 1961, to which page/line numbers in parentheses refer. A few textual corruptions have been silently emended. Page/line numbers for quotations from, and references to, Joyce's other works are preceded by the symbols listed below:

CM   *Chamber Music*, ed. William York Tindall, New York, 1954.

SH   *Stephen Hero*, ed. T. Spencer, J. J. Slocum, and H. Cahoon, New York, 1963.

D   *Dubliners: Text, Criticism, and Notes*, ed. R. Scholes and A. W. Litz, New York, 1969.

AP   *A Portrait of the Artist as a Young Man*, ed. C. G. Anderson, New York, 1964.

FW   *Finnegans Wake*, London, 1964. (Incorporating the 'Corrections of Misprints.')

CW   *The Critical Writings of James Joyce*, ed. E. Mason and R. Ellmann, London and New York, 1959.

The following further abbreviations are used in footnotes:

Budgen   Frank Budgen, *James Joyce and the Making of 'Ulysses' and other writings*, rev. ed., London, 1972.

Ellmann   Richard Ellmann, *James Joyce*, London and New York, 1959.

Gilbert   Stuart Gilbert, *James Joyce's Ulysses*, new ed., London, 1952.

JJQ   *James Joyce Quarterly* (Tulsa, Oklahoma, 1964–   ).

Letters,
I, II, III   *Letters of James Joyce*, 3 vols., ed. Stuart Gilbert and Richard Ellmann, London and New York, 1966. (The pagination of the revised version of Vol. I differs slightly from that of the first edition of 1957.)

Sultan   Stanley Sultan, *The Argument of Ulysses*, Columbus, Ohio, 1964.

*Surface
and Symbol*   R. M. Adams, *Surface and Symbol: the Consistency of James Joyce's Ulysses*, London and New York, 1962.

Thornton   Weldon Thornton, *Allusions in Ulysses: an Annotated List*, Chapel Hill, N.C., 1968.

Except in the essay on 'Calypso', quotations from the *Odyssey* are given in the translation by S. H. Butcher and A. Lang, *The Odyssey of Homer done into English prose*, London and New York, 1890. In 'Calypso' Mrs Glasheen has used another translation familiar to Joyce, that by Samuel Butler, *The Odyssey, Rendered into English Prose*, London, 1900, which suited her context better.

TELEMACHUS

Bernard Benstock

Even if we approach *Ulysses* armed with only *A Portrait of the Artist as a Young Man,* the 'Telemachus' portal seems to be deceptively simple. There are few discernible tigers at the gate and those have been prepared for by the developments in the last chapter of *A Portrait.* Various factors contribute to making this opening chapter of *Ulysses* easier than the preceding work: the time span of the chapter is tight and coherent; the dramatis personae are presented with either sufficient introduction or continuation and elaboration; all the characters are developed as fully rounded individuals, rather than as straw men set against the dominant personality of the protagonist; and a 'sweet reasonableness' of style pervades. The narrative voice is sufficiently detached from the scene and apparently has not been fortified with basic items from Stephen's vocabulary and diction. Unities of time, place, and action are adhered to, and if Stephen's pronounced system of aesthetics (AP, 215) is credited, 'Telemachus' appears to have attained the level of the dramatic:

> The dramatic form is reached when the vitality which has flowed and eddied round each person fills every person with such vital force that he or she assumes a proper and intangible esthetic life. The personality of the artist, at first a cry or a cadence or a mood and then a fluid and lambent narrative, finally refines itself out of existence, impersonalises itself, so to speak. The esthetic image in the dramatic form is life purified in and reprojected from the hu-

man imagination. The mystery of esthetic like that of material creation is accomplished. The artist, like the God of the creation, remains within or behind or beyond or above his handiwork, invisible, refined out of existence, indifferent, paring his fingernails.

Not that the narrative voice is without the distinctiveness that we have noticed in A *Portrait*: 'Stately, plump Buck Mulligan' as a descriptive phrase has a dignity-cum-pomposity befitting the Buck and might well be his own self-descriptiveness at work. In these opening moments, while Mulligan remains alone, narrative tone is maintained close to the character, and even after he has paged Stephen and called for him to ascend the stairs, the tone is sustained: 'Solemnly he came forward and mounted the round gunrest' (3.9). The full-throated sounds in *solemnly* and *mounted* and *round* are stately and plump. Mulligan's mock blessing of his surroundings is expansive enough to include 'the awaking mountains' (3.11), a pathetic fallacy that complements the Mulligan ego which views itself as responsible for that awakening. With the entrance of Stephen Dedalus the tone changes. Mulligan as priest pretends to be seeing the devil in Stephen's dishevelled appearance and he makes hurried signs of the cross while 'gurgling in his throat' (3.13), a phrase that moves away from Buck's self-description to a description of what Stephen is hearing. In viewing Stephen as 'displeased and sleepy' (3.14) the narrator has accepted Stephen's version of himself (his behaviour can be justified by his having been roused out of bed, having had his sleep disturbed), while the hissing and sputtering in the words themselves create the appropriate mood. Stephen's disposition is mirrored in his attitude as he looks 'coldly' (3.15) at Mulligan's 'shaking gurgling face' (3.15), the repetitions now firmly establishing the tone as Stephen's. But Buck refuses to relinquish the advantage that he began with: he took possession of the gunrest first, he summoned Stephen, he actively blessed while Stephen passively sulked; and the tone soon reverts to him. It is from his own point of view that he covers the bowl 'smartly' (3.19) and speaks 'sternly' (3.20) and cries out 'briskly' (3.30) and looks 'gravely' (3.32). The tensions of this colloquy between Mulligan and Dedalus are now established, the narrative voice constantly adding weights on each side of the scales throughout this part of the chapter.

The one intrusive element in these early exchanges is the word

'Chrysostomos' (3.28). Greek for 'golden mouthed', it appears immediately after the narrator has described Buck's 'even white teeth glistening here and there with gold points' (3.27). As a comment on Buck's dental work it is redundant; as a narrative comment it is out of place. The function of the word in the paragraph is as an editorial comment but not from the objective narrator: instead it is apparently within Stephen's mind and is the first instance of the use of the stream-of-consciousness technique in *Ulysses*. Although only a subliminal flash, it is the first of a series of one-word designations for Mulligan in Stephen's mind; the chapter ends with his labelling Buck as 'usurper' (23.24) and later that afternoon at the National Library Stephen's tag for him is 'Catamite' (204.22). ('Chrysostomos' and 'usurper' provide a frame for the 'Telemachus' chapter, from Stephen's point of view about Buck Mulligan.)

The Chrysostomos that Stephen has in mind is St John Chrysostomos, the Church father famed for his rhetorical skill (in Joyce's schema he designates theology as the 'art' of the chapter), but the irony lies in the metallic gold in Mulligan's affluent mouth; by contrast, Stephen's mouth is full of decayed teeth. Mulligan's epithet for him, 'Toothless Kinch' (22.28), reverberates in his mind several hours later when he contemplates his rotting teeth: 'My teeth are very bad. Why, I wonder? Feel. That one is going too. Shells. Ought I go to a dentist, I wonder, with that money? That one. Toothless Kinch, the superman. Why is that, I wonder, or does it mean something perhaps?' (50.34). That it is St John Chrysostomos, rather than the secular Chrysostomos, is proved when we learn Buck's full name, Malachi Roland St John Mulligan (417.40), and, since one Christian John suggests another, Buck is also playing the role of the Precursor, John the Baptist. Buck precedes Stephen (whose name is derived from the Greek for 'crown') up the tower, summons him forth, blesses him, and predicts that together they could bring forth marvellous changes: 'God, Kinch, if you and I could only work together we might do something for the island. Hellenise it' (7.12). He has usurped the role assigned by Stephen in *A Portrait* to Cranly, but just as Stephen now feels that Cranly has betrayed him, so he mistrusts Mulligan's 'mission', and his next inner comment follows Buck's suggestion that they work as a team. The arm that has been put around him provokes the thought, 'Cranly's arm. His arm' (7.15), and Stephen will later acknowledge that Mulligan

is the third in a line of 'whetstones' beginning with his brother:
'Where is your brother? Apothecaries' hall. My whetstone. Him,
then Cranly, Mulligan' (211.21). And to reemphasize Mulligan as
Precursor, Joyce names him Malachi, Hebrew for 'Herald'.

The stream of consciousness technique begins quietly and
modestly in 'Telemachus', with only the diary entries at the end of
A Portrait to prepare the way. Yet there the reader discerned
Stephen's thoughts as volitionally selected, carefully edited, literarily
patterned. Now the thoughts are presented as they occur to him and
in context, within the frame of the experience that stimulated the
thought. The first extended instance occurs when Mulligan raises
the issue of Stephen's dead mother and quotes Swinburne on the
sea as 'our great sweet mother' (5.9). Stephen's thinking is now
involved with recollection, rather than the thought-response earlier
to the gold points in Buck's teeth. The narrative voice moves extremely close to Stephen's mind when it informs us that 'pain, that
was not yet the pain of love, fretted his heart' (5.31)—how close
this is to Stephen's thought process can be seen from the previous
sentence, which noted that Stephen was gazing at 'the fraying edge
of his shiny black coat-sleeve' (5.30), *fraying* providing the sound
pattern for *fretted*. A lull in the conversation then allows him the
freedom to recall a dream he has had of his dead mother; the
literary allusion has given it shape. From the dream recollection of
the ghost, however, Stephen's mind continues the process: the immediate image of the sea ('The ring of bay and skyline held a
dull green mass of liquid', 5.38) evokes the image of 'green sluggish
bile' (5.40) which his mother vomited up during her illness. Thus
all occasions inform against Stephen.

From voluntary recall to involuntary association the technique
progresses, from a flash reaction to a developed series of responses.
Having a mirror held up to his face causes momentary introspection:
'As he and others see me. Who chose this face for me? This dogsbody to rid of vermin. It asks me too' (6.28). As in the previous
instance, Stephen's myopia (he has broken his glasses again)[1] causes
him to see first only the immediate environment, the frayed cuff,
before he looks beyond. The cracked mirror presents only its im-

[1] See 'Circe', 560.2, and David Hayman, *Ulysses: the Mechanics of Meaning*,
Englewood Cliffs, N.J., 1970, p. 19.

perfection at first, described by the close narrative voice as 'hair on end' (6.28), until Stephen glances behind the crack to his own reflection, upon which he then reflects. Buck had already addressed Stephen as 'poor dogsbody' (6.2), an epithet that Stephen accepts for himself, and his use of Robert Burns's 'as others see us' from 'To a Louse' makes that dogsbody vermin-ridden. The killing of lice in Stephen's clothing had occurred in the last chapter of A *Portrait*, while the image of a dead dog prepares the reader for the dog's body on the strand in 'Proteus'.

Joyce's rather sparing use of stream of consciousness in 'Telemachus' indicates that unlike such predecessors as Edouard Dujardin and Dorothy Richardson, Joyce viewed it as a technique and not as a genre or as a factor governing the overall style of his novel. In *Les Lauriers sont coupés* and *Pilgrimage*, inner monologue controls the dramatic material of the entire work: all experiences stem directly from Daniel Prince's mind as they are being perceived, or are narrated from Miriam Henderson's immediate point of view as they are happening. Joyce chose to play off a still dominant narrative voice, whose inflections could vary with character and situation, against the infrequent but significant instances in which the thoughts of his characters intruded. Nor was he unaware of the poetic possibilities of the technique (which for Dujardin, imbued with the principles of Symbolist poetry, was its greatest asset), and on occasion Stephen has his flights of poetic fancy, particularly in nostalgic recollection. Dujardin's slight novel begins with Prince's invocation of scene and mood (here in the Stuart Gilbert translation):

Evening light of sunset, air far away, deep skies; a ferment of crowds, noises, shadows; spaces stretched out endlessly; a listless evening.

And, from the chaos of appearance, in this time of all times, this place of places, amid the illusions of things self-begotten and self-conceived, one among others, one like the others yet distinct from them, the same and yet one more, from the infinity of possible lives, I arise. So time and place come to a point; it is the Now and Here, this hour that is striking, and all around me life; the time and place, an April evening, Paris; an evening of bright sunset, a monotone of sound, white houses, foliage of shadows; a soft evening growing softer, and the joy of being oneself, of going one's way; streets, crowds and, in air far aloft, outstretched, the sky; Paris is singing all around me, and languorously composes in the mist of apprehended shapes a setting for my thought.[2]

As depth psychology (the other end of the spectrum from poetry in the range of possibilities for the technique of interior monologue) this is totally unrevealing; its emphasis is in its poetic aura. Since Joyce was so forceful in crediting Dujardin as the source of his use of the technique (presumably having bought *Les Lauriers* from a railway kiosk in the early spring of 1903 in Paris), perhaps some vestige of Dujardin's poetic purpose can be seen in 'Proteus', the chapter in which Stephen's interior monologue dominates almost to the exclusion of narrated action, when Stephen recalls the Paris he had known:

> Paris rawly waking, crude sunlight on her lemon streets. Moist pith of farls of bread, the froggreen wormwood, her matin incense, court the air. Belluomo rises from the bed of his wife's lover's wife, the kerchiefed housewife is astir, a saucer of acetic acid in her hands. In Rodot's Yvonne and Madeleine newmake their tumbled beauties, shattering with gold teeth *chaussons* of pastry, their mouths yellowed with the *pus* of *flan breton*. Faces of Paris men go by, their wellpleased pleasers, curled conquistadores. (42.27)

If this is Dujardin, it is Dujardin run through the garden and into the troughs of Zolaism. Joyce's choice of naturalistic detail and his ironic determination transform the Paris 'impression' from poetic lyricism to dramatic irony. (Nor does one need the novel to create poetry out of a Paris sunscape; E. E. Cummings was doing so in verse in the early 1920s: 'Paris; this April sunset completely utters/ utters serenely silently a cathedral/ before whose upward lean magnificent face/ the streets turn young with rain'.)

If Dorothy Richardson, innocent of Dujardin and poetry, intended deep psychological insight in her *Pilgrimage*, the secret is safe with her in the grave. Her own claims are more modest: she seeks to present an inner life, and a decidedly feminine one, which permits only a single kind of truth, however limited by its individuality. The technique as it evolved permitted only the perspective of an involved narrator and her occasionally spontaneous—and therefore disconnected—thoughts:

[2] Edouard Dujardin, *We'll to the Woods No More*, tr. Stuart Gilbert, Norfolk, Conn., 1938, pp. 5–6.

Late at night, seated wide awake opposite her sleeping companion, rushing towards the German city, she began to think.

It was a fool's errand. . . . To undertake to go to the German school and teach . . . to be going there . . . with nothing to give. The moment would come when there would be a class sitting round a table . . . at the old school, full of scornful girls. . . . How was English taught? How did you begin? English grammar . . . in German? Her heart beat in her throat.[3]

In its basic honesty Dorothy Richardson's technique is convincing as Miriam's self-revelation, but it continually compounds the prosaic fallacy: it dies as literary art, long before Miriam ever comes to life as anything other than a subjective character constantly accusing herself and constantly apologizing for herself. By contrast, Stephen Dedalus emerges as a multiple enigmatic as he attempts to understand aspects of himself. In one of the few long sections of stream of consciousness in 'Telemachus', Stephen reacts internally to Haines's casually delivered remark that history is somehow to blame for the centuries of unfair treatment suffered by the Irish. Stephen's reaction is oblique but psychologically valid in terms of his defensiveness, his silence and cunning, his shoring up against the ruins:

The proud potent titles clanged over Stephen's memory the triumph of their brazen bells: *et unam sanctam catholicam et apostolicam ecclesiam:* the slow growth and change of rite and dogma like his own rare thoughts, a chemistry of stars. Symbol of the apostles in the mass for pope Marcellus, the voices blended, singing alone loud in affirmation: and behind their chant the vigilant angel of the church militant disarmed and menaced her heresiarchs. A horde of heresies fleeing with mitres awry: Photius and the brood of mockers of whom Mulligan was one, and Arius, warring his life long upon the consubstantiality of the Son with the Father, and Valentine, spurning Christ's terrene body, and the subtle African heresiarch Sabellius who held that the Father was Himself His own Son. Words Mulligan had spoken a moment since in mockery to the stranger. Idle mockery. The void awaits surely all them that weave the wind: a menace, a disarming and a worsting from those embattled angels of the church, Michael's host, who defend her ever in the hour of conflict with their lances and their shields.
Hear, hear. Prolonged applause. *Zut! Nom de Dieu!* (20.41)

[3] Dorothy Richardson, *Pilgrimage*, New York, 1967, p. 29.

Haines's silly piece of oversimplification ('It seems history is to blame', 20.40) produces in Stephen a complicated series of waves as response. His Irish Catholicism, which has withstood centuries of such English simplicity, suggests itself in its most complex forms, and his subtle mind is capable of expressing those complexities. Church history teaches the triumph over secular and disruptive forces that have for centuries challenged orthodoxy, but proud though Stephen may still be about such supremacy, he cannot help but ally himself with the brilliant heretics. Not the mockers, Mulligan's ancestors, but the intellectually obsessed sceptics. Glorying in the heritage of both the defenders of the faith and the sincere detractors, Stephen allows himself to be carried away with secret pride, until his sense of irony deflates his rhetorical overenthusiasm. Haines, not for a second privy to Stephen's thoughts, blithely continues his inane apology: 'Of course I'm a Britisher, Haines' voice said, and I feel as one' (21.19).

Even at this level of complexity the Joycean stream of consciousness in this first chapter allows for further variations. One of the most complex treatments in 'Telemachus' appears early in the chapter when Mulligan is still attempting to conciliate Stephen and enlist him in the campaign to Hellenize Ireland. The arm he has placed around Stephen has met with a cold response, as we gather from Stephen's mental comparison of Buck with the previous betrayer, and as we can also gather from Mulligan's blunt question: 'Why don't you trust me more? What have you up your nose against me?' (7.16). He is even willing to turn against Haines, if Stephen requests it, and suggests, 'I'll bring down Seymour and we'll give him a ragging worse than they gave Clive Kempthorpe' (7.18). What follows is once again recollection, almost a small vignette out of the past:

> Young shouts of moneyed voices in Clive Kempthorpe's rooms. Palefaces: they hold their ribs with laughter, one clasping another. O, I shall expire! Break the news to her gently, Aubrey! I shall die! With slit ribbons of his shirt whipping the air he hops and hobbles round the table, with trousers down at heels, chased by Ades of Magdalen with the tailor's shears. A scared calf's face gilded with marmalade. I don't want to be debagged! Don't you play the giddy ox with me!
>
> Shouts from the open window startling evening in the quadrangle. A deaf gardener, aproned, masked with Matthew Arnold's

face, pushes his mower on the sombre lawn watching narrowly the dancing motes of grasshalms.

To ourselves . . . new paganism . . . omphalos. (7.21)

As flashback this scene is deceptive: the locale is obviously Oxford, the mind is Stephen's. But Stephen has never been to Oxford and therefore cannot be dredging up this incident from first-hand memory. At best this is second hand, inspired by Mulligan's earlier assertion in attempting to flatter Stephen, 'You know, Dedalus, you have the real Oxford manner' (4.19). Stephen has either heard of the famous ragging from Mulligan and is basing his re-creation of it on such anecdotes or he is hypothesizing the events from his own imagination. The first possibility is the more likely, especially when we see the skill with which Stephen can 'imagine' the visit to the Gouldings (in 'Proteus') based on past experiences.

In the Oxford vignette Stephen has placed himself both *within* and *beyond* the action. The first paragraph transmits directly from the events within the room, the ragging itself, accompanied by the comments of the participants and the cries of the victim. The second paragraph locates the narrative voice at the window looking outward and viewing the calm, natural surroundings (the gardener deaf to the violent sounds from the room, concerned only with the grass). By contrast Stephen has made a definite choice: he opts for the serenity without rather than the 'shouts of moneyed voices' within to which he, too, would prefer to be deaf. The scene has played itself out in his imagination in response to Mulligan's offer to 'rag' Haines. Stephen is averse to violence, even the presumably good-natured hazing that Buck suggests. His conclusion, then, is to reject any such move against Haines, and he relents completely: 'Let him stay. . . . There's nothing wrong with him except at night' (7.34). His quarrel is in fact with Mulligan and not with Haines, as the key words that end the monologue indicate. Any cabal that involves him with Mulligan is dangerous: the exclusiveness of their own private Sinn Fein, the suspect sexual entente between them, the mystic rites that join them in conspiracy against everyone else, including Haines. By creating the Oxford scene in his mind Stephen makes his conscious choice: the enemy is Mulligan.

Inherent in the stream of consciousness technique is the looseness of free association; and, parallel with the emergence of the interior monologue, Joyce developed the symbolic structure of his novel. Animal imagery gives the 'Telemachus' chapter its organic unity and paves the way for the augmentation of one of the major motifs of *Ulysses*. Buck's nickname and the description of his face as 'equine in its length' (3.16) are some of the earliest indications, but the cluster of animal images comes into focus with the Mulligan comment recalled by Stephen, 'O, it's only Dedalus whose mother is beastly dead' (8.19). The dead beast forms one facet of the motif, as suggested in Stephen as dogsbody, and in its association with him and the drowned man expected to be washed ashore that day in 'Bullock harbour' (21.25), an avatar of Icarus who flew and fell. The Stephen who saw himself as the hawklike man in *A Portrait* had the previous night dreamed of flight ('Last night I flew. Easily flew. Men wondered', 217.32), recalling the dream at the steps of the Library soon after remembering his mythological self: 'Fabulous artificer, the hawklike man. You flew. Whereto? Newhaven-Dieppe, steerage passenger. Paris and back. Lapwing. Icarus. *Pater, ait.* Seabedabbled, fallen, weltering. Lapwing you are. Lapwing he' (210.35).

The dead animal is also echoed in the black panther of Haines's nightmare, the panther that he attempted to shoot in his dream. A. M. Klein's identification of the black panther with Christ[4] makes the crowned Stephen a Christian sacrificial animal as well, and the target of Mulligan's Ballad of Joking Jesus ('my father's a bird', 19.4), but even more specifically in the third of Mulligan's stanzas:

> Goodbye, now, goodbye. *Write down all I said*
> *And tell Tom, Dick and Harry I rose from the dead.*
> *What's bred in the bone cannot fail me to fly*
> *And Olivet's breezy . . . Goodbye, now, goodbye.*
>
> > (19.16)

And not only is the dead dog on the strand in 'Proteus' an aspect of Stephen as the dead god (the god/dog reversal), but so is the 'crowned' bather who emerges from the water at the end of 'Telemachus': his 'garland of grey hair' (22.5) is repeated toward the very end when we learn that he is a priest. Stephen's decision not to return to Mulligan's tower is directly linked with his appearance:

[4] A. M. Klein, 'The Black Panther, A Study in Technique', *Accent*, X (Summer 1950), 139–155.

The priest's grey nimbus in a niche where he dressed discreetly.
I will not sleep here tonight. Home also I cannot go. (23.19)

It is Haines, the Englishman who has nightmares and blames
history for Ireland's woes (causing Stephen to decide that 'History
. . . is a nightmare from which I am trying to awake', 34.22), who
is actually from Oxford, but Mulligan has insisted that Stephen
has the true Oxford manner, and in the Library Stephen acknowledges for himself the 'manner of Oxenford' (217.39). In anticipation
of Stephen as 'bullockbefriending bard' (36.2), bearing Mr Deasy's
letter on hoof-and-mouth disease, the Ox-cattle-cow-bull motif becomes the strongest of the animal images in 'Telemachus', centring
in particular in the imagined Oxford scene with Clive Kempthorpe:
Haines is called 'the oxy chap' (7.8); Clive has a scared calf's face
when he cries out, 'Don't you play the giddy ox with me!' (Clive
as sacrificial calf is but a parody of Stephen, the 'Bous Stephanoume-
nos, Bous Stephaneforos' of A Portrait.) The confrontation with the
milkwoman in the middle section of the chapter, however, reinforces the political reverberation of the motif, since she is imagined
by Stephen among her 'dewsilky cattle' personifying Ireland: 'Silk
of the kine and poor old woman, names given her in old times'
(14.2). The identification is especially irksome to Stephen because
the old milkwoman seems to ignore him and respect Mulligan and
Haines: 'A wandering crone, lowly form of an immortal serving her
conqueror and her gay betrayer' (14.3).

The Homeric parallels that become major corollaries in the
Bloom sections of the novel are still relatively dormant in 'Telemachus'. The essential purpose of the parallels here is to introduce the
Joycean Telemachus himself, the disinherited Stephen of 16 June
1904. Having once escaped Dublin in voluntary exile, Stephen has
been pulled back by the news of his mother near death, and now
maintains himself precariously in Sandycove, in a Martello tower,
perched on the edge of the Irish mainland, jutting into the sea. Even
Haines notices the resemblance to Elsinore: *That beetles o'er his
base into the sea,* isn't it?' (18.25). Stephen's position is made even
more precarious by his quarrel with Mulligan and discomfort with
Mulligan's guest, and he resolves to leave and not return. Although
Stephen has paid the rent for the tower, he surrenders the key to
Buck, having already resigned himself to being dispossessed: 'He
wants that key. It is mine, I paid the rent. Now I eat his salt bread.

Give him the key too. All. He will ask for it. That was in his eyes'
(20.19). Mulligan is fulfilling his Homeric role as Antinous, the
chief suitor, usurping Telemachus's kingdom and offending him by
making his futile impotence so obvious, except that in *Ulysses* the
Joycean Telemachus *insists* on being dispossessed.

That Stephen-Telemachus is in search of a father has become
a critical commonplace. Yet there is little evidence in the first chapter
of any such quest. Only the intimation of a *Hamlet* theory concocted
by Stephen 'proves by algebra that Hamlet's grandson is Shakespeare's grandfather and that he himself is the ghost of his own
father' (18.10). When Haines, who is somewhat dense and has been
conditioned by his reading in Celtic folklore to expect almost anything from the Irish, takes the 'he himself' literally to mean Stephen,
Mulligan laughs, 'O, shade of Kinch the elder! Japhet in search of
a father!' (18.17). By now three allusions are operative, father-son
relationships from the classics and the Bible: Odysseus-Telemachus,
King Hamlet-Prince Hamlet, Noah-Japhet. This heavy accumulation
of literary and biblical underpinning is mockingly undercut by a more
local allusion, Captain Frederick Marryat's novel of 1836, *Japhet in
Search of a Father*, where the heroic quest is reduced to a sentimental
papa-hunt. When Stephen proclaims to himself the determination
to cede the Martello tower to its squatter-usurper, he adds, 'Home
also I cannot go', a rejection of his consubstantial father, Simon
Dedalus. The psychological quest implied in 'Telemachus' must
therefore exist on a level concomitant with Hamlet-Telemachus-
Japhet, rather than on the mundane level depicted in the Marryat
novel.

Although Stephen has willingly and even contemptuously chosen
exile for himself, he nonetheless smarts under the pain of being disinherited. In the tower at Sandycove he lives precariously on the edge,
endangered, like Hamlet, by a variety of factors (Joyce's allusive
method often suggests more than it states, and the full speech from
which Haines extracted the descriptive phrase contains the full complex):

> *What if it tempt you toward the flood, my lord,*
> *Or to the dreadful summit of the cliff*
> *That beetles o'er his base into the sea,*
> *And there assume some other horrible form,*
> *Which might deprive your sovereignty of reason*

And draw you into madness? think of it.
The very place puts toys of desperation,
Without more motive, into every brain
That looks so many fathoms to the sea
And hears it roar beneath.

(I.iv.69ff)

Instead of the loyal Horatio warning against the danger at the outer edge of the ramparts, Mulligan plays the perverse tempter. He calls Stephen up to the summit of the tower, which his 'Omphalos' designation links with the maternal umbilical cord, and points Stephen toward the menacing sea: 'Isn't the sea what Algy calls it: a grey sweet mother? The snotgreen sea. The scrotumtightening sea. *Epi oinopa ponton.* . . . She is our great sweet mother. . . . Our mighty mother. . . . But a lovely mummer. . . . Kinch, the loveliest mummer of them all' (5.5–27). By hypnotic repetition Buck lures the sleepy, displeased Stephen toward the precipice, meanwhile introducing the recollection that Stephen had refused to kneel at his dying mother's bedside. The mother-sea as a china bowl of green mass of vomit freezes Stephen at the edge, even though the dream-ghost of the dead Mrs Dedalus reappears before him.

When Mulligan leaves the summit and descends, Stephen is alone for the first time, and the incipient danger grows progressively greater as he gazes out to sea with his myopic eyes. The narrative voice now moves very close to the protagonist, and at first the sea is calm ('Stephen stood at his post, gazing over the calm sea towards the headland', 9.5). But the 'toys of desperation' move in to take possession of him: 'Sea and headland now grew dim. Pulses were beating in his eyes, veiling their sight, and he felt the fever of his cheeks' (9.6). Only Mulligan's voice calling him to breakfast and distraining him from brooding breaks the spell, but his use of the word 'brooding' (9.19) sets off a new wave of recollections, the Yeats song that he had sung for her during her illness. Perhaps the lyrical power of the song has its soothing effect, for the immediate reaction is tranquil and distancing, and the sea is viewed in its benign beauty:

Woodshadows floated silently by through the morning peace from the stairhead seaward where he gazed. Inshore and farther out the mirror of water whitened, spurned by lightshod hurrying feet. White breast of the dim sea. The twining stresses, two by two. A hand plucking the harpstrings merging their twining chords. Wave-white wedded words shimmering on the dim tide. (9.25)

Nowhere else in 'Telemachus' have narrative voice and stream of consciousness been so indelibly blended. Here the psychological response to a given stimulus finds its most poetic wording within Stephen's imaginative mind.

The spell is shattered by a cloud effacing the sun, and bitter reality returns. The bay is now in shadow, a 'deeper green' (9.33), and Stephen regains the horrid image that had previously evoked his mother's spirit. The sea is once again a 'bowl of bitter waters' (9.33) and the same song that had soothed him in sunlight now brings forth harsh reality in shadow. Gradually his mind moves from painful thoughts to pleasant memories of the live Mrs Dedalus: 'Folded away in the memory of nature with her toys' (10.10); but soon 'memories beset his brooding brain' (10.10) and the recollections contain both pleasant and unpleasant aspects of that past life. Mulligan has left his shaving bowl behind on the parapet and its presence, even within Stephen's limited peripheral vision, plays its part in the materials of his memories. The 'bowl of bitter waters' had already intruded; now he remembers 'her glass of water from the kitchen tap when she had approached the sacrament' (10.11) and soon he is once again enveloped by the dream of her decayed body and cemetery odours and the words of the prayer for the dead. His violent reaction brings him close to the dreadful summit:

Ghoul! Chewer of corpses!
No mother. Let me be and let me live. (10.25)

When Mulligan for a second time calls him to breakfast, Stephen is saved from the spectre. How close he came to being deprived of reason can be seen from his reaction: 'Stephen, still trembling at his soul's cry, heard warm running sunlight and in the air behind him friendly words' (10.30). Mulligan, the gay betrayer and offender and usurper, is a welcome relief from the menace of tempting flood, and Stephen descends gladly into the interior of his tower, but not before he notices Buck's shaving bowl: 'The nickel shavingbowl shone, forgotten, on the parapet. Why should I bring it down? Or leave it there all day, forgotten friendship' (11.16). Now, in the new sunlight, it recalls the 'boat of incense' (11.21) that he had carried at Clongowes, and in this pleasanter but ambiguous light Stephen brings it down with him.

Stephen, interred in the 'gloomy livingroom' (11.24), appears to be the prisoner of the tower, and Mulligan, officiating in his ecclesiastical dressinggown, to be his jailor. Stephen is nevertheless the keeper of the keys and the bringer of light, and it is he who will find egress from captivity; his is the exile's volition, and although he resents being evicted by his tenants, he knows that he has the freedom of choice. The key that he surrenders to Buck is the key that can get Mulligan only *into* the cell.

In the gloom of that cell the conqueror Haines is without identity, not quite a person. He is only a vague shadow and a disembodied voice until the light comes into the room. Even later, out in the open air, Haines fades to become a voice that Stephen hears breaking into his thoughts ('Of course I'm a Britisher, Haines' voice said', 21.19). The narrative voice, here again immediate to Stephen, denies Haines his physical identity, as Stephen attempts to shut him out of his consciousness. But once Stephen is again out in the open air in the third part of the triptych, he is no freer than in the first part: there Mulligan had commanded the menacing seas about him and now Haines is in command. Although Stephen locks up the tower and pockets the key, he soon finds himself a drab figure between the two bright personages of Mulligan and Haines: 'In the bright silent instant Stephen saw his own image in cheap dusty mourning between their gay attires' (18.27). Haines chirps on about *Hamlet* (as an Englishman he can feel smugly comfortable with Shakespeare within the English literary tradition: 'It's a wonderful tale', he says of it). In a momentary aside Stephen recognizes the Conqueror for what he is: 'Eyes, pale as the sea the wind had freshened, paler, firm and prudent. The seas' ruler, he gazed southward over the bay' (18.32). As the spokesman for 'Rule, Britannia', Haines can assume that the sea is his domain, and just as Mulligan had threatened Stephen with the sea as mother (and by extension Mother Ireland), Haines can reduce him to insignificance by personifying the sea as Stephen's political master. Stephen accepts a cigarette from Haines's silver case, and hours later will recall the servitude he displayed before him: 'We feel in England. Penitent thief. Gone. I smoked his baccy. Green twinkling stone. An emerald set in the ring of the sea' (186.34)—the green stone in Haines's case echoes John of Gaunt's paean to England, which usurps Ireland's claim to be the Emerald Isle. And when the trio approach the sea, Mulligan plunges in for his swim, Haines sits and smokes, waiting to digest his breakfast, and hydrophobe Stephen, who has assiduously avoided a bath for eight months, walks away toward his schoolhouse in Dalkey.

It is the sea that dominates this Martello-Tower-and-Environs chapter of *Ulysses* as the symbol of Stephen's disinheritance. As a maternal image it unites with the ignorant and servile milkwoman to deny Stephen his Ireland (an Ireland that he must for his own sense of integrity reject, for which he cannot kneel in prayer at the hour of her dying). In its political guise it belongs to the insensitive Sassenach Haines, who can patronize the Celts and smile at Stephen as 'wild Irish' (23.11). Stephen's epigram of two masters, 'I am the servant of two masters . . . an English and an Italian' (20.27), linked Mother Church and Great Britain personified as Queen Victoria when Stephen mused, 'A crazy queen, old and jealous. Kneel down before me' (20.30). And Mulligan's mummer presented the menace of still another sea, the Icarian in which Icarus had drowned, while his fellow conspiracy with Stephen to Hellenize Ireland suggests the danger of Greek love. Stephen permits himself to return Mulligan's bowl, seeing himself then as the bearer of the bowl of incense at Clongowes Wood: 'I am another now and yet the same. A servant too. A server of a servant' (11.22). When he dismisses Mulligan as a catamite, Stephen indicates his suspicions, especially since the word is derived from Ganymede, the cupbearer. The sullen Stephen of the 'Telemachus' episode escapes the imprisoning tower, flees from Mulligan and Haines, abjures the sea, and makes his way back from the edge of the precipice eventually to Dublin, the process depicted in 'Proteus'. Spiritually disinherited, he temporarily returns to the source of his discontent, where a new aspect of the paralytic entrapment will become apparent during the course of the Odyssey proper and the Nostos, and a fresh necessity to fly by the nets, once he has killed the king and the priest in his mind (589.28).

Telemachus doesn't thank Nestor
[note for the Eumaeus Chapter,
BM Add. MS 49975]

NESTOR

E. L. Epstein

The 'art' of 'Nestor', according to Joyce's table of organization, is history.[1] In this chapter, Stephen teaches history, as well as literature and mathematics, to a class in a private school, and discusses a number of subjects, some of them historical, with the headmaster of the school while drawing his pay. History, indeed, is much discussed in 'Nestor', and many later passages in *Ulysses* depend for their interpretation upon an understanding of the chapter.

Joyce, despite his apparent coolness toward spectacular historical events, lived in dramatic times. *Ulysses* was begun during the First World War (the 'Nestor' chapter was written in Locarno in November to December 1917) and the first sections of *Finnegans Wake*, the Roderick O'Conor and the St Kevin sections in particular, were written during that period of the Irish Civil War when a Rory O'Connor could be sentenced to death by a Kevin O'Higgins.[2] The 'Nestor' chapter provides essential material for the understanding of

[1] Gilbert, p. 110.

[2] Ellmann, p. 801. Ellmann quotes Walton Litz as putting the composition of King Roderick O'Conor after 20 March 1923, and St Kevin in July–August 1923. However, the idea for the *Wake* occurred to Joyce in 1922, during his stay at Nice, 17 October–12 November (Ellmann, p. 728). After July 1922, the Irish began their civil war; on 12 August 1922, Arthur Griffith died and the fratricidal war began, reaching a climax with the ambush of Michael Collins (22 August 1922) and the execution of Rory O'Connor (captured 30 June, executed 8 December 1922).

Joyce's matured concept of the flow of time interpreted in general human terms.

In Book III of the *Odyssey*, Telemachus consults with Nestor. Telemachus initially feels his youth as a handicap in speaking to a man of Nestor's rank and experience, but eventually with Athene's aid he makes a good impression. The impression Nestor makes on Telemachus is more difficult to determine. Telemachus refers to him to his face in polite terms as 'great glory of the Achaeans', and 'one who above all men knows judgments and wisdom'. Later, in Book XVII, Telemachus declares that Nestor 'was diligent to entreat me lovingly, as a father might his son'. As Joyce notes, however, Telemachus never thanks Nestor for his information, which is, indeed, not very helpful to him. (In Book IV Telemachus praises Menelaus, whose information is more to the point than Nestor's.) After his return from Menelaus, in Book XV, Telemachus politely evades Nestor's hospitality, asking Nestor's son Peisistratus to leave him on the beach lest 'that old man keep me in his house in my despite, out of his eager kindness'. Telemachus does this despite his promise to Menelaus to 'salute in [Menelaus's] name Nestor, the shepherd of the people'. For some reason Telemachus has changed his mind and broken his promise to Menelaus. A cynical modern might suspect that Telemachus finds Nestor tedious.

Nestor appears as a Bronze-Age Polonius in many nineteenth- and twentieth-century burlesques, among them the works of Daumier, Offenbach, and John Erskine; the author of the latest of these burlesques of history, Richard Armour, says of Nestor that he 'knows almost everything except when to stop talking'.[3] Homer may not have meant this to be the reader's impression of Nestor: in Bronze-Age conditions, it must have been sufficiently rare for a valiant man to live to a great age; consider Achilles. However, Homer's treatment of Nestor is certainly ambiguous enough to allow the cynical interpretation some validity.

Joyce, as if to imitate Homer's famous objectivity, leaves his and Stephen's opinion of Mr Deasy in doubt for a while, as the chapter opens. There is a hint of disapproval in the adjective 'illdyed' applied to Mr Deasy's hair, but it is probably not to be taken as such; more

---

[3] Richard Armour, *The Classics Reclassified*, New York, 1960, p. 6.

likely, it is a metaphorical description of Mr Deasy's old blond brindle rather than a hint at cosmetic alteration. Other mildly pejorative epithets applied to him in the early pages refer to his fussy pace across the football field, his habit of talking without listening, and his 'old man's voice', all on page 29, but these are not Stephen's comments about him; these are auctorial assertions.

Soon, however, Stephen begins to move against Mr Deasy in his mind. He forces himself to 'answer something' to Mr Deasy's flat wisdom (30.17) and sardonically identifies the source of Mr Deasy's advice from Shakespeare to 'put but money in thy purse' as Iago. It is an open question whether Stephen's response, 'Good man, good man', to Mr Deasy's declaration that an Englishman's financial independence is his proudest boast (30.40) is completely ironic, or is, rather, a surprised acknowledgment of Mr Deasy's unexpected penetration into the English character. Stephen seems impressed enough by Mr Deasy's statement to recover it from his memory and develop it in his Shakespeare lecture in the library (204.30ff). Stephen refuses, however, to accept Mr Deasy's Orange view of history, conjures up mocking pictures in his mind of Mr Deasy's ancestor riding to Dublin on a patriotic mission (31.37), snubs his anti-Semitism (34.17) to no effect, and finally baffles him into slack-jawed wonder, at which Stephen asks himself, 'Is this old wisdom?' (34.20) Stephen sees there is nothing of wisdom to be gained from Mr Deasy, or from teaching: 'And here what will you learn more?' (35.14) The 'lions couchant' on the pillars of the gate, 'toothless terrors', are symbolic to him of Mr Deasy since they bring Mr Deasy into his mind ('Still I will help him in his fight', 36.1–2). Stephen's resentment at Mr Deasy's old foolishness is revealed in his reaction to Mr Deasy's chase after him with his silly joke: 'Running after me. No more letters, I hope' (36.5). Finally, Joyce leaves the reader with the vision of the old man coughing and laughing and dancing, with the sun casting rewards on his 'wise shoulders', a pathetic, golden figure of fun (36.21).

Later in the book the tone becomes much less respectful toward him; the reader and Stephen discover the reason for Mr Deasy's fierceness toward difficult wives in his own fierce wife, 'the bloodiest old tartar God ever made', who threw soup in a waiter's face (132. 23). Finally, Mr Deasy appears as the old clown he is in Stephen's hallucination in the 'Circe' chapter, coming in dead last on 'the favourite', a broken-winded dark yellow or orange nag,[4] Cock of the North, with gaiters like Deasy's, stumbling on the rocky road to Dublin. Mr Deasy firmly reiterates his ancestor's motto, 'Per vias rectas', which may contain a rectal pun,[5] but his wife-battered personality shows up in 'his nailscraped face' and the Irish stew that 'leopards all over him' in mockery of the sun's coins dancing on his shoulders; evidently his wife did not confine her violent food-throwing demonstrations to waiters (573.26). Since this hallucination is Stephen's and not the narrator's we must conclude that Stephen ends with contempt for Mr Deasy. Joyce is, in sum, less polite than Homer, who merely hints through Telemachus that Nestor's speech is at best time-consuming.

What does Stephen expect from Mr Deasy? What is Mr Deasy's place in the structure of Ulysses? He does not simply represent a past that Stephen despises. Stephen does not despise the past; he feels a strong need for knowledge about his city and his country. In the 'Aeolus' chapter, Stephen says gravely to himself, 'Dublin. I have much, much to learn' (144.30) and in the Scribbledehobble notebook, under 'Aeolus', Joyce has written 'Mark, learn, and inwardly digest', perhaps as a description of Stephen's attitude.[6] It was the past of Dublin that Stephen perceived in that metempsychotic moment in A Portrait when he saw the ghost of the Dublin of the Danes peer out through the vestments of the present (AP, 167, 168–169). No, Stephen by no means despises the past. Yet he does despise Mr Deasy. Something more than a guardian of the past must be symbolized by him.

We are all in the debt of Professor Adams, who, in Surface and Symbol, so carefully checks Mr Deasy's historical facts and finds them to be, as we suspected, a string of egregious blunders.[7] This inaccuracy, combined with the debilitation of old age, immediately

---

[4] An 'isabelle nag' is primarily of the colour called *jaune d'Isabeau*, named after a valiant woman who refused to change her underwear until a siege was lifted; the underclothes eventually came out *jaune d'Isabeau*.

[5] See A. M. Klein, 'A Shout in the Street', in *New Directions 13*, New York, 1951, p. 341.

[6] Thomas E. Connolly (ed.), *James Joyce's Scribbledehobble*, Evanston, Ill., 1961, p. 96. The ultimate source of this phrase is *The Book of Common Prayer*, Collect from the Second Sunday in Advent.

[7] *Surface and Symbol*, pp. 20–24.

suggests a parallel to Mr Deasy in another work of Joyce and provides a clue to his meaning.

The Four Old Men in *Finnegans Wake* combine triviality, inaccuracy, garrulity, and the deficiencies of age in a manner more exaggerated than appears in the figure of Mr Deasy, but otherwise quite similar. In addition to these characteristics, they share Mr Deasy's interest in money—he lectures Stephen on the benefits of thrift, even showing him his little machine for coins; he has money cowries on his desk, and at the end of the chapter the sun throws coins on his shoulders in reward for his defence of 'the light'. The traditional avarice of old age is also present in the Four Old Men. In Book I, chapter 6, of the *Wake*, their attempt to ring a harmonious chime for Ireland ends in a dreadful jangle of upper partials through which a savage wrangle over money can be clearly discerned —'pay name muy *feepence*, moy nay non Aequalllllll!' (*FW*, 141.4-7) The Leinster oldster mentions 'the mills' money he'll soon be leaving you' (*FW*, 140.28–29); at the end of the Tristan chapter, the Ulster oldster opens his love-song to Issy with the mention of £999,-000,000 in the Bank of Ulster (*FW*, 398.32–33), and the Leinster-man mentions as his greatest claim to her attention his ability to beg coppers for her (*FW*, 399.18–19). It would seem, therefore, that the Four Old Men represent a generalization of Garrett Deasy's characteristic traits of avarice and historical triviality. With this as a clue, it is possible to see what Deasy means in *Ulysses*. Like the Four Old Men, the Nestor-figure stands for history in its most trivial aspects, as an academic subject based upon the falsifying memory of the past, an avaricious gathering in of trifles, entirely missing the essence of the life of man through purblind probing into non-essentials.

Deasy, therefore, represents a general view of the life of man which is inadequate for Stephen and, one may say, for Joyce. With this in mind, the reader finds the sections of the Nestor chapter beginning to fall into place.

The chapter opens *in medias res* with Stephen inefficiently presiding over a history lesson. He does no more than test the students' memories, both in the history lesson and later in the recitation of *Lycidas*. History as a function of memory is subject to decay, as in the case of Mr Deasy; Stephen begins to ruminate about

other views of history. As Cochrane's memory fails him Stephen
realizes the futility of Nestor-history based on memory and advances
Blake's view of history to himself:

> Fabled by the daughters of memory. And yet it was in some way if
> not as memory fabled it. A phrase, then, of impatience, thud of
> Blake's wings of excess. (24.7)

Pyrrhus's famous statement is a historical fact, and yet to Stephen it
seems more than a product of memory; it bears a different significance. Blake preaches excess or impatience—he declares that the
road of excess leads to the palace of wisdom, that the tigers of wrath
are wiser than the horses of instruction, that it should be enough! or
too much! and that the cistern contains, the fountain overflows, all
in 'The Proverbs of Hell' and all counselling imprudence in the
search for wisdom. Stephen modifies Blake's 'excess' to 'impatience';
'impatience' or 'excess' leads to a true knowledge of the life of man.
Mr Deasy's God who deliberately manifests himself at the end of
history, and to whom the memory-facts of history lead inexorably,
is too stodgy for Stephen or for Blake. Blake says, in his notes on 'A
Vision of the Last Judgment',[8] that the last judgment is not fable
or allegory (with which Joyce seems to classify Nestor-history) but
rather 'Vision', a fact graspable only by the 'daughters of Inspiration', not by the 'daughters of Memory'. Pyrrhus's statement is to
Stephen such a visionary fact, its significance not entirely graspable
by the daughters of his Memory (even a 'glorious, pious and immortal memory', 31.23). God to Stephen, therefore, is not the final
term in a process each step of which is retroactively graspable by
memory, but rather a 'shout in the street', some totally unexpected
and unforeseeable manifestation. The phrase of Pyrrhus causes a
sudden moment of vision in Stephen, an image of the Last Day:

> I hear the ruin of all space, shattered glass and toppling masonry,
> and time one livid final flame. (24.9)

(The resemblance of this vision to a scene of the First World War,
a building hit by artillery bombardment, is probably due to the date
of composition.) This vision recurs at the climax of Ulysses, the
striking at the light in 'Circe', where it signalizes the end of the
world for Stephen as a son, and the beginning of his world as a

---

[8] See Thornton, pp. 27–28.

father (583.4).[9] Joyce provides a gloss for this section in his essay on
James Clarence Mangan:

> Poetry, even when apparently most fantastic, is always a revolt
> against artifice, a revolt, in a sense, against actuality. It speaks of
> what seems fantastic and unreal to those who have lost the simple
> intuitions which are the test of reality; and, as it is often found at
> war with its age, so it makes no account of history, which is fabled
> by the daughters of memory, but sets store by every time less than
> the pulsation of an artery, the time by which its intuitions start
> forth, holding it equal in its period and value to six thousand years.
> No doubt they are only men of letters who insist on the succession
> of the ages, and history or the denial of reality, for they are two
> names for one thing, may be said to be that which deceives the
> whole world. (CW, 81)

'History' is the 'art' of the 'Nestor' chapter; Joyce's concern is to
make it seem a false art, 'the denial of reality'. Mr Deasy represents
this false art; like the Four Old Men, he insists on the 'succession of
the ages' to the manifestation of God. (Later, John Eglinton, another
limited pedant, insists that 'the ages succeed one another', 206.30.)

Stephen muses on this vision of history and tries to reject it.
Less emotionally secure than Joyce at the time of the Mangan essay
(1902), he fears history as a nightmare from which he is trying to
awake (34.22–23); he finds it difficult to override the facts of
his life, and sees himself as a helpless victim of Mr Deasy's history,
moving like a football team to a goal:

> Again: a goal. I am among them, among their battling bodies in a
> medley, the joust of life. You mean that knockkneed mother's dar-
> ling who seems to be slightly crawsick? Jousts. Time shocked re-
> bounds, shock by shock. Jousts, slush and uproar of battles, the
> frozen deathspew of the slain, a shout of spear spikes baited with
> men's bloodied guts. (32.31)

The barely disguised World War I imagery—bayonets, grenade
blasts, mud, trench warfare—conceals a characteristic act of Stephen
and of Joyce, the hypostatization of a process into an image. Static
or detemporalized reality is the province of the artist: he catches the
timeless moments in the flow of time, and, like a geometer, traces
'the curve of an emotion' through these points, in a style that robs
the expression of these timeless moments of the natural kinesis of

---

[9] See E. L. Epstein, *The Ordeal of Stephen Dedalus*, Carbondale, Ill., 1971,
Chapter 3.

language.[10] The 'deathspew' of the slain is 'frozen'; the frenzied
activity of the battlefield is concentrated into a synaesthetic 'shout'
of spear points 'baited' with entrails. (The adjective 'frozen' modifying 'deathspew' and the adjectival clause modifying 'spear spikes'
both turn upon the frozen verbal activity of past participles, 'frozen'
and 'baited'.) The violence of the battle of life is frozen, as with an
instant snapshot, into an image, a fragment of reality shorter in
time than the pulsation of an artery, a vision of the artist. While
Stephen is demonstrating the true static or hypostatic way to apprehend human history to himself, the incarnation of feeble old
kinetic fable-history is fumbling with his writing-machine on an important question of cattle disease.

Mr Deasy's anti-Semitism is not merely a surface character-trait
of this silly old man; it is an integral part of the symbolic structure
of the chapter and of the book. Deasy represents history as memory,
as fact-by-fact plodding toward the inevitable manifestation of God,
with the earthly rewards of thrift or avarice thrown in as temporal
rewards for prudence. Vico declared that the Jews as the people of
God are not subject to the cycles of history,[11] and Stephen seems
to allude to this in his passage on page 34, remembering the Jewish
stockbrokers in Paris. Stephen sees in their 'full slow eyes' that they
are playing a part, that the mercantile disguise covers a timeless people. That is, among other reasons, why he counters Mr Deasy's
assertions with his own.

Other symbolic elements tie up with this aspect of the Jews as
the people of visionary history. Stephen feels a strong affinity between his 'darkness' and 'mummery' and that of the Jews and of the
Moors, to whom the Jews are linked ('Averroes and Moses Maimonides'):

Across the page the symbols moved in grave morrice, in the mummery of their letters, wearing quaint caps of squares and cubes. Give

[10] 'But for such as these [true artists] a portrait is not an identification paper
but rather the curve of an emotion'. (From the original essay 'A Portrait of
the Artist', written on 7 January 1904, reprinted many times, the latest being
in Chester Anderson's Viking Critical Edition of A Portrait, New York, 1968,
pp. 257–266.) The relation of this static view of the perception of the growth
of a personality, the perceiving of individual instants in a lifetime as points
on the curve of a graph, has obvious resemblances to Joyce's theories of epiphany
and the perception of beauty.

[11] Klein, 'A Shout in the Street', p. 345.

hands, traverse, bow to partner: so: imps of fancy of the Moors. Gone too from the world, Averroes and Moses Maimonides, dark men in mien and movement, flashing in their mocking mirrors the obscure soul of the world, a darkness shining in brightness which brightness could not comprehend. (28.11)

The 'brightness' is that of Stephen's enemies—Garrett Deasy, the pet of the sun, Buck Mulligan, 'tripping and sunny like the buck himself' (4.5), with his 'light untonsured hair, grained and hued like pale oak', his glistening gold and white teeth (3.17, 28), and his anti-Semitism, Haines with his pale eyes (18.32) and *his* anti-Semitism, Privates Carr and Compton with their 'blond copper polls' (430.35), John Eglinton's 'rufous' hair (184.31), Richard Best's brightness and lightness (186.2, 191.22)—all the major enemies of Stephen glow with light or are otherwise marked with paleness and lightness. Stephen himself feels a great affinity for darkness; he has felt it ever since the early chapters of A *Portrait*. Now it separates him from the sunny day-heroes with their day-philosophies:

. . . in my mind's darkness a sloth of the underworld, reluctant, shy of brightness, shifting her dragon scaly folds. (26.1)

'You find my words dark. Darkness is in our souls, do you not think?' (48.31) Stephen worries about the darkness that seems to be so congenial to him, but he cannot embrace the forces of the sun. Eventually, when driven to it, he smashes at the light (literally) when he feels that God is forcing him to submit, in the 'Circe' chapter.[12]

All of this is foreshadowed by Stephen's defence of the Jews, the 'dark' people in the 'Nestor' chapter; they bear the prophetic vision of history that the bright ones cannot comprehend; they bear the prophetic moment of illumination that the externally illumined ones lack. 'They sinned against the light' says Mr Deasy, and Stephen asks 'Who has not?' which puzzles the old son of light considerably (34.3, 17). That Ireland never 'let in' the Jews is historically inaccurate; but as evidence of the triviality of the Irish historical imagination, and a symbol of its grave limitations, it could hardly be better. Mr Deasy represents the Ireland into which he has not admitted fruitful visionary darkness, and is therefore a tedious empty old man, a Nestor of much less worth than the stately Homeric original.

[12] For an extended treatment of this theme, see Epstein, *The Ordeal of Stephen Dedalus*, passim.

Like Stephen, Joyce was an eager student of his time, of his place. In the *Scribbledehobble* notebook, under 'Nestor', Joyce asserts the importance of the understanding of geographical place and historical time for the understanding of human history—'nature develops the spirit in place, history in time'.[18] In his essay 'Ireland, Island of Saints and Sages', Joyce again asserts the importance of time and place, and the overriding importance of a visionary grasp of these dimensions:

> Nationality (if it really is not a convenient fiction like so many others to which the scalpels of present-day scientists have given the coup-de-grâce) must find its reason for being rooted in something that surpasses and transcends and informs changing things like blood and the human word. The mystic theologian who assumed the pseudonym of Dionysius, the pseudo-Areopagite, says somewhere, 'God has disposed the limits of nations according to his angels', and this probably is not a purely mystical concept. Do we not see that in Ireland the Danes, the Firbolgs, the Milesians from Spain, the Norman invaders, and the Anglo-Saxon settlers have united to form a new entity, one might say under the influence of a local deity? (CW, 166)

It is useless for Mr Deasy's historical imagination to examine Irish history; he will never see anything but alien invasions. It takes Joyce's mystic nationalism to touch the heart of the development of the Irish nature in space and time. In *Finnegans Wake* Joyce follows this programme in great detail—the Dane Earwicker, the Norman Persse O'Reilly, the Anglo-Saxon Mr Porter, and the primitive Irishman Tim Finnegan all merge into Ireland, 'under the influence of a local deity', Finn MacCool. The *Wake* is the proof that Deasy is wrong and Dedalus is right.

It is in the *Wake* that Nestor-history is finally revealed as futile. In Book III, chapter 3, the Four Old Men hold an inquiry on (literally) fallen Man. Fallen Yawn contains all the past of Ireland and of the world within him, but all the Four Old Men can do is to ask feeble questions to which they receive doubtful and evasive answers. Occasionally they get much more than they bargain for: at one point all the anguish of Irish history bursts out at them, raw and flaming, like a stream of lava accidentally released by careless miners (FW, 499–501). The screams of terror of Irish peasants run

[18] *Scribbledehobble*, p. 87.

down and slaughtered by Cromwell and the yeomen, the terrible sincerity of Swift's, Parnell's, Tristan's cries from beyond the grave that they were true and betrayed, the call to Patrick from the people of Ireland and the cry of his heart in response, all of these seem to be random noise to the four worthless old pedants, and they tune it out, anxious only to get the bare facts. When, despite them, the truth about fallen, sinning, tremendously creative Man begins to emerge, they sink back astonished with cries of 'Hoke!' (FW, 552) at the revelations of visionary history. Just so does Mr Deasy retreat baffled before history not of his making, before the darkness shining in brightness.

The theme of the 'Nestor' chapter, then, is the problem of the proper way to regard the stream of human history. Although Joyce resolves the question in Stephen's favour, this does not mean that Stephen is entirely triumphant in the chapter. At base, he is correct about history, but he suffers intensely from the emotional confusion brought on him by his own 'history', the circumstances of his mother's death and of his anomalous position in Dublin. Poor, lousy, with hollow teeth and borrowed clothes, his pretensions to be the lord of his land seem fantastic. Yet, this is the only sense in which Buck can be an 'usurper'—if Stephen, like Hamlet, is a disinherited prince.

His 'history' attacks him savagely and continuously. Stephen's heart is not in his teaching. He is abstracted and distant to the boys; he only asks them for the bare facts and for the bare words of Lycidas, while he spends his time in bitter musings. His riddle contains an indirect reference to his plight—the fox burying his grandmother under a hollybush 'probably . . . killed her', as Stephen later admits (559.12). Also, oddly enough, he is jealous of his pupils, rich, little middle-class boys, with a wealth of sexual experience that Stephen envies:

> Yes. They knew: had never learned nor ever been innocent. All. With envy he watched their faces. Edith, Ethel, Gerty, Lily. Their likes: their breaths, too, sweetened with tea and jam, their bracelets tittering in the struggle. (24.42)

Stephen's sexual problem is both physical and spiritual. As a mature twenty-two-year-old male he desires a sexual connexion which is more than that with a prostitute; spiritually, woman to him is still the girl on the beach in A Portrait, an angel from the courts of life, a symbol of the earthly reality to which he has sacrificed the security and peace of the priestly life. Now he has neither security nor the possession of femininity. In the 'Proteus' chapter this theme surfaces once more:

> She trusts me, her hand gentle, the longlashed eyes. . . . The virgin at Hodges Figgis' window on Monday. . . . Touch me. Soft eyes. Soft soft soft hand. I am lonely here. O, touch me soon, now. What is that word known to all men? I am quiet here alone. Sad too. Touch, touch me. (48.35)

In its most anguished form the question emerges again at a dreadful moment, when Stephen is confronting his mother's ghost with horror:

STEPHEN

> (*Eagerly.*) Tell me the word, mother, if you know now. The word known to all men. (581.5)

He is asking his mother from beyond the grave for aid in his sexual quest, in the quest for the symbol of the physical world which he is to transform into art.

Therefore, although the day is still young in the 'Nestor' chapter, Stephen's problems are well developed, and await only his drunkenness and further demoralization to attack him again.

In the 'Nestor' chapter Stephen exhibits the emotional pattern that has characterized him from the earliest chapters of the *Portrait*: deep down, at bottom, he has never changed—he clings to his vision of himself as the artist-god, destined from the first to transform his 'anmal matter' Ireland (*FW*, 294.F5), which 'belongs' to him, into imperishable art. His apprehension of his subject matter is aided by his idea of history as visionary and graspable only by timeless moments of vision. On the surface, however, he is dreadfully disturbed by the emotional currents set up by the attack of his environment on his vocation, and by his human confusions. Stephen's surface confusions of purpose provide a rich source of irony for Joyce, but, as in *A Portrait*, the essential elements of the artist's soul guide its development irresistibly through the dangerous currents of history seen as a stream of surface events. All of *Ulysses* is, in a sense, devoted to allowing Stephen's basic certitude to rise to the surface, through the roiled waves of emotion, to allow the artist to triumph, in however unclear a sense, over his unruly subject matter, to assert his command over visionary history and the flux of time.

PROTEUS

J. Mitchell Morse

Protein. . . . 1868. [. . . f. Gr. πρωτεῖος, primary, prime (so named as a fundamental material of the bodies of animals and plants). . . .] *Chem.* Any one of a class of organic compounds, consisting of carbon, hydrogen, oxygen, and nitrogen, with a little sulphur, in more or less unstable combination.

OED

Some colloids consist of well-defined molecules, with constant molecular weight and definite molecular shape, permitting them to be piled in a crystalline array. Crystalline proteins include egg albumin (MW 43000) and hemoglobin (MW 68000).
Linus Pauling, *General Chemistry, Third Edition*, W. H. Freeman and Company, San Francisco, 1970, p. 294. © 1970.

The proteiform graph itself is a polyhedron of scripture.
FW, 107.08.

The essential thing about the ever-living Proteus is that he doesn't *imitate* fire, water, animals, etc., but *is* and by turns *manifests himself as* fire, water, animals, etc. He is all nature, potent, latent; through changing forms he manifests the rolling heaving neverchanging everchanging all. His name signifies Primal or Elemental; before the Greeks knew him, the Egyptians had called him Ketos—Whale or Sea Monster; in Greece he became a partly human and on occasion intelligible sort of Leviathan or Behemoth. In Paradise the elect will doubtless digest and assimilate him along with those mere monsters; at that eternal beatific feast, not of reason but of illumination, all monstrous incomprehensible absurdities will be comprehended at last; meanwhile, Proteus is hard to approach and harder still to grasp; he can be forced to answer specific questions, but never volunteers a corollary; and he yields the truth only after having exhausted all appearances.

Being a reluctant prophet (like Jonah, who, having no conscious prophet motive, preferred to sleep, but whose ineluctable gift forced him to go to the bottom of the sea and into 'the belly of Hell'), Proteus comes ashore at high noon, the time of greatest light, not to prophesy but to sleep, surrounded by a protective herd of stinking seals: 'bitter is the scent they breathe of the deeps of the salt sea'.

Mortals therefore approach Proteus only when they are strongly constrained to. But the supremely great artists are as strongly constrained as Menelaus, who lay in ambush for Proteus among the seals although their 'deadly stench' distressed him sore, and as Jonah, who to his horror came to know something of the beast from the inside. Driven by conscious choice of will or by an unconscious tendency, the purposeful man, the artist, the prophet, is neither put off nor absorbed by the beast; he must on the one hand become identified with the beast, mere nature, the universe, the unconscious, the indifferent all-embracing all; but on the other hand he must recover from and renounce that identity; keeping his intelligible human purpose in view, he must assert and maintain his singularity, his separateness, his critical consciousness, his personal horror; for to be absolved is to lose one's consciousness of the experience, in effect to lose the experience itself; and in order to do his work he is constrained to experience the beast more fully than most men do.

I believe that in the 'Proteus' chapter of *Ulysses* Joyce shows us Stephen Dedalus beginning to realize that if he is ever to be a serious artist rather than an arty dilettante he must experience the beast. Hitherto he has been trying to avoid the experience.

Consider the differences between his twilight walk on Dollymount Strand in *A Portrait* and his noonday walk on Sandymount Strand in *Ulysses*. His interview with the director of Belvedere College is to his walk on Dollymount as his interview with Mr Deasy is to his walk on Sandymount. On Dollymount, having rejected the fading twilight promise of institutionalized spiritual power, he embraces without reserve the equally delusive promise of an equally conventional, mechanical, and perfunctory though uninstitutionalized spirituality—romanticism. He doesn't realize that its day too is sunken and that it too is moribund in moribund gestures. On Sandymount, having rejected Mr Deasy's confident noonday self-interest as a way of life, but having consented to join him in a disinterested effort to restore their country's vitality, he seeks in vain a way of expressing, with direction, force, and effect, his own form-less, undirected, and ineffectual vitality. He is beginning to want to know the deathless Proteus by holding fast to all his changing manifestations. He seeks fluid, wavelike forms that will express im-mutable laws through infinite mutations, the clarity of eternal forms through their opaque but ineluctable modalities. In this chapter he doesn't succeed. Stephen Dedalus never succeeds. Only Joyce will succeed. The chapter, written by Joyce and brilliantly successful, shows us Stephen still in the dark amid the blaze of Joyce's noon.

After his interview with the director of Belvedere in Chapter IV of A *Portrait*, Stephen looks toward 'Findlater's church'—a Presbyterian church, due ultimately to the Cromwellian invasion, built by a rich wholesale grocer—and sees a quartet of young men stepping along to the music of a concertina, very much like the quintet of young men in 'After the Race', one of whom, the son of a rich butcher, was being exploited by the others, and whose song, 'Cadet Roussel', was about a rich young man who drank and gambled his estate away and reduced himself to beggary. Both are manifestations of the beast Stephen is reluctant to grapple with. The next manifestation Stephen sees is a wooden Virgin Mary in a faded shrine in a slum; then by association he thinks of a dimwitted man digging in a slum vegetable garden; finally, in his own slum house, he finds his brothers and sisters sitting around a messy kitchen table, singing with their living voices a song that, as art, was dead when it was written but whose continued existence is a fact of life. Whatever these various figures may symbolize for Joyce, Stephen shrinks and withdraws from the disorder and misery they unsym-bolically represent, even while telling himself that he prefers them to the ordered progression of duties and rewards represented by the director. As yet he has no notion that such images can become the materials of his art; he is still the dilettante who ten years earlier had ignored the tram, the steaming horses, the driver, the conductor, and even the girl beside him, and by way of expressing his love had written her a poem that 'told only of the night and the balmy

breeze and the maiden lustre of the moon', without 'all those elements which he deemed common and insignificant' (*AP*, 70). He
still rejects such elements—the 'uncouth [*i.e.*, unknown] faces' and
ill-fitting clothes of the Christian Brothers, his contemporaries whose
parents are too poor to send them to Jesuit schools (*AP*, 71, 165–
166). His new poem for the girl is a villanelle (*AP*, 222–224). He
still dreams of himself as a poet writing in dainty mediaeval modes
and living the picturesque raffishness of Robert Louis Stevenson's
Villon or Rimbaud's 'Ma Bohème'. His romantic tendency is strongly
confirmed by a sudden vocation as he watches the birdlike girl on
Dollymount Strand. His incipient naturalistic tendency is overwhelmed by an adolescent mysticism personified in the girl: Dedalus's
chosen artistic medium, unlike Joyce's, is a stale poetic prose like
that of Oscar Wilde's fairy tales:

> Her bosom was as a bird's, soft and slight, slight and soft as the
> breast of some darkplumaged dove. But her long fair hair was
> girlish: and girlish, and touched with the wonder of mortal beauty,
> her face. (*AP*, 171)

But the sun is setting, the light of romanticism is dying, as at
the end of 'Araby' and as in *Finnegans Wake*, 472.22: 'Thy now
pallid light lucerne we ne'er may see again'.

In the next chapter of *A Portrait*, walking through mud flats
and industrial and commercial streets, Stephen escapes into fatuous
dreamy memories of literature: 'the girls and women of Gerhart
Hauptmann' with 'their pale sorrows . . . ; the cloistral silverveined
prose of Newman . . . ; the dark humour [*i.e.*, the dainty-sweet
melancholy] of Guido Cavalcanti . . . ; the spirit of Ibsen . . . , a
spirit of wayward boyish beauty; and . . . the dainty songs of the
Elizabethans', notably of Ben Jonson (*AP*, 176). By means of such
reveries he puts out of his mind 'his father's whistle, his mother's
mutterings, the screech of an unseen maniac' (*AP*, 175). He thinks
of his friend Cranly's common speech and of the shop signs in the
street as 'heaps of dead language' (*AP*, 178). He has far to go before he will realize that they are the stuff of life, the hard material
of art, and that his own preference for Wilde's easy inversions is a
preference for dead language. Throughout the rest of the novel he
continues to reject with scorn the living language all around him
and to compose his own thoughts in an ideal, idle, dead language

that is easy enough to handle because it enables us to ignore the hard
question, 'Just what do you mean, in terms of fact, action, consequences? Be specific'. His conclusion is a burst of meaningless adolescent rhetoric:

> Away! Away!
> The spell of arms and voices: the white arms of roads, their
> promise of close embraces. . . . Welcome, O life! (AP, 253)

This is meaningless because Stephen has never welcomed life or
willingly encountered the reality of experience or eaten its fried
bread with any gust or even with any detached interest. This is of
course understandable; nevertheless he is in fact running away from
the only life he knows and cutting himself off from the only experience he knows. At the end of *Ulysses*, having quit his job, declined the offer of another, broken with all his friends, relatives,
and acquaintances, and rejected Bloom and Bloomism, he is about
to run away again. For an artist of Joyce's temperament in Joyce's
early circumstances, flight and the sacrifices it entailed were undoubtedly necessary; but in order for Stephen Dedalus to grow into
James Joyce he had to turn and grasp the beast: the concrete, the
specific, the consequential, the dog that may very well bite. In
'Proteus' we see Stephen sorting out some of the elements that will
be involved in a complex decision whose complexity he is only beginning to suspect.

He reproaches himself briefly for having been distracted by lust
(40.19–26), but recovers quickly in the next line; he reproaches himself at length, repeatedly and without any effective reply, as a confessor might reproach a dull-witted sinner, for having distracted
himself with dreams of intellectual vanity (40.28–40, 41.28–39,
42.7–14), the whole business of dressing and acting the romantic
part of a famous writer or at least of a young man who has been
to Paris and speaks French. By association he recalls his Paris conversations with Kevin and Patrice Egan, and the futility, as it
seems to him, of political action (41.14–27, 42.37–44.10). He thinks
Kevin Egan wants to get him involved in the Fenian cause (43.9).
Whether Stephen thinks of Aristotle or Arthur Griffith or Hamlet
or the midwives or the drowned man or the dog, it is always in
relation to himself: '*Lui, c'est moi*' (41.38). He misses the point
of his own test of the solipsist theory (37.32): though the world

was there all the time without him, he has not learned to see it except as a reflexion of himself or an influence on himself or a threat to himself. He listens not to the waves of the sea but to the 'fourworded wavespeech' of his own sibilant urine (49.29), and sees in the writhing seaweeds only a metaphor, involving the pathetic fallacy, of his own discouragement (49.36). Joyce is the one who sees the lacefringe of the tide (46.13) without self-indulgence, as something to be observed and described. Joyce is the writer here; Stephen is still looking at himself in mirrors (40.29–30).

The big change in this chapter is one that has already taken place, outside the book: from the solipsistic Stephen, who cannot see others except in relation to himself, to the amused though sympathetic Joyce, who observes Stephen as well as his other creatures with a high degree of detachment. But the chapter is full of other changes, which are of its essence: not only the well-known ones of the dog and the waves, but many that are chiefly matters of literary play. Joyce, who consciously plays the role of godlike creator all through the book, is in this chapter a playful Proteus. We have it on the very best authority that Leviathan is not only strong but also comely, joyful, fearless, proud, and playful (Job, 41:12, 22, 33, 34; Psalms, 104:26). Let us recall Joyce's reply to Frank Budgen's amazed question about the word 'almosting': 'That's all in the Protean character of the thing. Everything changes: land, water, dog, time of day. Parts of speech change too. Adverb becomes verb'.[1] In the same way the mediaeval Italian pronoun *color* (*coloro*) (37.8) becomes the modern English noun *colour*.

The game begins immediately, with the opening phrase: 'Ineluctable modality of the visible' (37.1). A pleasant phrase: it calls the tongue, palate, and lips trippingly into play; it appeals to us oral types who care for words; its prancing syllables, which might be used as a test for the influence of alcohol, require of us a certain physical precision and seem to involve a corresponding intellectual precision: they seem to promise a precise meaning—but that is a delusion. What we have here, in fact, is a general formula, which can represent equally well Plato's doctrine that we are imprisoned in the phenomenal world, a world that affords us at best only crude approximations of reality, and Berkeley's commonsensical doctrine

[1] Budgen, p. 55.

that the external world is the real world, there being no evidence of
any underlying abstract substance, whether of formless matter or
of immaterial form. But the sentence that has begun so vaguely becomes precise in its concluding phrase, 'thought through my eyes'
(37.2). This is Aristotelian, and Berkeleyan. In its respect for the
concrete and particular it foreshadows the method of 'The Parable
of the Plums' in 'Aeolus', that parody of the *Dubliners* stories. That
is to say, it hints the future metamorphosis of Stephen Dedalus into
James Joyce.

But in this Protean chapter Stephen's thought changes direction
in the very next sentence, 'Signatures of all things I am here to
read, . . .' (37.2), which alludes to the mystic Jakob Boehme. The
phrase 'coloured signs' (a Berkeleyan idea, though I don't find it put
in just these words) leads Stephen to a phrase of Aristotle's, which
occurs in the first treatise of the *Parva naturalia*, 'On Sense and
Sensible Objects', 439a: 'It is the nature of light to exist in a limit-
less transparency; but it is obvious that there must be some limit to
the transparence in bodies, and it is plain from the facts that this
limit is actually colour; for colour either has its existence in the
limit or else is the limit itself'.[2] Stephen's word *adiaphane* (37.9),
which I suppose means 'opacity', doesn't occur in Aristotle's text.
A few lines later Stephen seems to change its meaning to 'darkness',
which in the Loeb Classics translation signifies Aristotle's *skotos*:
'You are walking through it howsomever. . . . I am getting on
nicely in the dark. . . . the black adiaphane' (37.12, 17, 29). The
formula 'A very short space of time through very short times of
space' (37.13), whose meaning, if any, escapes me, is a perfect
example of slippery, rippling, reciprocal form, looping back through
itself like the infinity sign. Counting his steps in time through
space, in space through time, Stephen thinks of the sequence
(*nacheinander*) and the simultaneity (*nebeneinander*) of events,
incidentally changing adverbs into nouns without bothering to
capitalize their initial letters (37.14, 17). Having discussed what I
think is the significance of these terms in 'Karl Gutzkow and the
Novel of Simultaneity',[3] I shall not repeat the discussion here. In

[2] Loeb Classical Library, *On the Soul, Parva Naturalia, and On Breath*, p.
225.

[3] *JJQ*, II, 1 (Fall 1964). See also Fritz Senn, 'Esthetic Theories', *JJQ*, II, 2
(Winter 1965), 134–136.

the next few lines Stephen's walking stick is changed into a sword, his legs into Buck Mulligan's legs, the word *nebeneinander* into solid ground under his feet, Blake's Los into Plato's demiurge, and Sandymount Strand into Blake's way out of time into eternity, where the *nebeneinander* and the *nacheinander* are one. The sea shells, having been used in ancient times as money, remind Stephen of Mr Deasy, whose table bears a mortar containing a collection of shells, including 'money' shells (29.36–40), and by an unstated transition he moves from the prints of horses on Mr Deasy's walls to some verses about Madeline the mare, whose trochees he calls iambs and by arbitrarily deleting a syllable turns into iambs (37.26–27). Immediately afterwards he indicates that he has been testing, or pretends to have been testing, the popular misconception that Berkeley's *esse est percipi* denies the reality of the external world—a misconception that changes Berkeley's actual doctrine beyond recognition (37.28–32). Stephen's later statement to the effect that Berkeley took the veil of the temple out of his shovel hat (48.25–27) indicates that he has finally succeeded in understanding Berkeley. That is a major change, whose importance can hardly be overestimated, even though Stephen is not helped by his new understanding. There is clear evidence in this chapter that Joyce knew at least *An Essay Towards a New Theory of Vision* (Dublin, 1709), *The Theory of Vision, or, Visual Language* (London, 1733), and the third and fourth dialogues of *Alciphron*; and it seems likely that he knew *A Treatise Concerning the Principles of Human Knowledge* and the vindicatory *Three Dialogues of Hylas and Philonous*. His view of the popular misconception is indicated by the episode 'Paddrock and bookley chat', (*FW*, 611.2–613.14), in which Berkeley might as well be speaking pidgin English for all Saint Patrick understands.[4] The conciliatory conclusion of the philosophical heliots (*sic*)—'Yet is no body present here which was not there before. Only is order othered. Nought is nulled. *Fuitfiat!*'—implying that Berkeley's *esse est percipi* merely reverses Locke's *nihil est in intellectu quod non antea fuerit in sensu*—is pure nonsense, implying that Joyce thought few people would ever understand Berkeley.

At the beginning of 'Proteus' Stephen seems to reject Berkeley; but the Berkeley he seems to reject is something the real Berkeley

---

[4] Cf. *Alciphron*, Fourth Dialogue, Section 11, second paragraph.

never was, a solipsist. If anyone inclines toward solipsism it is Stephen, who for a moment, thinking of himself as Hamlet, pretends that the tidal flat (44.10–11) is a cliff beetling over the sea (37.16)—thus not only changing the altitude but also changing Sandymount to Elsinore.

Thus, in less than a page, Protean Stephen, not knowing who he is or where he is going, has identified himself with Aristotle, Boehme, Hamlet, Blake, perhaps Lessing, perhaps Gutzkow, and an upside-down Berkeley; the language of his thought changes momentarily into Greek, Italian, and German, and he wilfully changes parts of speech and patterns of rhythm into other parts and other patterns. The whole chapter is a chapter of such changes.

The sentence, 'Bald he was and a millionaire, *maestro di color che sanno*' (37.8), obviously refers to Aristotle. But it doesn't correspond to any of the ancient testimony we have. Diogenes Laertius, not a witness himself but a compiler of stories, reports conflicts and contradictions wherever he finds them; he lets stand uncontradicted the story that Aristotle 'dressed his hair carefully', and with one exception every bust or larger statue of Aristotle that I have seen shows him with a full head of hair. The purported will that Diogenes Laertius records, though certainly that of a well-to-do-man, is hardly that of a millionaire. Ancient testimony, written or sculpted, is of course dubious: the same story is told of different men, conflicting stories are told of the same man, different versions of the same story differ in important details, etc.; but in this case I have found no written testimony at all that Stephen could have had in mind. I therefore suggest that the sentence 'Bald he was and a millionaire' refers not to the master of those who know but to another philosopher. The phrase 'coloured signs' (37.4) suggests Berkeley, who said that the eye doesn't see—the retina doesn't receive—objects themselves, but only the light reflected from or emanating from them, 'in all its modes and colours', so that to say we see an object is to confuse the sign with the thing signified;[5] and since Berkeley in *Alciphron*, Third Dialogue, Section 13, objects to Shaftesbury's ethics on the same grounds as to Aristotle's, and since moreover Shaftesbury was bald and a millionaire, I think we have here a rapid fluid Protean change involving all three philosophers. We

[5] *The Theory of Vision, or, Visual Language*, Sections 39–45; cf. *An Essay Towards a New Theory of Vision*, Sections 51, 65–66.

should not overlook the possibility that Stephen was thinking meta-phorically, to the effect that Aristotle, though bald in style, was rich in thought; but neither of these possibilities precludes the other.

The plural *Frauenzimmer* (37.35), which originally meant 'ladies', now means 'wenches', 'bitches', 'drabs', 'sluts', 'slovens'; none of the three German dictionaries I have consulted says it means or ever has meant 'midwives'; as for the 'shelving shore' (37.35), Skeat in his *Etymological Dictionary* says, 'We speak of a *shelving* shore, *i.e.* a shallow or sloping shore, where the water's depth increases gradually'. Thus the midwives, 'coming down to our mighty mother' (37.37), are presumably returning the 'misbirth' (37.42) to the mother, reversing their function.

The earthly Adam, 'made, not begotten' (38.10), according to the Cabbala was made by the uncreated heavenly Adam Kadmon, himself a metamorphosis of God. Stephen blends them into one, identifies himself with them, and changes the act of copulation that produced him into a manifestation of the *lex eterna*, the divine substance in which Father and Son are consubstantial. Since he thinks of himself as the unique Saviour, he cannot bring himself to think the word 'contransubstantiality', which involves the heresy that the Father and the Holy Ghost also are changed into bread and wine (38.10–21), a heresy that Arius combatted by embracing the heresy that they are not consubstantial. In finding the word un-thinkable, Stephen becomes identified with Arius; at the same time, he insists on the consubstantiality of all men.

There are many transubstantiations in this chapter. Stephen's Uncle Richie Goulding—a pretender, who calls the firm of Collis and Ward, for which he works, 'Goulding, Collis and Ward' (88.23) —is transubstantiated into one of Gilbert and Sullivan's gondoliers, who both turn out after all to be what they seem; and Stephen himself imagines that if he visits Uncle Richie he will be taken for a bill collector (38.39, 39.1). The phrase 'coign of vantage' (38.39) suggests that Uncle Richie's house is Macbeth's castle, and the mem-bers of his family birds. This too seems farfetched to me: it im-plies that Uncle Richie is Macbeth, and it violates the law of parsi-mony by overlooking the simpler explanation that Stephen is full of such tags. But Joyce's effects were often deliberately farfetched. And also facile, as in Uncle Richie's humorous transmogrification of a nondescript or perhaps nonexistent chair into 'our Chippendale

chair' (39.22), the transmogrification of Uncle Richie himself into
Verdi's Ferrando (a minor character in an opera even sillier than
The Gondoliers about changelings and compound errors of identity),
and Stephen's simultaneous changing of Ferrando's *'All'erta!'* into
a warning to himself that Uncle Richie ('We have nothing in the
house but backache pills') may try to touch him for a quid
(39.25–27). So that we can be even more farfetched and say that
Stephen's conclusion, 'Beauty is not there' (39.35), being a rationali-
zation of his real reason for not going there, is also a Protean change.
In the same way we can say that Stephen's warning to himself,
'By the way go easy with that money like a good young imbecile'
(38.26), is first hinted in 'Go easy. Bald he was and a millionaire'
(37.6), Stephen both identifying himself and contrasting himself
with Shaftesbury.

Wielding Ockham's razor as judiciously as our nature allows,
we cut our way through the thickets of fantasticality as well as we
can. Each of us, as a good Aristotelian, has doubtless compiled a
catalogue more or less raisonné of more or less plausible transformations. Almost every line yields at least one; let us make a selection
that will point in one direction. Such plausibility as most of the
following transformations have will depend of course on the fact
that they take place in Stephen's mind, not in the outer world.

Transformations of Stephen

In the following pages Stephen becomes, among other things, a
basilisk: a monster hatched from a rooster's egg by a snake (40.4).
The basilisk seems to be a conglomeration of John Calvin (who
even as a child was of such a nature that his schoolmates nicknamed
him 'the accusative case', and whose name means 'bald') with a
reformer of more humane temperament, William of Ockham—to
say nothing of Elisha, Joachim, Swift, and the swimming priest of
'Telemachus' (22.4–5, 22.7–9, 23.19, 40.2).

In yearning toward a girl he has refrained from picking up
(and whom I shall discuss at greater length in the section on other
transformations), Stephen identifies with her to such an extent
that we can only attribute to both of them the imagined words
'Touch me. . . . O, touch me soon, now. . . . Touch, touch me'
(49.4). The repetition of one word four times in three lines is

surely not accidental or without purpose or significance. Aristotle on touch has this: 'The first essential factor of sensation, which we all share, is a sense of touch. . . . The medium of tangible things is the flesh. . . . Without a sense of touch it is impossible to have any other sensation. . . . It is obvious, then, that without this, their only sensation, animals must die; for it is impossible for anything but an animal to possess this, nor need an animal possess any sense but this. . . . The faculty of touch then consists of earth'.[6] Thus, by not permitting himself to pick up the girl, Stephen is both losing and saving himself. On the one hand, like Mr Duffy of 'A Painful Case', he is cutting himself off from the flesh, the earth, the beast, the merely instinctual, the presocial precritical precortical id, with which an artist must consciously have contact if he is to have any understanding of life; on the other hand, he is avoiding the danger of being committed to it and absorbed into it—as I shall indicate when we come to the girl in the next section of this catalogue.

Stephen's hat becomes a leaf; his eyelashes become peacock feathers, through which he watches the sun approaching or crossing the meridian (49.11–12); he identifies with Mallarmé's faun, a figure of recurrent deluded ungratified desire, an artist despite himself, who creates nymphs out of the air, changes swans into naiads, embraces Venus, etc., all by blowing an arid rain of sounds through his pipes, and who doesn't know whether he is awake or dreaming or an animal or a poet or a fool: it seems fairly clear that Stephen identifies with Mallarmé to the extent that Mallarmé identifies with the faun. And perhaps it is worth pointing out that in one of the frivolous quatrains of 'Offrandes à Divers du Faune' Mallarmé promised to popularize his friend Edouard Dujardin.[7] Stephen's word 'tawny' (49.15), if it is not, as I suspect it is, part of another quotation, may have been suggested by the faun's 'tawny hour'—'l'heure fauve'.

In the next paragraph Stephen calls Buck Mulligan's castoff shoes, which he is wearing, 'a buck's castoffs' (49.17), a phrase that inevitably suggests antlers and cuckoldry and implies that Mulligan has betrayed or is betraying or will betray him with Haines. The references to Esther Osvalt (49.21) and to Wilde (49.23), as Herbert Howarth has pointed out, suggest that their relationship is homo-

---

[6] *On the Soul, Parva Naturalia, and On Breath*, pp. 75, 135, 199, 201, 221.
[7] *Oeuvres Complètes*, Pléiade, p. 112.

sexual, involving the transformation of at least one of them into a quasi-woman.[8]

Stephen becomes the son of the drowned man with whom he has refused to identify (50.4, 19); at the same time he becomes Ferdinand, son of Alonso in *The Tempest*; finally, by identifying with 'all dead', including all humanity, living and dead, male and female, he identifies with the drowned man after all, entering the whirlpool (50.11–18). He is nevertheless consciously aware of Proteus in the form of a shoal of minnows gorged on the dead man's genitals (50.11–12). As the chapter ends, he becomes in rapid succession all that he has been or may be or would be or would not be: Christ (50.23), Lucifer (50.24–25), Hamlet again (50.25), Buck Mulligan (50.25), the cocklepickers and Adam and Eve (50.26–27), Berkeley and the turning world itself—'Evening will find itself in me, without me' (50.29)—a gentleman poet flattering a dull-witted queen, whether Victoria or Kathleen ni Houlihan matters not at all (50.32), a scurrilous yellow journalist (50.32), a toothless superman (50.36–37), and a hermaphrodite looking back over his/her shoulder like Lot's wife (51.4).

Thus he begins to achieve the extremely difficult self-resolving contradiction of genius: to identify with the beast but retain his critical consciousness: to reach an understanding like that of Jonah, who experienced the beast from the inside but was not absorbed by it. Jonah lived to prophesy the God-given victories of the wicked King Jeroboam (II Kings 14:25), and was cited as one whose experience foreshadowed the death and resurrection of Christ (Matthew, 12:39–41, 16:4; Luke, 11:29–30).

Other Transformations

Uncle Richie's little daughter Crissie, as 'Papa's little bedpal. Lump of love' (39.14), becomes his wife or mistress. I'd hesitate to say so but for the identity of ALP and Issy in the id of HCE; but Stephen makes the transformation or equivalence quite consciously; it is as unmistakably clear as his own nastiness.

[8] 'The Joycean Comedy: Wilde, Jonson, and Others', *A James Joyce Miscellany, Second Series*, ed. Marvin Magalaner, Carbondale, Ill., 1959, pp. 179–194. Cf. Marie Delcourt, *Hermaphrodite: Mythes et rites de la Bisexualité dans l'Antiquité classique*, Paris, 1958– , especially the rere regardant illustrations on pp. 90, 92.

Temple, Mulligan, and Foxy Campbell (the heresy sniffer in *A Portrait*) become Houyhnhnms, presumably to Stephen's Yahoo (39.41–42). These roles foreshadow those of Shaun and Shem in *Finnegans Wake*.

A porter bottle on Sandymount becomes a sentinel on Pharos (41.6).

Kevin Egan, the wild goose, becomes the Holy Ghost; his son, Patrice, becomes both Christ and a bunny (41.16–19).

The boulders on the beach become mammoth skulls (42.22–23), shells of dead Behemoths.

The smells of bread and absinthe become the 'matin incense' of Paris (42.28–29), suggesting not only the French word for 'morning' but also a morning religious service in which the bread and absinthe are the body and blood of Christ. But the kerchiefed housewife's acetic acid (42.31), whatever she may do with it, has the power to turn wine into vinegar.

I'm afraid the 'Paris men' are Parises, 'wellpleased pleasers' of whorish Helens. They are also Italians (42.28) and Spaniards (42.34).

Two Helens, breakfasting, 'newmake their tumbled beauties' (42.30–31); since the verb 'newmake', used in connexion with eating, suggests the grave mediaeval noun 'refection', these whores are, for the nonce, nuns, a change that recalls to us a scurrilous *double-entendre* Hamlet addressed to Ophelia. Moreover, the name of one of them, Madeleine, is a form of Magdalen, the name of a well-known whore who became an ascetic; the other's, Yvonne, is a feminine form of John, and I can make little of it, except that both girls have gold teeth like Buck Mulligan, whom Stephen has called John Chrysostomos. In the ancient world eloquent people were not only called 'golden mouth' but were also said to have honey flowing from their mouths, and here are our two whores with mouths full of custard that has turned to pus.

The phrase 'Noon slumbers' (42.35) recalls old Proteus himself.

The old terrorist Kevin Egan's cigarette tobacco becomes gunpowder, the match with which he lights it a fuse (43.22).

The waitress evidently thinks Stephen is a Dutchman, but Kevin Egan thinks her question 'Hollandais?' refers to Dutch cheese, and ungrammatically says, '*Non fromage*', meaning '*Pas de fromage*' (42.40). This is conjecture on my part; it's the only way

I can make sense of Kevin Egan's elliptical speech, unless indeed the waitress's question did mean 'Dutch cheese?' and Kevin, misunderstanding her, said, 'No, we are Irish', and then corrected himself and said, '*Non fromage*'. Either way, things get confused and changed around. Kevin Egan's misuse of the word 'postprandial' (43.2) changes the lunch, if only verbally, into a dinner, and the time from midday to evening. He identifies Stephen with Simon Dedalus (43.10). Etymologically, his fustian shirt is Egyptian; its colour, sanguine, is French by way of Latin, and signifies bloody, bloodthirsty, and hopeful; and its tassels, Latin again, are Spanish. Verbally, he turns Queen Victoria into an ogress; and his conversation is afflicted with a circumstantiality that changes the subject from sentence to sentence (43.10–21).

The hat of this fierce Irish nationalist, who believes in God and is presumably a Catholic (41.23–24), is that of an Ulster Protestant nightrider (43.23–24). The walls of his lonely room are covered with a strange damask: 'damascened with flyblown faces of the gone' (43.38). It is doubly strange in that Stephen uses the word 'damascened', which has to do with colouring and inlaying steel, for 'damasked'. Stephen changes Kevin's limited daily round into a truncated version of the stations of the cross (43.35–36). Kevin Egan becomes a Jew in Babylon; Stephen becomes the author of Psalm 137 (44.9). Haines becomes a panther (*i.e.*, a Christ figure) as well as a sahib or magus; Mulligan becomes a hunting dog as well as an informer and a guide (44.24). A silted-up boat becomes a coach stuck in sand (44.34); the sand and stones become dead language (44.35, 38–39). Berkeley says the conclusion of his theory of vision is 'that *Vision is the Language of the Author of Nature*',[9] and that although 'The proper, immediate object of vision is light, in all its modes and variations' (Section 44), nevertheless God speaks to us through all visible things. He shows them to us through 'light and colours, with their several shades and degrees; all which, being infinitely diversified and combined, do form a language wonderfully adapted to suggest and exhibit to us the distance, figures, situations, dimensions, and various qualities of tangible objects— . . . just as words suggest the things signified by them'. His spokesman, Euphranor, freely admits Alciphron's ob-

---

[9] *The Theory of Vision*, Section 38.

jection, 'I see, therefore, in strict philosophical truth, that rock only in the same sense that I may be said to hear it, when the word *rock* is pronounced'.[10] Stephen, however, throughout this chapter, tends to confuse words with things. He makes no use of his intellectual perception that he shouldn't. The whole technique of the chapter is the pretence that things change when words change— though some things do in fact change. Thus the misbirth becomes Moses (45.7–8) only verbally, but a sandbank dwindles in fact (46.7).

The dog becomes many animals, among them a leopard (47.2) and a panther (47.3); and since these are well-known symbols of Christ, here we have another opportunity to be wonderfully far-fetched.

The Gypsy patois of the cocklepickers becomes language 'no whit worse than' the monkish Latin of Aquinas, whose hymn *Pange lingua gloriosi corporis mysterium* Stephen liked because it was 'intricate and soothing' (AP, 210), and also perhaps because it celebrated the mystery of transubstantiation. (Cf. AP, 169.1–10, 221.14– 16.) The words of Aquinas and the cocklepickers alike are nuggets, beads, pebbles, calculi, small, light, manageable (47.29–31), unlike the clumsy language of dead giants or a loutish God (44.38–45.2).[11] This lesson in philology foreshadows the evolution of language in 'Oxen of the Sun'; but since the boulders as language suggest the way we take the sign for the thing signified, I believe that Stephen's Sir Lout is either every man who makes such a naive mistake, or God failing to live up to Berkeley's conception of him, or both.

But though Stephen doesn't accept Berkeley's theological interpretation of the phenomena of vision, he continues to try to understand Berkeley's natural explanation of them; and at least with regard to the perception of distance, he succeeds. The following passage four pages later is explicitly Berkeleyan:

> The good bishop of Cloyne took the veil of the temple out of his shovel hat: veil of space with coloured emblems hatched on its field. Hold hard. Coloured on a flat: yes, that's right. Flat I see, then think distance, near, far, flat I see, east, back. Ah, see now. Falls back suddenly, frozen in stereoscope. Click does the trick. (48.26)

[10] *Alciphron*, Fourth Dialogue, Sections 10 and 11.
[11] Cf. Budgen, pp. 52–53.

Berkeley says distance is a relationship among objects, not itself an object that reflects light; that therefore we don't see it, but learn from experience—experience of 'the connexion between the proper objects of sight and the things signified by them'—to estimate it and adjust our ideas accordingly: e.g., that a castle on a hill far away, which seems to our eyes to be two inches tall, doesn't change its size with our distance from it, but that God makes an apparent change by way of informing us of our distance from it; and that the system of such apparent changes constitutes an 'Optic language', whose rules, though as arbitrary as those of human language, are as regular. We learn the language so early that we are not aware of having learned it, and through want of reflection tend to take the signs of things for the things themselves. Stephen's phrase 'Coloured on a flat' seems to owe something to the following exchange between Euphranor and Alciphron:

> *Euph.* Tell me, is not the visible appearance alone the proper object of sight?
> *Alc.* It is.
> What think you now (said *Euphranor*, pointing towards the heavens) of the visible appearance of yonder planet? Is it not a round luminous flat, no bigger than a sixpence?
> *Alc.* What then?
> *Euph.* Tell me then, what you think of the planet itself. Do you not conceive it to be a vast globe, with several unequal risings and valleys?
> *Alc.* I do.
> *Euph.* How can you therefore conclude that the proper object of your sight exists at a distance? [12]

That is to say, we see flat, 'then think distance'. We see the signs, then think the things; and our uninstructed or unreflective naïveté thinks we see the things—e.g., that we see distance, or, as the author or authors of Genesis thought, that the stars and planets are what they seem, little lights.

The virgin at Hodges Figgis' window, 'Wrist through the braided jess of her sunshade' (48.38–41), illustrates Joyce's own practice of fetching symbols from afar. Why the rare word 'jess' instead of 'strap' or 'loop', either of which would be at least as accurate and much more accessible? When Joyce uses one word rather than another, there is always a reason. The *OED* tells us that the word

[12] *Alciphron*, Fourth Dialogue, Sections 9–11.

'jess' signifies 'A short strap of leather, silk, etc., fastened round each of the legs of a hawk used in falconry; usually bearing on its free end a small ring or varvel to which the swivel of the leash is attached'. We need only recall that Dedalus thinks of his mythic patron as 'the hawklike man' (210.35) to realize that the virgin's jess is a symbol of the same kind as the cord of the crossblind that the director of Belvedere in A Portrait loops into a snare. Likewise, the virgin's imagined 'stays' (corset) and 'suspenders' (garters) are symbols of restraint and propriety, the 'curse of God' (49.1) that Stephen defies.

The waves of mingled sea water and urine flow 'greengoldenly' (49.26); the word may have been suggested to Stephen by L'Après-midi d'un Faune, two lines of which refer to 'the sea-green gold of distant / Verdures'—'l'or glauque de lointaines / Verdures'. However that may be, the waters become beer or ale or stout (49.32) and a flower of foam (49.33), foreshadowing Bloom's image of a flood of porter with flowers of froth (79.35–40), and just possibly Bloom's 'languid floating flower' (86.42).

The sea weeds become women, perhaps enchanted women (49.35–39), and a loom. The moon becomes a woman, 'a naked woman shining in her courts', drawing a toil—i.e., a net, a snare—of waters, tempting men lasciviously in love with death (50.2–3). Here, I believe, we have an ironic identification of Diana with 'the froeken, bonne à tout faire, who rubs male nakedness in the bath at Upsala. . . . Lascivious people' (43.16); and also with the bawds of the Barbican in Dryden's MacFlecknoe:

> Where their vast Courts the Mother-Strumpets keep,
> And, undisturb'd by Watch, in silence sleep.

a transformation of the subterranean submarine depths in Cowley's Davideis, I, 79–80:

> Where their vast Courts the Mother-Waters keep,
> And undisturb'd by Moon in Silence sleep.

Stephen's gaze moves from the sea at his feet to the sea farther out. 'Five fathoms out there' (50.4). The drowned man therefore becomes Alonso in The Tempest (50.4), Stephen's father, and Lycidas (50.8). Also a porpoise (50.8), a bag of gas (50.11), and a sleeping leper (50.16–17), whose brown eyes have turned blue

(50.19; cf. *FW*, 418.31). Stephen sums up all seachanges: 'God becomes man becomes fish becomes barnacle goose becomes feather-bed mountain' (50.13). But there are metaphorical and theological as well as biological changes here. God doesn't become man in the same way that imperious Caesar becomes clay or a king goes a progress through the guts of a beggar. That is a different kind of becoming, and the word 'becomes' has a different meaning, whether we believe that the incarnation was an actual event or a metaphorical condensation of the gradual democratization of God, who in the early days had been incomprehensible and fearsome but under more civilized conditions had become more humane and even, finally, human. But in either case, when God, having become man, then becomes fish, that is no ordinary fish, such as the one Hamlet's beggar ate. It is a literate Greek fish, an *ichthys*, the result of an artful transubstantiation by which the flesh (or the fish, if you prefer) is made word: an early Christian acronym made up of the initial letters of the formula Iesous CHristos THeou[h]Yios Sauter: Jesus Christ God's Son Saviour. Whether or not Stephen is consciously playing this word game, Joyce certainly is. And this brings us to the third section of our catalogue, which deals chiefly with verbal patterns.

Varieties of Variation

Proteus is the god not only of alteration but also of alternation, pattern, and persistence: he is the sea, which though never the same for two successive moments has always been the same. Joyce's 'Proteus' chapter is full of changes that represent recurrent patterns with variations: the dynamic stability of living things.

We have already seen an example of playful changing about in 'A very short space of time through very short times of space' (37.13). Likewise, in Stephen's imagination, William of Ockham hears the dringdringing bells of his own mass and another mass that another priest is celebrating at another altar in the same church (40.9–18). In Joyce's contrapuntal description, the two priests perform a solemn dance: 'Down, up, forward, back', lifting, kneeling, dringdring, dringdring, not in unison, alternating, the same but different. Two pages later we see another contrapuntal dance, this time explicitly farcical in the manner of the *Commedia del'Arte*:

'Belluomo rises from the bed of his wife's lover's wife' (42.30). A similar reciprocal or push-pull movement occurs in the sentence 'Faces of Paris men go by, their wellpleased pleasers' (42.31). Another dance is the reversal of motion brought about by the old silent-movie technique of reprinting a section of film in reverse order: the Post Office usher having been shot to bloody bits with a bang shotgun, the bits and buttons reassemble themselves—'all khrrrrklak in place clack back'—and the usher shakes hands with Stephen (42.1–6).

Other transformations involve different uses of the same word. The use of the word 'shells', for example, both literally as in 'crackling wrack and shells' (37.11), 'a damp crackling mast, razorshells, squeaking pebbles' (40.42), and 'a loose drift of rubble . . . silly [*i.e.*, empty] shells' (50.6), and metaphorically, as in 'Human shells' (41.10) and 'My teeth are very bad. . . . Shells' (50.34), constitutes a small motif, not intellectually significant, but against the background of the sea poetically just. There is a temptation to think that the cliché 'Human shells' may refer not only to the retired seamen (41.9) but also to the 'two crucified shirts' on the 'dryingline' (41.8), and even (Will somebody please lead us in a word of prayer?) to the 'Broken hoops' (41.6) near 'Ringsend' (41.9)!

There is a different kind of play with different meanings in the phrase 'the stagnant bay of Marsh's library' (39.36), not only because of the name Marsh but also because the word 'bay' in one of its meanings signifies a recess or alcove, and because Marsh's library, as I think Richard Kain once told me, is stagnant by the will of its founder, whose personal library it was: no books may be taken out, and none may be added to it.

Finally, there is the metamorphosis of literary styles, to which I have already referred, and which both reflects and produces the endless metamorphosis of our ways of thinking. The difference between the language of Sir Lout on the one hand, and those of the cocklepickers and Thomas Aquinas on the other, is indicated not only by the rhythms of the phrases but also by the sounds of the individual words. The sentences 'I'm the bloody well gigant rolls all them bloody well boulders, bones for my steppingstones. Feefawfum. I zmellz de bloodz odz an Iridzman' (44.40) are heavy, clumsy, slow, inaccurate, because they are cluttered with excess words that

Coleridge would have called 'blank counters',[13] they are full of oc-clusive *b*'s, *d*'s and *dz*'s, and instead of a comma after 'Feefawfum' there is a full stop that stops the utterance dead in the middle, for no reason but slowness of wit. It is inconceivable that Sir Lout could say or think 'Ineluctable modality'. On the other hand, the sentences 'Monkwords, marybeads jabber on their girdles: roguewords, tough nuggets patter in their pockets' (47.30) have a quickness of rhythm that expresses agility of mind. Such agility is not apparent in the cocklepicker, however: everything about him suggests heaviness, slowness, clumsiness—even his 'blunt bootless inaccurate kick'—and the one sentence he utters, 'Tatters! Out of that, you mongrel' (46.32), has none of the qualities Stephen imagines the speech of rogues to have. Stephen is still, for all his struggles, romancing. He has yet to meet the midwife of his own thought, Leopold Bloom.[14]

[13] *Biographia Litteraria*, end of Chapter XVII.

[14] In this chapter there are many indications that Stephen has affinities of personality with Bloom. They have been pointed out in a valuable article by Erwin Steinberg, ' "Lestrygonians," A Pale "Proteus" ', *Modern Fiction Studies*, XV, 1 (1969); in another, 'The Proteus Episode: Signature of Stephen Dedalus', *JJQ*, V, 3 (Spring 1968), Steinberg shows how Aristotle, Blake. and Boehme are integrated in Stephen's thought.

CALYPSO

Adaline Glasheen

This house, this cave in Eccles street, Dublin, ought to be a little good place—food and fire, bed with a warm female in it, jakes with a man whose digestion is unperturbed. But things are not what they seem. Custom and ceremony of Mr and Mrs Bloom are awry.

For one thing, domestic roles are exchanged. Mrs Bloom lies abed, giving orders—'Hurry up with that tea. I'm parched'. Bloom brings her breakfast and letters, promises to exchange one smutty book for another. No real drudgery is required of him, but Mrs Bloom seems mistress of the house and Bloom stands at the bedside like a detached, respectable upper-servant, calm to the very bowels.

As a father and husband, calm is what Bloom could not be on the morning of 16 June 1904, for he knows that his fifteen-year-old daughter, Milly, and his wife, Molly, are about to give themselves to besieging males.

> A soft qualm regret, flowed down his [Bloom's] backbone, increasing. Will happen, yes [to Milly]. Prevent. Useless: can't move. Girl's sweet light lips. Will happen too [Molly]. He felt the flowing qualm spread over him. Useless to move now. Lips kissed, kissing kissed. Full gluey woman's lips. (67.16)

In 'Calypso', this resigned and dismal passage is the only comment Bloom makes about his unchaste, ungoverned women. It directly expresses his lack of strength (softened backbone), and his paralysis (can't move), his voyeurism; and it implies his resignation.

'Calypso' does not of itself explain why Bloom lacks backbone and cannot move. His easy resignation of his wife to another man is understandable, because in 'Calypso' Mrs Bloom is described as sluttish, gross, blown. She and her bed and bedroom are frowsty and frowsy. There is no suggestion that Bloom shares bed, bedroom, or comes near this quintessential wife-who-is-no-longer-young-as-she-used-to-be. How so unpalatable a woman has got a lover is a mystery, but so putting-off and antisexual is Mrs Bloom that the reader does not wonder that Bloom is calm in her presence, mildly repelled by sight and smell of her. Bloom says not an unkind word to her, nor of her, but facts speak for themselves. Having looked at wife, he looks at art, represented by *Bath of the Nymph* which hangs over the bed, and delivers his terse, dry verdict: 'Not unlike her [Molly] with her hair down: slimmer' (65.13). This echoes *Odyssey*, V, 214ff, where Ulysses tells the nymph, Calypso:

> I am quite aware that my wife Penelope is nothing like so tall or so beautiful as yourself. She is only a woman, whereas you are an immortal.

Bloom is called away by the smell of his burning pork kidney with which he knows delighted fleshly communion—'toothsome pliant meat'. Nowhere in 'Calypso' is it suggested that Mrs Bloom is toothsome pliant meat. Few wives of sixteen years are toothsome.

But this is Molly Bloom at 33. Details of her past and present loveliness will flower in Bloom's imagination all day long until the rejected frump of 8 A.M. becomes a lass unparalleled: 'skin so delicate white like wax' (84.37); 'Know her smell in a thousand. Bathwater too. Reminds me of strawberries and cream' (375.4); 'Beautiful on that *tre* her voice is: weeping tone. A thrush. A throstle' (93.27); 'That's where Molly can knock spots off them. It is the blood of the south. Moorish. Also the form, the figure' (373.22); 'opulent curves, none the worse for wear' (653.26); 'Would I like her in pyjamas? Damned hard to answer' (381.13). Etc., etc. Molly's larger-than-life glamour is Bloom's own creation, but there is independent testimony to her human female attractions.

As soprano and woman Molly is admired by the men of Dublin, is the one possession for which they envy Bloom. Menton says: 'She was a finelooking woman. I danced with her, wait, fifteen seventeen golden years ago, . . . And a good armful she was. . . . She had plenty of game in her then. . . .' 'Has still', Ned Lambert says (106.18–31). Lenehan says, 'Hell's delights! She has a fine pair [of breasts], God bless her. . . . He shut his eyes tight in delight' (234.31). Etc., etc. None of these Dubliners claims to have known Molly sexually or speaks of her as unchaste till the unnamed narrator of 'Cyclops' tumbles to her current connexion with Boylan (319.28).

Molly has just attached Hugh 'Blazes' Boylan, free-spending, dashing bachelor, cynosure of female eyes. Locally successful bounder, conquering hero in any old opera, Boylan sails grandly past sirens (or barmaids) that would detain him and goes straight to having straightforward sex with Molly, while Bloom, eating his liver and bacon at the Ormond, winds a rubber-band around his fingers 'gyved them fast' (274.10). Proved, over-proved to be toothsome, pliant meat, Mrs Bloom is also gifted with a beautiful voice and has long sung professionally in Dublin. Managed by Bloom, her career was, till lately, in the doldrums, but now Boylan is taking her and other artists on a singing tour of Ulster.

And Bloom himself gives the lie to his morning rejection of Molly. When he comes home at night, he gets into bed (revealed for the first time as his bed, also) and gives a long kiss to 'the plump mellow yellow smellow melons of her rump. . . '. (734.38)

How are we to harmonize unpalatable Mrs Bloom of 'Calypso' with toothsome Mrs Bloom of everywhere else in *Ulysses*?

Surely, Molly has, like many a wife of sixteen years, 'Let herself go'. Surely, too, female attractions exist in the eye of the beholder and at 8 A.M. Bloom beholds her with a jaundiced eye—sour grapes. Another man has got Molly, so she is not worth the having.

So far as 'Calypso' goes these are sufficient reasons for Bloom's disenchantment with Mrs Bloom abed at breakfast time—she is not young as she once was, she is about to be unfaithful. But the reasons will not do to explain why Bloom deserted fertile sex with Molly ten years before when she was as young as twenty-three and had not been unfaithful.

I think, therefore, we must assume that in 'Calypso', which is his own 'mature narrative', Bloom is lying.

A truth-telling Ulysses is—like a home-loving Ulysses—a contradiction in terms. Homer's Ulysses lies all the time to everybody; he tells small lies and big lies. It is the thing he does best, lying. And when he has told a circumstantial, believable tale about being a Cretan murderer, Athena caresses him for it:

> 'He must be indeed a shifty lying fellow', said she, 'who could sur-pass you in all manner of craft . . . full of guile, unwearying in deceit . . . that is why I cannot desert you in your afflictions; you are so plausible, shrewd and shifty. . . '. (*Odyssey* XIII, 291ff.)

Bloom, too, is an accomplished liar, master of the false matter-of-fact. Describing the events of his day to Mrs Bloom, he omits

> . . . to mention the clandestine correspondence between Martha Clifford and Henry Flower [Bloom's *nom de plume* in an obscene, simpering exchange of letters with an unknown pen-pal] . . . the erotic provocation and response thereto caused by the exhibitionism of Gertrude [Bloom's response was to masturbate to ejaculation] . . . he included mention of a performance by Mrs Bandman Palmer of *Leah* [Bloom did not attend it] . . . an invitation to supper at Wynn's [which did not take place] . . . . (735.11)

Here Bloom emulates Ulysses (*Odyssey*, XXIII, 337ff.), who, telling his adventures to Penelope, does not utter the name of admired Nausicaa, says nothing of having shared Circe's bed for a year, Calypso's for seven years.

Bloom's account of 16 June falls on unbelieving ears, for Molly says to herself:

> . . . he [Bloom] came somewhere Im sure . . . either it was one of those night women if it was down there he was really and the hotel story he made up a pack of lies to hide it. . . . (738.41)

But the unwary reader of 'Calypso' has no reason to doubt Bloom's veracity in making himself out the unoffending victim of bossy, unat-tractive Mrs Bloom. He is a victim, and a victim worthy of respect be-cause he does not let ill-usage demoralize him. His interior monologue is consistent, believable, civilized, disarmingly humble. Even his defe-cation, as Mr Thornton observes, 'contributes importantly to our impression of Bloom as a man without "pomp and pride" '.

So Molly-unpalatable rouses sympathy for Leopold-domestic-saint. He behaves so well to his fat shrew of a wife. Would we behave as well? Likely not. And thus begins our sense of Bloom's moral superiority. 'Calypso' gives the impression, never lost, that

Bloom is a reasonable, charitable man, more than charitable when it comes to his faithless wife, for he goes on loving her and suffering in that love, thus keeping steadily before us the fact of Molly's adultery and failing to inform us that he left Molly in the sexual lurch ten years before.

That Bloom is a very believable man is sufficiently proved by the simple faith with which readers—myself among them—used to accept as real the twenty-six lovers for which Bloom, in a scene in 'Ithaca' recalling Jesus and Magdalene, forgives Molly.

Foster Damon, 1929: (Mrs Bloom) 'has shamelessly given herself to a succession of lovers'. Harry Levin (1941): 'twenty-five others have shared her bed with Bloom'. Edmund Wilson (1948): (Mrs Bloom has) 'a prodigious sexual appetite'. Mitchell Morse (1959): 'She has had a long series of lovers. . . . She is a dirty joke'.

I think it very funny and intelligent of Bloom to contrive to look a saint when blasting his wife's reputation, saying, in effect, that what Boylan got was a piece of soiled goods. (This harks back to 'Calypso', page 62, where Bloom picks up an armful of Molly's dirty linen and litters the bed with it.) And the blasting-forgiving of his wife is all the funnier, cleverer, and more caddish when you know (what Mr Ellmann was first to make clear) that most of the suitors on the list are lies and Bloom knows they are lies. Indeed, Bloom's impudence and daring are grown since morning, when, in servile guise, he pointed out but one lover of Mrs Bloom's and that a potentially real one. At night, in forgiving temper, Bloom draws the really long bow.

No sooner is the cuckold revenged (731–732) than the admirer of St Bloom is told blandly, coldly that Molly's conjugal rights have been inhibited, her fertility limited because for '10 years, 5 months and 18 days' her husband has not engaged in complete carnal intercourse, with 'ejaculation of semen within the natural female organ' (736.13). Bloom's absence from fertile sex with Molly is, of course, equivalent to Ulysses' absence from Penelope.

Men and women are sure to differ about who more gravely injured the other—is it Bloom by his ten-year absence from 'complete' sex or Molly by two days' adultery (as Mr Ellmann counts) in those ten years? I think Joyce doesn't give a damn for Bloom's failure to pay . . . *il debito amore/lo qual dovea Penelope far lieta* . . . or for Molly's unfaiths. The Blooms have affronted each other's sexual pride—too bad, surely. But their great sin is against human fecundity. They have not replaced their dead son, Rudy.

'Ill just give him one more chance', Molly says (780.6) when she is prepared, as ordered, to get up early on the morning of 17 June and bring Petruchio his breakfast in bed. Molly is willing, always was willing to give Bloom one more chance, or, as it seems to me, as many chances as he is prepared to take. Molly is physically attractive, sexually willing, capable of having children, as is shown in 'Penelope' by her menstrual flow. The flow shows she is not pregnant by Boylan; her adultery with Boylan shows she is not sexually frigid, but is 'a seedfield that lies fallow for the want of a ploughshare. . . '. (409.33) Joyce wrote of Molly:

> . . . it seems to me to be perfectly sane full amoral fertilisable untrustworthy engaging shrewd limited prudent indifferent *Weib*. *Ich bin das Fleisch das stets bejaht*.[1]

'It' is not a very interesting woman, but a sexual magnet whose perfection is insisted on, so that no individual quality of hers—save one fault alone—can be advanced as reason or excuse for Bloom's having absented himself. Molly's fault is the fault of beautiful Ann Hathaway in 'Scylla and Charybdis'—she is pushy about sex, too enthusiastically yes-saying. The grace of docility has been denied her. Her beauty and fertility are wasted because she is too ignorant, loutish, and self-satisfied to suspect that the most taking of female ways is: 'Be it done unto me, according to thy word'. When the name of the game is fertility, Mina Purefoy with her (is it?) nine children, enlarged glands, bunions, varicose veins has the better part, for her husband has stayed the course. Bloom left Molly when she was twenty-three, leaves her again at thirty-three for a pork kidney.

Being a seductress is, therefore, Molly's mode of sin against fertility, equivalent to Bloom's abstaining from fertility for ten years. 'Can't move', he tells us in 'Calypso'; in 'Circe' (550) he announces his death; but it was a dummy that drowned; Bloom is alive and farting, only shamming dead.

If 'Calypso' were a story in *Dubliners*, we would know very well what ails Bloom of the softened backbone—'Can't move'. *Dubliners* is Joyce's *Journal of the Plague Year*. If Bloom were in *Dubliners* (he nearly was) he would be one among many, stricken by the

---

[1] *Letters*, I, 170.

mysterious paralysis endemic to Ireland and centred in Dublin. The etiology of the disease is unknown, the termination sure—Bring Out Your Dead!

'Calypso' is, however, but an imitation of a *Dubliners* story. Things and people look fixed in 'Calypso', but the fixity is a fraud, a technical deception, a mockery of the dead nature of *Dubliners*. *Ulysses* is a restless book in which things and people cease to be still, and, if they do not attain life, they attain movement and metamorphosis and surprising identities. And the most restless thing in the book, the most elusive, is the male will which is Ulysses, 'a name for roaming'.

Like many an army veteran in foreign parts, Bloom does not want to go 'home', i.e., return to his wife's natural female organ and beget a child. It is Bloom's duty as a husband, but, ready deviser, reluctant fertiliser, he makes excuse after excuse for continuing absent, device upon device for shirking his duty. When one excuse is undercut, he makes another—my wife is unpalatable, bossy, unfaithful; I am too ugly and aging; I am paralyzed, dead; why don't we just adopt Stephen Dedalus?

Bloom is a healthy man of thirty-eight, attractive to Josie Breen, Gerty MacDowell, Nurse Callan, and to Molly herself. Molly says that when he was young he was 'too beautiful for a man' (743.41), and is at present a husband that's 'fit to be looked at' (763.4). Bloom is not physically impotent, as is shown in 'Nausicaa' when he masturbates and ejaculates his seed on to barren ground which is not home. Nor is Bloom repelled by Molly's person, for until Boylan proposed to Molly two weeks before 16 June (167.19) Bloom was accustomed to come on Molly's barren backside (740.8). Bloom is not, therefore, sexually paralyzed, but is perverse in his unwillingness to beget.

On 16 June 1904 it takes two sins, adultery and onanism, to show that the Blooms are a sexually viable pair, and that it is a disorder of Bloom's will that keeps them infertile.

It is all very well for Bloom to prove he is no woman's slave, instead a free man who can do what he likes with what's his own. But Bloom has also to answer to an angry God who has commanded Jew and Christian alike 'Be fertile and multiply'. And for ten years Bloom has answered, 'I will not serve'. Thus, for all his show of humility, Bloom is proud and disobedient as Stephen.

The command to fertilize a waste land is given (for the how-many-eth time?) in 'Calypso' (60–61). Its terms and timing suggest that, though Bloom sins, God, like Molly, gives him another chance to choose to be fertile. But the choice is not forever—man and earth grow old.

Bloom is coming away from the butcher-shop, which is the equivalent of war at Troy and of the cattle raid at Trinacria, which defiance of divine dietary command Joyce interpreted as 'the crime committed against fecundity by sterilizing the act of coition'.[2] Of his own choice and for himself, Bloom has bought a pork kidney for breakfast, defying the dietary command of the God of the Jews.

Also in the butcher-shop Bloom, himself an ad-man, picks up an advertisement which urges him to invest in the cultivation of a sandy tract in Palestine—come back to Zion—'your name entered for life'. The advertisement becomes a vision of Zion cultivated and bearing the fine fruits that throughout *Ulysses* signify Molly Bloom in an ideal state of high cultivation. Bloom is attracted by ad and vision, but says: 'Nothing doing. Still an idea behind it' (60.27).

A second vision follows close on Bloom's rejection of the first: Zion waste, dead womb, and sunken cunt, God's anger raining down in brimstone on Sodom and Gomorrah. Bloom is frightened: 'Grey horror seared his flesh. . . . age crusting him with a salt cloak' (61.21). He blows his cool and hurries 'homeward' with the intention of mending his infertile ways, perhaps also running like Jonah from God's anger.

Note the violence and intensity of Bloom's physical response to the vision of Zion waste: 'Grey horror seared his flesh. . . . Cold oils slid along his veins, chilling his blood . . .' . Contrast this intensity with the 'soft qualm regret' that Bloom experiences when he thinks of Molly possessed by another man.

Bloom, we learn later on, does not believe in 'the existence of a supernatural God' (634.12). Judaism, Protestantism, Roman Catholicism, Bloom has spurned these superstitions and has chosen to be a resolute Secularist—reason, practical morality, the improvement of society. Threatened by an angry God, Bloom is sustained by those old rugged schoolmen, Paine, Bradlaugh, Ingersoll—every phenomenon has its natural cause. Before Bloom reaches his front door, he has reduced the hell-fire vision to 'bad images', caused by

[2] *Letters*, I, 139.

want of exercise (61). His repressive modern consciousness is what
Bloom guards more straitly than his home whose door he left un-
locked. Stormed by the wild outside, his consciousness stands fast,
and the invader is repelled by 'the bow of reason'.

'Be fruitful and multiply'. 'Nothing doing'. Though heavy with
seed, Bloom passes by the healthy, living flesh of his wife, and
chooses once again to enjoy the bad dead flesh of the pork kidney,
a meat forbidden by his tribal god, unacceptable as a sacrifice.

'No' to the cultivation of Zion is repeated a third time in
'Calypso' when Bloom regards his parched, unprosperous back
garden and thinks of improving it.

> Want to manure the whole place over, scabby soil. . . . All soil
> like that without dung. . . . Reclaim the whole place. Grow peas.
> . . . Lettuce. . . . Still gardens have their drawbacks. . . . He
> walked on. . . . He kicked open the crazy door of the jakes.
> (68.10)

Though heavy with dung, Bloom passes by the starveling garden
and deposits his riches—bowels that fertilize, urine that relieves
drought—in a jakes which contains, keeps riches from the earth,
is a man-made place, not clean, in poor repair, its very name recalling crazy, suicidal Ajax, no friend to Ulysses.

'The king was in his countinghouse'. Complacent and miserly,
Bloom sits on his throne in the waste land and commits 'premedita-
tive defecation' (728.36), and he enjoys it as, later on, he enjoys pre-
meditative masturbation.

To Zion, wife and garden, Bloom refuses to give of himself.
As time goes on, the bad husbandman turns hypocrite: after spill-
ing his seed on rocks by the sea, he preaches in 'Oxen of the Sun'
against those gentiles who mock fecundity, and he is rebuked.

> It ill becomes him to preach that gospel. Has he not nearer home a
> seedfield that lies fallow for the want of a ploughshare? . . . an
> exotic tree which . . . in its native orient, throve, . . . but trans-
> planted . . . its roots have lost . . . vigour while the stuff that
> comes away from it is stagnant, acid and inoperative. (409.32)

It is hard to guess how Bloom's conduct in time to come will
be affected by this preaching, by the visions of Zion, by having
been himself changed into pork and sacrificed. His strong efforts
to adopt Stephen, a gentile, do not look much like listening to

ancestral voices and their God. When Stephen flatly refuses, on racial grounds, to be Bloom's adopted son or son-in-law or lover of Molly (689–692), another such sacrifice as little Harry Hughes, Bloom proves himself ready with another device for avoiding fertility, and creates in his wife's mind an entirely imaginary Stephen Dedalus, which phantom drives out flesh-and-blood Boylan.

Thus, while we see him, Bloom never gives up the good fight for his own disengagement, but he shows prudence in the breakfast he orders Molly to fetch him on the morning of 17 June: eggs and tea, Findon haddy (smoked fish) and hot buttered toast (764.7). No pork kidney to tempt Bloom from his wife or provoke his God to anger—the breakfast is kosher.

Bloom is more sorely tried than Ulysses because Ulysses has nothing to forgive his wife; Bloom is braver and wiser than the Shakespeare of *Ulysses* who cannot forgive his wife. Having slain the suitors and cleansed his mind of hatred, Bloom translates for-giveness-in-mind to forgiveness-in-flesh when he gets into bed and gives Molly's bottom a kiss of peace (734.38). But kissing Molly's bottom is not being 'home' again. Her bottom is the part of Molly that Bloom never left off physical contact with. Molly calls it 'the usual kissing my bottom' (739.21) and recalls 'the last time he [Bloom] came on my bottom when was it the night Boylan gave my hand a great squeeze' (740.8), that is, about two weeks before 16 June. The kiss of peace then signifies only that Bloom has returned to such incomplete and infertile carnal relations as he had with Molly before she and Boylan agreed to love (167.19). Forgiveness is better than hatred, but it is not the same thing as getting a child.

Will Bloom choose to come 'home' and *viver come bruti*, or will he, like Dante's Ulysses (*Inferno*, XXVI, 55ff) hold himself superior to domestic duty, die for the cause of male freedom and self-reliance? As I make it out, the question abides; Bloom avoids choice or keeps his choice secret. On one page of 'Ithaca' we are told that it is 'absurd' to think that the Blooms, now disunited 'are obliged to reunite for increase and multiplication' (726.17). Two pages later we are told that Bloom may sail away from home again; far away he will 'hear and somehow reluctantly, suncompelled [son compelled] obey the summons of recall' (728.2). This suggests Bloom is moved by forces in the sky or his unconscious, and exists only in motion going to or coming from. But as soon as the suggestion of eternal voyaging has been made, Bloom asserts his will by neither going nor coming, but deciding to rest (728.15ff). It is significant that the great question of *Finnegans Wake* is: will Finnegan cease his resting? Awesomely mysterious is the will of the male. Quaint and grave is the unresolved last labour that God imposes on his Bloom—procreation.

No matter why Bloom left 'home', no matter what Molly has been doing in his absence, the fact is sure—Bloom has been a long time in other places and has met up with other dear charmers who detain him. The charmers correspond to Homer's Calypso and Circe, who are identified in the schema of *Ulysses* as 'nymph' and 'whore'. Just as Penelope's rivals are not flesh-and-blood women but unchanging goddesses, so Molly's rivals are not flesh-and-blood, but, as we learn in 'Circe', *données* of the male brain, states of his excitation: Calypso is the ideal purity that lures a man to defile her, Circe the ideal filth that lures a man to be defiled, to wallow companionable in 'the slimepit and the mire'. They are de Sade's Justine and Juliette, and I also suppose them to be an elaborate commentary on the nature of art, which is notoriously inimical to domestic duties.

To provide these critters' gorgeous trappings, Joyce did for 'Circe' a grand ransack of the world's treasure-hoard of perverse, polymorphous, male eroticism so that they are temptation adequate to explain Bloom's ten-year absence from home. In 'Calypso', however, the goddesses are only potentials; as it were, they are those 'little pills like putty' described by W. B. Murphy in 'Eumaeus':

> —I seen a Chinese one time . . . that had little pills like putty and he put them in the water and they opened, and every pill was something different. One was a ship, another was a house, another was a flower. (628.26)

Circe or her picture is under the bed, animal tamer and tamed:

> *Ruby: the Pride of the Ring.* Hello. Illustration. Fierce Italian with carriagewhip. Must be Ruby pride of the on the floor naked. . . . *The Monster Maffei desisted and flung his victim from him with an oath.* Cruelty behind it all. (64.25)

In 'Circe' Bloom becomes Ruby, a female and an animal, tamed by Bello, a fierce Italianate sort. Continuing his interior monologue, Bloom next sees:

The *Bath of the Nymph* over the bed. Given away with the Easter number of *Photo Bits*: Splendid masterpiece in art colours. . . . Three and six I gave for the frame. She [Molly] said it would look nice over the bed. (65.11)

I do not think it random, and I do think it funny, the configuration of rival queans: Calypso over, Penelope on, Circe under the bed—virgin goddess, earthly wife, hellish whore. Any man can take pride in assembling a harem lively and accomplished as this one, and if the nymph Calypso seems safest of the houris, she proves to be most lethal.

Bloom, at any rate, considers her safe. In 'Lestrygonians' he thinks of ideal beauty as represented by casts of classical statues in the Kildare street museum:

Suppose she [a plaster-cast goddess] did Pygmalion and Galatea what would she say first? Mortal! Put you in your proper place. Quaffing nectar at mess with gods, golden dishes all ambrosial. Not like a tanner lunch we have, boiled mutton, carrots and turnips, bottle of Allsop. Nectar, imagine it drinking electricity: gods' food. . . . And we stuffing food in one hole and out behind: . . . They [gods and/or statues] have no [organs of excretion]. Never looked. I'll look today. (176.29)

To these immortal lovelies, Bloom flees in panic to avoid meeting Boylan in the street. 'Cold statues: quiet there. Safe . . .' (183.23). Art is traditionally a refuge from Life, and amid art Bloom rapidly recovers himself and would have offended by unveiling goddesses' secrets, but is prevented by Buck Mulligan passing through the museum. Casting up accounts before going to bed at night Bloom lists among the 'imperfections in a perfect day. . . . A provisional failure to . . . certify the presence or absence of posterior rectal orifice in the case of Hellenic female divinities' (729.29). He has forgotten that in 'Circe' the Nymph says she is one of those statues who '. . . as you saw today, have not such a place and no hair there either. We are stonecold and pure' (551.2). And she goes on unpleasantly to prove that indeed she has not (553ff).

When Bloom meets the Nymph in the brothel, he is emotionally shipwrecked and looks to her for refuge. He is on all fours and in tears, having been turned into a pig and a female tamed by Bello, burnt on the sacrificial pyre as Bloom burned his breakfast pork. For Bloom, it has been a mostly enjoyable Sade-Masoch game with himself in masochistic role; but excesses became too excessive; and Bloom talked of going home.

The Nymph does 'Pygmalion and Galatea' (note the double or male and female role, for she is Bloom and Bloom's creation) and descends from her oak frame. She is kind at first, but it rapidly develops that she has bones to pick with Bloom. Bloom who was Bello's female victim finds himself reproached by the Nymph for having been the brutal male tormentor of her shrinking female self. When Sade and Masoch romp, roles are interchangeable, sexes shifty. What is interesting and rather unexpected—the Nymph suffered, or says she suffered outrage at Bloom's hands that is approximately the outrage Ulysses suffered when shipwrecked on Calypso's isle. By Homer's account, Calypso found Ulysses in distress, took him to her bed, pestered him every night for seven years with unwelcome sexual attentions: '. . . though he [Ulysses] was forced to sleep with her in the cave by night, it was she, not he, that would have it so' (*Odyssey*, V, 152).

Why Ulysses, so ready of devices, submits himself passive, victim to seven years of nights of fates worse than death is not explained; but the episode gives a sense that Homer could a tale unfold that would harrow. In *Ulysses* (545–554) Calypso, outraged by the slandering hints of Homer, forces Bloom to reveal What Really Happened for Seven Years in the Ogygian Cave, or at any rate to agree with her account. Her bill of grievances aims to break Bloom's spirit by shaming him with the sins of his flesh. The sins run from snoring to coming on the warm female bottom, and the nymph's clear young needling voice rises in an ecstasy of Manichean snobbery.

> Mortal! You found me in evil company . . . I was hidden. . . . I was surrounded [Gilbert, p. 126, says *Calypso* means 'I hide or I veil' and *Ogygia* means 'I surround'] by the stale smut of clubmen, stories to disturb callow youth. . . . Rubber goods. . . . My bust developed four inches in three weeks. . . . [she was in *Photo Bits*] You bore me away, framed me in oak and tinsel, set me above your marriage couch . . . kissed me in four places. And with loving pencil you shaded my eyes, my bosom and my shame. . . . What have I not seen in that chamber? What must my eyes look down on? (545.6–547.3)

Bloom does not deny her impeachment, though it is at odds with his statement (65.14–15) that he hung up *Bath of the Nymph* in response to a whim of Mrs Bloom's. Instead he conciliates by prais ing her, dispraising his wife. Prosecuting attorney, super-ego, mother confessor, the Nymph unveils Bloom's lies and evasions.

First, Bloom says, he hung her up in his bedroom because he adored her, 'a thing of beauty, almost to pray' (546.10). Why then, Classical-and-Sacred-Art wants to know, did he snore, fart, use foul language in her presence? I suppose she is talking about the introduction of rude acts and words into *Ulysses.*

Bloom's wife—'she'—is not immortal, not a thing of beauty— 'Frailty, thy name is marriage' (546.21)—and he goes on, inferentially, to compare the present state of his wife with the unbeautiful, dilapidated domestic objects, seen in the bedroom at eight in the morning: she is soiled like her personal linen, loose like the quoits of the old brass bed, untrustworthy like the broken commode, absurd like the one-handled chamber pot—and overweight—'Goddess, my wife Penelope . . .'

The Nymph disposes of this excuse, so convincingly put forward in the 'Calypso' section—'My wife is not as young as she used to be'—by recapturing for Bloom two scenes from his past.

First, Bloom is reminded that when he was a callow youth of sixteen, long before he knew Molly or the dismal bedroom, he profaned Classical-and-Sacred-Nature by dropping his seed on her 'virgin sward', when having a fantasy of Lotty Clarke, the actress (549). 'O! Infamy!' Bloom summons up the phrase 'natural phenomenon', he was precocious, very young, easily roused. Pathetically, he adds, 'No girl would when I went girling. Too ugly. They wouldn't play' (550.2).

The second past recaptured demolishes this excuse. Bloom is shown as not too ugly for Molly to play with him on Ben Howth. Yes, but, as Bloom says, 'Circumstances alter cases' (550.10). After playing with Molly he was all amort and ran away, not from a 'dull, stale, tired bed', not from a frowsty bedroom without a view. Bloom ran away from a fresh, beautiful young girl, from a coupling in the most idyllic surroundings and in the open air.

Bloom ran away to sea, pretended to be dead or physically incapable of returning home to the natural female organ. He is not dead, but alive and farting and spending time playing at being

Circe's-victim-Calypso's-tormentor. Molly chose him. He chose the goddesses. Till this night the goddesses seemed safe.

But Circe tried to turn him into a woman, and, as it now begins to seem Calypso wants to turn him into a eunuch. She is under the false impression that in the Kildare street museum Bloom saw and admired her unflawed marble hinderparts. She, therefore, tries first to seduce him, is lofty and lascivious, curls her body about:

> We immortals, as you saw today, have not such a place and no hair there either. We are stonecold and pure. We eat electric light.
> (551.2)

Bloom thinks she wants to hear him confess to more male enormities. He shows no enthusiasm for stonecold bottoms, but confesses enthusiastically to worship of the warm bottom of the human female, Molly.

> *Peccavi!* I have paid homage on that living altar where the back changes name. . . .
> It overpowers me. The warm impress of her warm form. . . . So womanly full. It fills me full. (551.16, 552.8)

Smirching Purity, Shocking the Nymph is fun and games with Bloom, a stylized mode of the erotic. He is, therefore, displeased when the Nymph, having failed to interest him in pure and stonecold bottoms, drops seduction and tries exhortation. She sheds classical guise and appears as a sacred Christian female, an eyeless nun—eyeless, I suppose, so as not to see Bloom's wickedness. 'No more desire', she says. 'Only the ethereal' (552.21).

In the Smirching Purity game, I don't doubt, a nun is the *ne plus ultra* of naughty sensation, and Bloom has at home in a drawer, an erotic photocard showing the anal violation of a nun (721.28). Purity is to remain passive, be profaned—that is playing Bloom's game. This girl-evangelist—'No more desire'—is not Bloom's type. She turns him off. She also turns him (is it metamorphosis or miracle?) from pig to man again.

Once Bloom was a bill collector and didn't manage to collect money owed by the Tranquilla convent. It was a sweet, pretty young nun who refused to pay him, roused him to pleasant desire which, as he thinks, she perceived (155.2ff). The eyeless Nymph usurps the semblance of the young nun and announces herself:

Tranquilla convent. Sister Agatha. Mount Carmel, the apparitions
of Knock and Lourdes. No more desire. . . . Only the ethereal.
(סעב.בס)

By calling herself Sister Agatha, the Nymph means, I suppose,
that she is a virgin martyr like St Agatha of Sicily, possessor of
a miracle-working veil. When St Agatha refused the advances of the
Roman governor, she was horribly tortured, imprisoned in brothel,
burned at stake.

Disconcerting for a man to meet up with a sex-fantasy that
preaches sexual cold; disconcerting for Pygmalion to hear Galatea
burst into praise of his marble statue; highly disconcerting for a
man to find a Christian virgin martyr rise up against him in a
brothel, especially when he has easily, gaily confessed to having
tormented her. Bloom has, therefore, every reason for wanting to discredit her, prove she is not indeed an apparition of the Virgin, as
was seen at Mount Carmel, and Lourdes, and at Knock in County
Mayo.

The Nymph is also the eminent Irish poet, Æ, or let us say,
his Muse. It is Æ who first calls up the word 'ethereal' in Bloom's
mind. He has seen Æ coming from lunch at a vegetarian restaurant,
in the company of an ill-dressed female.

> . . . vegetarian. . . . They say it's healthier. Wind and watery
> though. Tried it. Keep you on the run all day. . . . Dreams all
> night. . . . Those literary etherial people they are all. Dreamy,
> cloudy, symbolistic. I wouldn't be surprised if it was that kind of
> food you see produces the like waves of the brain the poetical. . . .

> *The dreamy cloudy gull*
> *Waves o'er the waters dull.*
> (166.40)

Earlier on Bloom has composed the distich:

> *The hungry famished gull*
> *Flaps o'er the waters dull.*
> (152.34)

Which is an honest description of a flesh-and-blood gull, but influenced by sight of Æ, Bloom's hungry gull becomes dreamy
cloudy. It is Æ's recension that the Nymph-Nun quotes as if it
were her own when trying to convert Bloom from the flesh.

> No more desire. . . . Only the ethereal. Where dreamy creamy
> [see 172.31] gull waves o'er the waters dull. (552.21)

She makes Bloom angry because nothing is more irritating to man or poet than to have his high flights brought up against him, unless it is having his poetry appropriated by someone else without acknowledgment. It is clean against her intention but Sister Agatha and her veil work a miracle: Bloom leaves off being a pig.

Wanting Bloom to be pure spirit, stonecold, she says, 'No more desire. Only the ethereal'. And in response, Bloom who has been on all fours 'half rises' (552.24), meaning he doesn't rise to the level of spirit where she wants him, but rises to the level that lies half way between beast and angel.

Getting half way up from all fours is a strain on mammalian anatomy, and Bloom's back trousers' button snaps, saying 'Bip!' (for biped?). The half-rise is a movement of rejection, a protest against the Nymph's 'Only the ethereal'. Bloom says to her coldly:

> You have broken the spell. The last straw. If there were only ethereal where would you all be, postulants and novices? (553.7)

The Nymph has caused Bloom to snap the bonds—Bip!—of an erotic spell that held him long; she frees him from a curse, drug, sin, fantasy, succubus, game played with himself, Art, lie, obsessional psycho-sexual state. Call it what you want to, Sister Agatha's miracle removes Bloom from all fours where anything goes and returns him to the distressed cold level of the mundane where dignity is threatened by the loss of a back trousers' button.

Bloom is not grateful to her for making him a man again, which is very human of him. Ready as always, only just risen from pig position, Bloom has wit to turn the tables and put the female in the wrong. 'You have broken the spell' means 'It was you, not me, made the magic go out of our relationship'. He goes on to play on 'nun' as a religious and 'nun' as a whore, bringing up an argle-bargle of obscure accusations of sexual malpractice in convents (553), stuff he must have found in books like *The Awful Disclosures of Maria Monk* (235.18). And against the Nymph's plea for 'No more desire' he brings the Wife of Bath's argument about there being only the one way to keep the supply of virgins coming.

Himself guilty of sexual malpractice, himself absent from fertility, as he later admits, Bloom is not in the moral position for censuring the behaviour of others. But without blush or hesitation he repeats the tactic of the 'Calypso' section—always blame the woman. There is something very doughty about Bloom who at

need seizes any bloodless weapon and bashes it about in defence
of his *amour-propre.*

'No more desire. Only the ethereal' It is equivalent to Calypso
saying: 'Ulysses, let me make you immortal' (*Odyssey*, V, 136).
Like Bloom, Ulysses is untempted and leaves Ogygia without an
expression of gratitude for seven years bed and board or for Calypso's
at last actively helping him to go home. Far from feeling gratitude,
Bloom, ever ingenious, makes out that he, like Ulysses, did a lot
of years' nightly work in a female's bed and has not got paid money
for it. Like a whore with a tightwad and insatiable client, Bloom
rails at the Nymph.

> What's our studfee? What will you pay on the nail? You fee men
> dancers on the Riviera, I read. . . . sixteen years of black slave
> labour behind me. And would a jury give me five shillings alimony
> tomorrow, eh? Fool someone else, not me. (554.1)

Well, the Nymph has had her try at spiritual unmanning, and
Bloom has refused to will his spiritual castration. The bloody
malevolence that Ulysses senses in Calypso breaks out of the Nymph-
nun and she seeks physical revenge for the failure of her stonecold
hinderparts and the ethereal to get her a man. If she can't have
Bloom, he'll be worth no one's having. The spiritual Lady of *Comus*
becomes Spenser's Britomart, a mailed and aggressive Chastity.

> THE NYMPH
> . . . Wait, Satan. You'll sing no more lovesongs. . . .
> (*She draws a poniard and . . . strikes at his loins.*) . . .
>
> BLOOM
> (*Starts up, seizes her hand.*) . . . No pruning knife.
> The fox and the grapes, is it? . . . (*He clutches her veil.*) . . .
>
> THE NYMPH
> (*With a cry, flees from him unveiled . . .*) . . .
>
> BLOOM
> (*Calls after her.*) . . . (*The fleeing nymph raises a keen.*) (554.13)

N.B.: after the Nymph strikes at Bloom's loins, Bloom does
no more to her than start up and seize her hand to prevent her
castrating him; clutch her veil, so that, running away, the Nymph
unveils herself. Yet many have the impression that in this scene
Bloom assaults the Nymph, tries to rape her or rough her up. But
restrained hand and clutched veil do not physical assault make.

I guess this and other misreadings of 'Circe' to result from ingestion of pornographic matter, which, for the reader (for Bloom and Stephen too?), is a dizzying witch's brew. Few who read 'Circe' with empathy proper to the material, remain so staid of nerve and cold of blood as to be capable of tranquil and accurate apprehension.

Bloom responds to the poniard, as he responds to everything, with restraint, with a refusal of the invitation to join in the game when it reaches the very pitch of titillation. He refuses to be wounded, he does not wound. For, if the reader is hot and drunk with something, Bloom (superior in recuperative power) is cold sober and has been sober since—'Bip!'—he refused spiritual castration by snapping a vulgar button, mock to highflown delicacy. And he is still cold and alert when Delicacy comes at him with a knife.

Circe would turn him into a female, Calypso into a eunuch. The goddesses bode no good, threaten Bloom's ability to get a son on his wife, or even to maintain his integrity as *l'homme moyen sensuel*. But when Bloom breaks the bonds of erotic delicacy and takes control of erotic pain, he is suddenly a formidable man. He drives the Nymph from him with a shower of billingsgate and money grievances. Then he tames the animal tamer, dismisses the charms of Circe-Cohen—'Mutton dressed as lamb'—and calmly retrieves his potato from Zoe. Even when victor over a gaggle of sex-fantasies, Bloom's is a bloodless victory.

All the pushy, bossy goddesses turn meek as kittens, thus providing a finer satisfaction than playing about with a poniard. Emotional satisfaction is given because it is females who are cowed; moral satisfaction is given because it is not females, but aberrant parts of the whole male which he has personified as females. Bloom is the rival goddesses and his victory over them is his victory over himself, a worthy foe. We leave it to some liberated woman to decide with what justice aberrant parts of a man are personified as women.

Also, and it is to Bloom's credit as a perspicacious man, he is not taken in by a pretty face; he refuses 'the ethereal' while yet the Nymph presents a front of unstained, immortal beauty and wooes him soft away from ungraceful wallowing of body and mind to her own apparent and declared state of 'stonecold and pure. We eat electric light'. But the Nymph is false. On one page she says, 'No more desire'; on the next reveals herself as Mrs Grundy with a pruning knife, who violently desires Bloom's genitals. 'Only the ethereal', she says, revealing herself to be neither stonecold and pure like classic statues, nor impalpable and pure like the 'apparitions of Knock and Lourdes'. Unveiled, she proves to be of a man-made, sham, palpable substance that is in poor repair.

> (*With a cry*, [the Nymph] *flees from him* [Bloom] *unveiled, her plaster cast cracking, a cloud of stench escaping from the cracks.*) (553.28)

It would be unholy neat if the '*cloud of stench*' were that ethereal substance ether, a nauseous, poisonous, drugging, anaesthetizing chemical compound which explodes when it meets with air. But, however horrid its stench, I can't be sure ether smells, like the Nymph, of butter, 'Onions. Stale [can be urine or the smell of a whore]. Sulphur. Grease' (554.6).

Whatever the physical chemistry of the stench, it is ichor gone stale and rancid in the veins of gods. Bloom has wondered if statues of goddesses have posterior rectal orifices, and the Nymph in true lying doubletalk, characteristic of the Greek oracles, tells him that immortals have not a place of excrement.

She neglects to tell him that, having no place from which the divine equivalent of blood, guts, and urine can be excreted, pressure of gassy substance increases till container cannot contain, cracks open, emits a bad smell which ought to be the odour of sanctity, but is the odour of corruption bursting out of a whited sepulchre.

The Nymph is a fair-seeming, frail vessel of stench and wrath, a plaster saint that, when anatomized, is revolting and imbecilic in her lack of cloacal common sense. She points the Blakeian moral: even for a sham *objet d'art* it is better to eliminate than to burst, better to be a sewer that carries off than a jakes that contains. Like Frankenstein's monster she runs amok and tries to destroy her creator. 'Virgins go mad in the end', Bloom prophetically and punningly supposes (368.10). He is prompt to restrain the crazed, costive female.

'Cat of nine lives!' Bloom calls her. The Nymph provoked him, cried false rape, revealed herself cheat and castrator and bad smell; but old patterns are made again in the male brain, old phantoms are tenacious of their queer existence. We are told Bloom will sail away again from home one day perhaps and receive as tribute: 'A nymph immortal, beauty, the bride of Noman' (727.33).

LOTUSEATERS

Phillip F. Herring

Euphoria as Kinetic Response

On the surface 'Lotuseaters' is one of the least interesting or eventful episodes of *Ulysses*, lying as it does in perfumed lethargy between the fecund smell of Calypso's bed and the morbid air of 'Hades', and consequently it has attracted little attention. The fifth episode is more than an interlude, however, because it forecasts Joyce's creative techniques in later sections, precipitates several major motifs in the novel, and provides us with a clear example of Joyce's use of the Homeric background.

At this point in *Ulysses*, roughly ten o'clock, Leopold Bloom leaves home to begin his circuitous voyage through Dublin. He walks south to the Westland Row postoffice, stops momentarily before the display window of the Belfast and Oriental Tea Company, has a daydream full of lush images of the Orient, and receives from the postmistress a flirtatious letter from Martha Clifford, with whom he corresponds under the pseudonym Henry Flower. On the street again, he meets C. P. M'Coy, is annoyed when his view of an attractive pair of legs is interrupted by a passing tram, and, after a perfunctory conversation, finds himself alone. Now Bloom reads his letter and learns that Martha wishes a rendezvous, an idea he prudently dismisses as unrealistic despite his knowledge of Molly's impending tryst. He pockets the enclosed flower, tears the envelope to pieces and proceeds to All Hallows Church, where a mass is in progress. Here the dominant image patterns of euphoria, perfume, and flowers converge in Bloom's mind as he observes a ritual he only partially understands. The next stop is the chemist, where Bloom orders Molly's lotion and buys a cake of lemon soap. Continuing his walk, he meets the racing enthusiast Bantam Lyons, lends him a newspaper so that he can gauge the potential of the horses running in the Ascot Gold Cup Race, and unconsciously gives him the tip on 'Throwaway' that is to cause Bloom much embarrassment in 'Cyclops'. As the 'Lotuseaters' episode ends, Bloom is plodding toward the Hammam for his bath.

The imagery and action of *Ulysses* interrelate all the episodes of the novel, causing each chapter to grow more or less naturally out of the previous one, thus swelling the progress of a design previously begun. A raindrop falling on any part of this vast spiderweb vibrates the total structure. One finds, rather predictably, that in order to begin an analysis of 'Lotuseaters' one must step back a pace to 'Calypso', the first episode of the 'Odyssey' section and the first in which Bloom appears. Although the reference is still cryptic in 'Calypso', the central act of Bloom in 'Lotuseaters', the reading of Martha's letter, has its origin in the earlier chapter: 'He peeped quickly inside the leather headband. White slip of paper. Quite safe' (56.40). Almost immediately following this we see the first sequence of images of the orient—the major motif of 'Lotuseaters'— precipitated by Bloom's reflection on time and the sun's apparent movements.

It is important to note that in 'Calypso', as in *Ulysses* generally, the images Bloom calls forth in his musings on the Orient spring mostly out of his knowledge of Molly's youth in Gibraltar and his current marital conflict: he often thinks of her father Major Tweedy, veteran of the Battle of Plevna (56.32), moustached like the pantomime character Turko the Terrible (57.22, 596.21), and dreams of Molly in Turkish costume (381.11, 439.8). By implication Bloom's memory is also being nourished by Hozier's *History of the Russo-Turkish War* and *In the Track of the Sun* (709.5, 16, 36). The associative connexion in his mind is thus fixed in the following way: Major Tweedy with Turkey and the Crimean War, together with Molly and her early years in Gibraltar. All of it provides Molly with an exotic aura Bloom finds decidedly attractive.

Motifs in Wagnerian music dramas have denotative meanings, and emerge or subside as the plot dictates a particular passion; so too does the Oriental motif in *Ulysses*. It denotes exotic sensualism, mostly of the sexual variety (cf. 476, 477), and it usually involves Molly, who is still very much at the centre of Bloom's sexual fantasies. (Notice that while the Orient suggests sensuality to Bloom, the reverse is not necessarily true. Gerty MacDowell, for example, is hardly the houri of his imagination.) Joyce made this traditional linking of the exotic-Orient motif with sexual fantasy as early as 'Araby', where the young boy's major discovery is precisely that his quest has sexual implications. But it is still a bit premature for us to make such a connexion. In 'Calypso' the exotic images of turbans, mosques, and Balkan wars merge, too, with visions of the model farm at Kinnereth, the Agendath Netaim land scheme in Palestine, and Bloom's identity problem.

On subsequent readings, the student of *Ulysses* may find Bloom's longing for the Promised Land (an integral part of the Oriental motif) assuming an increasingly ironic dimension. 'Bleibtreustrasse' (60.25) beckons the Wandering Jew to the homeland, but when Bloom, 'adorer of the adulterous rump' (530.22), arrives there in 'Ithaca' he discovers the Promised Land to be the proximity of faithless Molly's posterior (734.25). The wanderer's circumambulations, as in *Finnegans Wake*,[1] take him through infinite time and space (especially in 'Ithaca') and, in connexion with 'metempsychosis', which grants Bloom his archetypal identities, through such *personae* as Henry Flower, Rudolph Virag and the humiliating transformations of 'Circe', through Dublin's two hemispheres and, finally, to his wife's bed.

Curiously enough, the infinity sign—∞—frequently seen in Joyce's notes for the later episodes of *Ulysses*, may symbolize Bloom's voyage and his destination.[2] There are, of course, eight sentences in 'Penelope', where circularity permeates both structure and symbolism. This configuration may even be the secret of the marriage bed

[1] See Clive Hart, *Structure and Motif in Finnegans Wake*, London and Evanston, Ill., 1962, chapters IV and V, on Joyce's use of spatial cycles in *Finnegans Wake*.

[2] A glance at a map of Dublin will show that the city proper is circumscribed by canals and the North and South Circular Roads, and, with a little imagination one can picture a reclining posterior. In 1904 the river Liffey, which divides the city, would have carried away a good part of the city's sewage.

which ultimately convinces Penelope that the dirty wanderer in her house is truly Odysseus.[3]

In *Ulysses*, however, Bloom's journey is more than a geometric design; as Joyce learned from Giordano Bruno, antagonistic forces separate and bring together again. Stephen says, 'There can be no reconciliation . . . if there has not been a sundering' (195.7). Bloom forgets his housekey, symbolic of his manhood and authority, and is denied use of the front door; and like Moses he is forbidden admittance to his particular Promised Land.[4] Still his voyage represents a firm step toward a reconciliation of his multiple identities and in marital terms. To be more specific, his trajectory on 16 June 1904 has flung him out of his usual orbit, enabling him to experience deep frustration, humiliation, fear, punishment, and catharsis, so that he can accept with a new and balanced equanimity the human condition as he finds it. Man's debased position, when seen in comic terms, makes possible an appropriately debased act of acceptance: the kissing of a woman's arse. This is not just the spontaneous act of a perverted mind. Even if a (k)nightly ritual, it means acceptance of an unfaithful wife, a hostile alien society (and the outcast's role within it), and the essential depravity and imperfectibility of mankind. It may be the end of illusion and the beginning of cynicism, but Bloom now presumably has the psychological stability to accept life and endure it. The oriental motif takes its place in the pattern of *Ulysses*: the 'melonfields north of Jaffa' (60.20) have become the 'yellow smellow melons' of Molly's rump (734.38). Eastern and western hemispheres, as well as sexual conflicts, have been momentarily reconciled, the wanderer has returned, and unity replaces multiplicity.[5]

In 'Lotuseaters', however, Bloom is not yet acquiescent, but rather euphoric and emotionally inert. The primary reasons for this

[3] *Odyssey*, XXIII, 166ff. Interestingly enough, upon recognizing the Ithacan shore, his own particular 'Promised Land', Odysseus 'kissed the earth' (XIII, 354).

[4] See Jackson I. Cope, '*Ulysses*: Joyce's Kaballah', *JJQ*, VII, 2 (Winter 1969), 101–102.

[5] That Joyce habitually delighted in contemplating the human sexual anatomy in spatial and temporal terms is obvious from the 'children's games' section of *Finnegans Wake* (cf. FW, 293) as well as in his reference to the four cardinal structural points of the 'Penelope' episode (*Letters*, I, 169–170). See also his gestation chart for 'Oxen of the Sun'. Bloom's humble acquiescence distinguishes him from Stephen, whose indignation at the ugliness of the Dublin environment can provide him with creative energy but makes assimilation impossible.

are the early hour (he is digesting his breakfast), his mental preparation for the bath (and possible masturbation), and the numbing
effect of Boylan's letter to Molly. Milly's letter (66.1), suggesting
that she too is contemplating a love affair, will add to his discomfort. The euphoria is but a thin veil for Bloom's deep sense of
frustration at this point in the novel, a mood which somehow in-
fects, or is communicated to, his environment in 'Lotuseaters', and
is subtly telegraphed to the reader by means of imagery and narrative technique. (Notice that the episode is called 'Lotuseaters'
which suggests an affinity between this ambience and the paralytic
one which inhibits the characters of *Dubliners*. Bloom succumbs to
the effects of the lotus, as Odysseus does not, but there are others
like him in the chapter.) We can, I believe, best penetrate Bloom's
psychological state in 'Lotuseaters' by pinpointing specific circumstances that form his mood in the early part of the novel.

In a sense, much of Joyce's work has to do with the fall of man
from a state in which illusions function to shape and control his
view of the 'real world'. When environmental forces gain momentum,
forcing a sensitive character to see things clearly for the first time,
he typically feels a strong sense of social isolation. This is precisely
the mood of Leopold Bloom as he leaves 7 Eccles street. In 'Lotuseaters' he still bears the marks of Joyce's earlier heroes, but in the
process of deepening his characterization Joyce seems to add a
dimension that I find missing in Bloom's antecedents—a genuine
sense of moral responsibility which will not prevent him from attaining reconciliation and inner peace within the superficial confines
of social alienation.

Let us consider for a moment the ways in which Bloom's frustration exhibits itself. His reveries constitute a *Drang nach Osten,*
a subconscious, partially sincere desire to escape from his marital
predicament, from the hostile Dublin environment, to the land
of his ancestors (which would make him the Jew he thinks he ought
to be), a new land where perhaps his scientific and social schemes
(dramatized in 'Circe') could be implemented; in short, a place
where Bloom could flower, prosper, gain fulfilment, be appreciated.
His stop at the tea-store window pushes his reveries farther east to
Ceylon, and contributes to the lethargic mood which will lead him
to the Hammam. (If he cannot act decisively at least he can posit
soothing buffers against the pain of reality.)

Notice too that the 'technic' of 'Lotuseaters', as Joyce rather obscurely described it to Stuart Gilbert, is Narcissism, and the 'organ' is the genitals. Probably the most immediate cause of Bloom's narcissistic reveries is the suppressed awareness of his impending cuckoldry. His preoccupation is of a sexual nature, and his frustration is thus appropriately expressed in sexual terms, specifically in the unfolding of several masturbatory fantasies and in womb-flight to the engulfing warmth of the baths. Ultimately even the frustration is frustrated, since Bloom must wait until 'Nausicaa' to gain any sort of sexual release; but to this problem we will return later.

Since presumably Bloom could have stopped by the postoffice at any time during the day, the fact that he chooses to do so now must be significant. His flirtation by post provides him with solace at just the right moment. He may now contemplate a love affair as a retaliatory measure, as 'proof' of his undiminished sexual attraction (ego salve), and as an unusual opportunity to have a fresh encounter, with just cause and a minimum of risk. Bloom did not, of course, begin his flirtation because of Boylan's letter, and he is too prudent to use Martha to even the score, but the letter does present him with this enticing option. It will now become a preoccupation during the course of Bloom's day.

To say that Bloom is prudent hardly explains it all. As we become better acquainted with him we see that by nature he looks for intellectually satisfying solutions to problems posed by the external world; i.e., he believes in 'Lotuseaters' that his social and familial situation is not likely to become more tolerable, but that the frustration that alienation causes can be alleviated by an active fantasy life. Imagined or contemplated love affairs with Martha Clifford, Gerty MacDowell, etc., revitalize wounded masculine ego without undue complication. So too does his imagined triumph over the 'Citizen' in the 'Cyclops' episode. These, then, are acceptable alternatives to further involvement in the quagmire of extrafamilial relationships. Bloom is interested in *real* economic and social reform, but on the personal level he is willing to accept solutions that do nothing more than bolster his self-confidence.[6]

Let us now look at the letter he receives:

[6] Admittedly these are in part schemes for self-aggrandizement. Stephen on the other hand, says 'We can't change the country. Let us change the subject' (645.18).

Dear Henry,

I got your last letter to me and thank you very much for it. I am sorry you did not like my last letter. Why did you enclose the stamps? I am awfully angry with you. I do wish I could punish you for that. I called you naughty boy because I do not like that other world. Please tell me what is the real meaning of that word. Are you not happy in your home you poor little naughty boy? I do wish I could do something for you. Please tell me what you think of poor me. I often think of the beautiful name you have. Dear Henry, when will we meet? I think of you so often you have no idea. I have never felt myself so much drawn to a man as you. I feel so bad about. Please write me a long letter and tell me more. Remember if you do not I will punish you. So now you know what I will do to you, you naughty boy, if you do not write. O how I long to meet you. Henry dear, do not deny my request before my patience are exhausted. Then I will tell you all. Goodbye now, naughty darling. I have such a bad headache today and write *by return* to your longing

MARTHA.

P.S. Do tell me what kind of perfume does your wife use. I want to know. (77.32)

Notice that Martha Clifford's letter bears the same relationship to Bloom's circumstances that his euphoria does to the ambience of 'Lotuseaters', and Bloom's odyssey to the mythic world of Homer; the letter is not in itself symbolic, rather it resonates meaning through the hallways of memory. Stephen says a genius's 'errors are volitional and are the portals of discovery' (190.22), but Joyce knew also that the errors of women such as Martha and Molly, though involuntary, are equally revealing. Strictly speaking, however, Martha's errors indicate only her class and (lack of) education; that is, read in isolation from the text, her letter is in no way symbolic. But when we read into it thematic correspondences from the world of Leopold Bloom, we find it resonating meaning that is strangely coincidental. The chastizing tone seems calculated to appeal to Bloom's perverse nature, and the errors call attention to Joyce's puzzling method. 'I do not like that other world' tells us nothing about Martha because there is no frame of reference. She does not appear in the novel and Bloom has never met her. Is it then one of Joyce's private amusements? Is 'that other world' Hades, our next port of call after 'Lotuseaters' (cf.: 'I pray for you in my other world', 581.16); or a mischievous reference to the Homeric correspondences which the title *Ulysses* invites us to probe; or is it possibly a subtle call for action to one who is satisfied merely to dream of love? We get nowhere trying to impose limits, but I think we should not hesitate to leave closed a door to which Joyce has hidden the key. We should merely note the tease and remember that the importance of the letter is in its boosting of Bloom's ego and its channelling of the direction of his thought at various times during his day.

Martha's letter is also interesting as an example of fictionalized autobiography. Ellmann discusses Joyce's brief flirtation and correspondence with Martha Fleischmann in Zürich in 1918 to 1919,[7] an obvious parallel to Bloom's with Martha. Less obvious analogies may be drawn with the notorious letters of 1909 from Joyce to Nora, two of which contain invitations to flagellation.[8] A letter of 1912 from Nora,[9] though closer to the interior monologue style of 'Penelope', is even less grammatically correct than Martha's. Feminine identities tend to merge in Joyce's work, but the most interesting ones have their basis in Nora.

In Martha's letter, and at numerous other points in *Ulysses* (especially in 'Lotuseaters') Joyce is using a sort of 'cave of echoes' technique in which verisimilitude cannot really be measured against the tradition of realist fiction. The origins of his technique are to be found rather in (1) music, where theme, parallel, motif, and allusion are judged in terms of aesthetic or emotional appeal rather than logic or experience, and in (2) symbolist poetry, with its concern for evocation, suggestion, correspondence, synaesthesia, and 'that other world' in general. When viewed in this tradition 'Lotuseaters' and the episodes it anticipates technically take on a consistency all their own, where Bloom's frustration kinetically affects the external world through character, action, and imagery. As is often seen in Wallace Stevens's poems, it is perception (here conditioned by mood) that imposes order on the reality of the moment. In 'Anecdote of the Jar', for instance, our perception of the jar against the backdrop of nature seems to reshape the 'slovenly wilderness', but we remain aware that this is an optical trick. In 'Lotuseaters', Joyce goes a step further. He controls not our perceptions, but Bloom's. Not only does Bloom evaluate experience and

---

[7] Ellmann, p. 463.
[8] *Letters*, II, 268, 273–274.
[9] *Letters*, II, 296.

suggest archetypal patterns, he also influences, *affects*, the external world by reordering it so as to illuminate his particular concerns.

If, for the moment, we accept the world of 'Lotuseaters' as *the world*, or even Joyce's mimetic representation thereof, we may conclude that neurosis has the power to rearrange perceived reality. To deny it, one would presumably have to justify what I have called 'resonance', or an order of corresponding coincidences, by allusion to a controlling supernatural force such as Berkeley's God, upon whom the existence of the phenomenal world depends. At any rate, the interaction of Bloom's neurosis with this malleable external world is counterbalanced by an active fantasy life that seems to be the daytime equivalent of Freud's dream world: as servant of Bloom's neurosis, fantasy life functions as an alternate world of wish-fulfilment. When it overpowers his reasoning faculty, as it does in 'Circe', nightmares walk on stage and deny him the capacity to distinguish between reality and fantasy. (In *Ulysses*, where the character is recompensed for his ordeal by purgation and some psychic rehabilitation, hallucination is temporary and functional. In the world of Kafka's fiction, in which neurosis similarly causes reality to merge with fantasy, we find the ultimate horror. Where reality *becomes* nightmare, or vice versa, even the possibility of catharsis is denied.

Another product of this complicated phenomenology in *Ulysses* is, of course, motif. We have seen a typical example in the flagellation threat in Martha's letter. Though Bloom has a masochistic streak and feels vaguely culpable for his *separatio a mensa et a thalamo* (204.1), on the psychic level this letter does help to precipitate Bella Cohen's mistreatment of him in a fantasy scene of 'Circe' (528ff).

Notice too that the pseudonym Henry Flower resonates. 'Flower' is a variation of 'bloom' which is a translation of the Hungarian name Virag. Flowers are associated with romance, are expressions of love, which suggests sexual communion. Bloom thinks of his penis as a floating flower (86.42), and the latent connotation of his name apparently fascinates Martha just as Paul de Kock's name does Molly. One can chart resonance in many directions.

Consider the timely meeting of Bloom and his fellow pariah C. P. M'Coy (73ff). M'Coy is a mirror image of Bloom gone to seed; in fact, according to Ellmann he is modelled on an actual prototype of Bloom.[10] He too is a canvasser for advertisements, has a wife who sings soprano, is socially isolated, and leads a life in which hope is continually shattered by the apparent futility of action. The curious appropriateness of this meeting in 'Lotuseaters' suggests that M'Coy is actually a shadowy forerunner of the chimeras in 'Circe', who are projections of Bloom's psychological state. Bloom shuns him, ostensibly because he is impatient to read the letter, but subconsciously he senses an affinity such as he never does with his Homeric counterpart. Dlugacz, in 'Calypso', has made him uncomfortable for the same reason (60). Bloom thinks of M'Coy 'You and me, don't you know? In the same boat. Softsoaping. Give you the needle that would' (76.13). As Bloom's gaze wanders during this interlude the reader becomes aware that Joyce has interwoven even more coincidental correspondences. A valise is being hoisted on to an 'outsider' carriage (M'Coy is both an outsider and a notorious borrower of valises); a stylish lady entering the carriage is presumably 'off to the country' (74.13) (on the next page we are told that Molly has a singing engagement in Belfast); a tram, an unwelcome intruder like Boylan, interposes itself, and Bloom is denied the fulfilment he seeks. 'Watch! Watch! Silk flash rich stockings white. Watch!' foreshadows both the musical technique of 'Sirens' and the dramatic action of 'Nausicaa' and 'Circe', where the themes of voyeurism and frustration are again interdependent. The irony is interestingly complex. Beginning in 'Lotuseaters', Bloom enters the boudoirs of the imagination to escape the frustration of marital estrangement, only to find that he is balked there as well.

The conversation now turns to musically talented wives (74–75), and again Bloom's subconscious evokes analogies: 'Love's Old Sweet Song' appropriately suggests infidelity and unrequited love; and there is an ad which hints lewdly at Bloom's dormant sex life and impending cuckoldry:

> *What is home without*
> *Plumtree's Potted Meat?*
> *Incomplete.*
> *With it an abode of bliss.*
> (75.1)

---

[10] Ellmann, pp. 385–386.

Bloom will later remove crumbs and fibres of potted meat from Molly's bed (731.15), but unlike Boylan he will brush no 'cobwebs off [any] quims' (564.17).

In order to reassure himself, Bloom, ordinarily of a more charitable disposition, disparages M'Coy by suggesting that if he is not a homosexual ('Think he's that way inclined a bit') he may likely be a pimp (76.19). Ironically enough, this is just the sort of innuendo Bloom himself will encounter later in the day; in slandering his prototype he is slandering himself. Later (235.11) M'Coy will blanch and act strangely after Lenehan tells him about fondling Molly on the way home from a party while Bloom unconsciously played the Swiftian Laputan pointing out the stars and comets (Cf. also 282.19): 'Every word is so deep, Leopold' (76.36).

Call it metempsychosis if you will, but Stephen thinks, 'We walk through ourselves, meeting robbers, ghosts, giants, old men, young men, wives, widows, brothers-in-love. But always meeting ourselves' (213.18). He too has had a M'Coy-like encounter when he contemplated Cyril Sargent in the Dalkey schoolroom: 'Like him was I, these sloping shoulders, this gracelessness' (28.28). Later Stephen will argue consubstantiality in Shakespearean drama (188, passim) and, in order to absolve himself from the responsibility of repaying Æ a borrowed pound, will theorize about molecular change and human identity (189). Apparently one can also decline to meet oneself.

Let us now look at Bloom's fellow 'lotuseaters' as enumerated by Joyce in his schema.[11] As with M'Coy, the oat-crunching horse Bloom passes mirrors his sexual incapacity: 'Gelded too: a stump of black guttapercha wagging limp between their haunches. Might be happy all the same that way' (77.6). Even the cabbies who drive them seem emasculated: 'no will of their own' (77.14). Catholics hear mass in Latin, which 'stupefies them first' (80.35), and in the mass Bloom thinks of eunuchs: 'One way out of it' (82.26). He notes the Catholic belief in the 'Lourdes cure, waters of oblivion, and the Knock apparition, statues bleeding. Old fellow asleep near that confession box. Hence those snores. Blind faith. Safe in the arms of kingdom come. Lulls all pain. Wake this time next year' (81.12). This narcotic stupor also includes soldiers: 'Half baked

[11] Hugh Kenner, Dublin's Joyce, London, 1955, and Boston, 1956, p. 226.

they look: hypnotised like. Eyes front. Mark time' (73.2). Bloom
as bather is immersed and inert in the amniotic fluid of the baths,
in narcissistic communion with himself. Finally, the list includes the
passive spectators of cricket (86.26).

Clearly the list is incomplete. The imagery of drowsiness extends from 'Calypso' (where Molly is still in bed) to 'Hades', through
the land of the living dead to the cemetery. (Legend has it that
Hades was himself impotent.) If the Midas touch made gold of
ordinary things, Joyce makes the cognition of Bloom transform the
experience of everyday life to suit the prevailing mood of the 'Lotuseaters' episode. This can be demonstrated in nearly every paragraph,
and to catalogue all the occurrences would be tedious. Here are
some of the more interesting examples: 'smoking' is a form of
escapism: 'Cigar has a cooling effect. Narcotic' (78.29; cf. 71, 77,
304). The pubs of Dublin also provide refuge from reality, and we
see Guinness stout winding 'through mudflats all over the level
land, a lazy pooling swirl of liquor bearing along wideleaved flowers
of its froth' (79.38). Patriotic songs such as Ben Dollard sings in
'Sirens' might also have merited a reference in 'Lotuseaters' (like
politics à la 'Ivy Day in the Committee Room'), since they evoke
misty-eyed nostalgia for days when heroic action was more common
in Ireland. So far the list of 'lotuseaters' includes smokers, drinkers,
soldiers, cabbies, cabhorses, would-be lovers, and communicants; to
these we can add children playing games before 'ruins and tene-
ments' (77.21), a drowsy cat (77.25), 'heathen Chinee' (who reject the opiate of the masses in favour of the genuine article, 80.6),
naive missionaries (presumably) in their foggy idealism, and the
indolent Mr Hornblower (86.23). Of course Bloom's own profession—advertising—preys upon dreamers such as Martha Clifford,
who has begun corresponding as the result of Bloom's newspaper
ad: 'Wanted smart lady typist to aid gentleman in literary work'
(160.11).[12]

---

[12] The biblical story of Mary and Martha (Luke 10: 38–42) as Bloom remembers it from a painting (79.6) is hinted at in 'Lotuseaters'. Marion and
Martha are, of course, the two women foremost in Bloom's thoughts here. The
story is relevant because it shows stasis rewarded. Jesus defended Mary, who sat
idly by and listened to the Master while her sister Martha bustled about serving
the meal. So, too, will the indolent, supine Molly Bloom effortlessly retain the
devotion of her husband and vanquish the enterprising Martha Clifford (just as
Bloom will Boylan). In 'Nausicaa' Gerty seems to be two Marys: the Blessed

If pubs, music, and religion help the Irish to escape tedium, so do such sporting activities (Joyce listed only cricket in his schema) as horse-racing and betting (85–86). A cyclist 'doubled up like a cod in a pod' (86.19) cleverly suggests vehicular escape and foreshadows the womb-flight imagery connected with the Hammam.

Joyce seems to be straining his ingenuity somewhat in intensifying the symbolism of Bloom's infantile regression to 'womb of warmth' (86.37). Bloom is, of course, meeting himself (Henry Flower) in the bath when he contemplates his 'languid floating flower', a meeting that is foreshadowed in the M'Coy scene. An early allusion to Bloom as Messiah is seen where he considers communion with himself ('This is my body', 86.35), and since masturbation does not take place (368.17) this particular communion may be described as a form of *autocoitus interruptus* (now who is straining?). In 'Nausicaa' frustrated communion is reflected in the benediction service, but there Bloom carries through with the sexual impulse that originates in 'Lotuseaters'. Shortly before the end of 'Lotuseaters' Bloom has witnessed Holy Communion; now he will become the Host ('This is my body'), and, in an offstage scene in the Hammam, will simultaneously decline it. In a strange way the Plumtree's Potted Meat ad also seems relevant here, and once again the motif points in several directions: Boylan will serve Molly potted meat and make Bloom's home complete for a time; Bloom is thereby made domestically superfluous in this sexual trinity and must perforce seek to become at one with himself; in the tub, with mind wandering, he is, in a sense, potted meat as well; and finally, we have a perfect thematic bridge over the Lethe, river of forgetfulness, to 'Hades' ('that other world') and Glasnevin Cemetery, dominion of potted meat.

Foreground and Background

Structurally and thematically, 'Lotuseaters' points unwaveringly toward the 'Nausicaa' episode. Though the effect is more cumulative in 'Nausicaa', each is a study in frustration, the cause of which is a specific event in the previous episode. In 'Calypso' Bloom receives the shock of Boylan's letter; in 'Cyclops' he is disparaged sexually

---

Virgin (346, etc.), and, since she seeks to win favour in a sitting position, the Mary of the above story.

(as M'Coy had been) and racially, and is forced to flee Barney
Kiernan's pub amid threats and confusion. The two subsequent
episodes in each case serve partially to rehabilitate Bloom's image
of himself, reassuring him of his unimpaired magnetism (Martha's
letter; Gerty's undies), while showing the reader how persistently
he acts out the abnormal sexual behaviour which has made his
cuckoldry (and perhaps wittolry) inevitable. As we have seen, the
truth about Bloom is to be found not only in what he thinks, says
and does, but in imagery and ambience as well. In both episodes we
see him flirting with a woman, yet (like Homer's Penelope) prudently maintaining his distance. Martha Clifford wishes to know
the kind of perfume Molly uses; Gerty wafts perfume to Bloom via
a handkerchief. In 'Lotuseaters' Bloom ogles a pretty pair of legs, but
is frustrated by a tram; in 'Nausicaa' he sees as much as he needs
to satisfy his voyeuristic taste. On the primary level 'Nausicaa' provides a resolution: 'Did me good all the same. Off colour after
Kiernan's, Dignam's. For this relief much thanks' (372.30), but on
the secondary level the reader learns that masturbation itself is a
confession of frustrated desire.

In 'Nausicaa' Joyce thus makes a mockery of the fervently religious tones of romantic adoration characteristic of 'Araby', and
more specifically parodies Stephen's voyeuristic encounter with the
girl on the beach in A Portrait (171–172): 'Her image had passed
into his soul for ever and no word had broken the holy silence of
his ecstasy. . . . A wild angel had appeared to him . . .' (AP, 172).
Both of these earlier scenes seem largely devoid of the ironic perspective implicit in the scenes in 'Nausicaa' and the Marian allusions to Gerty MacDowell.

Although the numerous references to thoughts and events of
'Lotuseaters' (368, 369, 372, 374, 377, 381) lend credence to the
theory that these episodes were meant to be complementary sexual
fantasies, it is a parallel that Bloom himself apparently never imagines. He has at last gained sexual release, but the general pattern
of Bloom's day shows Joyce telegraphing the message that masturbation is no substitute for sexual union. It is only self-deception, a
voyage from Aeolus; nothing is resolved or can be until Bloom is
called to account for his reprehensible practices in 'Oxen of the
Sun' and undergoes psychotherapy in 'Circe'. On the sexual level
'Nausicaa' thus completes 'Lotuseaters'; on another it carries forward
the motifs of euphoria and frustration. At the end of his post-

ejaculatory reveries Bloom remains undisturbed by his failure to complete 'I . . . AM. A.' (or, similarly, coition) and he falls asleep (as
Stephen does after his ecstatic vision of the girl on the beach in
A Portrait), oblivious to the mocking tones of the cuckoo clock.
First for Stephen in A Portrait, then for Bloom, the scenes on the
beach have had a narcotic effect in that their momentary sense of
well-being bears no relationship to the reality of the moment. This
is, of course, the central irony of 'Nausicaa' (and of A Portrait):
the disparity between the protagonist's view of his situation (expressed in thought patterns; usually optimistic) and that which
Joyce subtly reveals to the reader (through imagery, ambience,
parallels, resonance, narrative tricks; thoroughly ironic). It is parallax,
in other words. And, finally, it is because Bloom and Stephen are
so determined to go about their daily routines in spite of ever-
present anxieties that the climactic scenes of purgation in 'Circe'
become a psychological inevitability.

To attain a still deeper understanding of 'Lotuseaters' we must
delve into the mythic background and attempt to reconstruct
Joyce's view of the Homeric episode. His Greek was never good
enough to read Homer in the original, but he did copy down and
memorize significant terms in Attic Greek, and he was certainly
conversant with some of the more important scholarship. In any
event, he had a considerably more sophisticated orientation than one
derives from The Adventures of Ulysses, the Charles Lamb adaptation which set him dreaming as a schoolboy.[18] Probably the best
place to begin is with the version Joyce found most appealing in his
maturity: the Butcher and Lang translation. There the 'Lotuseaters'
passage is brief enough to be quoted in its entirety:

> Thence for nine whole days was I borne by ruinous winds over
> the teeming deep; but on the tenth day we set foot on the land of
> the lotus-eaters, who eat a flowery food. So we stepped ashore and
> drew water, and straightway my company took their midday meal by
> the swift ships. Now when we had tasted meat and drink I sent
> forth certain of my company to go and make search what manner
> of men they were who here live upon the earth by bread, and I
> chose out two of my fellows, and sent a third with them as herald.
> Then straightway they went and mixed with the men of the lotus-
> eaters, and so it was that the lotus-eaters devised not death for our
> fellows, but gave them of the lotus to taste. Now whosoever of them
> did eat the honey-sweet fruit of the lotus, had no more wish to

[18] Ellmann, p. 47.

bring tidings nor to come back, but there he chose to abide with the lotus-eating men, ever feeding on the lotus, and forgetful of his homeward way. Therefore I led them back to the ships weeping, and sore against their will, and dragged them beneath the benches, and bound them in the hollow barques. But I commanded the rest of my well-loved company to make speed and go on board the swift ships, lest haply any should eat of the lotus and be forgetful of returning. Right soon they embarked and sat upon the benches, and sitting orderly they smote the grey sea water with their oars.[14]

The translation requires little comment: the language is rich, poetic, and, for the late nineteenth century, quaint. As for the relevant commentary, Joyce studied the glosses to the text, classical scholarship, and at least one encyclopaedia; many of the ideas he thought useful for the mythic superstructure of his novel were recorded in one of the notebooks now in the Buffalo Joyce collection.[15] The two primary sources for his notes on Homer seem to have been W. H. Roscher's *Ausführliches Lexikon der griechischen und römischen Mythologie* (6 vols., 2 supp. vols., Leipzig, 1884–1937) and Victor Bérard's *Les Phéniciens et l'Odyssée* (2 vols., Paris, 1902).

Roscher's work was useful because of the alphabetical presentation of often chapter-length entries on mythological subjects, and the methodical referencing of later scholarly and literary views of each classical subject in question. It was here, for instance, that Joyce obtained important information on post-Homeric accounts of the unfaithful Penelope.[16] In the 'Lotuseaters' entry in Roscher, which fills not quite a page, Joyce would have found first a plot summary of this section of the *Odyssey*, then notes on the later Greek and Roman tendency to equate the lotus with 'forgetfulness'. Lotuseaters, some thought, habitually slept for six-month periods. Roscher also cites the split between those commentators who attempted to pinpoint Lotusland on the North African coast and who viewed the *Odyssey* as a historical account, and those writers who saw Homer as a poet seeking to obscure his hero's route across the 'winedark sea'.[17]

[14] *Odyssey*, IX, 82–104.

[15] See my edition of '*Ulysses* Notebook VIII.A.5 at Buffalo', *Studies in Bibliography*, XXII (1969), 287–310.

[16] See also my article entitled 'The Bedsteadfastness of Molly Bloom', *Modern Fiction Studies*, XV (Spring 1969), 49–61.

[17] The reader might also wish to compare Alfred Lord Tennyson's poem 'The Lotus-eaters', though Joyce does not seem to have made use of it.

Victor Bérard's theory that the *Odyssey* is Semitic in origin was obviously an important factor in Joyce's decision to make his own hero a Dublin Jew. In the eighteen-page chapter on 'Lotuseaters' (vol. II, pp. 95–113) Bérard argues that, whereas we now normally identify people according to colour, race, and language, navigators of old often did it on the basis of diet; thus 'lotuseaters', and 'fisheaters' would have been a quite ordinary racial classification. By calculating the probable trajectory of Odysseus's nine-day voyage, harvesting pertinent references from ancient and modern scholarship, and following the trade-winds in his yacht, Bérard was able to document the common view that the 'lotuseaters' inhabited the island of Djerba, which is off the Tunisian coast. He says that they were an ordinary, honest Berber people whose fruit diet was determined more by necessity than choice. They lived in a simple way Rousseau would have admired, cultivating their orchards, trading, at peace with all men, without lawcourts or the paraphernalia of government. All things considered, the idyllic life of the 'lotuseaters' and the abundance of their fruits (or wine made therefrom) would alone seem to have been enough to tempt weary seafarers into deserting their ship.

Of course, Homer did not speak of life style, only of the narcotic effect of the lotus on crewmen from Odysseus's ship. Bérard, though insistent about the authenticity of Lotusland, refused to be seduced by the fruit itself. In the *Odyssey*, he says, the poet made a pun on *lotus* and *Lethe*, and the resulting hybrid was the 'fruit of forgetfulness'. Supposedly the Greek poet allowed himself this liberty because he was transmitting a Semitic poem in which the word *lotus* had a distinctly foreign connotation. For the Greeks it meant a 'prairie herb', a 'clover' (Bérard's *trèfle* = shamrock?), and was neither a fruit nor intoxicating in nature. Homer may not have understood that the Semitic word meant 'perfume'. At any rate, Joyce found Bérard's explanation interesting enough to take notes:[18]

> On a voulu reconnaître dans le nom du *lotos* (fruit) un mot sémitique לוט, *lot*, dont λωτός serait en effet l'exacte transcription ל = λ; ו = ω; ט = τ; . . . dans l'Écriture לוט, *lot*, désigne une espèce de parfum, qui nous est fort mal connu. (Vol. II, p. 103)

Again we see the importance to Joyce of historical and philological accuracy as he imagined it. It is a tribute to Bérard that Joyce ac-

[18] See '*Ulysses* Notebook VIII.A.5', 295.

cepted the Hebrew origin of the word *lotus* and transfused his 'Lotuseaters' episode with perfume, elevating it to a motif of primary
importance even though it is absent in the *Odyssey*.[19] 'Forgetfulness'
is also present, but, as was demonstrated earlier, it takes the form
of 'euphoria'.

This still leaves us with the problem of deciding exactly what
the lotus *plant* signified to those who followed Homer. To say that
he made a pun is not to say that no fruit by that name existed.
According to Bérard, Herodotus said the fruit was like the date, but
tastier and more aromatic; Theophrastus identified it as the jujube,[20] as did Georg Autenrieth in his *A Homeric Dictionary*:
('Said to be a plant with fruit the size of olives, in taste resembling
dates, still prized in Tunis and Tripoli under the name Jujube'.)[21]

What Joyce thus learned in his studies was that there were
conflicting views about what the lotus could have been. He had a
licence, if he needed one, to find whatever correspondences pleased
him. There are in the 'Lotuseaters' episode of *Ulysses* many species
of 'lotuseater' and an abundance of sources for euphoria. Despite
this multiplicity, he seems to have borrowed from Bérard one concept of specific importance in formulating a modern symbolic
equivalent for lotus—the dietary-racial one. The diet that unites
Catholic Ireland racially, Joyce concluded, is the communion wafer
—'opiate of the masses'. It is ironic that what unites the rest of
Catholic Ireland should exclude a different kind of 'lotuseater', Leopold Bloom. His own neurosis palls for the moment in juxaposi-
tion to the ceremony he describes in naïvely comic terms, terms he
would not have recognized as Bérardian-Marxian:

> Something like those mazzoth: it's that sort of bread: unleavened
> shewbread. Look at them. Now I bet it makes them feel happy.
> Lollipop. It does. Yes, bread of angels it's called. There's a big idea
> behind it, kind of kingdom of God is within you feel. First com-
> municants. Hokypoky penny a lump. Then feel all like one family

[19] For a short study of perfume and Bloom's lemon soap as it relates to the
theme of infidelity in *Ulysses* see George H. Gibson's 'The Odyssey of Leopold
Bloom's Bar of Soap', *Furman Studies*, XIII (May 1966), 15–19.

[20] Cf. *Ulysses*, 590–591, where Edward VII has first a red, then a white
jujube in his mouth. In notebook V.A.19 in the Buffalo collection, a primitive
draft of the Circe episode, King Edward sucks red, yellow, and white jujubes.
Joyce was surely enjoying a private joke here. See also 151.5.

[21] Norman, Okla., 1958.

party, same in the theatre, all in the same swim. They do. I'm sure
of that. Not so lonely. In our confraternity. . . . Blind faith. Safe
in the arms of kingdom come. Lulls all pain. (81.3)

After the mass he begins to think of communion in personal terms:
he says 'This is my body' (86.35) as he pictures himself in the bath,
and he imagines 'the dark tangled curls of his bush floating, floating
hair of the stream around the limp father of thousands, a languid
floating flower' (86.40). Again we see the protean qualities of lotus;
now it has become the water-lily of Egypt, but even here Joyce
seems to be toying with the idea of lotus as uniting element, because it is also *lingam*, the masculine principle that links mankind
throughout the ages.

In conclusion, it might be wise to cast a cold eye on the place
'Lotuseaters' occupies in the scheme of *Ulysses*. It must be studied
above all as an early episode in a novel which becomes increasingly
experimental and complex. It sets the course toward more important
chapters that define the conditions of Leopold Bloom's psychology
in terms implicitly universal. Technically the fifth chapter is a
quietly experimental predecessor of the later *tours de force* such as
'Sirens' and 'Oxen of the Sun', though as a transitional chapter it
is comparable to the colourless 'Eumaeus' episode. In one way
'Lotuseaters' is oddly deceptive: it reveals the nature of Bloom's
particular brand of paralysis as if he were a character in *Dubliners*,
but like Homer's lotus it seems calculated to stupify the unwary
crewman before the voyage has well begun. Bloom is a 'lotuseater',
to be sure; his narcotic reverie, on the other hand, will be short lived.
Joyce neglects to emphasize at this stage of *Ulysses* that Bloom, like
Throwaway (85–86), is a typical 'dark-horse' whose adaptability will
enable him to conquer debilitating self-doubts and send him across
the finish line to win his lady's favour.

HADES

R. M. Adams

The hero's descent into Hell, in the *Odyssey*, takes place relatively late in the epic (Book XI of XXIV); it occurs in the midst of a set of fearful, desperate adventures, and for Odysseus it constitutes at the same time a soul-testing experience and a revelation of his future destiny. His path toward Hades has taken him through ever-darkening perils (Lotuseaters, Cyclops, Circe) threatening stupefaction, devouring, and transformation into a beast. In Hell itself he meets not only his old comrades-at-arms (some of whom, like Agamemnon, he had not known to be dead), but his mother who describes to him, in tears and despair, the agony of her own death. Returned at last from the dark land of the Dead, Odysseus must still pass the Sirens, Scylla and Charybdis, and the perils represented by the Oxen of the Sun, before he is brought to Calypso's isle and so back to where his story began, with his solitary casting ashore on the coast of Phaeacia, and his coming to the court of Alcinous.

By contrast, Leopold Bloom gets to Hell quickly and easily, not by any means in an atmosphere of struggle and anguish. What he finds there, though scarcely agreeable, neither harrows nor inspires him in any personal or intimate way. During the drive to the cemetery, he reflects, to be sure, on his father and his father's suicide; but there is nothing in the chapter like Odysseus's passionate scene with his mother—or, for that matter, like the meeting of Aeneas with Anchises or with proud, silent Dido. The real *descensus Averni* of Joyce's book—in short—is reserved for the chapter known as 'Circe'; there we see a really haunting vision of Bloom's psychic underworld, compared with which 'Hades', though overcast and perhaps obsessed, is essentially a daylight chapter. This is said, not to diminish the episode, simply to define its quality. It has been prepared for by only two episodes involving Bloom, becalmed 'Calypso' and soporific 'Lotuseaters'; while deepening and darkening their tonalities in ways to be described, it takes care not to pre-empt the sinister, violent, and macabre tones that will be needed toward the end of the book. 'Hades' is preparation and amplification, perhaps initiation; it is not climax. The chapter is not even particularly prophetic. During his journey to Hades, Bloom, unlike Odysseus and Aeneas, receives neither enlightenment nor direction as to his future course. He is a stranger to most of the rituals performed during it, and there is a strong implication that little illumination could be had from them, even if he were a believer. He is not intimately involved with any of the people who share the chapter with him; quite the contrary. The trials and tests that Bloom passes are real enough, but their connexion with the rest of the book is thematic and indirect, not practical or (so to speak) narrative. The chapter has many overtones and reverberations that spread through the rest of the novel, but is not itself a major point for their intertwining.

Genesis

Unlike most episodes of *Ulysses*, much of the material of 'Hades' can be related genetically to specific, well-defined public events, at which James Joyce is known to have been physically present. The chief of these is the death and burial of Mr Matthew Kane, who provides many hints in the novel for the character of Martin Cunningham. On 10 July 1904, Mr Kane, who for many years had been Chief Clerk of the Crown Solicitor's Office in Dublin Castle, went swimming from a boat off Kingstown Harbour, and suffered a stroke, dying in the water. On 13 July his body was borne in a cortège from Kingstown to the southeast of Dublin (the town is now called Dun Laoghaire), to Glasnevin in the northwestern suburbs of the city. Like Paddy Dignam in the novel, Matthew

Kane had five young children, and after the funeral a meeting was held at which a sum of money was subscribed to take care of them. Unlike the meager funeral of Paddy Dignam, that of Matthew Kane was largely attended, for he had been a popular figure and very well liked. Among the mourners present, according to the *Freeman's Journal* for 14 July 1904, p. 2, were J. S. Joyce and J. A. Joyce, A.B., as well as John Wyse Power, Alf Bergan, Alfred H. Hunter, Tom Devlin, Long John Clancy, John Henry Menton, Louis A. Byrne, and Sir Frederick Falkiner, all of whom figure in the novel, either under their own or under borrowed or modified names.[1] An H. E. Thornton, who may or may not have been Ned Thornton, the original of Mr Tom Kernan, was also present; the Reverend Father Coffey officiated. No fewer than three brothers-in-law attended, P., J., and R. Kavanagh, whom Joyce economically compressed into one, Bernard Corrigan (647.36). Mrs Kane was surprisingly absent, as is Mrs Dignam in the novel, evidently for the sufficient reason[2] that her husband had some time before put her into an institution for alcoholics. Since he had already given Matthew Kane and his dipsomaniac wife substantial existence in the novel as Martin Cunningham and his dipsomaniac wife, Joyce was obliged to invent characters for Paddy Dignam and *his* wife; and this he did, but minimally. Paddy is but a fading little ghost with a red face, his wife scarcely more than a snubnosed sniffle (568.8ff). Martin Cunningham is a much more rooted figure than Paddy Dignam, has more characteristics, gestures, expressions, functions, a more complex history. Paddy Dignam, on the other hand, operates in the novel by his very anonymity and frailty; the only thing people remember about him is his drinking and a job he once had with John Henry Menton. Bloom recalls so little about Paddy Dignam that the vacancy becomes a significant part of Bloom's own character: only a man of unusual sympathies would turn out for the funeral of a friend whom he had known so slightly.

Matthew Kane's funeral was crowded with mourners from all walks of Dublin life; their names nearly fill a crowded column in

[1] Joyces are of course Dedaloi in the novel; John Wyse Power is split into Jack Power (probably with the addition of some traits from Tom Devlin) and John Wyse Nolan; Long John Clancy becomes Long John Fanning, and Alfred Hunter contributed generously to the character of Bloom. The other characters occur in the novel under their own names.

[2] Stanislaus Joyce, *My Brother's Keeper*, London, 1958, pp. 225–226.

the *Freeman's Journal*. The meanness and meagerness of Paddy Dignam's burial Joyce achieved partly by a process of simple subtraction, partly by conflating Matthew Kane's funeral with two other funerals he had attended at Glasnevin, those of his brother George and his mother Mary (March 1902, and August 1903). Small but significant portions of the 'Hades' chapter were adapted from earlier descriptions of these funerals, the first represented in *Stephen Hero* under the guise of Isabel Dedalus's funeral, the latter limited to an episode described in a separate epiphany. But the funeral of Matthew Kane shaped in most of its particulars the narrative structure of the chapter.

Not only did Joyce take over the Matthew Kane funeral as the narrative core of his chapter; apart from making the scene more paltry, he found very little occasion to modify his raw materials. The Dignam residence is placed at 9 Newbridge avenue, Sandymount; it was vacant in 1904, but conformed with the direction actually taken by the Kane procession. These funeral cavalcades were traditional in Dublin life, as the very characters in the novel remark (88.1–2); the passage of this one across Dublin can be traced street by street, sometimes building by building, landmark by landmark. The story of Reuben J. Dodd's reward for the rescue of his son, and that of the Childs murder case, are suggested naturally by the sights and circumstances of the journey, and repeat popular Dublin fantasies, if not histories. Corny Kelleher is an imaginary employee of an actual employer; John O'Connell served in real life, and to public acclaim, the post he is shown occupying in the novel; Parnell and Daniel O'Connell occupy in Glasnevin the sepulchres they are shown occupying in the book, and popular imagination fostered the sort of messianic expectations that are described as centering on the one, and the sort of reverent-irreverent legends that are repeated about the other.[3] The core of the chapter is solid social

---

[3] Daniel O'Connell died at Genoa, 15 May 1847, in the course of a pilgrimage to Rome; his heart, in a special urn, was forwarded to the Eternal City, where it rests in the Irish College. O'Connell's presence impinges on the events of this chapter in several different areas. One of his great terrors during his last hours was that he would be buried before he was properly dead (cf. 111.15–20). He is also related to Bloom by the circumstance that in 1844 he was imprisoned for agitation in the Richmond Penitentiary on the South Circular Road, opposite Raymond Terrace, where the Blooms were living when Rudy was begotten. On the wall of the jail over the door was engraved the useful motto, 'Cease to do evil—learn to do well'. Denis Florence McCarthy wrote, under this title, an indignant poem on the Liberator's imprisonment; and, early

fact worked out in elaborate detail. But around this armature Joyce
has woven a set of intricate and occasionally moving overtones. The
first and most obvious layer of these overtones comprises the Homeric
and Virgilian parallels, in which the chapter is particularly rich. We
may as well list them all together, for convenience's sake.

Classical Parallels

In the course of their journey across Dublin, the mourners for
Paddy Dignam cross four streams, the Dodder, the Liffey, the Grand
Canal, and the Royal Canal; they parallel the four traditional rivers
of the underworld, Styx, Acheron, Cocytus, and Phlegethon. John
O'Connell, the superintendent of the cemetery, is Hades or Pluto,
King of the Underworld, and the wife whom he showed 'gumption'
in marrying (according to Bloom's macabre reflections, 107.42–108.3)
is therefore Proserpina. Simnel cakes, sold at the entrance to the
cemetery, are referred to as dogbiscuits because drugged cakes flung
to Cerberus were necessary to get Aeneas past the three-headed
watchdog (100.37–38); Father Coffey, 'bully about the muzzle', 'with
a belly on him like a poisoned pup' (103.28, 31), is evidently Cerberus himself. Corny Kelleher can only be Charon. The shades of
the famous dead are represented by statues that the carriage passes;[4]

---

on in 'Hades', Bloom recalls the actual morning of Rudy's begetting, when
Molly was 'watching the two dogs at it by the wall of the cease to do evil. And
the sergeant [originally, in the *Little Review*, this figure was called "the warder"]
grinning up' (88.7–9). Bloom, thinking of Daniel O'Connell, this 'big giant in
the dark', recalls hearing someone say he was a 'queer breedy man great catholic
all the same' (108.7); he's evidently alluding to the sort of story that Yeats
was also alluding to in a famous Senate speech of 11 June 1925 when he reported, 'it was said about O'Connell in his own day, that you could not throw
a stick over a workhouse wall without hitting one of his children'. The descendant
of this potent fertility emblem is not only blessed with a couple of keys (like
Keyes, Bloom thinks, 107.4, 35, but also like Hades/Pluto himself), he's managed to get along very well with women—who, after all, will 'kiss all right if
properly keyed up' (108.12). Despite his macabre occupation, he is married,
and 'eight children he has anyway' (108.19). Thus, everywhere we look, Daniel
O'Connell is associated with dark, underground, fabulous fertility. On the plane
of classical parallel, this potent buried muscleman is doubtless an Irish Hercules,
but he can hardly help making one think of Giant Finn as well.
   [4] In order, they are Sir Philip Crampton (92.12), Smith O'Brien (93.11),
Daniel O'Connell (93.39), Sir John Gray (94.8), and Lord Nelson (95.9). All
the statues stand at the centre of town, where the occupants of the funeral
carriage would naturally see them; all entered the book at the same time, as
inserts on a set of proofs. Joyce obviously thought of them as a unit.

they contrast with the foundation stone laid down for Parnell, to
whom no statue has yet been erected, but who is present to all
minds as a recently deceased hero. There is no special reason why
he should not be thought of as recently dead Agamemnon, done in
by Captain Willie O'Shea, an Aegisthus in husband's clothing.
Daniel O'Connell is undoubtedly Hercules. The elusive figure of
Macintosh, released by a chance word from Bloom to wander through
the rest of the book (112.7), may well parallel the seemingly pointless figure of Theoclymenos.[5] Martin Cunningham, whose drunkard
wife 'leads him the life of the damned' is Sisyphus or Ixion; his
existence would 'wear the heart out of a stone' because every week
he has to start over again, 'shoulder to the wheel' (96.35–37). The
drover who switches his herd of cattle past the funeral cortège is
Orion driving wild beasts over the fields of asphodel (97.33–39);
the old tramp (99.39–41) sitting on a curbstone emptying dust and
stones out of a boot is one of the fifty daughters of Danaus, condemned (for murdering their husbands at the request of their father) to gather water in a sieve. Prometheus is probably the fellow
looking for his liver (106.1–2). Like Elpenor (whose name Bérard
glosses as 'the fiery-faced'), fiery-faced Paddy Dignam gets to
Hades faster than Odysseus in his swift ship. John Henry Menton
snubs Bloom, as Ajax in Hell snubs Odysseus; even a recollection
of jolly Mat Dillon's convivial evenings conjures up the memory of
Tantalus glasses (115.15), to reinforce an earlier use of the verb
(108.17).

Bloom Alone

All these tricks and games of classical correspondence (summarized in good part from Stuart Gilbert)[6] fill the periphery of
the episode with elaborate fancy-work; but at the heart of it there
is a great hollow resonance. And that is the real development of this
chapter, the sounding of that resonance, the deepening and darken-

---

[5] Joyce himself called Stuart Gilbert's attention to the discussion of Theoclymenos in Victor Bérard's *Les Phéniciens et L'Odyssée*; but the parallel seems a
little strained, since in the epic Theoclymenos attaches himself to Telemachus,
not Odysseus. Joyce thought of more parallels than he could use in his novel;
for example in the Italian schema for the novel (at the Lockwood Memorial
Library in Buffalo), a character named 'Eriphyle' is listed for 'Hades'; she's
in the *Odyssey* all right, but never came through into *Ulysses*.
[6] Gilbert, pp. 143ff.

ing in Bloom's mind of an immense emptiness. If, in our imaginations, we momentarily take this chapter out of the book, moving Bloom directly from the bath to the newspaper office, we shall surely be surprised and perhaps distressed to see how much we have lightened and trivialized his being—how far we have moved him toward the Charlie-Chaplin pole of his existence; how much of his interior distance has been foreshortened. Stephen Dedalus, disagreeable as he often is, has been allowed in 'Proteus' to sound some rich and complex chords; now Bloom, in 'Hades', after two relatively superficial manifestations, comes forward.

Many different incidents in the chapter serve to make us aware of Bloom's loneliness as a wanderer. During the funeral cortège, he acts the part of an outsider, a latecomer, a half-rejected and scarcely tolerated hanger-on. His story about the son of Reuben J. Dodd is rudely taken out of his mouth by Martin Cunningham. Antisemitic outbursts against Dodd ('of the tribe of Reuben', says Martin Cunningham, 93.41; 'Drown Barabbas!' cries Mr Dedalus, 94.27) are expanded into the insinuation that Bloom as a Jew is in some sort of complicity with Jewish money-lenders like Dodd:[7]

> —We have all been there, Martin Cunningham said broadly. His eyes met Mr Bloom's eyes. He caressed his beard, adding:
> —Well, nearly all of us. (94.9)

Identified thus, in the space of a few seconds, with Judas Iscariot and Barabbas, Bloom also carries on his shoulders the mythic bur-

---

[7] In real life, it appears, Reuben J. Dodd was not Jewish, but he is consistently so throughout the novel (e.g., 183.1-2). The phrase 'of the tribe of Reuben' is customarily applied to Judas Iscariot (see the Encyclopaedia Britannica, 11th ed., 'Judas'). In this whole matter, it seems likely that Joyce was working off a family grudge against the Dodds, since his father had had unhappy financial dealings with Dodd senior, and James had gone to school with, and there snubbed, Dodd junior. Oddly enough, it seems likely that though the Dodds weren't Jewish, the man who saved young Dodd from the Liffey (and was rewarded with 2s.6d.) was; his name was Moses Goldin. The story is told anachronistically in the novel, since young Dodd didn't fall (or jump) into the Liffey till 26 August 1911; Joyce probably got it from an account in The Irish Worker of 2 December 1911, which Ellmann reproduces, pp. 38–39. Though one must beware of overstating Joyce's sympathy with the Jews, it's possible that he meant an irony to be felt here, where the real-life situation is exactly reversed in the telling—Dodd's meanness attributed to his Jewishness, the rescuer's heroism ascribed implicitly to his Irish generosity. One sees an analogous irony in Lenehan's charge (337.15) that Bloom is 'defrauding widows and orphans' at the very moment when, unlike everyone else in Barney Kiernan's, he is exercising himself to help them.

dens of the Wandering Jew, as will be made explicit by the citizen
(338.27). And much of the suspicious dislike with which he is
regarded in Dublin goes back to the superstitious feelings about
Jews implicit in this legend—they are alien, unlucky, doomed to
suffer forever the divine displeasure. On the other hand, Bloom's
very matter-of-factness often serves to set him apart from his companions. When he observes that a quick death is preferable to a
slow one, they stare at him in stunned disquiet (95.29–34). When
he remarks, with his usual equal-handed practicality, that cattle and
corpses ought to be transported on special trams to the slaughter-
house and the cemetery (98.12–15), his ideas are bluntly rejected.
Unaware Mr Power talks brutally and boldly about the disgrace of
having a suicide in the family, to the pained humiliation of Bloom,
who is particularly conscious of his father's suicide because of an
approaching anniversary, 27 June (113.9–10). At the cemetery,
Bloom is left to talk and associate for such comfort as he can get
(it looks meagre but is in fact substantial, as we shall discover),
with dull Tom Kernan, the central figure of 'Grace'. (Mr Kernan,
as we learn in that story, had converted rather half-heartedly to
Catholicism on the occasion of his marriage; as we see him now,
it's evident that the reinoculation with religious values described in
the Dubliners story, hasn't 'taken'.) Several figures who were not in
fact at the funeral (Stephen Dedalus, B.A., C. P. M'Coy, and—
Macintosh) get credit in the public prints for having been there
(647.40–43); but Bloom, who was not only there himself but the cause
of two of the others being described as there, is represented in the
press only as a misprint. He is brutally snubbed by John Henry
Menton; and Joe Hynes, who has borrowed money from him (119.33–
34), doesn't know his first name and asks crudely 'What is your
christian name?' (111.34).[8] Deeper than any of these on-the-whole
trivial misadventures, there is the gloomy emptiness of Bloom's
encounter with the raw fact of death, unrelieved by religious con-
solation of any sort. During the greater part of the religious service
held over Paddy Dignam's body, Bloom's mind is elsewhere. He
experiences hardly anything of its exterior aspects beyond the priest's

[8] The point was first made in the opening lines of the chapter, when Martin
Cunningham addressed Mr Dedalus as 'Simon', and then Mr Bloom as 'Bloom'
(87.4–9); it is underlined when Hynes unhesitatingly knows the first name of
M'Coy, even though he isn't present and absconded long ago from his job at
the Freeman: 'Charley' (111.37). Only Molly is on a first-name basis with her
husband, and she turns 'Leopold' into the half-derisive 'Poldy'.

toad belly and croaking voice, and what he does experience he fails
to understand:

> The priest took a stick with a knob at the end of it out of the
> boy's bucket and shook it over the coffin. Then he walked to the
> other end and shook it again. Then he came back and put it back
> in the bucket. As you were before you rested. It's all written down:
> he has to do it. (104.7)

These comments of Bloom's, short interior summaries of feeling
after fragments of the religious ceremony, are particularly curious
because we can't be confident of the spirit informing them: does
the weight of their satire fall on Bloom or on the ceremony? At
the end of the service, Bloom hears the priest consign Dignam's
spirit to his maker, '*In paradisum*', and he thinks: 'said he was going
to paradise or is in paradise. Says that over everybody. Tiresome kind
of a job. But he has to say something' (104.25). It's probable that
this kind of response is meant to represent Bloom's limited, practical,
factual mind; he has about as much sense of religious awe as an old
shoe, and damps out all the splendours and consolations of the
Christian faith (if not all of its terrors), as if they had never existed.
On the other hand, Bloom's crawly imagination spares him few of
the grisly details of physical corruption and disintegration; he follows the rat, the worm, and the process of decay into the very
kernel of the grave, and gives himself, along with the reader, a
fine case of the blues, thereby. It's not to be supposed that Joyce is
here preaching a sermon: 'This is what death is like for a man
who does not believe in the sacraments and comforts of the Christian ministry'. Bloom has his share of graveyard pluck, and can
resolve toward the end of the episode, 'They are not going to get
me this innings' (115.8). Still, it's undeniably a test of moral courage
that he has passed, and the more impressive because, though he
doesn't have any sense whatever of religious assurance, he is haunted
throughout the chapter by an amazing assortment of ghosts, spooks,
and hobgoblin doppelgängers.

Ghosts

It is probably natural that 'Hades' (an episode described as using
the primary technique of 'incubism')[9] should carry out, more

---

[9] Joyce seems to have meant by the word not merely possession, as by a
demon or incubus, but oppressed meditation, obsession.

than any other unit of *Ulysses*, that major theme of *Dubliners*, that
Ireland is a land of walking ghosts and barely vitalized corpses.
Wherever we look, there sprouts a spook. Apart from serving as
Irish counterparts of fallen classical heroes, O'Connell and Parnell
linger on as ghosts to haunt their epigonic successors. Legends are
still recited about them, and they have left scarecrow relatives whose
meagre stature sets off their own epic dimensions. (John Howard
Parnell was a city marshal, John O'Connell superintendent of a
cemetery.) The Dublin dead constantly control the Dublin living, if
not directly, at least through the complex patterns of memory and
association: 'we obey them in the grave' thinks Bloom (90.21).
Simon Dedalus is haunted by thoughts of his dead wife, as Bloom
is by thoughts of his dead father, his dead father's dead dog, and
his own dead son. Little Peake, the almost-invisible clerk at Crosbie
& Alleyne's establishment (in 'Counterparts') is revived for a moment as Bloom scans the obituary column (91.17–18), but it doesn't
seem to be the same person, just a namesake. Another living, half-
verbal ghost is the old man selling bootlaces near the statue of Smith
O'Brien (93.15–23); Bloom recalls that he used to be a solicitor,
used to have an office in Hume street, in the same house as Molly's
namesake, Tweedy, crown solicitor for Waterford.[10] Again, unhappy Mrs Sinico, from the *Dubliners* story 'A Painful Case', recurs
to Bloom's mind at the cemetery (114.41); he had attended her
funeral at Glasnevin less than a year before—and here again the
memory lingers. The ugly face of death represented by the Childs
murder case has reverberations throughout the latter part of the
book ('Oxen of the Sun', 'Circe') as well as in 'Hades' itself; ghostly,
ghastly memories still linger around the Childs house, and though
Samuel Childs was properly acquitted (for lack of evidence), the
house in which the murder took place stands wrongfully condemned
(100.10). Joe Cuffe and Wisdom Hely, former employers, remind
Bloom of his own dead selves (97.41, 114.9), as the droves of cattle
and sheep suggest masses of humanity being herded toward the

[10] The connexion with himself which Bloom's imagination makes through
the name 'Tweedy' lingers long in his mind and sinks deep: an imaginary murder-
case, constructed in fantasy around thoughts of the Childs murder case, has as
its clue a shoelace (100.16); and when he is being tortured by Bello, in the
depths of the 'Circe' episode, to confess 'the most revolting piece of obscenity
in all your career of crime' (538.2), Bloom sees among the mute, inhuman faces
that throng forward 'Bootlaces a penny'

grave. All occasions do inform against poor Bloom; cheese, he thinks, is the 'corpse of milk', and 'every Friday buries a Thursday' (114.23, 109.37). 16 June was, of course, a Thursday.

The technique of incubism also works through a whole panoply of depressive metaphors, macabre puns, and gloomy colours. 'Brown', 'grey', and 'dull' are particularly frequent adjectives. We recall from 'The Dead' that Mr Browne is a sombre figure in that story, and Gabriel Conroy worries about whether he should quote Browning; evidently that colour is particularly sinister. Here in 'Hades', it is Mervyn Brown (104.1) who has told Bloom about the gas-filled crypt of Saint Werburgh's church; the boatman aboard the barge, which is compared to the *Bugabu*, tips to the passing cortège a brown strawhat (99.23), and the tramp in front of Jimmy Geary's shakes out a 'dustbrown yawning boot' (99.41).[11] Even more play is made with the word 'grey'. This is the colour of the obese elderly rat that troubles Bloom's sight and imagination after the funeral (114.13, 15), it is the colour of Paddy Dignam's dead face (98.32), the colour of Bloom's suit that needs turning by Mesias (110.17), the colour of various people's hair (93.31, 107.40, 42), even of the air over the cemetery (104.34). It occurs further in connexion with Sir John Gray (94.8) and the Greystones concert that Molly had to give up when she became pregnant (89.12).[12] As for 'dull', Bloom reflects as the cortège passes down Sackville street that this side of the street is full of dull business by day and squalor by night (95.35–40); the bootlace-seller is dullgarbed (93.15), and

---

[11] Mervyn Brown, who lived in Harcourt street about the time the Blooms were nearby on Lombard street, west, was a pianist, professor of music, and organist at several different churches about Dublin. Joyce may have wanted his name for symbolic reasons, but took care to give him good, practical reasons for knowing Bloom as well as Saint Werburgh's. Daughter of Wulfhere, ancient King of the Mercians, Saint Werburgh gave her name to the church which is now one of the oldest in Dublin, and houses in its crypt the body of Lord Edward Fitzgerald. The church's special feature is not its organ, but the Geraldine monument and a fine Gothic pulpit. Joyce evidently hinted at the organ in order to suggest a wind machine for making music from corpsegas. 'Aboard the Bugaboo' is listed by Hodgart and Worthington, *Song in the Works of James Joyce*, New York, 1959, as a popular song; a bugaboo or bugbear is a spook.
[12] When he appears briefly in 'Circe', already partly ghouleaten but still pursued by that obscene rat (472.14–19), Paddy Dignam is grey of face and wears a brown mortuary habit. G. R. Mesias was an actual merchant tailor, with a shop at 5 Eden quay (279.35–36), but Joyce clearly delighted in the overtones of his name.

Paddy Dignam's hearse-horse looks back at the coffin with a dull eye (101.9).

In addition to these rather obvious devices of colour and tone, the prose of the chapter is saturated with half-felt metaphors and images involving death, engulfment, hell, and the devil. Just as Bloom, in 'Lestrygonians', when he is hungry, draws his hidden metaphors from various foods, so here he is obsessed, even in the metaphoric substructure of his thought, with circumstances and imagery of mortality. A perfunctory but representative list of these expressions might include: 'doubledyed ruffian' (88.32), 'lowdown crowd' (88.31), 'watered down' (89.18), 'trenchant' (91.4), 'dead nuts' (91.6), 'bone in their skulls' (91.31), 'terrible comedown' (93.21), 'there is no carnal' (93.35), 'drink like the devil' (95.25), 'dead side of the street' (95.35), 'slipped down' (97.7), 'dead march' (97.21), 'dead meat trade' (98.2), 'dropping barge' (99.10), 'cycle down' (99.16), 'dropping down' (99.22), 'yawning boot' (99.41), 'place gone to hell' (100.11), 'harpy' (101.17), 'dead weight' (101.22), 'mortal agony' (101.28), 'few bob a skull' (102.33), 'an infernal lot' (103.41), 'every mortal day' (104.19), 'gazed gravely' (104.35), 'followed the barrow' (104.38), 'damn all of himself' (106.2), 'went off' (106.6), 'dead letter office' (107.39), 'churchyards yawn' (108.5), 'a devil of a lot' (109.3), 'the coffin dived . . . the men . . . struggled up and out' (110.20–21), 'Ivy day is dying out' (111.5), 'dead against it' (114.25–26), 'devilling for the other firm' (114.28), 'rooted dislike' (115.18), and 'mortified' (115.20).

Much-mooted Macintosh is a spook of another species. Who he 'is' in the sense of a flesh-and-blood figure outside Bloom's momentary perception of him and recurrent fantasies about him, we are deliberately not told. Indeed, Joyce is so ostentatious about not telling us, that it doesn't seem in the least uncomfortable to accept the notion that he is an enigma without an answer. We might be fortified in this unambitious assumption by noting that Joyce, in that schema for the novel which he drew up in Italian, refers to some character in this chapter—to whom does the word apply better than Macintosh?—as 'L'Ignoto'. The desire to push beyond this point has led to a variety of speculations, more or less specific, more or less probable, more or less useful to the reading of the book. Macintosh is Joyce himself, who sometimes wore a dirty raincoat; he is Theoclymenos, as noted above; he is Mr James Duffy of 'A

Painful Case', returned to haunt the grave of Mrs Sinico; he is Charles Stewart Parnell returned from the grave; he is the Wandering Jew; he is Jesus Christ on the road to Emaus, or any other sacred *revenant* whose name one chooses to inscribe on his blank calling card. The novel itself offers no unequivocal grounds for choosing among these various alternatives—as the very diversity of options makes evident. But the two extreme alternatives (as often in Joyce) seem more compatible with one another and with the rest of the novel than those middle-of-the-road 'explanations' that are really no improvement on the original problem itself. If Macintosh is Mr Duffy or James Joyce, his presence in *Ulysses* is either messy or cute. But if he is an unknown, unrecognized god, he strikes a dark and resonant chord with the sense of loneliness and search that everyone feels in the face of death. His being in this sense Everyman in no way conflicts with his being, in another sense, Noman. The chief symbolic link is made via Bloom's vague reflection on the sudden mysterious disappearance of Macintosh: 'Well of all the. Has anybody here seen? Kay ee double ell' (112.14). Apart from reference to the anachronistic song, this phrase may involve allusions to the Book of Kells, to Kino's eleven-bob trousers, through 'Kay ee' to the key Bloom has lost and for which he is looking, through 'El' to the Hebrew name of the Lord, and to the cabalistic tradition of identifying K with 11 as the symbol of resurrection.[13]

Even if he is a god, Macintosh is probably a sinister and unlucky god, and any identification of him with a god which depends on the number eleven is blurred by his further association with the pattern of twelve/thirteen. There are, it appears, eleven mourners at the grave of Paddy Dignam, plus the officiating priest. Cunningham, Dedalus, Power, and Bloom came in the first coach; Lambert, Hynes, and Kernan in the second; Menton, Corrigan, and Dignam junior in the third; while Corny Kelleher and Father Coffey have been at the cemetery all morning. Bloom tots up everybody (110.22), and finds twenty of them; but this includes the gravediggers, whose numbers have not been told—whose numbers, in fact, are revealed only casually, indirectly and later (112.16), when a 'seventh gravedigger' comes by to pick up a spade. Thus Macintosh is number

[13] I summarize here, with some omissions, from Robert A. Day's impressive monograph, 'Joyce's Waste Land and Eliot's Unknown God', Madison, Wis., 1971, p. 155ff.

thirteen, or Bloom is number thirteen (110.10–11)—actually the presence of Macintosh makes everybody number thirteen; and this is death's number because (presumably) it represents the twelve disciples plus Christ. Elsewhere in the novel (185.1, 296.39, for example), we find Joyce acutely aware that in any assembly of Irishmen, the thirteenth will inevitably betray or inform on one of the others. The completion of this fateful pattern at the moment when Dignam's body is lowered into the grave is formalized by the braying of a donkey, considered by the Romans an animal of ill omen and associated during the middle ages with the doubting apostle, Thomas.[14]

This offsetting arrangement of symbols, linked peripherally or by overtones only, where the Unknown God may also be Judas, where he is represented by two overlapping number codes, and reinforced by a remote symbol of another morally obtuse disciple (both Judas, Thomas, and perhaps Balaam's ass are used at only a fraction of their full valency) illustrates the ghostly and atmospheric management of overtones in this grey episode. On occasion, a simple impression of natural objects serves to suggest an invisible world, as in the beautifully rhythmic incantation of the cemetery-approach: 'The high railings of Prospects rippled past their gaze. Dark poplars, rare white forms. Forms more frequent, white shapes thronged amid the trees, white forms and fragments streaming by mutely, sustaining vain gestures on the air' (100.22). One can have the spectacle as simple trees (cypress, we pause to note, would have made a wholly different impression), but for mere trees they are rather agitated and animate; one can have them as ghosts, but for ghosts they are pale, vain, and mute—one could blink them away, or dismiss them with a shake of the head. 'I do not like that other world', Martha Clifford wrote, and Bloom doesn't like it either (115.5–6), but both he and the reader are often troubled with intrusive intimations of it which brush and flicker across their disturbed vision. It is a very gassy chapter indeed.

[14] Joyce evidently had some acquaintance with Angelo de Gubernatis's elaborate collection of *Zoological Mythology* (1872), in which the lore of the ass, as well as that of the dog, is spread out for all to see; but de Gubernatis says nothing of the shamefaced ass who slinks away to die, and who thereby connects in Bloom's mind with 'poor papa'.

Heart

Against all these chilly spooks and ghastly though insubstantial phantoms, the chapter takes as its symbolic resource the image of the heart. Functioning or failing to function, the organ is deeply woven into the texture of the prose; heart failure was responsible for the death of Dignam (95.22), as broken hearts were responsible for those of Mrs Dedalus, Daniel O'Connell, and Parnell (105.2–3, 95.40). Athos, Rudolf Virag's old dog, died because he 'took it to heart' (90.22), and Queen Victoria, putting a few violets in her bonnet after Albert's death, showed that she was vain 'in her heart of hearts' (102.16). Thinking of the Catholic attitude toward suicides, Bloom recalls that 'they used to drive a stake of wood through his heart in the grave' (96.30), and moves on to reflect that Martin Cunningham's life would 'wear the heart out of a stone' (96.35–36). Almost all these references to hearts are depressing in their connotation, having to do with failings of hearts or heart failure; we are not surprised that Bloom, humming *Là ci darem*, stops short just on the verge of the ill-omened word: '*Mi trema un poco il*' (93.27).

But in his one intimate exchange with, or approach to, Bloom, Mr Tom Kernan, apparently without intending to do so at all, effects a striking retrospective rearrangement of the connotations of the word 'heart':

> Mr Kernan said with solemnity:
> —*I am the resurrection and the life.* That touches a man's inmost heart. (105.30)

Bloom agrees, politely enough, that it does, but he doesn't really believe the phrase. It won't accomplish much for the fellow in the six by two with his toes to the daisies. Yet, strangely enough, the connotative meaning of the word 'heart' has been turned around by Mr Kernan's quotation of Jesus' words on the occasion of the raising of Lazarus (John, II:25); and henceforth in 'Hades' it almost always has a favourable implication. We hear of John O'Connell's 'goodheartedness', (107.32), and of how jokes warm 'the cockles of his heart' (109.8). Shakespeare's jesting gravediggers show 'the profound knowledge of the human heart' (109.15). The mourners, when the funeral is over, take 'heart of grace' (111.26) as they move away from the grave; and, on the very last page of the chapter, we are told that Mat Dillon had a 'heart of gold really' (115.15).

There are a couple of exceptions, whether apparent or real, to this very striking turnabout. Humane Bloom thinks at one point (111.18) that there ought to be some law or procedure to protect against burial alive—a procedure to 'pierce the heart' of the corpse; and this suggestion, however well-intentioned, is surely macabre in its feeling. On 113.5, he recalls a song, 'Old Ireland's Hearts and Hands' (the circumstances suggest a sarcastic attitude), and on 113.34ff he thinks of the Sacred Heart of Jesus, which a figure of the Redeemer is evidently displaying. The symbol here was evidently important to Joyce (he lists 'Sacro Cuore' in the 'Italian' schema at Buffalo), but for a variety of reasons, we probably should not take it with full seriousness.[15] As a matter of fact, it's not at all easy to calculate the spirit behind this very potent symbol; but even if we view it as negatively as may be, the shift in tonal values surrounding the word 'heart' before and after Mr Kernan's solemn quotation is very striking indeed. Like Martha Clifford, and indeed like Bloom himself, Mr Kernan may well be something of a sacred idiot, the bearer to others of tidings whose import has never crossed his own mind. Bloom and Kernan are 'in the same boat' (105.23), as Bloom and C. P. M'Coy were 'in the same boat' (76.13); they are perhaps three men in a boat or tub, like those sacred simpletons Winken, Blinken, and Nod. On a more exalted level, Mr Kernan, as the unconscious vessel of a degenerate sort of 'Grace' may even be a modern avatar of blind Tiresias, able, like his predecessor, to see for others, but not for himself.[16]

[15] Bloom's response to the image ('Heart on his sleeve') is by no means reverent; the Order of the Sacred Heart was fostered by the Blessed Margaret Mary Alacoque, whom Mulligan treats with scant respect elsewhere (202.4); and both Mrs Dedalus and King Edward invoke the Sacred Heart in the depths of the 'Circe' episode (582.18–20; 599.16). Bloom's fragmentary reflection that 'Ireland was dedicated to it or whatever that' (113.36) can scarcely be anything but a sardonic reference to someone's pious exaggerations. Yet none of these citations is conclusive; it is probably more to the point that the cult of the Sacred Heart, like the Memorial Society of the Little Flower (91.20), would be likely to offend Joyce's severe and unsentimental taste.

[16] Another mark of Tom Kernan's prophetic character lies in the catchwords to which he is said (91.3–7) to be addicted. 'Trenchant' doesn't amount to very much, and in fact he uses the word just once (287.15); but 'retrospective arrangement', which he uses twice (241.4, 277.18–19), and which is echoed several other times, is a stronger term in itself, and seems much more idiosyn-

Interconnexions and Correspondences

For certain descriptive details of the cemetery scene, Joyce took advantage of his own previous writings: the fact is of interest, not because it alters radically our understanding of the passages involved, but because it suggests the emotional undercurrents that Joyce's hard, cold style is dominating. In particular, one four-sentence paragraph of the chapter had a rather involved history before it turned up in *Ulysses*. As Bloom and his companions enter the gates of Glasnevin, they encounter another party on their way out:

> Mourners came out through the gates: woman and a girl. Leanjawed harpy, hard woman at a bargain, her bonnet awry. Girl's face stained with dirt and tears, holding the woman's arm looking up at her for a sign to cry. Fish's face, bloodless and livid. (101.16)

In its original version, this passage was one of Joyce's epiphanies; Stanislaus Joyce tells us[17] that his brother wrote it about their mother's funeral (mid-August, 1903) two or three months after the event. In that form it read:

> Two mourners push on through the crowd. The girl, one hand catching the woman's skirt, runs in advance. The girl's face is the face of a fish, discoloured and oblique-eyed; the woman's face is small and square, the face of a bargainer. The girl, her mouth distorted, looks up at the woman to see if it is time to cry; the woman, settling a flat bonnet, hurries on toward the mortuary chapel.[18]

In *Stephen Hero* (p. 167), Joyce used the same passage with very slight modifications (such as the tense of the verbs and the substitution of 'pinched' for 'small' in describing the woman's face) in a scene describing the burial of Stephen's sister Isabel. The changes made to incorporate the paragraph in *Ulysses* are clearly more substantial. 'Leanjawed harpy' carries out some of the underworld themes of 'Hades', besides being sharper and quicker than the first version. The strongest metaphor, 'fish's face', and the strongest adjective, 'livid', are withheld till the very end of the passage; and the

cratic in context. It applies in fact to the whole of *Ulysses*, and suggests again that Mr Tom Kernan is capable of meaning much more than he understands.

[17] *My Brother's Keeper*, p. 235.

[18] R. E. Scholes and R. M. Kain (eds.), *The Workshop of Daedalus*, Evanston, Ill., 1965, p. 31. See also the review by David Hayman in *JJQ*, II, 1 (Fall 1965), 240–243.

essential quality of the scene, which is the grubby, slavish dependence of the girl on the woman, even in the expression of her own feelings, is brilliantly focussed.

The meagreness of Isabel Daedalus's funeral in *Stephen Hero* (modelled as it is on George Alfred Joyce's funeral in real life) contributed largely to the meagreness of Paddy Dignam's. Like Father Coffey in 'Hades', the priest in *Stephen Hero* has a great toad belly and a croaking voice. Joyce, writing *Stephen Hero* in the person of an omniscient third-person narrator, describes the priest shaking an 'aspergill' over the coffin, while Mr Bloom, through whose innocent eyes the scene is viewed in *Ulysses*, calls it 'a stick with a knob at the end of it' (104.7). Simon Daedalus weeps sloppily over his dead child in *Stephen Hero*, as over his dead wife in *Ulysses*; and on the way back from the cemetery, the *Stephen Hero* funeral party stop at Dunphy's Corner for a drink, as Bloom predicts the *Ulysses* party will do (98.41–42). Another figure who seems to have carried over into *Ulysses* from the earlier book is that 'William Wilkinson, auditor and accountant', whose corpse Bloom silently calculates might be worth three pounds, thirteen and six (108.33–35). *Stephen Hero* describes in considerable detail a Mr Wilkinson, who was a tall, one-eyed friend of the Daedalus family—a man from the north of Ireland, who travelled for an ironmonger, made available part of his house to the Daedalus family, and attended the funeral of Isabel. Wilkinson's appearance in 'Hades' seems too pat to be altogether coincidental; it exemplifies the way in which, for certain sparse yet sometimes significant details, Joyce deliberately cannibalized his own earlier writing. But it is a biographical, not a literary fact; it alters hardly at all our reading of the text of the chapter.

Another set of buried connexions has the effect of relating the mind of Bloom to that of Stephen Dedalus through indistinct but perceptible parallels. On the narrative level, 'Hades' brings about Bloom's first crossing-of-paths with both Stephen (88.6) and Boylan (92.19); neither figure leaves many direct traces on Bloom's mind. He does wonder for a moment if after his death Molly would marry Boylan, concluding that she very well might (102.12–13); about Stephen he hardly reflects at all. Yet his general thoughts are often strangely in harmony with those Stephen has formed, if not expressed, elsewhere. 'Drowning they say is the pleasantest' Bloom reflects (114.30), echoing Stephen's 'Seadeath mildest of all deaths known to man' (50.19). Seeing a gravedigger coiling up a coffinband after the burial, Bloom thinks 'His navelcord' (112.30), recalling Stephen's vision of the midwives carrying 'a misbirth with a trailing navelcord' (38.1), which he later supposes they have tucked 'safe among the bulrushes' (45.8). Bloom's 'found in the river bed clutching rushes' (96.31), though by its context it suggests the demise of Ophelia, carries overtones of the birth of Moses, as well. And this is not unnatural, for Bloom, like Stephen, is acutely aware of the cyclical pattern of life, where birth and death merge. 'In the midst of death we are in life', he thinks (reversing Martin Cunningham's half-platitude at 96.14). 'Both ends meet' (108.16): they do indeed, and very easily. Bloom reflects that the young intern who dressed his bee-bite has moved from the deadhouse at the *Mater Misericordiae* to the lying-in hospital: 'from one extreme to the other', as he summarizes (97.30). Even the rat wriggling under a plinth reads Bloom a lecture on the Eternal Return: 'Who lives there? Are laid the remains of Robert Emery. Robert Emmet was buried here by torchlight, wasn't he? Making his rounds' (114.17). From Emery the modern corpse to Emmet the ancient one (from stone to ant and back again) the ranging rodent acts his role in the process by which 'God becomes man becomes fish becomes barnacle goose becomes featherbed mountain' (50.13). (Mr Tom Kernan has an interesting set of analogous reflections on Robert Emmet, 240.27ff). Bloom, who is like Shakespeare 'all in all' (212.29) appears to be suffused with Shakespearean tags throughout the chapter. 'Love among the tombstones' nicely summarizes the action of 'Romeo and Juliet' (108.15), there is an apposite quotation from 'Julius Caesar' (109.27), the jesting gravediggers are summoned from 'Hamlet' (109.14), and the play itself is laid under casual contribution in the phrase 'when churchyards yawn' (108.5: *Hamlet* III.ii.407). What would happen 'if we were all suddenly somebody else' (110.24) is a question very present to Bloom's mind, not just at the moment when he forms this phrase, but throughout the chapter. At various stages in its development, we notice, he himself is not only Leopold Bloom, but L. Boom, C. P. M'Coy,—Macintosh, and Dear Henry, a rather impressive assortment of variously acquired artificial and representative personalities. Surely it is no accident that a peculiar phrase from his private meditations, 'damn the

thing else' (105.39) turns up within two pages on the tongue of
Martin Cunningham (107.32).

   In effect, Bloom is a diffused personality—not merely dim and
hazy around the edges, but with chunks of other personalities' in-
corporated with his, and vice versa. In later chapters of the book he
will turn transparent, become mythical, and disintegrate entirely; in
this chapter he is being built up; but the negative process of dissolution is already under way in selected spots around his periphery.
When other people's words turn up in Bloom's monologues, or his in
theirs, it isn't a 'dropping out of character' but a deliberate dropping
of character into some other continuum. A classic instance, far too
obvious not to be deliberate, is the appearance of Stephen's words
about Gerard the herbalist in the midst of a Bloom monologue in
'Sirens' (280.26–27); but one could also point to the way Bloom's
meditation on 'the jews they said killed the christian boy' (108.30)
looks forward to Stephen's recital, on pp. 690–691, of the legend of
little Harry Hughes.

   Among the themes which can be seen to linger on in 'Hades'
after their enunciation in earlier chapters, one ought to mention
those of sleep and the east. Father Coffey shakes sleep over the
corpse (104.16), drunken Mrs Cunningham performs in Bloom's
recollection a song from a music-hall show *The Geisha* (96.40–42),
and the chapter is dotted with thoughts about the opium grown in
Chinese graveyards (108.27–28), whores in Turkish graveyards
(108.13), a book about *Voyages in China* (114.24), a Parsee tower
of silence (114.29)—not to mention Rudolf Virag's dog Athos, who
is named for a Greek mountain as Bloom himself is named for an
Irish one, or the way in which C. P. M'Coy 'levanted' (111.42)
with the cash of a few ads. In addition to carrying out the oriental-
ism of 'Lotuseaters', this imagery serves to associate eastwardly oriented Bloom with the rising sun and the subsurface overtone of
resurrection that runs through the chapter. There is even a moment
when Bloom, foreseeing the ritual stop on the journey home for a
drink at Dunphy's, reflects that what they get there will be the
'elixir of life' (98.42)—usquebaugh, which has been known to raise
Irishmen from the dead.[19]

_____

   [19] The whole question of drink, which bulked so large as a social issue in
Ireland around the turn of the century, is crucially if ambiguously related to
the events of the chapter. Paddy Dignam is dead of drink after having lost his

On occasion, an apparently ordinary word planted in the course of 'Hades' flowers into fuller and more deeply dimensioned meaning later in the book. This isn't, at its best, simply a matter of thematic repetition; the two passages, related by the repeated word, reflect from one another a meaning that isn't properly present in either one of them considered in isolation. When the funeral cortège is about to get under way, Bloom sees an old woman staring out a window; and his thoughts move on to the interest that women take in preparing corpses on their deathbeds for imminent burial: 'Job seems to suit them. Huggermugger in corners. Slop about in slipperslappers for fear he'd wake. Then getting it ready' (87.18). The word 'slipperslapper' gets double resonance here from the circumstances under which it occurs nearly 400 pages later in 'Circe'. 'Is this Mrs Mack's?' Bloom asks Zoe Higgins, and she answers casually, 'No, eightyone. Mrs Cohen's. You might go farther and fare worse. Mother Slipperslapper'. The first and most obvious overtone contributed by the first passage to the second is that Bloom has come to a house of death, but there are also reverse connexions, via Cohen, with old Cohen's bed, bed 'of conception and of birth, of consummation of marriage and of breach of marriage, of sleep and of death' (731.9). Still more interesting and impressive is the way Joyce has handled the theme of the corpse as buried divinity destined to be resurrected, torn apart, and devoured by the faithful. Reading *Ulysses* with *Finnegans Wake* in mind, we can scarcely fail to be aware of this theme as a powerful element in the earlier novel.

In fact we find all sorts of references to cannibalism and corpseeating on both sides of the 'Hades' chapter. 'Lotuseaters' takes us to the performance of a mass where Bloom as comparative anthropologist reflects largely on the practice of god-eating in Christianity and elsewhere (80.34–38). And on the other side, 'Lestrygonians' is full and forthright on the same process—see, for example, 171.31–40. But within 'Hades' itself, Joyce carefully touches only the fringe and outskirts of the theme—and his delicacy of touch

---

job because of drink (102.42); prudent Molly says the last word on the social drinking that leads inevitably to this end: 'and they call that friendship killing and then burying one another' (773.33). Richie Goulding has clearly set his foot on the same path (88.23–30). But Joyce also represents a heroic dimension in Irish drinking—it is a kind of tribal communion, a celebration of the revival of a buried god. The two attitudes, like equally violent, equally opposed attitudes toward woman, seem to exist side by side in Joyce's mind, as in the novel.

invites our admiration. Bloom reflects briefly, at the beginning of the chapter, on the vitality of corpses which, even after being clipped and trimmed, 'grow all the same after' (87.23); he reads the obituary column (91.15ff) in the same paper where he has previously seen (75.1–4) an ad for Plumtree's Potted Meat; but he does not tell us till two chapters later that the two incongruous items stood side by side, so that the phrase 'Dignam's potted meat' forms, as if automatically, in his mind (171.34). Though he has thought in 'Hades' of the corpse decaying into 'kind of a tallowy kind of a cheesy' (108.39), and that cheese is 'the corpse of milk', (114.23), those words are allowed to sink into the reader's mind without further emphasis, and only make connexion with the Gorgonzola that Bloom eats in Davy Byrne's (172.16) through a set of tenuous and latent relationships. Lastly, those interesting 'crustcrumbs' that the travellers find in their mildewy coach (89.29–30) recall not only Richie Goulding's worthless backache pills (88.34), but also perhaps the remnants of a sacramental feast. As he enters the bed, Cohen's old bed again, the bed of birth, marriage, adultery, and death, Bloom will again encounter 'some crumbs, some flakes of potted meat' (731.15), and again, I think, the earlier passage must be read in the light of the later one.

Perfunctories

Many local details of the chapter can be 'verified' in the most prosaic of ways, by a diligent thumbing through of Thom's Dublin Directory or of the daily Dublin newspapers. The sort of trivia thus uncovered include street addresses, restaurants, churches, sporting events, theatrical performances, municipal officials, and various commercial enterprises—all of which constitute the pabulum of meditation or conversation in the course of the chapter. Many of the characters active in this section of the book carry over from short stories in *Dubliners*, notably 'Ivy Day' and 'Grace', but also including 'A Little Cloud' and 'Counterparts'. Old Mrs Riordan (97.25), from whom Bloom hopes to get an inheritance, was a friend of the Dedalus family, Dante Riordan in the *Portrait*. Ned Lambert, John Henry Menton, Corny Kelleher, and Paddy Leonard first appear or are first mentioned in this chapter. The total absence of description or comment when they are first 'introduced' allows them to slide into the narration almost unnoticed.

As with most of these early chapters of *Ulysses*, we do not have a true holograph of 'Hades'. There is a typescript with Joyce's corrections on it in the Poetry Collection of the Lockwood Memorial Library in Buffalo, New York;[20] but it is definitely later than the version printed in *Little Review* (September 1918). Then there must have been one other typescript or set of proofs between this typescript and the first proofs we have toward the volume *Ulysses*. Finally, we have a set of rather rich and abundant proof sheets.[21] As usual with Joyce, the effect of all these changes was increment, accretion. Almost nothing that got into the book was ever taken out. Thus, in *Little Review* the chapter makes about 884 lines of type as against 1,176 roughly equivalent lines in the Modern Library edition. It was enlarged by more than 25 percent. The sort of thing that got added was miscellaneous. The statues of central Dublin entered the novel as a unit on proof sheets; the refrain that runs through Bloom's mind from 'The Pauper's Drive' ('Rattle his bones /Over the stones/ Only a pauper/ Nobody owns', 96.12) with its various echoes and reverberations, was inserted on a typescript. The potentially important paragraph in which a streetorgan plays (five years before it was written) 'Has Anybody Here Seen Kelly?' (97.18–30), entered the book some time after the typescript was prepared but before the first proofs we now possess. When he added new material, here as elsewhere, Joyce did so sometimes to expand and diversify, sometimes to sharpen the point of what he had already written. His method of composition was unusual chiefly in allowing the material to grow in considerable measure from the inside out.

Conclusion

It's arguable that every third chapter in *Ulysses* is a particularly strong, rich, or vivid one (the full list would give us 'Proteus', 'Hades', 'Scylla and Charybdis', 'Cyclops', 'Circe', and 'Penelope'). Whether this is true or not, it is clear that 'Hades' stands out from its immediate neighbours ('Calypso' and 'Lotuseaters' on one side,

[20] V.B.4, in the Spielberg catalogue.
[21] V.C.I., 6a, 6b, 6c, 7a, 7b.

'Aeolus' and 'Lestrygonians' on the other) as darker and more lyrical in its feeling, more structured and less desultory in its action. Bloom, in the course of it, is less alone physically, more alone spiritually; the sense of life's empty forms, and of a restless imagination groping and probing beneath them is more profound. The black clouds and oppressive weights of Bloom's nightmare existence are reserved for 'Circe'; but in 'Hades' he passes (partly by pluck, partly by luck, and partly perhaps by sheer insensitivity) a psychic test of sufficient seriousness to put him on the way toward equipoise with the Stephen Dedalus of 'Proteus'.[22]

[22] This chapter was written before the publication of Richard Ellmann's *Ulysses on the Liffey*, Oxford, 1972, an elegant, sinuous little volume which in several ways confirms, extends, modifies, and occasionally counters my conclusions. The most important extension, I think, is a set of dialectical oppositions that balance Bloom's motion, physical and spiritual, through 'Hades', against Stephen's motion in 'Proteus'. Some of Professor Ellmann's other dialectical pyrotechnics seem less integrally connected with the novel; this one is basic. A point of confirmation is found in the essential pattern of sinking and then rising within the chapter, which I connect with the reversal in the use of the word 'heart', but which Professor Ellmann relates to an even more exciting sentence in 'Proteus', that which begins 'God becomes man', (50.13). On this sentence and its manifold implications, Professor Robert A. Day has written an extraordinarily provocative study, which (through his kindness) I have seen, but which, as with Professor Ellmann's book, I have not used to alter my conclusions. Finally, when Professor Ellmann sees 'Hades' as portraying the Viconian third age, democratic, ordinary, and unassuming, I confess to feeling modified and even a little countered. For it seems to me that Bloom is elevated toward the end of the chapter. In his humility, which is visible, he becomes the vessel of a 'higher' vision, of which the paradigm (transformation through metaphor of the everyday to the mythical) is found in the last phrase of that crucial 'God becomes man' sentence in 'Proteus'. Thus these 'third' chapters ('Proteus' and 'Hades') incorporate, as I see it, not only the third Viconian age, but also the ghost of a *ricorso*.

In these several directions, my argument clearly needs some filling out as well as some pulling back and a little tucking in. But I should sprawl all over several other chapters if I now tried to revise: and in any case, when the next good book on *Ulysses* appears, there will be still further patching and mending to do. It has therefore seemed simplest merely to append this *caveat lector*.

AEOLUS

M. J. C. Hodgart

A crucial event takes place at this point in the narrative: Bloom does some work. Work in *Ulysses* is a rare process. There is plenty of activity, many miles are travelled, many elbows raised, but bread-winning productive work, 'servile' work of the kind that may not be performed on the Sabbath, is minimal. Barmaids, curates, whores, and beggars ply their trades, and in the background there are glimpses of the navvies, draymen, and tramwaymen who represent the labouring classes of Dublin. Stephen does a nominal hour as schoolmaster, taking a class from 10 to 11 (if that can be called work), and is duly paid. Bloom does a little housework at the beginning and the end of the day, and a little shopping in the middle, and performs several corporal works of mercy such as feeding the seagulls; but only in 'Aeolus' does he earn money by exercising his profession as advertising consultant, when he enters the newspaper office to see about the renewal of an advertisement for his client Alexander Keyes. Later he does a little research in the Library toward the layout and copywriting for this campaign; and his budget, £1.7s.6d. for the day, includes the credit item 'Commission recd. *Freeman's Journal*' (711). Otherwise Bloom, Stephen and the other main characters have world enough and time for an endless amount of drinking, conversation, meditation, and erotic pleasure. This is consonant with the economic history of Dublin, where almost nothing was manufactured except porter and biscuits; it was a port, chiefly for the export of cattle, a shopping centre for all Ireland, a centre for administration, services, and education—a city of consumers. In 'Aeolus' they consume, greedily, the written and spoken word.

A short prologue evokes the transportation systems of Dublin: of people (the Dublin United Tramway Company), of post (the Royal Mail), and of porter (Guiness drays). Bloom is seen first in an office of the *Freeman's Journal and National Press*, talking to 'Red' Murray; then in the printing works, talking to the foreman Councillor Nannetti, and Hynes; next he goes to the editorial office of the *Evening Telegraph*, a paper associated with the morning *Freeman's Journal*. Inside a group of hangers-on, 'Professor' Mac-Hugh, Simon Dedalus, and Ned Lambert, soon to be joined by J. J. O'Molloy, are discussing the first specimen of rhetoric, a newly reported speech by one Dawson. The group are joined by the editor Myles Crawford and the parasite Lenehan; Dedalus and Lambert leave. Bloom comes in to make a telephone call and leaves. Professor MacHugh makes a short speech on the subject of Rome (equals England) versus Greece (equals Ireland). Accompanied by Mr O'Madden Burke, Stephen enters, and asks the editor to publish the letter from Mr Deasy. The main debate then begins, on the topic of the Ancients versus the Moderns: Crawford asserts that there are no modern journalists or orators as good as the old ones, instancing Ignatius Gallaher's coup in reporting the Phoenix Park Murders, and the great orators of the eighteenth century. There is a short speech in reply by J. J. O'Molloy, who produces as the second specimen of rhetoric a speech by the barrister Seymour Bushe. MacHugh caps this with what he considers an even finer speech by John F. Taylor (third specimen). Stephen puts the motion 'that the house do now adjourn' to a pub (143.35). As they walk to Mooney's, Stephen begins to deliver his own speech, 'The Parable of the Plums'. Bloom approaches the editor in the street, fussing about the Keyes advertisement, and is rudely rebuffed (K.M.R.I.A.). Stephen finishes his parable to his uncomprehending audience. As an epilogue, the whole tramway system of Dublin comes to a halt, because of an electrical failure, while at the centre of this system, Nelson's column, Stephen, and his companions also halt, the professor peering aloft at the onehandled adulterer.

The Homeric correspondences to this story are neither difficult to discover nor very profound. At the beginning of Book X, Odysseus describes how their next landfall was the floating island of Aeolia. They were entertained for a month by Aeolus, king of the winds; on their departure Aeolus gives Odysseus a bag containing all the dangerous winds, bound with a silver cord, and sends him on his way with a friendly zephyr. Thanks to this wind Odysseus sails nearly home to Ithaca, and is actually in sight of the island by night, when he falls asleep. His companions, thinking that the bag holds treasure, undo it, and the winds break out and drive the ship back to Aeolia. (It was, of course, all Odysseus's fault, since he ought to have trusted his comrades enough to tell them what was really in the bag.) Aeolus naturally loses his temper with Odysseus, curses him, refuses to help him again, and drives him away. Myles Crawford, the editor, is the King of Wind; he first dismisses Bloom in a kindly enough manner: 'Begone! he said. The world is before you' (129.22). But when Bloom importunately comes back to him, he rebuffs him with a cruel snub. There is little to be added to Stuart Gilbert's commentary on the other Homeric associations, such as the noise of the newspaper office and of Aeolus's palace. The most obvious are the physical winds and draughts in the office and street, references to literal wind, and the large number of metaphors of which wind is the vehicle. Here are some of them (those asterisked were added to the *Little Review* text): for the wind, flatulence, balloon, zephyrs, gale days, windfall, what's in the wind, reaping the whirlwind, veer about, get the wind of, weathercocks, breath, blows over, *windbag, *blowing out, *blow out, *the draught, There's a hurricane blowing, blowing, on the breeze a mocking kite, the vent, *his first puff, *storm, *wheeze, *fanned, breath of fresh air, *Inspiration, Windy Arbour, breath of life, shape of air, trees blown down by that cyclone, *il vento*, divine afflatus, *belch, *spirit, gone with the wind, the four winds, take my breath away, windy Troy, breathless, *caught in a whirl, bellows, a little puff, squalls, raise the wind.

More significant are the non-Homeric parallels suggested by this metaphor, which point to one of the basic allegorical structures of the book. Here the English language and indeed many other languages play into Joyce's hands, as they did into Rabelais's and

Swift's.[1] A dictionary gives the following meanings of Hebrew *ruach*: 'breath, wind, air, breeze, blowing; animal life, spirit, ghost, soul, mind, intellect, passion'. The Greek *anemos*, 'wind', has many Indo-European cognates in the same semantic field, including Latin *anima* 'air, breeze, the breath, principle of animal life', and *animus* 'spiritual principle of human life, rational soul, disposition, courage, pride, vehemence, wrath'. The etymology of 'spirit' and 'inspiration' shows the same confusion of literal and metaphorical, or rather that primitive religious beliefs have been fossilized in language: Latin *inspirare* 'to breathe into, blow upon, excite, inflame, to arouse by divine influence'; *spiritus*, 'breath, breeze, breath of life, life, soul, mind, spirit, energy, courage, pride, arrogance'.[2] Wind, therefore, may be flatulence, over-blown rhetoric or false inspiration, but it may also be the true inspiration of religion and art. A central theme in *Ulysses* is that of the Trinity, God the Father, God the Son, and God the Holy Ghost (Old English *gast*, 'life, spirit, soul'). As always in Joyce, religion provides metaphors for the process of artistic creation. At the beginning of the book, the Trinity is separated; Bloom the Father and Stephen the Son are divided and consequently sterile. At the end, Stoom and Blephen, the two halves of the artist, become mystically identified, and the Trinity is completed, made Holy and Undivided, by the Holy Spirit, the inspiration of the book itself. Hence Stephen is able to walk out of the book, at last able to begin writing it. When we meet him in 'Aeolus' he is still uncreative: Myles Crawford gives him yet another reminder that he has done nothing yet. But just as the Old Testament, and even the writings of the pagans, in the view of traditional theology, contain prophecies of the Trinity and of the completed mission of Christ, so in 'Aeolus' there are foretastes of the godlike creative power to come.

In every chapter in which Stephen appears there is a correspondence with the Gospel story or *Vita Christi* and to the seasonal Liturgy based on that story, though the order does not always follow that of the Bible. Thus, as A. M. Klein has shown, the first chapter, 'Telemachus', is the Baptism of Christ; 'Nestor' combined

---

[1] Rabelais, Book 4, chapter 43: 'How Pantagruel landed at Ruach or Windy Island'; Swift, *The Mechanical Operation of the Spirit*.

[2] *Langenscheidt's Hebrew-English Dictionary; The Universal Dictionary of the English Language*, ed. H. C. Wyld.

Jesus among the teachers (Luke 2) with Jesus in the Temple (Matthew 21); 'Aeolus' is the Ministry of Jesus, and in particular the Sermon on the Mount.³ Stephen-Christ speaks in parables, and there are references to the Sermon on the Mount ('sufficient for the day is the newspaper thereof', Matthew 6), to the wise and foolish virgins (Matthew 25) and to weeping and gnashing of teeth (Matthew 7). Stephen's teachings fall on deaf ears, just as the seed falls on stony ground (Matthew 13), and as the plumstones of his Parable fall on the pavements of Dublin. The whole of *Ulysses* is a parable, for him who heareth the word and understandeth it; he indeed beareth fruit.

Whenever Bloom appears, from 'Calypso' to 'Circe', there is a similar correspondence with the books of the Old Testament. Thus in 'Calypso' he begins as one of the patriarchs of *Genesis*, while 'Lotuseaters' is clearly about the Egyptian Bondage. In 'Aeolus' the references to Moses are overt: Bloom thinks about the Passover, two of the speeches are about Moses, and Stephen's parable has the subtitle 'A Pisgah Sight of Palestine' (149.25). The entry into the Promised Land is frustrated by the normal paralysis of the Dubliners (of which the becalmed tramcars are an emblem); just as Odysseus gets a glimpse of his own promised land of Ithaca before the contrary winds blow him back to Aeolus's island. But there is at least a promise of Canaan, even though it remains doubtful if the Irish will ever achieve a meaningful political freedom or Bloom reestablish his rule in his own home. The figure of Moses is central to the political theme of *Ulysses*, and to the sustained parallel between the Jews and the Irish. Joyce uses the old cliché comparing Charles Stewart Parnell to Moses, leading his people out of British bondage, and gives it a vast extension of meaning. Parnell's presence is as pervasive in *Ulysses* as in the *Portrait* or *Finnegans Wake*. Parnell was the only Irish political figure whom Joyce admired, and his aloofness set Joyce's own life style: he is the archetype of both the God of Creation and of the Artist, 'paring his fingernails'. Joyce

³ I do not know if other writers in this book agree with me, but I am convinced that 'Scylla and Charybdis' corresponds to the Entry into Jerusalem (Palm Sunday). It is generally agreed that 'Oxen of the Sun' and 'Circe' correspond to the Last Supper (Maundy Thursday) and the Crucifixion (Good Friday) respectively; 'Eumaeus' is the Descent into Hell, and 'Ithaca' moves from Easter Saturday to the Resurrection on Easter Sunday. Klein, A. M. 'The Black Panther (A Study in Technique)'. *Accent*, X (Spring 1950), 139–155.

also equates him with Christ, the uncrowned king, whose kingdom was not of this world.[4] The implication is that there can be no true victories in the world of politics, and the only triumphs are those of the creative imagination. The equation 'Stephen = Christ = Moses = Parnell' is fundamental to *Ulysses*. Joyce's allegorical method, of which that equation is an example, is based on the 'typology' invented by the Fathers of the Church and developed by the mediaeval theologians. When the Christians took over the Jewish Scriptures they had to make them meaningful in terms of Christian doctrine. They did so, where they could not find prophecies of Christ's coming, by hunting for ingenious correspondences between Old and New Testament personages and events. The whole of the Old Testament narrative was seen as a shadow play, in which the characters unknowingly acted out the events of Christ's life: thus, Joseph in the pit prefigured Christ in the tomb. I think that Joyce considered Odysseus as acting out the events of Bloomsday, though it is usual to put that the other way round. The Fathers claimed that typology had been invented by Jesus himself, in the mysterious words of John, 3:14: 'And as Moses lifted up the serpent in the wilderness, so must the Son of Man be lifted up'. The comparison between Moses and Christ is used in the Good Friday Reproaches, which Stephen parodies in 'Oxen of the Sun'. The art of the 'Aeolus' chapter is rhetoric, which can be taken to mean the whole art of writing; and by his open emphasis on Moses, Joyce is not only developing a leitmotif, but stating something about the way in which *Ulysses* is written and in which it ought to be read.

The charge brought against another of Joyce's heroes, the protomartyr Stephen, was that of speaking blasphemously against Moses (Acts 6:11). Of course, Stephen's parable, like most of *Ulysses*, is highly blasphemous in the literal sense, but on the anagogical level Joyce saw Stephen, and himself, as bearers of the highest spiritual truth. When he made the first gramophone recording of a passage from *Ulysses*, he chose a piece of 'Aeolus', his own freely and beautifully rewritten version of a speech he had heard John F. Taylor give years before (24 October 1901) at his university's Law Students

---

[4] See M. J. C. Hodgart 'Ivy Day in the Committee Room' in Clive Hart (ed.), *James Joyce's Dubliners: Critical Essays*, London and New York, 1969, pp. 115–121.

Debating Society. Ironically, Taylor was defending the revival of
the Irish language, an issue on which Joyce's views were negative.
But metamorphosis is normal Joycean procedure: the passage is
transformed into a truly inspired statement of Joyce's artistic credo:

—But, ladies and gentlemen, had the youthful Moses listened
to and accepted that view of life, had he bowed his head and bowed
his will and bowed his spirit before that arrogant admonition he
would never have brought the chosen people out of their house of
bondage nor followed the pillar of the cloud by day. He would never
have spoken with the Eternal amid lightnings on Sinai's mountain-
top nor ever have come down with the light of inspiration shining
in his countenance and bearing in his arms the tables of the law,
graven in the language of the outlaw. (143.7)

The art of the chapter is rhetoric, a subject that now seems tedious
to nearly all readers, critics, and writers—but it was not so to Joyce
or to his contemporaries. The art of making persuasive speeches is
an ancient and much-loved tradition of the Irish, especially the
making of political speeches, whether at the graveside of dead lead-
ers or from the dock. I have read that until recently every Irish bar-
man in London kept under the bar a collection of condemned felon-
heroes' speeches,[5] and another selection of Irish oratory was edited
by Joyce's friend T. M. Kettle.[6] Most of the great orators in the
English language, like most of the great English dramatists of the
last three centuries, have been Irish; and speech is an art cultivated
at all levels of Irish society, to a degree unequalled in the English-
speaking world. At the end of O'Molloy's quotation from Bushe
('. . . which if aught that the imagination or the hand of sculptor
has wrought in marble of soultransfigured and of soultransfiguring
deserves to live, deserves to live' 140.14), 'Stephen, his blood wooed
by grace of language and gesture, blushed' (140.21). He thinks of
the emotional effect of oratory, as when Daniel O'Connell spoke to
an audience of one million at Tara. In his instinctive response,
Stephen is Irish, alltooirish; not long before this chapter was written
Pearse had made Easter Week inevitable by his speech at the

[5] This was probably Speeches from the Dock edited by T. D., A. M., and
D. B. Sullivan. This has gone through many editions since it was first published
in the 1890s; a revised edition was published by Gill and Macmillan, Dublin,
1968.
[6] Irish Orators and Oratory, London, Dublin, and Belfast (ca. 1914).

graveside of O'Donovan Rossa in 1915: 'but the fools. the fools, the fools!—they left us our Fenian dead. . .' .[7] Even Bloom shows himself to be a connoisseur of rhetoric, at the end of 'Sirens' when he quotes the end of Robert Emmet's speech from the dock, 1803: 'When my country takes her place among the nations of the earth, then and not till then, let my epitaph be written. I have done'.[8]

Classical rhetoric is 'the craft of speech'; it teaches how to construct a discourse artistically.[9] Of this craft 'Aeolus' is a compendium and, as is usual in Joyce, a systematic parody. Stuart Gilbert gives a huge list of the figures of speech illustrated in the chapter, from Metonomy, Chiasmus, and Metaphor to Hapax Legomenon. This was probably based on a list given to him by Joyce, since it is unlikely that Gilbert or anyone else but the author could have discovered all these figures. Even so the list is not exhaustive and not completely accurate; and I have not yet discovered what Joyce's sources were.[10] Joyce does not of course confine himself to figures of speech; as Gilbert notes, he also provides examples of the three main *kinds* of oratory, according to Aristotle: the deliberative (political, hortative, advisory); the forensic (legal); and the epideictic (declamatory, ceremonial, oratory of display or panegyric, which Gilbert calls 'expository'). In reverse order of appearance, these are the speeches of Taylor, Bushe, and Dawson. The five divisions of the classical *Ars* are *inventio, dispositio* (or 'organization' of the discourse), *elocutio* (style), *memoria,* and *actio* (delivery also called *pronuntiatio*), all of which are illustrated in the chapter. *Inventio* means the discovery of arguments, either non-artistic proofs (laws, witnesses, contracts, tortures, oaths) or artistic proofs: the last are based on the rational appeal (logos), the emotional appeal (pathos) and the ethical appeal (ethos). No one speaks very rationally in 'Aeolus' and what logic there is lies in the enthymeme, which I shall discuss separately; the pathos of Taylor's speech is manifest, while the ethical appeal is used a great deal. This is based on the

---

[7] Quoted in Sean O'Casey, *The Plough and the Stars,* Act II.

[8] 'Written. I have./ Pprrpffrrppfff./ Done' (291.11).

[9] E. R. Curtius, *European Literature and the Latin Middle Ages,* tr. W. R. Trask, London, 1953, Chapter 5, gives the best general description of classical rhetoric.

[10] Professor Brian Vickers in a private communication has pointed out some of the errors. There is much research still to be done into the rhetorical sources of 'Aeolus', on the part that rhetoric played in the Jesuit educational system.

esteem in which the speaker is held; as usual in Ireland, the truth of a statement is judged not by its logical consistency or correspondence with the facts, but with the character of the person who makes it. Throughout the chapter the characters pass strong spoken and unspoken judgments on others, e.g., Crawford speaks of Mr Deasy (another rhetorician) and O'Molloy says to Stephen 'Professor Magennis was speaking to me about you. . . . He is a man of the very highest morale' (140.27), the headline, or rather caption, repeating 'A MAN OF HIGH MORALE' (that is, ethics). I shall try to show below that the whole chapter is based on the rules for *dispositio*.

Elocutio includes the classification of styles into low, middle, or high (for the purposes of instructing, moving, and pleasing), all of which are illustrated, and the figures of speech. *Memoria* is essential to the orator, and Joyce was justly proud of his own fabulous memory. He relied on memory partly for his most famous piece of rhetoric, the sermon in the *Portrait*, as he did for the Bushe and Taylor quotations, both being versions of what he had personally heard in his student days.[11] *Actio* (*hypokrisis*) includes the orator's art of gesture, which supplied another basic theme for the chapter; but this so strongly affected the whole narrative technique that it will have to be discussed separately below.

Joyce calls the technique of 'Aeolus' 'enthymemic', thus producing one of the most irritating minor problems in the interpretation of *Ulysses*. For neither Joyce nor anyone else seems to know exactly what an enthymeme really is. The Greek *enthymema* 'a thought, argument' is derived from *enthumesthai*, 'to consider, reflect upon' and that in turn from '*thumos*', 'mind'; but its special meaning comes from Aristotle, who discusses it under the heading of *logos*, that is, of arguments possessing rational appeal. In one view it is the rhetorical equivalent of the syllogism: in logic, the syllogism is a device for proceeding from two premises, major and minor, to a conclusion, e.g. 'All men are mortal' (major), 'Socrates is a man' (minor), therefore 'Socrates is mortal' (conclusion). To ask a rhetorical question, what can be the rhetorical equivalent of that? One answer is that it is 'an argument based on what is true for the most part: "good men do not commit murder; Socrates is a good

[11] Ellmann, pp. 94, 95. Cf. Ellmann, p. 207: 'The image of himself making a public self-defence with the eloquence of Seymour Bushe and John F. Taylor never quite left Joyce'.

man; therefore Socrates did not commit murder" '.[12] It is not certainly true that good men do not commit murder, but only very
probably true. So 'the essential difference is that the syllogism leads
to a necessary conclusion from universally true premises but the
enthymeme leads to a tentative conclusion from probable premises'.[13]
Hence, more loosely, the enthymeme may be 'an argument based on
probable premises as distinct from a demonstration' (OED). But
the word has come to have a second and very different meaning,
that is, of a truncated syllogism, with one premise suppressed, the
simplest example being Descartes' *Cogito, ergo sum* (which omits
the major 'all thinking beings exist', a ridiculous tautology); another
example is 'we are beggars and therefore cannot be choosers'. The
second meaning presumably came from Aristotle's statement that
'the enthymeme must consist of few propositions, fewer often than
those which make up normal syllogisms'.[14] I suppose his reason for
saying that is that it is tedious for an orator to take his audience
step by step through an entire syllogism. It could be that Joyce meant
that the whole chapter was enthymemic in sense 1, in that nothing
is certainly demonstrated; it can't be proved by syllogisms that
Irish = Hebrew or Stephen = Christ. But he also used sense 2,
e.g. 'We were weak, therefore worthless' (suppressing the major,
'all those who are weak are worthless'—which the Gospel says is
untrue in any case). The example of an enthymeme in Gilbert's
list seems to me to be wrong: 'If you want to draw the cashier is
just going to lunch' (119.27), says Bloom to Hynes; but that is
just an elliptical sentence, from which the words 'you had better
hurry, because' have been deleted; and in fact Bloom has tactfully
deleted another, undeniably true, proposition, 'and since you owe
three shillings, will you please repay me'—which is an intolerably
difficult sentence to say to anyone. The chapter abounds with these
tactful ellipses; everything is left hanging in the air. The richest
example of reasoning is on page 117, but I cannot decide whether
it is an enthymeme or a true syllogism. Bloom and Red Murray see
the publisher Brayden enter.

[12] G. A. Kennedy, *The Art of Persuasion in Greece*, New York, 1963, p. 97,
quoted by Brian Vickers, *Classical Rhetoric in English Poetry*, London, 1970,
p. 62.
    [13] E. P. Corbett, *Classical Rhetoric for the Modern Student*, New York,
1965, p. 61, discussing Aristotle, *Prior Analytics*, I, 27.
    [14] *Rhetoric*, I, 2, quoted by Corbett, p. 62.

—Don't you think his face is like Our Saviour? Red Murray whispered. . . .

Our Saviour: beardframed oval face: talking in the dusk Mary, Martha. Steered by an umbrella sword to the footlights: Mario the tenor.

—Or like Mario, Mr Bloom said.

—Yes, Red Murray agreed. But Mario was said to be the picture of Our Saviour. (117.23)

That seems to be a way of proving rhetorically, if not logically, that not only Stephen = Xt, but Brayden = Xt, Mario = Xt, and by extrapolation every human being = Xt, a proposition set out in 'Circe'.

The structure of the chapter follows the traditional rhetorical structure of a speech. The authoritative formulation is in the treatise *Ad Herennium*, which I shall quote from Brian Vickers's lucid exposition.[15] There are seven sections within a speech: *exordium, narratio, divisio, confirmatio, refutatio, confutatio,* and *conclusio.* 'The introduction [*exordium*] is the beginning of the discourse, and by it the hearer's mind is prepared for attention'. This is the prologue, with trams, mail, porter drays in circulation. 'The Narration or Statement of Facts sets forth the events that have occurred or might have occurred'; or as Red Murray says '—There it is' (116.27). The narration, beginning with Bloom in the newspaper office, is summarized above. 'By means of the Division we make clear what matters are agreed upon and what are contested, and announce what points we intend to take up'. The first matter agreed on is that Dawson's is a poor specimen of rhetoric. The second matter agreed on is that in all things except plumbing the Romans (British) were inferior to the Greeks (Irish). The matter disagreed on (136ff) is that the modern journalists and orators are inferior to the ancient or to those of the recent past. The next heads in the *Ad Herennium* are *confirmatio* (proof) and *refutatio*: 'Proof is the presentation of our arguments, together with their corroboration. Refutation is the destruction of our adversaries' arguments'. Crawford presents his argument, corroborating it with the story about Ignatius Gallaher; he is refuted first by O'Molloy and then by MacHugh, whose only proof is to produce outstanding specimens of modern rhetoric. 'The Conclusion is the end of the discourse, formed in accordance with

[15] *Classical Rhetoric in English Poetry,* London, 1970, pp. 65ff.

the principles of the art'. There would appear to be no conclusion
to the debate, since the point at issue, like the 'enthymemes' and
elliptical sentences of the chapter, is left hanging in the air. But
this inconclusiveness is only apparent, since the fragmented discourse
is in fact brought to a conclusion by Stephen's Parable of the Plums.
The discourse is taken on to a higher plane, since the Parable, for
all its absurdity, is true imaginative art, in contrast to merely brilliant
oratory; and because Stephen speaks with Christlike simplicity. The
Fathers contrasted the high style of the pagan rhetoricians unfavour-
ably with the *sermo humilis* of the Gospel, the only proper style for
the spreading of God's word. The parable contains, in its ludicrous
narrative, dark sayings and hidden mysteries which are close to the
heart of the book. The two Dublin vestals (Martha and Mary) are
the two midwives seen by Stephen on the beach in 'Proteus' (37.33),
where he first names one of them Florence McCabe. Her gamp is
named after the famous umbrella of Sarah Gamp, who was not only
midwife but layer-out of corpses. Representing the two phases of
Woman that preside over birth and death, they reappear in 'Oxen
of the Sun' 'The aged sisters draw us into life . . . over us dead they
bend. First saved from water of old Nile, among bulrushes . . .'
(394.13). The Mosaic reference suggests that they are the midwives
of the New Ireland, and the layers-out of its stillborn corpse. They
spit out the plumstones, which will die on the stony ground, unless
fertilized by the urine of Bloom's humanity and Stephen's art. Thus
they exemplify the major Waste land-Fertility theme, which receives
its fullest treatment in 'Oxen of the Sun'. At the end, they are too
tired to move 'or to speak' (no more rhetoric); static on a phallic
monument, they gaze up in paralysis at the phallic Nelson, the one-
handled adulterer.

> . . . That tickles me I must say.
> —Tickled the old ones too, Myles Crawford said, if the God
> Almighty's truth was known. (150.12)

But God's truth *is* at last, in the fullness of time, known; and the
debate on old versus new is concluded. The midwives have presided
over the birth of a miraculous Child, and now a great Modern writer
is among us.

The art of rhetoric, as noted briefly above, included *actio*,
which meant essentially the orator's gestures. This supplied a basic

theme for the chapter, and even a modification of its narrative technique toward the visual and the dramatic. The subject of gesture was much studied by classical theorists. Thus Cicero, after listing the basic emotions:

> On all these emotions a proper gesture ought to attend; not the gesture of the stage, expressive of mere words, but one showing the whole force and meaning of a passage, not by gesticulation, but by emphatic delivery, by strong and manly exertion of the lungs, not imitated from the theatre and the players, but rather from the camp and the palaestra . . . . But all depends on the countenance and even in that the eyes bear sovereign sway; and therefore the oldest of our countrymen showed the more judgment in not applauding even Roscius himself to any great degree when he performed in a mask; for all the powers of action proceed from the mind, and the countenance is the image of the mind, and the eyes are its interpreters.[16]

Cicero differs from the other great theorist Quintilian in minimizing the value of manual gesture, in which the orator's art approaches the mimetic art of the actor:

> As to the hands, without the aid of which all delivery would be deficient and weak, it can scarcely be told of what a variety of motions they are susceptible, since they almost equal in expression the powers of language itself; for other parts of the body assist the speaker, but these, I may almost say, speak themselves. With our hands we ask, promise, call persons to us and send them away, threaten, supplicate, intimate dislike or fear; with our hands we signify joy, grief, doubt, acknowledgement, penitence, and indicate measure, quantity, number and time. Have not our hands the power of inciting, of restraining, of beseeching, of testifying approbation, admiration, and shame? Do they not, in pointing out places and persons, discharge the duty of adverbs and pronouns? So that amidst the great diversity of tongues pervading all nations and peoples, the language of the hands appears to be a language common to all men. . . .[17]

These points are beautifully illustrated in 'Aeolus', a highly visual chapter, in which the characters are seen conversing in body-language as well as in words: it is a miniature textbook of non-

[16] On Oratory and Orators, tr. J. S. Watson, quoted in Actors on Acting, ed. Cole and Chindy, London, 1949, p. 24.
[17] Quintilian, Institutes of Oratory, tr. J. S. Watson, London, 1913, quoted in Actors on Acting, ed. Cole and Chindy, p. 29.

verbal communication by facial expression and bodily gesture. The mention of Michelangelo's *Moses* is relevant in this respect, the sculpture being outstanding for the representation of emotion and thought kinesically in 'frozen' bodily action. Despite Cicero's warning, many theorists have drawn parallels between oratory and acting, and Joyce would seem to follow them. 'Aeolus' can be read as a one-act play, with very full stage directions and minute instructions to the actors on how to use their bodies. This serves to remind us that *Ulysses* is an epic of the body, and the body plays its part in debate and discussion, just as it does in music (Bloom's *wind* adds a fugal voice to 'Sirens'). Bloom is himself based on the greatest mime of the silent movies, Charlie Chaplin: he has a Chaplinesque walk, which the newsboys imitate (129.31).

Gestures can have deictic, ruminative, and symbolic uses, among others: Bloom points 'backward with his thumb' as a hint to Hynes (119.28); foreman Nannetti scratches his armpit, then his ribs; Bloom crosses his fingers to illustrate the crossed Keyes ad (120.21). The debaters use a good deal of abrupt gesture, vividly presented, and there is some bodily contact. MacHugh lays a firm hand on Crawford's shoulder (127.23), and Crawford lays a nervous one on Stephen's (135.14). Crawford 'suddenly stretched forth an arm amply' (129.21) saying to Bloom 'begone'. There is a lot of stage business about offering and lighting cigarettes, apparently trivial actions which nevertheless promote the solidarity of the group and once again exclude Bloom. The more strictly rhetorical gestures include MacHugh's 'extended elocutionary arms' (131.9) in the middle of his discourse on Rome, and O'Molloy's ending his quotation from Bushe thus: 'His slim hand with a wave graced echo and fall' (140.17). Stephen responds strongly, 'his blood wooed by grace of language and gesture' (140.21). When MacHugh reaches the climax of oratory with his quotation from Taylor, he fiddles with his spectacles in a most elaborate manner (141.22), while his glances are minutely described, perhaps as a tribute to Cicero's emphasis on eyes. Aeolus-Crawford accompanies all his talk with violent movement, thrusting back his dicky 'with a rude gesture' (137.1); later 'his mouth continued to twitch unspeaking in nervous curls of disdain' (138.14); and finally it is he who mentions the supremely symbolic nonverbal gesture: 'Will you tell him he can kiss my arse? Myles Crawford said, *throwing out his arm for emphasis*' (146.32).

That is the ultimate act of obeisance; that it is used traditionally by the Devil's disciples shows us what kind of a king Aeolus really is. But even the gestures end in frustration, for at the end of so much hand-waving we are left with the image of the one-handled adulterer, his digits diminished.

The 'vision' of Stephen expressed in his parable, and its title 'A Pisgah *Sight* of Palestine', are also pointers to the visual nature of the chapter, which is heightened by the capitalised phrases that interrupt the text every few lines. These have usually been described as 'headlines', added at a late stage in composition to match the description of the newspaper office. But most of them are seen on closer inspection to be unsuitable for headlining: they are rather captions under imaginary illustrations, probably photographs, added by an anonymous sub-editor. The first, IN THE HEART OF THE HIBERNIAN METROPOLIS, is obviously the caption for a picture of Nelson's Pillar, with the trams starting from its foot, while near the end DEAR DIRTY DUBLIN is the caption for the view that the two vestals see from the top of the Pillar. The fourth, WILLIAM BRAYDEN, ESQUIRE, OF OAKLANDS, SANDYMOUNT, must be the title of a photo-portrait of the aforesaid Brayden. The sixth is rather different, being an extract from Hynes's account of Dignam's funeral then being set up in type, real or imagined by Bloom: WITH UNFEIGNED REGRET IT IS WE ANNOUNCE THE DISSOLUTION OF A MOST RESPECTED DUBLINBURGESS. This is followed by what could be an illustrated article on newspapers: HOW A GREAT DAILY ORGAN IS TURNED OUT and WE SEE THE CANVASSER AT WORK. Only about two are suitable for headlines: SHINDY IN WELLKNOWN RESTAURANT and LOST CAUSES/NOBLE MARQUESS MENTIONED, to which should, perhaps, be added the odd American-English ones near the end (reminding us that America has been the only promised land for many Irishmen). The penultimate is clearly visual in intent: HORATIO IS CYNOSURE THIS FAIR JUNE DAY. ('I *see*, the professor said'.) The last is neither headline nor caption but a mysterious voice from the sky proclaiming obscurely that the old ones have been tickled into a state of sexual excitement: DIMINISHED DIGITS PROVE TOO TITILLATING FOR FRISKY FRUMPS. ANNE WIMBLES, FLO WANGLES—YET CAN YOU BLAME THEM?

If it was Joyce's intention to heighten the visual qualities of the chapter by the use of gesture and photographic captions, it can be said that he was highly successful. The *purling rill* of rhetoric,

as it babbles on its way (123.25) obscures neither the vivid figures
of the debaters nor the strong key-images of the chapter, Moses,
the Pillar, the traffic of Dublin, which are as sharp as the images of
sower and grain, thorns and stony ground, in the parables. 'Aeolus'
is mainly concerned with the teachings of Jesus the rabbi, but like
the rest of *Ulysses* it celebrates the deeds of Jesus the wonderworker,
the greatest of whose miracles was restoring the dead to life. The
radiant visual imagery of 'Aeolus', as of many other chapters, is essential to the miracle of artistic recreation.

LESTRYGONIANS

Melvin J. Friedman

The 'Lestrygonians' episode was first published in the January 1919 number of the *Little Review*.[1] It was in interesting company: it appeared along with a Yeats play, *The Dreaming of the Bones*, written in the manner of Japanese Noh drama; a symposium on *Exiles*; and the first instalment of a story by May Sinclair, 'Mary Olivier: A Life'. The presence of May Sinclair is especially intriguing because she was among the first to acknowledge and label a new literary technique; in an article written the previous April for *The Egoist*, she had this to say about Dorothy Richardson's *Pilgrimage*: 'In this series there is no drama, no situation, no set scene. Nothing happens. It is just like life going on and on. It is Miriam Henderson's stream of consciousness going on and on. And in neither is there any discernible beginning or middle or end'. She might have said the same thing about Leopold Bloom's meanderings in *Ulysses*, espe-

---

[1] Curiously enough, it was left unfinished in this number. Margaret Anderson carried over the final four and a fraction pages into the double issue of February-March 1919, which was ostensibly a special number devoted to Remy de Gourmont. This disturbing habit of 'little magazines' to allow even short works to continue over into subsequent issues—after all 'Lestrygonians' runs only thirty-three pages in the 1961 corrected edition of *Ulysses*—is partly redeemed by Margaret Anderson's careful division of the parts. The January number leaves off with Paddy Leonard's final words, '—Ay, Paddy Leonard said. A sucking-bottle for the baby'. The February-March instalment starts with the next paragraph which finds Bloom outside in the street, once again his own man.

cially about his almost unbroken monologue in the 'Lestrygonians'
section. She might actually have used with some appropriateness a
favourite expression of Leopold Bloom, 'stream of life'—which is
one of the verbal leitmotifs of 'Lestrygonians'.

The novelist as narrator of objective facts is only intermittently
visible in this eighth chapter of *Ulysses* and even then his language
is often caught up in a syntax that belongs more to poetry than to
prose. And his omniscience is often in doubt. This narrator has no
separate identity; he never intervenes to comment or pass judgment
in propria persona in the manner of nineteenth century omniscient
storytellers in novels of Stendhal, Dostoevsky, Manzoni, or Jane
Austen. He even refrains from such insertions as 'he thought', 'he
said', or 'he felt', which we find in even so inward-looking a novelist
as Virginia Woolf.[2]

To give some examples of the presence and rhetorical identity
of this narrator: he can be absolutely colourless and anonymous,
describing Bloom's movements with reportorial detachment: 'He
crossed at Nassau street corner and stood before the window of
Yeates and Son, pricing the field glasses' (166.17). On the other
hand, his narrative movement can get caught up in the syntax of
Bloom's reverie and the result looks like this: 'With hungered flesh
obscurely, he mutely craved to adore' (168.37). Occasionally the
texture of the language is affected and we get an alliterative effect,
with accompanying syntactical confusion: 'Wine soaked and softened rolled pith of bread mustard a moment mawkish cheese'
(174.25). This last has nothing of the omniscient, assured narration
that is in control of external events; the syntax has completely broken
down and grammatical safeguards have deserted the language. In
fact, it is seemingly more removed from logical controls and closer
to a kind of post-Symbolist poetry than the bits of Bloom's inner
monologue that follow: 'Nice wine it is. Taste it better because I'm
not thirsty' (174.26).

This narrator—he might also be called an 'implied author'
(Wayne Booth's expression)—performs only limited service in
'Lestrygonians'.[3] He is sometimes around at the beginning of a

[2] See the brilliant discussions of narrative movement in *Ulysses* in S. L. Goldberg's *The Classical Temper*, London, 1961.

[3] We should heed Wayne Booth's valuable warning: '. . . we must never
forget that though the author can to some extent choose his disguises, he can
never choose to disappear'. (*The Rhetoric of Fiction*, Chicago, 1961, p. 20.)

paragraph to get Bloom across a street, to explain how he digests his gorgonzola cheese sandwich and wine, or to set the time. He can, as we have seen above, remain perfectly detached or else lose identity in the flow of Bloom's monologue. The important thing to remember is that he never speaks for himself and that his voice does not have any special timbre—like that of the intrusive story-tellers of nineteenth-century fiction. He is emphatically not a shaping influence on the principal narrative movement of 'Lestrygonians' although he participates in that movement by supplying it with an external dimension. He is needed to relieve the impressionism of Bloom's monologue by supplying it with a set of spatial and temporal *points de repère*.

Most commentators on *monologue intérieur*, from Dujardin on, have indicated this need to set the monologuist firmly in both time and space. Dujardin's little book on the subject was written more than forty years after the publication of his novelette *Les Lauriers sont coupés* (1887)—the Symbolist-inspired work that Joyce announced was essential to the writing of *Ulysses*. Dujardin's first-person, Daniel Prince, sets the temporal and spatial circumstances of his monologue in the second paragraph of *Les Lauriers*: . . . *et, autour de moi, la vie; l'heure, le lieu, un soir d'avril, Paris, un soir clair de soleil couchant*. . . . He gets even more precise in the third paragraph: . . . *L'heure a sonné; six heures, l'heure attendue. Voici la maison où je dois entrer, où je trouverai quelqu'un*. . . . Joyce resists these easy formulas in *Ulysses* and very carefully turns over the stage directions to the narrator we have been speaking of. Thus we find in 'Lestrygonians' this transitional sentence of objective third-person narration: 'He [Bloom] raised his eyes and met the stare of a bilious clock' (173.1). Joyce realized better than Dujardin how one's consciousness reacts to external pressures of time and space, and felt the need of an occasional intruding third person to relieve the flow of monologue. Dujardin tried to muffle this third-person authorial presence by placing all awareness of external events within Daniel Prince's monologue; Joyce retained this view from the 'outside'.

Les Lauriers sont coupés, with all its amateurish attempts at rendering consciousness, manages to give us an accurate and compelling look at Prince's *état d'âme*. There are actually several intriguing comparisons to be made between his April wanderings in

Paris between 6 P.M. and midnight and Bloom's Lestrygonian movements between 1 and 2 P.M. on his June day in Dublin. Ezra Pound
called Bloom *l'homme moyen sensuel* and *l'homme qui croit ce
qu'il lit dans les journaux*; Daniel Prince is much the same thing
but in a *symboliste* setting. As Leon Edel put it so well: 'The type
of mind Bloom has is not unlike that of Daniel Prince in *Les
Lauriers sont coupés*. He sees immediate images and reflects upon
them immediately; he has a literal, fact-accumulating mind. He has
absorbed all kinds of data and all manner of clichés. Through him
we become aware of the city, in the concrete images it flashes into
his mind'.[4] The 'Lestrygonians' chapter of *Ulysses* is filled with
Bloom's unrequited physical needs (both sexual and culinary). He
recalls longingly the sensually satisfying moments with Molly. During his conversation with Mrs Breen he pays particular attention to
her 'womaneyes' and thinks of what she was like in her more attractive days. He looks ahead to the vicarious pleasure involved in answering Martha Clifford's suggestive letter. In the matter of food
Bloom also behaves with the same despair of the present and sensual
anticipation of the future as he exits hurriedly from the Burton
restaurant ('Couldn't eat a morsel here', 169.33) and makes his way
to Davy Byrne's 'Moral pub'.

Daniel Prince also has women and food on his mind through
his six-hour monologue. Not only does Prince think constantly of
his liaison with Léa—which is as chaste as Bloom's current relations
with Molly—but he also ogles every attractive woman in sight. He
enjoys a certain fugitive gastronomic bliss in the *Café Oriental,
restaurant*. A refrain which passes through his mind while in the
restaurant is *Et toujours la même triple passion. . . . Vive le vin,
l'amour et le tabac. . . .* (The ellipses are such a necessary part of
Dujardin's use of *monologue intérieur*.) He, too, dotes on past sensual joys and fondly anticipates the future, but despairs of the boredom of the present. Daniel Prince accommodates himself to that
hole in time which he must pass through before his next meeting
with Léa. This is, in fact, the main subject of *Les Lauriers sont
coupés*: it is a novel about the interim between past and future
pleasures and the need to adjust to that in-between time.

If Bloom has an in-between, hole-in-time period of his day, it
is during the 'Lestrygonians' section: 'This is the very worst hour of

[4] *The Modern Psychological Novel*, New York, 1964, p. 84.

the day. Vitality. Dull, gloomy: hate this hour. Feel as if I had been
eaten and spewed' (164.38). It is his time for contemplation just
as the 'Proteus' section was Stephen Dedalus'.[5] His inner monologue
is, as we have already suggested, the controlling movement of the
section, a movement which is frequently broken in upon by a narrative third person. Most of Bloom's thoughts in 'Lestrygonians' are in
the area of consciousness that Freud labelled the preconscious; thus
the transition from third to first person is often barely noticeable
and both are made to seem a part of Bloom's 'stream of life'. The
smoothness of the transition reminds us again of how much Joyce
has advanced beyond the monologue of Les Lauriers sont coupés
in which the 'I' works too hard and does too many things that properly belong to the third person. Yet one can appreciate how much
Joyce learned from Dujardin's insistent use of the first person, which
differed so markedly from most previous first-person fiction with its
obtrusively confessional nature. Novelists who held on to the omniscient third person felt the need for elaborate stage directions
before they could enter a character's mind. Dujardin, avoiding these
unnatural circumlocutions, is in Prince's mind from the opening
paragraph, which is no more than a series of impressions separated
by commas and semicolons and with no reference to person: Un
soir de soleil couchant, d'air lointain, de cieux profonds; et des foules
confuses; des bruits, des ombres, des multitudes; des espaces infini-
ment étendus; un vague soir. . . . The je actually doesn't appear for
the first time until we are six lines into the second paragraph. But
from then on we are at its mercy. It becomes the most kinetic element in Dujardin's syntax; it has a way of turning up unexpectedly
when one is least prepared for it.

Joyce is much more sparing in his use of the first person. In
the tenth line of 'Lestrygonians' we finally get this: 'Bloo . . . Me?'
And this comes out of a confusion. Bloom has been presented with
a throwaway by a young man and begins reading it. He hurriedly

[5] For an excellent comparison between these two chapters of Ulysses, see
Erwin R. Steinberg, ' "Lestrygonians," A Pale "Proteus"?', Modern Fiction
Studies, XV (Spring 1969), 73–86. See also Steinberg's 'Characteristic Sentence
Patterns in Proteus and Lestrygonians', in New Light on Joyce from the Dublin
Symposium, ed. Fritz Senn, Bloomington, Ind., and London, 1972, pp. 79–98,
which appeared after the completion of this essay. See, finally, Steinberg's recent
seminal book, The Stream of Consciousness and Beyond in 'Ulysses', Pittsburgh,
1973.

glances and sees only the 'Bloo' in 'Blood of the Lamb': his immediate reaction is that the handout may have some reference to himself. Bloom, for good reason, is especially sensitive to this kind of thing and through most of 'Lestrygonians' (one can say) *il se promène, lisant au livre de lui-même*—Mallarmé's remark about Hamlet, quoted in the library scene of *Ulysses*. Bloom is Hamletian only in the sense of perpetually reading from the 'book of himself', of having almost the vocation of finding the way to 'self'.

We have sustained this comparison with *Les Lauriers sont coupés* for so long because Dujardin's is perhaps the surest narrative model we have for 'Lestrygonians', the chapter of *Ulysses* in which the inward turnings of Bloom's mind are most in evidence. There are also essential differences to be pointed out. While *Les Lauriers* depends on an insistent first person, 'Lestrygonians' acknowledges the limits of the 'I' by introducing an 'objective' narrative voice to locate Bloom's monologue in time and space and to control its direction. Bloom's 'I' is often the blundering sort we identified above in the confusion over the Blood of the Lamb. We can go for long stretches without encountering it at all. Bloom finds the way to self by passing judgment on what he sees outside; his first person is often muted by the shock of a world which, he feels, constantly needs interpreting and explaining. Bloom is a man (as Théophile Gautier once said about himself) for whom the exterior world most emphatically exists. His mind, in 'Lestrygonians', is rather like Mrs Breen's handbag—with its 'chipped leather', 'Soiled handkerchief: medicinebottle'.—frayed, shopworn, chaotic. It is a mind, finally, which basks in the reflected rays of everything it has known and experienced, ranging from densely physical passions to the proud heritage of *Judenkultur*, half assimilated, and bits of Shakespeare and Da Ponte, half learned.

Richard M. Kain has already perceptively pointed out that 'one of the striking features of Joyce's style is the unusual fluidity with which it turns from the outer to the inner world'.[6] This is the kind of versatility one looks for in the most skilled applications of *monologue intérieur*, which is always as much concerned with the outside as with the inside. Bloom's pronominal uses mirror this preoccupation with the outside; there are probably more third-person pronouns in 'Lestrygonians' than first-person. There is even the occasional use

[6] *Fabulous Voyager: James Joyce's 'Ulysses'*, rev. ed., New York, 1959, p. 131.

of the second person: 'If you leave a bit of codfish for instance'
(151.25); 'How can you own water really?' (153.29). This use of
the 'you', by the way, is quite different from what Dujardin, in his
Le Monologue intérieur, called *une première personne déguisée*.[7]
Bloom is clearly not substituting the 'you' for 'I' as Dujardin did himself in *Les Lauriers sont coupés*, or as Valery Larbaud did later in
Mon plus secret conseil, or Michel Butor did fairly recently in *La
Modification*. The only pronoun which could properly replace the
'you' in Bloom's monologue is 'one'. This is a much more natural
use of the second person, say, than the one Joyce's friend Larbaud
uses in *Mon plus secret conseil: Lucas, il faut vous habituer à cette
idée*. Lucas, the monologuist of the story, addresses himself in the
second person, something Leopold Bloom abstains from in 'Lestrygonians'.

A close look at a passage from 'Lestrygonians' will pinpoint these
various narrative modes we have been discussing:

> His downcast eyes followed the silent veining of the oaken
> slab. Beauty: it curves, curves are beauty. Shapely goddesses, Venus,
> Juno: curves the world admires. Can see them library museum
> standing in the round hall, naked goddesses. Aids to digestion. They
> don't care what man looks. All to see. Never speaking, I mean to
> say to fellows like Flynn. Suppose she did Pygmalion and Galatea
> what would she say first? Mortal! Put you in your proper place.
> Quaffing nectar at mess with gods, golden dishes, all ambrosial. Not
> like a tanner lunch we have, boiled mutton, carrots and turnips,
> bottle of Allsop. Nectar, imagine it drinking electricity: gods' food.
> Lovely forms of woman sculped Junonian. Immortal lovely. And
> we stuffing food in one hole and out behind: food, chyle, blood,
> dung, earth, food: have to feed it like stoking an engine. They have
> no. Never looked. I'll look today. Keeper won't see. Bend down
> let something fall see if she. (176.24)

This is set off in the text as a separate paragraph. It is interesting
thematically because it represents an excellent blending of the ancient and modern, in a very Joycean way. As one reads it one might
well be reminded of a sentiment expressed by Flaubert in a letter to
Louise Colet: 'Is there anyone more in love with antiquity than I,
anyone more haunted by it, anyone who has made a greater effort to

---

[7] For a brilliant and exhaustive study of the second person, see Bruce A.
Morrissette, 'Narrative "You" in Contemporary Literature', *Comparative Literature Studies*, II, 1 (1965), 1–24.

understand it? And yet in my books I am as far from antiquity as possible'. The above paragraph, although it is written by a man 'in love with antiquity', is still in many respects 'as far from antiquity as possible'.

To concentrate more on the style and narrative devices: The first sentence is the voice of the narrator of objective facts, this time playing a very restrained, reportorial role. The poetic turn, 'silent veining', saves it from passing unnoticed. The second sentence is almost as regular syntactically as the first. The mildly free associative arrangement of parts gives us the clue that the telling has shifted to Bloom's mind. It is Bloom's mind that sets up the equation between beauty and curves. Dujardin would probably have used the 'I' at this point or introduced some painfully mannered device to convince the reader that he is observing Bloom's thoughts in their condition of becoming. The colon is used here much as it is used in the rest of the passage—as an internal divider, more decisive than the comma but not functionally very different. The colon appears with surprising frequency in this passage. From the second sentence through the end of the paragraph, by the way, we are uninterruptedly in Bloom's mind.

The equalizing, balancing role of the colon is especially evident in the third sentence. The syntax is irregular in the fourth sentence, indicating a breakdown in logical controls on the part of Bloom's mind. The fragment 'Aids to digestion' offers a transition between the elevated subject matter of the earlier part of the passage (with its nod toward antiquity) and the here-and-now concerns of Bloom's culinary needs, which have haunted the entire 'Lestrygonians' chapter.[8] The digestive leads into the sexual in the next sequence of the monologue, ending with the mention of Nosey Flynn (the fixture at Davy Byrne's who is a carryover from 'Counterparts').[9] We have now come full circle from the opulence of antiquity to the seediness of contemporaneity. Nosey Flynn is Joyce's Sweeney, who can get no closer to the world of classical mythology than the opportunity of

[8] This passage supports Eliot's famous remark that Joyce is 'manipulating a continuous parallel between contemporaneity and antiquity' ('Ulysses, Order and Myth', Dial, November, 1923). See also Harry Blamires' interesting reading of this passage in The Bloomsday Book, London, 1966, p. 72.

[9] In 'Counterparts' we are told: 'Nosey Flynn was sitting up in his usual corner of Davy Byrne's. . .' (D, 93).

ironical juxtaposition affords him. The 'I' appears for the first time in the Nosey Flynn sentence, and it is not a very decisive use of the first-person pronoun at that.

From this point to the end of the paragraph the contemporary and the ancient prove to be congenial bedfellows. If we are to accept Weldon Thornton's explanation for 'Pygmalion and Galatea' that it refers to 'W. S. Gilbert's play, *Pygmalion and Galatea* (1871), which played at the Queen's Royal Theatre, Dublin, in November, 1891',[10] then we can see in this casual mention a convenient modern experience of the mythical. The second person turns up shortly after this: 'Put you in your proper place'; here again 'one' can be substituted for 'you'—there is no disguised first person here.

Bloom reaches Olympian heights in the next sentence and then descends to the unappetizing quotidian in the one after that. After suggesting a ludicrous coupling of ancient and modern, Bloom returns to the 'Junonian' forms in the library and stays there until 'And we stuffing. . .' . There is a staccato movement in the rest of the paragraph which mirrors Bloom's anxiety about investigating the hinder parts of the statues in the museum. The final sequence, beginning with 'Bend down', contains three parts which would normally be separated by some form of punctuation; the urgency on Bloom's part to set about this tempting investigation, however, seems to account for the hurried-up, unfinished, restless, underpunctuated effect.

The passage we have looked at is fairly characteristic of 'Lestrygonians'. It begins with a sentence of omniscient narration and then turns into inner monologue. Bloom's awareness throughout is very close to consciousness. One feels that at any moment he could break into speech. The present paragraph is more than usually coherent for *monologue intérieur*; its digressions never take us very far from the juxtaposition between the beauties of antiquity and the sordidness (especially in respect to food) of the modern world.

The syntax is never elaborately distorted, neither in the sentence of objective narrative nor in the monologue. Frank Budgen quotes Joyce as pointing to the following lines from 'Lestrygonians' as an indication of what he could do with syntax: 'Perfume of embraces all him assailed. With hungered flesh obscurely, he mutely craved

[10] Thornton, p. 147.

to adore' (168.37). Joyce ends by saying, 'You can see for yourself
in how many different ways they [the words] might be arranged'.[11]
'Lestrygonians' is filled with these curious syntactical arrangements:
'Mr Bloom, quick breathing, slowlier walking, passed Adam court'
(167.26); 'His hand looking for the where did I put found in his
hip pocket soap lotion have to call tepid paper stuck' (183.38). (This
last construction, which comes at the very end of 'Lestrygonians', is
curious because it seems to bring together within the same syntactical
unit the partly omniscient narrator with the partly conscious monologuist.) There are other examples of these irregularities in word
order in the episode. But the displacements are relatively mild in
the paragraph we have been studying. Still this passage beautifully
illustrates what Joyce had in mind when he answered Budgen's query
about his search for the Flaubertian *mot juste:* 'I have the words already. What I am seeking is the perfect order of words in the sentence'.[12]

Indeed Joyce did have the words and knew how to use them
to maximum poetic advantage. We need only look at the opening
lines of 'Lestrygonians': 'Pineapple rock, lemon platt, butter scotch.
A sugarsticky girl shovelling scoopfuls of creams for a christian
brother. Some school treat' (151.1). We notice here one of Joyce's
favourite alliterative sounds 's' dominating the passage. (This sound,
as we recall, combined interestingly with 'f' to produce the final
paragraph of 'The Dead'.) 'Sugarsticky' is one of those telescoped
words that has such remarkable poetic suggestiveness; it also sets
the right gastronomic tone for Bloom's culinary wanderings in the
remainder of 'Lestrygonians'.

Until now we have been looking at two kinds of movement in
the eighth chapter of *Ulysses*: that of a third-person, unidentified
narrator who reveals various degrees of omniscience and that of the
inner workings of Leopold Bloom's mind. We have noticed the
shuttling back and forth between the two, with usually a sentence
or two of objective discourse and then a sustained bit of *monologue
intérieur*. We have said nothing as yet about the dialogue. Bloom
talks to Mrs Breen for three pages, to Nosey Flynn and Davy Byrne
for another three pages; a conversation takes place in Davy Byrne's,
after Bloom has temporarily left the scene to urinate (the only time

[11] Budgen, p. 20.
[12] *Ibid.*

he is not immediately present in 'Lestrygonians'), for two and a half
pages; Bloom talks to a blind stripling for a page. There are other
intermittent brief exchanges overheard by Bloom, with the speakers
not identified, adding up to another page. This all combines to
produce a quite substantial part of the thirty-three page 'Lestrygonians' section.

Of course, none of these dialogues is uninterrupted. Bloom's
monologue breaks in on all but the one that takes place when he
is not on stage; then we have infrequent stage directions issued by
the objective narrative voice: 'Nosey Flynn pursed his lips' (177.22);
'Davy Byrne, sated after his yawn, said with tearwashed eyes' (178.2);
'His hand scrawled a dry pen signature beside his grog' (178.17).
The most interesting of these is: 'Davy Byrne smiledyawnednodded
all in one' (177.38). Here the effect of three words run together indicates a condition in which the omniscience of the teller is in question and the objective stage directing seems to get caught up in the
next bit of dialogue: '—Iiiiiichaaaaaaach!' (177.39).

The most frequent habit in 'Lestrygonians' is for Bloom's monologue to interrupt conversation. The stage directions are still intermittently present but in these passages they seem less noticeable
than when Bloom is off stage. Thus after one almost uninterrupted
page of Bloom's conversation with Mrs Breen we have two paragraphs of inner monologue; then we return to dialogue for a half
page before the interruption of another snatch of monologue; and
so on to the end of the exchange between Bloom and Mrs Breen.

The two paragraphs of monologue following the first page of
dialogue with Mrs Breen reveal Joyce at his most lyrical. After some
small talk about the Bloom family and the death of Paddy Dignam,
Mrs Breen brings up the unhappy subject of her husband and his
current eccentricity: '—O, don't be talking, she said. He's a caution
to rattlesnakes. He's in there now with his lawbooks finding out the
law of libel. He has me heartscalded. Wait till I show you' (157.20).
This is followed by monologue which is introduced with the usual
examination of Bloom from the outside by a third-person presence:
'Hot mockturtle vapour and steam of newbaked jampuffs rolypoly
poured out from Harrison's. The heavy noonreek tickled the top of
Mr Bloom's gullet' (157.23). The texture of the language has obviously been richly affected by Bloom's gastronomic needs and an-
ticipations. Joyce fittingly used the word 'peristaltic' to explain the

movement of this kind of prose in his remarks to early commentators like Stuart Gilbert. Here is another instance where the omniscience of the third-person voice is in doubt. There is no distortion of syntax, just a running together of words and a fine sense of the suggestive quality of language—both audible and visual. Bloom's monologue, for the remainder of the paragraph, is fittingly concerned with various aspects of food; its attention turns in the next paragraph to the contents and condition of Mrs Breen's handbag, without noticeable transition and without the intervention of the implied authorial voice: 'Opening her handbag, chipped leather, hatpin: ought to have a guard on those things' (157.31). The monologue continues in this vein until Mrs Breen's conversation interrupts.

The dialogue in 'Lestrygonians' is fairly conventional, except for the insistent breaking in of Bloom's monologue. To put it differently, one might say—as we suggested at the beginning of this essay—that the eighth chapter of *Ulysses* is really Bloom's *monologue intérieur* interrupted by a narrator filling in objective details and by a series of dialogues which dramatize situation rather than consciousness (although there is some dramatizing of consciousness also). Dialogue and authorial or narrative presence then work to suggest an intrusion from without on Bloom's thoughts. Joyce, when most heatedly caught up in the flow of Bloom's inner monologue, will always insist on what is 'outside'. Conversation and narrative intervention are, in a sense, *entr'actes* which offer aesthetic reprieves from Bloom's 'steady monologue of the interiors'.[13]

[13] See Erwin R. Steinberg's illuminating essay, '. . . the steady monologue of the interiors; the pardonable confusion . . .' , *JJQ*, VI, 3 (Spring 1969), 185–200. See also his 'Introducing the Stream-of-Consciousness Technique in *Ulysses*', *Style*, II (Winter 1968), 49–58.

I have tried in this essay not to get involved in the complex matter of terminology and I have resorted to critical language about which there is some general agreement. For the most useful essays on the definition and description of the subject with which I have been concerned, see the following: Lawrence E. Bowling, 'What Is the Stream of Consciousness Technique?' *PMLA*, LXV (June 1950), 333–345; Robert Humphrey, *Stream of Consciousness in the Modern Novel*, Berkeley and Los Angeles, 1954; William York Tindall, 'The Stream of Consciousness', in *Forces in Modern British Literature*, New York, 1956, pp. 187–211; Erwin R. Steinberg, 'The Stream-of-Consciousness Novelist: an Inquiry into the Relation of Consciousness and Language', *ETC*, XVII (December 1960), 423–439; David Daiches, *The Novel and the Modern World*, Chicago, 1960; Shiv K. Kumar, *Bergson and the Stream of Consciousness Novel*, New York, 1963; Leon Edel, *The Modern Psychological Novel*, New York, 1964;

The January 1919 issue of the *Little Review*, which contained the longer section of 'Lestrygonians', was the first number of the magazine which ran into difficulties with the postal authorities. From then on, Margaret Anderson was under constant pressure from every variety of censorship and post-office oppression. An ironical footnote in the May 1919 issue alludes to her difficulties: 'To avoid similar interference this month I have ruined Mr Joyce's story by cutting certain passages [from "Scylla and Charybdis"] in which he mentions natural facts known to everyone'.[14] Finally, in order to safeguard the future of the *Little Review* Miss Anderson was forced to suspend serialization of *Ulysses* following the September-December 1920 number. The *Ulysses–Little Review* affair forms one of the darkest moments in American literary history. Jackson R. Bryer's interesting article supplies most of the details.

We know from Bryer's article that Ezra Pound had taken liberties with certain of the early episodes, especially 'Calypso', before forwarding them to Margaret Anderson. There is no evidence, as far as we know, to support any tampering with 'Lestrygonians'. Miss Anderson's own hand was only visible after the postal authorities intervened; in other words, 'Lestrygonians' would not have been affected by her deletions. Yet when we compare the corrected 1961 text of the eighth chapter of *Ulysses* with the *Little Review* version we find many significant differences.

We know from Richard Ellmann's *James Joyce* (see the chart on p. 456) that 'Lestrygonians' was sent to Pound on 25 October 1918 to begin serialization in the January 1919 number. The next we hear about it is when the Post Office Department intervenes to confiscate copies. None of this indecisive bit of literary history helps us account for the startling changes from magazine to book. Joyce's letters from 1919 through 1921, however, are filled with his misgivings about the difficult process of putting *Ulysses* between covers. He says, for example, in a letter to James B. Pinker on 7 December

---

Sultan, pp. 138–148; Frederick J. Hoffman, *Freudianism and the Literary Mind*, Baton Rouge, La., 1967; and Derek Bickerton, 'Modes of Interior Monologue: A Formal Definition', *Modern Language Quarterly*, XXVIII (June 1967), 229–239. Bowling, by the way, has some very convincing pages on *Les Lauriers sont coupés*. See also, finally, Harry Levin's brilliant book *James Joyce: a Critical Introduction*, Norfolk, Conn., 1941, and London, 1944.

[14] Quoted in Jackson R. Bryer, 'Joyce, *Ulysses*, and the *Little Review*', *South Atlantic Quarterly*, LXVI (Spring 1967), 153.

1919: 'The text hitherto published in *Little Review* is *not* my text as sent on in typescript. The book is to be published as I wrote it with a few additions on the proof'.[15] Here is the objection he expressed to Harriet Shaw Weaver on 25 February 1920: 'It would be creating trouble to set from the *Little Review* as many passages are omitted and hopelessly mixed'.[16] He has this to say to John Quinn on 11 March 1920: 'There must be no alterations whatsoever of my text, either that already consigned in typescript (the version in *The Little Review* is, of course, mutilated) or that added on proofs; and, in view of the six years' unbroken labour which the book has cost me, I must have a first proof and a revise of the whole book'.[17] 'Mutilated' is the key word here; Joyce was convinced, obviously, that his text was seriously tampered with and much work was needed to restore it to a state of aesthetic respectability.

Joyce becomes increasingly concerned with the matter of proofs. In a letter to John Quinn, dated 24 November 1920, he pinpoints the problem: 'The episodes which have the heaviest burden of addenda are *Lotus-eaters*, *Lestrygonians*, *Nausikaa* and *Cyclops*. Therefore I must stipulate to have three sendings of proofs. . .' .[18] Proofs are also the subject of some remarks made to Harriet Shaw Weaver on 30 August 1921: 'I have made a great deal of addition to the proofs so far (up to the end of *Scylla and Charybdis*)'.[19] Finally, to Valery Larbaud on 24 September 1921: 'You will scarcely recognise parts of *Ulysses* I have worked so much on them'.[20]

The letters abound in this kind of misgiving. Joyce was convinced that the serialized text in the *Little Review* thoroughly betrayed his artistry. He used the process of proofreading to rewrite large segments of his book, even when the *Little Review* text was reasonably untampered with, as in the case of 'Lestrygonians'. Most of the revision involved adding material, so that the eighth chapter in the published book is significantly longer than it was in the *Little Review* version.[21]

There are, indeed, a few examples of shortening the text. Much

[15] *Letters*, II, 456.   [16] *Letters*, I, 137.   [17] *Letters*, II, 459–460.
[18] *Letters*, III, 31.   [19] *Letters*, I, 171.   [20] *Letters*, III, 49.

[21] Joseph Prescott has done some excellent close work with the text of *Ulysses*; see especially his fine essay, 'Stylistic Realism in *Ulysses*', in *Exploring James Joyce*, Carbondale, Ill., 1964, pp. 106–134, 162–182. See also A. Walton Litz's pioneering study *The Art of James Joyce*, Oxford, 1961, and Adams's *Surface and Symbol*.

of this tightening occurs toward the end of the section. Thus 'Weight. Would he feel it if something was removed?' (181.27) read in the *Little Review*: 'Weight or size of it, something blacker than the dark. Wonder would he feel it if something was removed' (February-March, 1919, p. 60). 'Smells on all sides bunched together. Each person too' (181.40) read in the *Little Review*: 'Smells on all sides bunched together. Each street different smell. Each person too' (February-March, 1919, p. 60). There are very few of these areas where the *Little Review* text is longer than the book version.

Before looking at the kinds of additions Joyce made—and these are legion—we should glance at a few changes in phrasing. In the dialogue with Bloom, Mrs Breen says at one point: '—Go away! Isn't that grand for her?' (156.37). In the *Little Review* version she says with much less flair: 'Is that so?' (January, 1919, p. 32). 'O, leave them there to simmer' (160.10) was in the *Little Review* simply 'O, let them stay there' (January, 1919, p. 35). In his conversation with Davy Byrne, in Bloom's absence, Nosey Flynn uses the expression: 'You can make bacon of that' (177.23). In the *Little Review* it was expressed less colourfully: 'You may take that from me' (January, 1919, p. 48).

There are a few changes in words and in word order which seem not to matter a great deal: 'town' becomes 'world' (152.16), 'smart' becomes 'tasty' (158.23), 'country' becomes 'county' (173.16), 'museum library' becomes 'library museum' (176.26), 'wine' becomes 'stuff' (182.38), 'Grumpy' becomes 'Crusty' (183.3), 'Potato. Purse' becomes 'Purse. Potato' (183.35). The word 'men' turning into 'missionary', which results in 'White missionary too salty' (171.35), is clearly an improvement. Joyce also changes several names in the transference from the *Little Review* to the published book: 'Hyam's' becomes 'Kino's' (153.25), 'Dr Brady' becomes 'Dr Murren' (162.9), 'Charley Kavanagh' becomes 'Charley Boulger' (165.9).

Another observation might be made. Joyce's fondness f   n-
ning words together is noticeably curbed, though by no ·
lenced, in the final version of 'Lestrygonians'. There are ·
telescoped constructions in the *Little Review* text than
they have a way, when overused, of somewhat clutter'
of the prose. Controls, Joyce realized, were clearly ne
that became essential to his art in *Ulysses*. The f'
fully run together words in the 1961 text offe'

fining of Joyce's technique from the serialized version to the published book. We are grieved, however, to notice 'stickumbrelladust-coat' returning to three separate words in the final form of 'Lestry-gonians'.

Finally, the crucial matter of Joyce's additions: they enrich our view of Bloom's mind, of his 'stream of life'. We now have a more valuable sense (to quote May Sinclair on Dorothy Richardson once again) of 'life going on and on'. To give an admittedly extreme example of what Joyce has done: he set 'Poor Mrs Purefoy!' in a paragraph by itself in the *Little Review* (January, 1919, p. 36); in the final version he added to these three words some of the best inner monologue in 'Lestrygonians':

> Poor Mrs Purefoy! Methodist husband. Method in his madness. Saffron bun and milk and soda lunch in the educational dairy. Eating with a stopwatch, thirtytwo chews to the minute. Still his muttonchop whiskers grew. Supposed to be well connected. Theodore's cousin in Dublin Castle. One tony relative in every family. Hardy annuals he presents her with. Saw him out at the Three Jolly Topers marching along bareheaded and his eldest boy carrying one in a marketnet. The squallers. Poor thing! Then having to give the breast year after year all hours of the night. Selfish those t.t's are. Dog in the manger. Only one lump of sugar in my tea, if you please. (161.6)

Bloom's gastronomic needs, his interest in the scientific process, his devotion to the cliché, and his compassion are all expressed in this passage. It starts off characteristically with Bloom the incurable punster on display. (Bloom would probably have agreed with Beckett's Murphy whose gospel began: 'In the beginning was the pun'.) Although this addendum is longer than most in 'Lestrygonians', it does reveal the kind of thing Joyce added on to his final text. He was tirelessly attempting to give us the most convincing possible inner view of a man.[22]

---

[22] A valuable close study of 'Lestrygonians' appeared after the completion of this essay. See Chester G. Anderson, 'Leopold Bloom as Dr. Sigmund Freud', *Mosaic*, VI (Fall 1972), 23–43. Another perceptive essay on 'Lestrygonians' which appeared after the completion of my study is William M. Schutte's 'Leopold Bloom: A Touch of the Artist', *JJQ*, X (Fall 1972), 118–131.

SCYLLA AND CHARYBDIS

Robert Kellogg

The Dialogue

The soul of a city is its talk. Whether its body is resplendent
with avenues or is smudged with laborious grime the vital signs of
civic life are verbal: gossip, stories, speeches, and conversations of
every sort. The literary artist who would render a city must reproduce its talk. Of no city is this more true than of Dublin, and one
of the rarest moments in the fictional history of human talk is
'Scylla and Charybdis', the chapter Joyce specified as being 'dialectic'. That does not exhaust the categories for considering the narrative art of 'Scylla and Charybdis', but I will begin there, hoping
eventually to show how this episode, perhaps more than any other,
embodies an essential quality of Joyce's art: its interpenetration with
his life. Bloomsday, 16 June 1904, was the day Joyce first walked
out with Nora Barnacle. In the larger myth that comprised both his
life and his art, the soul's search for its father was mysteriously one
with a search for its bride.

Formally, 'Scylla and Charybdis' is a mock-Socratic dialogue,
with something of the Quaker meeting and theosophic seance
added. It combines the comic spirit of Aristophanes' *Clouds* and the
seriousness of the conversations of Socrates. Stephen's spoken part
of the dialogue is sometimes called his 'lecture' on Shakespeare.
But Mr Best, one of the participants, is probably more accurate

when, in speaking of the absent Haines, he says, 'I couldn't bring
him in to hear the discussion' (186.26). The Socratic discussion is
an instrument of education which is appropriate to the scene of the
chapter in the assistant librarian's office of the National Library.
In Joyce's time the real educational institution in Dublin for those
who did not attend Trinity College, which has its own great library,
was neither University College nor the Royal University. These were
in Eugene Sheehy's words merely examining boards. 'The real Alma
Mater at this time was the National Library in Kildare Street', he
wrote in *May It Please the Court*.[1] Here under the benign direction
of Thomas W. Lyster, 'the quaker librarian', the students and intel-
lectuals of Dublin met to read and talk.

Their conversation was not the formal dialectic of the philosophy
course but the living dialectic of the library steps and offices. Judge
Sheehy evokes the scene: 'We read for our examinations in the
Library upstairs, but there were rather prolonged adjournments to
the steps outside, where we heard the views on art and life and
literature of Joyce, Kettle, Skeffington, Arthur Clery, John Marcus
O'Sullivan, William Dawson, Constantine Curran and many other
well-read and cultured men'.[2] At the end of the discussion in
'Scylla and Charybdis' Stephen asks himself, 'What have I learned?
Of them? Of me?' It is an artist's question, looking forward to his
future reflection on the scene, rather than a literary critic's, intent
on reaching the truth about Shakespeare's plays, but the question
does acknowledge the primary expectation of dialectic. In 'Nestor'
Stephen admitted to Mr Deasy that he was not a teacher, 'a learner
rather'.

The burlesque, or mocking, element in 'Scylla and Charybdis'
is therefore of a special sort. Before the *entr'acte*, when Buck Mulligan enters (197.16), it does not derive from what the participants
say. Even if their dialogue may fall short of the highest conversational art of which Dublin society was and is capable, still it is informed, energetic, and intelligent. It is a conversation of which the
participants in real life would have little need to be ashamed, despite
the trivialities of Best and Lyster; (they seem to us trivialities printed
on the page of a masterpiece). The mockery in the first half comes
instead from Stephen, who shares with the chapter's narrator the

[1] Dublin, 1951, p. 12.
[2] *Ibid.*, p. 12.

attitude of his silent thoughts when they are directed toward his fellow discussants. The extent and variety of these private musings and mental associations, reported directly, without narrative comment or intervention, distinguish the chapter from the usual literary dialogue, making it more truly narrative and poising the external world of talk (which for Stephen is a form of action) against the internal world of thought and emotion.

The narrator of 'Scylla and Charybdis' is similar to the one who tells the first three chapters of *Ulysses* and all of *A Portrait of the Artist*. In giving us Stephen's experience from Stephen's point of view he lets much else go by the board, refraining from giving any more than the briefest and most matter-of-fact external views of Stephen. It has taken readers of Joyce some time to adjust to the effects of this extreme narrative partiality. Our first impression is that Joyce's own intellectual and aesthetic sympathies must be equally partial, and the biographical evidence lends strong support to this view. Stephen's aesthetic theories, as I shall show, are cribbed from early Joyce essays. Even his mannerisms and his appearance are startlingly like the young Joyce's. Inevitably, of course, there are a few differences—Joyce's swimming ability and joviality, for example—and these lead to a second impression, that Joyce's characteristic view of Stephen is ironic. The most probable explanation is that Joyce gives us a Stephen who is in fact extremely close to the actual Joyce at the same age, but that he does not (unlike most autobiographers!) give the young man the benefit of the older man's wisdom. Such irony as exists in Joyce's view of Stephen has been achieved, if this view is correct, through a remarkable effort both of artistic growth and of honesty.

The tone of Stephen's and the narrator's mockery of the other speakers in the dialogue is approximately that of Joyce's own commentary on the Dublin literary scene of 1904 in 'The Holy Office'. Stephen's irritation with the 'unprejudiced' blandness of Russell and the librarians, in their comfortable distance from the 'sea of troubles' and 'conflicting doubts, as one sees in real life' (184.4), to which Mr Lyster alludes at the beginning of the chapter, corresponds to Joyce's ridicule in the poem:

> For every true-born mysticist
> A Dante is, unprejudiced,
> Who safe at ingle-nook, by proxy,

Hazards extremes of heterodoxy,
Like him who finds a joy at table,
Pondering the uncomfortable.
                                        (CW, 150)

With the entrance of Buck Mulligan, crying 'Amen' to the final words of Stephen's most mystical utterance about Shakespeare as father, ghost, and analogue to God, Stephen's hard-won doctrines are themselves held up to ridicule. '—You were speaking of the gaseous vertebrate, if I mistake not? he asked of Stephen' (197.22–3). Mulligan's wit and energy captivate Stephen's hearers, whose imaginations his theorizing has already strained. The librarians are only too willing to grant Stephen a respite while they enjoy Mulligan and talk of other things. '—Yes, indeed, the quaker librarian said. A most instructive discussion. Mr Mulligan, I'll be bound, has his theory too of the play and of Shakespeare. All sides of life should be represented' (198.6).[3] Mulligan's side of Shakespeare's life, as might be expected, is its seamier one. He repeats an old libel that Shakespeare 'died dead drunk', and incorporates Edward Dowden in a new one to the effect that the Trinity professor once expressed a worldly acquiescence to 'the charge of pederasty brought against the bard' (204.13, 21). But Mulligan's entrance serves less to enrich the dialogue itself than to dissipate its intellectual intensity and link it to the plot of *Ulysses*. It is in the *entr'acte* that Stephen's failure to keep his drinking appointment with Mulligan and Haines is explained and that Bloom's dark silhouette appears in the corridor outside.

In 'Telemachus', where Mulligan's burlesquing humour was, through the 'art' of the episode, embodied in theological forms, Stephen associated him with the brood of mockers and the heresiarchs (21.8). This association is taken up again on Mulligan's entry, when a mocking version of the Apostles' Creed as it might sound according to the Sabellian heresy goes through Stephen's head (197.29–198.3). Mulligan, in turn, has accused Stephen of having 'the cursed jesuit strain in you, only it's injected the wrong way' (8.31). Neither young man is orthodox, in theology or in literature. But Stephen is earnest in both while Mulligan doesn't care. Stephen takes part in the discussion to learn—even if only from himself. Mulligan is looking for a good performance—even if only

---

[3] The 1961 text prints a comma after *discussion.*

his own. He is a materialist with a sense of humour, whose parodies are derived from an admirable store of learning and exquisite sensitivity to form, which turn on their heads the old pieties and sanctities, many of which Stephen deeply cherishes. As Stephen mocks Russell's mysticism Mulligan mocks Stephen's. The *entr'acte* signals, therefore, a shift of various sorts, philosophical and tonal, with Stephen's thoughts pivoting from an energetic rebuttal of ideas and opinions expressed by rather faintly drawn characters to a defensive stance against the hilarious blasphemy of his charming enemy, one of the most vividly portrayed characters in English literature.

The objective conflict among the speakers in 'Scylla and Charybdis'—what they actually say to each other—is intellectual. The chapter's 'organ' is the brain. The germ that generates the plot and imagery of the chapter, connecting it with the whole theme of *Ulysses*, is Stephen's argument about Shakespeare. He sets out to prove a proposition that to serious Shakespeare scholars must be as outlandish in its mere conception as it is beside the point: that Shakespeare identified himself with the ghost of Hamlet's father rather than with Hamlet. His main adversary is the sub-librarian John Eglinton, who warns him at the beginning, 'if you want to shake my belief that Shakespeare is Hamlet you have a stern task before you' (194.16). In a certain sense these two poles in the dialogue serve as Scylla and Charybdis, for by the end of the argument the opponents have reconciled the extremes:

—The truth is midway, he [Eglinton] affirmed. He is the ghost and the prince. He is all in all.
—He is, Stephen said. The boy of act one is the mature man of act five. All in all. (212.28)

The dialectic has been useful. Both men have learned; but Stephen has passed between a Scylla and a Charybdis of longer standing and greater significance than the two positions in this particular dialogue.

Stephen's theory is based on a reading of the same books that Joyce consulted in constructing his own Shakespearean theory of 1904, which he also told to Gogarty, Best, and Magee in the National Library (195.28–196.9).[4] The two theories, Stephen's and Joyce's, are apparently identical, except that Joyce was less willing than Stephen to admit that he did not believe his. The intellectual

---

[4] Ellmann, pp. 161 and 374–375, and William M. Schutte, *Joyce and Shakespeare*, New Haven, Conn., 1957, pp. 153–177.

subject matter allows Joyce to stick remarkably close to an actual event in telling this episode of *Ulysses*. It is important to his theme that the reader understand the strongest possible likeness to exist between the creating artist and the world of his creation, so that the narrative art of the chapter will itself be an illustration of its own theme.

According to the theory, the ghost's crying out for vengeance expressed Shakespeare's misery over Anne Shakespeare's adultery with his own brothers, Richard and Edmund. *Venus and Adonis* is evidence of Shakespeare's having been seduced originally by Anne, causing a wound to his sexual self-confidence that the sonnets document. In her sexual ascendancy over him Anne also lives on as Cleopatra and Cressida. *Richard III* and *King Lear* name the evil brothers Richard and Edmund. The death of Prince Arthur in *King John* is his son Hamnet's death. His mother's death resulted in the scene with Volumnia in *Coriolanus*, and her maiden name is preserved in the Forest of Arden. A reconciliation comes in the last plays, when Marina, Perdita, Miranda, and Imogene reflect the rebirth of family love in Shakespeare's own granddaughters (208.28–35). The aesthetic principle behind Stephen's theory in his belief that 'his own image to a man with that queer thing genius is the standard of all experience, material and moral' (195.39). In the discussion, he uses this principle to interpret the whole body of Shakespeare's work. Its main thematic significance in *Ulysses* derives, however, from its being also the aesthetic principle appropriate to an understanding of Stephen's and Joyce's life and art.

A Deeper Insight

Professor S. L. Goldberg has demonstrated brilliantly the extent to which Stephen's philosophical principles in 'Scylla and Charybdis' are indebted to Joyce's reading of Aristotle's *de anima*, which insists upon the primacy of sensation in human knowledge.[5] He has also shown convincingly that Aristotle's epistemology is related to what both Joyce and Stephen called the 'classical temper' in art. Aristotle, in the allegorical apparatus of the chapter, is one of the correspondences to the rock of Scylla. Because Professor Goldberg's reliable investigations are well known, I will consider myself a bit freer

[5] S. L. Goldberg, *The Classical Temper*, London, 1961, pp. 66–99.

than an entirely balanced view might warrant to explore at the outset the 'Charybdian' influence of the 'romantic temper' in Joyce's thought and in Stephen's Shakespeare theory. In going back to Joyce's early critical writings, I assume that they constitute a legitimate background to Stephen's thought and will allow me to contemplate a more interesting question of interpretation than the degree of irony in Joyce's mature view of the young Stephen: was the theological vocabulary in Joyce's and Stephen's aesthetic thought meant merely metaphorically, or was it intended to refer to a genuine mystical reality?

The subject of Plato versus Aristotle comes up early in the chapter. Even before Stephen speaks about his theory, the mystic Russell 'oracles' out of his shadow an opposition to using the facts of Shakespeare's life to interpret his art. 'Art has to reveal to us ideas, formless spiritual essences', he says. 'The supreme question about a work of art is out of how deep a life does it spring . . . . The deepest poetry of Shelley, the words of Hamlet bring our mind into contact with the eternal wisdom, Plato's world of ideas. All the rest is the speculation of schoolboys for schoolboys' (185.14). To Stephen's super-polite observation that Aristotle was once Plato's schoolboy, Eglinton joins Russell in preferring the master to his pupil. Stephen's mocking but silent response to Russell's 'formless spiritual essences' is a Mulligan-like burlesque of theosophical jargon. After an uncharacteristically warm exchange once more with Eglinton about their respective preferences for Plato and Aristotle Stephen mentally prepares for battle with a few calisthenics of definition and a review of positions:

> Unsheathe your dagger definitions. Horseness is the whatness of allhorse. Streams of tendency and eons they worship. God: noise in the street: very peripatetic. Space: what you damn well have to see. Through spaces smaller than red globules of man's blood they creepycrawl after Blake's buttocks into eternity of which this vegetable world is but a shadow. Hold to the now, the here, through which all future plunges to the past. (186.13)

Stephen's Mulliganism about the theosophists creepycrawling after Blake's buttocks would seem once and for all to dispose of the mysticism and Charybdian incoherence of the romantic temper. But for Joyce, who regarded Blake as the greatest of the romantic poets, the question was a more serious one, as, after the departure of

Russell and the entrance of Mulligan, I believe it also was for Stephen.

In Blake's personal life Joyce recognized a likeness to his own. In the surviving fragment of his sympathetic 1912 lecture on the mystical poet he wrote that 'like many men of great genius, Blake was not attracted to cultured and refined women. Either he preferred to drawingroom graces and an easy and broad culture . . . the simple woman, of hazy and sensual mentality, or, in his unlimited egoism, he wanted the soul of his beloved to be entirely a slow and painful creation of his own' (CW, 217). This seemingly inconsequential pattern, a 'great difference in culture and temperament that separated the young couple' (CW, 218), Joyce examined not only in his play *Exiles* but in his own life with Nora. It is the kind of bond among men of great genius which he took seriously, and which linked him imaginatively to Blake even when he turned away from his philosophy. Joyce also associated himself with Blake's 'madness', in opposition to an excess of 'the now, the here' in modern materialism. 'If we must accuse of madness every great genius who does not believe in the hurried materialism now in vogue with the happy fatuousness of a recent college graduate in the exact sciences, little remains for art and universal philosophy'. In such a world, 'with regard to art, then, those very useful figures, the photographer and court stenographer, would get by all the more easily' (CW, 220).

Closer in time to Stephen's thought in 1904 was Joyce's essay, 'James Clarence Mangan', published in *St. Stephen's* in 1902, in which he related the danger of materialism to the classical and romantic tempers, and hence to the aesthetic poles of 'Scylla and Charybdis'. Much of the essay's theoretical thought was assigned to Stephen in *Stephen Hero*. Either way, it bears on *Ulysses*. I would rather attribute its ideas to Joyce, however, than to a fictional prefiguration of the Stephen of *Ulysses*, although my general thesis is that the distinction scarcely exists when the thoughts of the two are from the same period. The dispute between the classical and romantic tempers 'has been ungentle (to say no more) and has seemed to some a dispute about names and with time has become a confused battle . . . *the classical school fighting the materialism which attends it*, and *the romantic school to preserve coherence*, yet as this unrest is the condition of all achievement, it is so far good, and presses slowly towards *a deeper insight which will make the schools at one'* (CW, 74).[6] Joyce went on in this essay to say that 'the highest praise must be withheld from the romantic school (though the most enlightened of Western poets by [whom according to Stanislaus Joyce he meant Blake] be thereby passed over)' (CW, 74–5). He was speaking historically. As for the future, an artist who might aspire to achieve the deeper reconciling insight would face the double dangers of the two tempers, materialism and incoherence, surely the most appropriate analogues to the rock of Scylla and the whirlpool Charybdis in Stephen's aesthetic theory.

In a letter to Grant Richards about *Dubliners,* Joyce said in 1906 that he had written his book 'with considerable care, in spite of a hundred difficulties and in accordance with what I understand to be the classical tradition of my art'.[7] The stories do exemplify the classical method defined in the Mangan essay: 'a method which bends upon these present things and so works upon them and fashions them that the quick intelligence may go beyond them to their meaning, which is still unuttered' (CW, 74). What I have called the 'Charybdian' strain in Joyce's thought comes in the very next sentence. 'So long as this place in nature is given us, it is right that art should do no violence to that gift, though it may go far beyond the stars and the waters in the service of what it loves' (CW, 74). At this point I find the clue helpful that Joyce gave in his allegorical chart of correspondences, opposing mysticism to dogma. In its simplest form it is an opposition of religious truth that is internal in the mind (mysticism) and religious truth that is external to the mind (scholasticism). Neither denies a spiritual reality beyond the stars and waters. They disagree only in their response to the gift of 'this place in nature'. It is here that Joyce differs from Blake. In the fuller original form of the 'red globules of man's blood' passage as it occurs in the 1912 lecture, Joyce wrote, 'Blake killed the dragon of experience and natural wisdom, and, by minimizing space and time and denying the existence of memory and the senses, he tried to paint his works on the void of the divine bosom' (CW, 222).

Through what deeper insight might the classical and romantic tempers become at one? Joyce would scarcely give way in his Aristotelean acceptance of the gift of 'this place in nature' from which the artist 'bends upon these present things'. On the other hand, he

[6] My italics.
[7] *Letters,* I, 60.

would share with Blake an abhorrence of being so caught up in the materialism that attends the classical tradition that 'the quick intelligence' might not 'go beyond them to their meaning'. Whichever approach an artist takes to the great eternal truths, Joyce would insist, as in the Mangan essay, that 'it must be asked concerning every artist how he is in relation to the highest knowledge and to those laws which do not take holiday because men and times forget them' (CW, 75). Those laws are not Plato's world of ideas, but they do recall Russell's dictum that great art should 'bring our mind into contact with the eternal wisdom'. A few sentences from the conclusion of the Mangan essay will illustrate how far Joyce's critical language was willing to incorporate that of mysticism in search of 'a deeper insight'. The first passage suggests Stephen's state of mind at the end of 'Scylla and Charybdis', when he achieves the peace of the Druid priests in Cymbeline:

> But the ancient gods, who are visions of the divine names, die and come to life many times, and, though there is dusk about their feet and darkness in their indifferent eyes, the miracle of light is renewed eternally in the imaginative soul. When the sterile and treacherous order is broken up, a voice or a host of voices is heard singing, a little faintly at first, of a serene spirit which enters woods and cities and the hearts of men, and of the life of earth—det dejlige vidunderlige jordliv det gaadefulde jordliv—beautiful, alluring, mysterious.[8] (CW, 83)

The second passage from the Mangan essay illustrates Joyce's willingness to grant that the truth of either the visible world or of the imagination itself may be a proper subject of intense imaginative contemplation:

> Beauty the splendour of truth, is a gracious presence when the imagination contemplates intensely the truth of its own being or the visible world, and the spirit which proceeds out of truth and beauty is the holy spirit of joy. These are realities and these alone give and sustain life. (CW, 83)

And, finally, a statement of the Dedalean optimism from which Bloom tacitly dissents in 'Ithaca' (666.34–6):

> In those vast courses which enfold us and in that great memory which is greater and more generous than our memory, no life, no moment of exaltation is ever lost; and all those who have written

---

[8] Ibsen's words mean 'this beautiful, miraculous earth-life, this inscrutable earth-life'.

nobly have not written in vain, though the desperate and weary have never heard the silver laughter of wisdom. Nay, shall not such as these have part, because of that high, original purpose which remembering painfully or by way of prophecy they would make clear, in the continual affirmation of the spirit? (CW, 83)

The influence of such mystical thought on *Finnegans Wake* is well known. There is no possibility that Joyce 'outgrew' this early Charybdian strain. Nor is it likely that anyone would argue for a Stephen with a much different temper, considering the amount of the Mangan essay that found its way into *Stephen Hero*. The reconciliation of the classical and romantic tempers within the same artist was not entirely a theoretical ideal. It would be produced by the imagination's simultaneous contemplation of both the truth of its own being and the truth of the visible world. In his 1903 review of the French translation of Ibsen's *Catilina* Joyce found that 'Ibsen has united with his strong, ample, imaginative faculty a preoccupation with the things present to him' (CW, 101). Hence Ibsen was capable of passing beyond these things. In 'Ibsen's New Drama', Joyce had in 1900 characterized the great Norwegian's art as one almost independent of the accidents of character and incident: 'The naked drama—either the perception of a great truth, or the opening up of a great question, or a great conflict which is almost independent of the conflicting actors, and has been and is of far-reaching importance—this is what primarily rivets our attention' (CW, 63).

Such 'naked drama' Joyce distinguished from 'Literature' in the early essay 'Drama and Life' (1900). It was not a distinction that he maintained for long as a critic, sending it the way of a similar one between 'literature' and 'poetry' in the Mangan essay, but it had its uses. Literature was a lower form than poetry and drama, primarily concerned not with great truths and changeless laws, of which human society is the embodiment, but with 'the whimsicalities and circumstances of men and women' which 'involve and overwrap' those laws (CW, 40). This early conception of drama and poetry as distinct from literature—art which primarily reveals the high and eternal truths of man, affirming and ennobling his humanity regardless of the ordinariness of his circumstances—is the nucleus of the deeper insight that reconciles the two tempers. In the Mangan essay Joyce attributed Blake's minimizing of time to all poetry, which 'sets store by every time less than the pulsation of an artery, the time in which its intuitions start forth, holding it equal in its period and value to six thousand years' (CW, 81). And in 'Drama and Life' he defined drama as 'strife, evolution, movement in whatever way unfolded: it exists before it takes form, independently; it is conditioned but not controlled by its scene' (CW, 41). The distinction among drama, poetry, and literature is related to the two tempers when one thinks of drama as eternal human truth embodied in the human community and revealed in various media through the imagination's intense contemplation of this visible world; and of poetry as eternal human truth produced through the intense imaginative contemplation of the truth of the individual imagination.

Joyce's critical writing at about Stephen's age reveals a consistent adherence to the minimal tenets of the classical temper, the artist's obligation to 'bend upon these present things'. But it also reveals an urge for reconciliation with the romantic temper and a nonpartisan willingness to adopt mystical language, to express an admiration for mystical poetry, and even to grant the high accolade of 'truth' to the product of the imagination's contemplation of the truth of its own being. 'His own image', Stephen believes in *Ulysses*, drawing upon Joyce's notion of poetry but also expressing something of the romantic temper, 'to a man with that queer thing genius is the standard of all experience' (195.39). A mystical vision that annihilates the senses and experience is threatened by incoherence; the classical preoccupation with 'the now, the here' is threatened by materialism. The artist who was a dramatist, a poet, and, above all, a literary artist, fearlessly involving his imagination in the whimsicalities and circumstances of men and women in society, without dimming his perception of both dramatic and poetic forms of truth, would be one who had reconciled the two tempers and who had found the deeper insight that 'the truth is midway' (212.28). Such an artist, surely Joyce's and Stephen's reconciling ideal at this time, was Shakespeare.

The 'Art'

The scene in the library opens with Mr Lyster's comforting purr: '—And we have, have we not, those priceless pages of *Wilhelm Meister?* A great poet on a great brother poet' (184.2). The dialogue we may assume is already in progress, accounting for Russell's 'oracled' opposition to academic speculation, even before we hear any. Literature is the general subject of the chapter; Mr Lyster also announces its special subject: a poet on a brother poet. But literature in Joyce's scheme is also the 'art' of 'Scylla and Charybdis', as theology had been the 'art' of 'Telemachus', meaning that it organizes the thoughts and actions of the characters and of the narrator. When Buck Mulligan went out on the upper stage of the Martello Tower in 'Telemachus' and began intoning the mass, the impulse to do so was his, and the narrator's contribution was limited to the decision to begin telling the story with that significant bit of mockery. But Russell and the librarians are blander characters than Mulligan. Were it not for the 'art' of the narrative, their actions would be too colourless to fit into the novel's symbolic patterns. Since the narrator in 'Scylla and Charybdis' reflects Stephen's point of view so faithfully, another way of saying this would be that through the narrator the scene is transmuted into the literary forms and modes that are at any particular moment the appropriate extension of Stephen's powerfully patterned imagination.

When Mr Lyster finishes his opening speech about seas of trouble and conflicting doubts, for example, the narrator describes his gait: 'He came a step a sinkapace forward on neatsleather creaking and a step backward a sinkapace on the solemn floor' (184.6). A moment later he 'corantoes off'. These dance steps are allusions to *Twelfth Night*, I.iii, as is the 'galliard' in which Mr Lyster later goes off to meet Bloom (200.27). The comic situation in Shakespeare's play deflates the original remark about Goethe's 'priceless pages', even though it is summoned through a description of the librarian's walk and his squeaking shoes, neither of which proceeds from his conscious will or has any objective relationship to literature. Stephen thinks of Mr Best for a moment toward the end of the chapter (215.42) as the handsome youth, whose hair Socrates toyed with in *Phaedo*, 89. His beauty contrasts throughout the scene with John Eglinton's stern primness: 'The sense of beauty leads us astray, said beautifulinsadness Best to ugling Eglinton' (204.23). Both men are unmarried, and with the introduction of the theme of homosexuality, 'Love that dare not speak its name', into the discussion of Shakespeare's sonnets (202.19), their bacherlorhood suggests the erotic atmosphere of the Platonic Academy.

Mr Lyster, whom the narrator consistently calls 'the quaker librarian', is fair game not so much from his own harmless idiosyncrasies but because he also personifies some of the general characteristics of his sect. 'Mr. Dedalus, your views are most illuminating', he says to Stephen (193.10), producing a moment later the question in Stephen's mind, 'Why did he come? Courtesy or an inward light?' Either might have motivated George Fox, for example, the founder of the Children of Light, whom William Penn characterized as 'civil beyond all forms of breeding in his behaviour'.[9] In addition to the Quaker's fundamental belief that everyone has within him a light sufficient for his salvation ('Mr Mulligan, I'll be bound, has his theory too of the play and of Shakespeare'), 'walking' had a religious significance in seventeenth-century English which Fox used when he wrote, 'I was taught how to walk [i.e., behave] to be kept pure'.[10] Unseemly behaviour was called 'disorderly walking' by the Friends and other 'strait walkers'. The inward light (which in this case shines in a poorly lighted office), the creaking neatsleather (George Fox was a shoemaker), and the renaissance dances, arousing visions of those disorderly walkers Sir Toby Belch and Sir Andrew Aguecheek, are wickedly focussed when Mr Lyster is perceived not only as an individual but as a type of Protestant teacher comically devoid of doctrine.

I am not sure that scholars have recognized the extent of Joyce's allusions to George Fox's *Journal* or the subtlety with which Stephen's thoughts and the description of Mr Lyster are blended. One of the most strikingly cryptic and beautiful passages of interior monologue in the chapter will illustrate the effect I have in mind. With an 'alarmed face' Mr Lyster asked Stephen whether he believed that Anne Shakespeare had been unfaithful to the poet. Clearly thinking of the librarian as a Quaker, Stephen wonders to himself about courtesy or an inward light, but responds aloud, apparently back on the subject of Shakespeare and Anne, by saying, '—Where there is a reconciliation . . . there must have been first a sundering'. Mr Lyster answers simply 'Yes', and Stephen then thinks: 'Christfox in leather trews, hiding, a runaway in blighted

[9] 'The Testimony of William Penn Concerning the Faithful Servant George Fox', printed in *The Journal of George Fox*, ed. Rufus M. Jones, New York, 1963, p. 63.
[10] *Journal of George Fox*, p. 66.

treeforks from hue and cry. Knowing no vixen, walking lonely in the chase. Women he won to him, tender people, a whore of Babylon, ladies of justices, bully tapsters' wives. Fox and geese. And in New Place a slack dishonoured body that once was comely, once as sweet, as fresh as cinnamon, now her leaves falling, all, bare, frighted of the narrow grave and unforgiven' (193.20).

The last half of the passage is obviously about Anne Shakespeare, one party to a reconciliation. But what about the first half? Stephen may well have Shakespeare in mind, but the interesting fact is that his imagery comes from Fox's description of himself in the *Journal*, revealing Stephen's sympathy for the troubled young Christian and associating Fox, through the medium of Mr Lyster, with Shakespeare's isolation. Fox was called 'the man in leathern breeches',[11] 'sat in hollow trees and lonesome places',[12] 'walked solitary in the Chase',[13] and won many 'tender people', including the women Stephen thinks of, to his religious beliefs. Fox used the word 'tender', according to his editor, of people who were 'religiously inclined, serious, and earnest in their search for spiritual realities',[14] as in the clause 'till people began to be acquainted with me, for there were many tender people in that town'.[15] Fox refuted those who said women have no souls, 'No more than a goose'.[16]

As the wise and common-sensical John Eglinton is by Stephen imaginatively associated with Socrates, Mr Lyster carries reminders of the saintly George Fox. Both teachers are thence subtly related to Shakespeare, Fox in the way I have just indicated, Socrates through his shrewish wife (190.28). Literature, therefore, is not only the subject of discussion in 'Scylla and Charybdis'; literary allusions in Stephen's thoughts and in the narrator's description also colour, through the chapter's 'art', our perception of the whole scene, both the immediate actions of the characters and their general parodic similarity to teachers and students of the historical and fictional past.

With the exception of Bloom, who carries out his aesthetic investigations with only slight intrusion into the episode, the characters in 'Scylla and Charybdis' were, in fact as well as in fiction, men of letters in contemporary Dublin. The theosophical poet George Russell, the sensitive and intelligent essayist William Kirkpatrick Magee, and Richard Best, a promising young scholar of

---

[11] *Journal of George Fox*, p. 139.   [12] Ibid., p. 79.   [13] Ibid., p. 69.
[14] Ibid., p. 70.   [15] Ibid., p. 71.   [16] Ibid., p. 77.

Celtic antiquity, are simultaneously characters in Ulysses and actual men. Joyce's habit of putting real people into his fictions has resulted in some curious ontological confusions. Richard Best is reported by Mr Ellmann to have responded, when reminded that he was a character in Ulysses, to the effect, 'I am not a character in fiction. I am a living being'.[17] One easily imagines the exasperation of the distinguished old scholar as he sought once and for all to declare his historical independence of the vacuous young librarian with the toyable hair. In addition to Russell and the three librarians at least a dozen other contemporary Irish writers are mentioned in conversation. Besides Wilde and Shaw and Yeats there are Judge Dunbar Plunket Barton, Dr George Sigerson, Padraic Colum, E. V. Longworth, Edward Martyn, Susan Mitchell, George Moore, George Roberts, Fred Ryan, and James Starkey ('Seumas O'Sullivan') from the local literary establishment. Buck Mulligan unfairly accuses Yeats of comparing Lady Gregory to Homer (216.28) and, by devious implication, Synge to Shakespeare (198.14–15), in the same mischievous spirit with which he tells about Dowden on Shakespeare's supposed pederasty. Mulligan's finest allusion to contemporary literature is the parody of Synge in which he tells about waiting for Stephen with Haines at the Ship and receiving the telegram. It goes in part: '—And we to be there, mavrone, and you to be unbeknownst sending us your conglomerations the way we to have our tongues out a yard long like the drouthy clerics do be fainting for a pussful' (199.37).

When they address each other in the library the characters call each other by their proper names. The narrator, however, in accordance with his 'art', refers to Russell and Magee, as does Stephen in his thoughts, by their literary pseudonyms, 'Æ' and 'John Eglinton'. The pseudonyms indicate that the two writers have themselves encouraged a degree of fiction to enter their lives. They 'mummed in names' (195.22). This drift, the actual becoming fictional in the process of narration, is underlined when the subject of names comes up in the discussion. The narrator, following the example of Buck Mulligan's conception of a play and consequent parturition (208.25), disappears momentarily and the scene is rendered dramatically. The result is that the proper names filter part-way back into the representation of the scene as speech headings, as though the narrator's

[17] Ellmann, p. 374.

departure signalled a slight objectification of the point of view. 'Mageeglinjohn' asks, 'Names! What's in a name?' and 'Quaker-lyster' irrelevantly asserts, 'But he that filches from me my good name . . .' (209.10-30). When the narrator returns he resumes his custom of calling Magee 'John Eglinton' and filching from Mr Lyster his good name, calling him as usual 'the quaker librarian'.

Joyce's narrative partiality to Stephen, and the consequent patterning of his fictional world in conformity to Stephen's imagination, requires a special alertness to whatever objective, novel-like information we may be given about Stephen's surroundings. The bravura of Stephen's and the narrator's private mockery of Lyster, Russell, Eglinton, and Best, woven out of several hundred literary allusions and Protean transformations of their names and words and actions distracts our attention from the scene as it may be thought to have objectively occurred. When Stephen speaks to Russell about inserting Mr Deasy's letter in the *Irish Homestead*, he adopts an outward manner of 'best French polish'. He is throughout the scene eager to impress and convince his hearers. They, on the other hand, are either rude, irrelevant, or disengaged. Especially painful to Stephen is Eglinton's invitation to Russell and Mulligan to come to George Moore's soirée that night, with no suggestion that Stephen would be welcome too (191.32), and Lyster's announcement that Russell is bringing out a volume of younger poets, again omitting Stephen (192.9). His isolation from the burgeoning society of Dublin literati is associated briefly in his mind with literary images, which convey his pain while keeping it relatively free of self-pity, 'Cordelia. Cordoglio. Lir's loneliest daughter'. Or if there is pity in the linking of the daughters of Lear and Lir with the Italian word for 'deep sorrow', it is the static emotion described in Joyce's *Paris Notebook* (13 February 1903) as the product of proper art, an aspect of 'sorrow comprehended in sorrow' (CW, 144). We know that Stephen more than gets his revenge on his tormentors in his private thoughts. In objective, social terms, however, he is mild, polite, the offended party. He is sensitive to his own behaviour, aware that he might himself be rude—if we may take the narrator's word for it—when he answers, 'Bosh!' to Eglinton's suggestion that Shakespeare made a mistake in marrying Anne Hathaway. 'A man of genius makes no mistakes. His errors are volitional and are the portals of discovery' (190.21). Irritatingly sententious perhaps, with its quibble on the distinction between 'error' and 'mistake', but Stephen's expletive and the following explanation come out in the heat of the chase, where impatience with what 'the world believes' hurts no one.

With its single lamp and surrounding shadows, the room where the dialogue takes place contrasts with the brightness 'in the daylit corridor' (200.27) where Mr Lyster talks with Bloom, and even more so with the holy atmosphere in the 'kind air' (218.5) of Kildare street outside the library. There is at times a mysterious and religious aura in the room. Eglinton looks over at Russell after teasing Stephen about one of his youthful boasts: 'Glittereyed, his rufous skull close to his greencapped desklamp sought the face, bearded amid darkgreener shadow, an ollav, holyeyed' (184.31). Left briefly alone, Stephen thinks, 'a vestal's lamp', as he contemplates the 'vaulted cell', with its 'warm and brooding air'. Here Eglinton 'ponders things that were not', 'what might have been', and 'things not known'. 'Coffined thoughts around me, in mummycases, embalmed in spice of words. Thoth, god of libraries, a birdgod, moonycrowned', Stephen muses. 'They are still. Once quick in the brains of men. Still: but an itch of death is in them, to tell me in my ear a maudlin tale, urge me to wreak their will' (193.29). The old thoughts are like the ghost of Shakespeare's play, but in Joyce's and Stephen's celebrated distinction between 'proper' and 'improper art' they are improper, because they urge him to some action (*Paris Notebook* 13 February, 1903; *CW*, 143). To adopt the religious language that either Joyce or Stephen might use, such thoughts, by exciting desire and loathing, are profanities in the sacred temple of art.

Because most of the literary activity of libraries and of men of letters falls short of the high status of proper drama and poetry, which produces rest or stasis in the beholder, it is mostly profane in this sense. Russell illustrates two extreme varieties of such profanity. His connexion with the *Irish Homestead* and with practical agricultural affairs shows literature at about its most materialistic. As a theosophist, on the other hand, his spiritual powers are exercised on a chaos of whirling souls: 'Filled with his god he thrones, Buddh[a] under plantain. Gulfer of souls, engulfer. Hesouls, shesouls, shoals of souls. Engulfed with wailing creecries, whirled, whirling, they bewail' (192.2).[18] Russell's literary activities are too Scyllan, his spiritual exercises too Charybdian. Judged by such exalted standards, most of the characters' literary interests can be objected to, which accounts for Stephen's secret attitude of mockery and hauteur.

His own practical literary values are equally at odds with the others'. He is eager to receive payment for his literary efforts. Eglinton tells him, '—You are the only contributor to *Dana* who asks for pieces of silver', adding that he probably won't have room for Stephen's theory in the next number anyway, because 'Fred Ryan wants space for an article on economics' (214.18). That *Dana* should publish articles about making money does not bother Eglinton. That an artist should be paid for his work does. Stephen's view is, of course, just the opposite. It is literature that ought to be sacred, not the material body of the artist. Nor should the sanctity of literary art be confused with the ordinariness of its subject, another topic on which Stephen is at odds with his contemporaries. Joyce's Holy Office as an artist was, according to the poem, to serve as a Holy Orifice, conveying the cloacal wastes which the idealistic niceties of his contemporaries forbid them from noticing. In their vaulted cells they will edit papers on economics and agriculture by the light of vestals' lamps, keeping their personal lives and their art at a safe distance from 'these present things'. By evoking the literary scene of Dublin in 1904, with details of its publications and performances, and by bringing actual men of letters into his story, either as characters or through conversational allusions, Joyce illustrates in 'Scylla and Charybdis' the aspect of art which Stephen attributes to Shakespeare in the dialogue: its acceptance of the gift of 'this place in nature'.

The 'Symbol'

In 'Telemachus' Buck Mulligan advertizes Stephen's theory to Haines, although he does not want to hear it rehearsed, being unequal at such an hour 'to Thomas Aquinas and the fiftyfive reasons he has made to prop it up' (17.39–41). 'It's quite simple', says Mulligan, 'he proves by algebra that Hamlet's grandson is Shakespeare's grandfather and that he himself is the ghost of his own

[18] The 1961 text reads *Buddh*.

father' (18.10–12). Mulligan humorously and heretically exaggerates, but his characterization is close enough to anticipate Stephen's words in the library: Shakespeare 'was not the father of his own son merely but, being no more a son, he was and felt himself the father of all his race, the father of his own grandfather, the father of his unborn grandson who, by the same token, never was born' (208.13). As for Stephen's being the ghost of his own father, Mulligan teasingly refers to his turning away from the elder Dedalus's Noah-like weaknesses by saying, 'O, shade of Kinch the elder! Japhet in search of a father' (18.17). The sense in which Shakespeare is the father of all his race is the analogy of the creative artist to the God of creation. Hence as artist Stephen, too, could become the father of his own father in a fictional work.

Inevitably when we contemplate Stephen's future artistic productions we are led to a consciousness of his being (through his identity with Joyce) the future author of the work in which he is himself a character—the father of himself, of Bloom, of Kinch the elder, all in all. 'Stephen Dedalus' was not merely Joyce's fictional name for a literary character very much like himself in 1904. In its more classical form, the name 'Stephen Daedalus' was at times in 1904 Joyce's own name. Over this name he published three short stories that year in the *Irish Homestead*, using the name also to sign letters to his friends. 'Stephen Dedalus' equals Joyce in the same way that 'Æ' and 'John Eglinton' equal Russell and Magee. It is a literary pseudonym which blurs the ontological gap between a character in fiction and a living being. Stephen in the library tells the others that he consists of the memory of his former self and the potentiality of his future self. It is a moment in which the narrative comes alive with self-consciousness, predicting its own future composition and uniting Stephen Dedalus in 1904 with James Joyce in 1918: 'In the intense instant of imagination, when the mind, Shelley says, is a fading coal that which I was is that which I am and that which in possibility I may come to be. So in the future, the sister of the past, I may see myself as I sit here now but by reflection from that which then I shall be' (194.29–34). During the discussion Stephen consciously made mental notes for the composition of the scene. When Mr Lyster finished his announcement about the collection of young poets he looked at Russell and the other two librarians as they sat around the lamp:

Anxiously he glanced in the cone of lamplight where three faces, lighted, shone.
See this. Remember. (192.12)

At the end, when Stephen discusses the possibility of publishing his Shakespeare theory he receives a useful suggestion from Mr Best: '—Are you going to write it? Mr Best asked. You ought to make it a dialogue, don't you know, like the Platonic dialogues Wilde wrote' (214.2).

The biographical evidence of Joyce's life in the years between 1904 and 1918 suggests that that which in actuality he came to be was a man in some respects like Leopold Bloom, by reflection from whom he saw himself as he sat in the library.[19] Bloom's life has elements in common with Stephen's version of Shakespeare's life and with Joyce's own. The relationship between Stephen and Bloom cannot really be 'proved by algebra' because it is not produced entirely by a simple logical analogy, but by some deeper pattern of imagination, some 'entelechy, form of forms', which unites Stephen, Joyce, and Bloom in life and in art. It is here in 'Scylla and Charybdis', in Stephen's argument about Shakespeare as father, that Joyce tells his reader in effect: 'I, too, am the father, the older man whom this young artist would one day become'. Even Stephen's definition of a ghost fits Joyce as well as it does Shakespeare: 'One who has faded into impalpability through death, through absence, through change of manners. Elizabethan London lay as far from Stratford as corrupt Paris lies from virgin Dublin. Who is the ghost from *limbo patrum*, returning to the world that has forgotten him? Who is king Hamlet?' (188.16). The ghost is the exiled artist betrayed in his native city.

Usurpation, exile, adultery, 'the note of banishment, banishment from the heart, banishment from home' (212.6) are, according to Stephen, continual themes in Shakespeare's plays. These themes unite not only Shakespeare but all of Joyce's heroes—Socrates, Christ, Fox, Ulysses, Parnell—with himself, whether in his various fictional disguises as Stephen Dedalus, Richard Rowan, and Leopold Bloom or as James Joyce, the ghostly haunter from abroad (Trieste-Zürich-Paris) of the usurpers and betrayers in Dublin. In

[19] Ellmann, pp. 384–385. Since Bloom appears too briefly in this episode, with neither his thoughts nor his spoken words reported, I have left the full documentation of this point to other writers in this volume.

real life, this isolated hero inflicted even on Nora his tormented accusations of infidelity: 'I have been a fool. I thought that all the time
you gave yourself only to me and you were dividing your body
between me and another. In Dublin here the rumor is circulated
that I have taken the leavings of others. Perhaps they laugh when
they see me parading "*my*" son in the streets'.[20] With justification
Nora might have complained on such occasions of a 'biographical
fallacy', only injected the wrong way: Joyce seeking through a preoccupation with his art to impose meanings on his life. The non-
fact of his wife's infidelity fascinated him. He lived with it for many
years, yearning perhaps for at least an imaginative image of himself
as cuckold to serve as a standard for those master spirits, Bloom and
Shakespeare, who could survive a betrayal urged by the beast with
two backs.

Stephen's thoughts about paternity are not confined to 'Scylla
and Charybdis'. Especially his musings on the mystery of the Trinity
—the Arian and Sabellian heresies as well as the orthodox dogma
of the Church—constitute a continuing theme in *Ulysses*. Arius
held that the Trinity consisted of three persons who were not consubstantial. Sabellius taught that the Trinity was one person with
three consubstantial modes. Stephen considers the possible useful-
ness of these heretical doctrines and rejects them (208.7–18). Instead, he supposes the orthodox filial relationship to exist between
the artist and a consubstantial second person whom he sends into
the world of his creation to mediate between it and himself. An
important effect of Stephen's 'theolologicophilolological' theorizing
is the self-consciousness it brings into the narrative, including itself
in its generalizations and leading us to conclude that Stephen and
Joyce are consubstantial, of one essence—but that they are also
separate persons, separated as they are joined, by time and the laws
of the two worlds they inhabit, the fictional and the actual. This
spiritual relationship between the artist and his creation illustrates
the sense in which Joyce and Stephen had the cursed Jesuit strain
injected the wrong way. The analogy to orthodox theology in their
aesthetic theory is rigorously exact in detail, but upside-down over-

---

[20] *Letters*, II, 233. I have no wish here to go into the very personal correspondence written during the two trips to Dublin in 1909, rather to establish
merely the fact that Joyce's life assumed patterns that his imagination had already made familiar.

all. Eternity and immutability are in Joyce's aesthetic the attributes
not of the creator but of his creation, into which he sends the son.
In the eternal world of art, therefore, the creator himself is but a
ghost, his own person being subject to the temporal order.

Stephen's doctrine of an aesthetic trinity can be documented
in the text of Ulysses, but another significant conceit in 'Scylla and
Charybdis' cannot: the rock and the whirlpool of the Homeric parallel. In Joyce's famous chart, which was printed nearly complete by
Stuart Gilbert in 1930, are listed the title, scene, hour, organ, art,
symbol, and technic for 'Scylla and Charybdis'. A fuller version of
the chart, printed by Hugh Kenner in Dublin's Joyce, contains an
additional column of 'correspondences', which Gilbert had included
in his discussions of the individual episodes. Not all Joyceans agree
on the legitimacy of using these helpful bits of external evidence
to construct interpretations of the work. Specifically, the interpre-
tive information that the chart supplies about 'Scylla and Charybdis'
is that the chapter's symbols, Stratford and London, correspond to
the Homeric rock and the whirlpool respectively, as do Aristotle in
opposition to Plato and dogma in opposition to mysticism. The
correspondences to Ulysses are Shakespeare, Socrates, and Christ.
Everything on the chart is in the text—except the Homeric parallels
themselves. In the Odyssey, Ulysses lost six men to the monster
Scylla, through the 'volitional error' of sailing close to the rock she
lived in, rather than commit the 'mistake' of destroying his whole
company in the whirlpool Charybdis.

Since the Homeric rock and whirlpool are not part of the text
of Ulysses they are not themselves subject to interpretation. There
is no need to ask what they 'mean' in the chapter. They are from
the reader's point of view at most a kind of allegorical commentary:
as the rock was to the whirlpool in the adventure of Ulysses, so
Stratford is to London in the life of Shakespeare. Such correspondences and analogies within the chapter accumulate, enriching each
other, and an exploitation of them in interpretation seems altogether legitimate if we are aware of its limitations. In my earlier
discussion of Joyce's urge to discover a reconciliation of the classical
and romantic tempers, I found useful not the Homeric images themselves but the dialectical relationship they expressed. In the Mangan
essay, Joyce said that the ancient gods die and come to life many
times, renewing the miracle of light eternally in the imaginative

soul, an idea that suggests that the characters in *Ulysses* really may in some sense be intended as reincarnations of the ancient heroes. I will not deny it; but that kind of genuinely symbolic, almost mystical, connexion among Stephen, Hamlet, and Telemachus, or among Bloom, King Hamlet's ghost, and Odysseus, has only obscure support in the text and will not concern me. I will side with Stephen, who tells his hearer that Aristotle 'would find Hamlet's musings about the afterlife of his princely soul . . . as shallow as Plato's' (186.4), even though it was precisely Plato whose musings about the afterlife for the first time describe the reincarnation of Odysseus as an ordinary man: 'And so it happened that it fell to the soul of Odysseus to choose last of all. The memory of his former sufferings had cured him of all ambition and he looked around for a long time to find the uneventful life of an ordinary man; at last he found it lying neglected by the others, and when he saw it he chose it with joy and said that had his lot fallen first he would have made the same choice'.[21] Nonetheless, I will consider the meaning of the chapter's 'symbol' by relying on the text itself and the allegorical analogies that Joyce stipulated in his chart, and not on any events in the life of Homer's hero.

Stratford and London stand in Stephen's imagination for ideas that can at times be paraphrased rather neatly as 'the facts of life' and 'the fictions of the imagination'. But pithy labels do not do justice to the depth of his conception of Shakespeare's spiritual and imaginative experience. Just before the *entr'acte*, Stephen tries to understand the new passion out of which Shakespeare wrote the sonnets of the dark lady. He refers again to a whirlpool (as he had done silently in thinking of Æ as an engulfer of souls). The association with a whirlpool is allegorically appropriate, since Shakespeare's was a 'London' experience, but the experience was also a 'fact of life', not a psychic fantasy. What, then, makes it Charybdian and Londonesque rather than Scyllan and Stratfordian? Stephen speaks of the lasting influence of Anne's conquest of Will: "The tusk of the boar has wounded him there where love lies ableeding. If the shrew is worsted yet there remains to her woman's invisible weapon. There is, I feel in the words, some goad of the flesh driving him into a new passion, a darker shadow of the first, darkening even his own understanding of himself. A like fate waits him and the two

[21] *Republic*, X, 620, tr. H. D. P. Lee, London, Penguin Books, 1955, p. 400.

rages commingle in a whirlpool' (196.31).[22] Whatever else Stephen
means—and I do not pretend to understand entirely the speech from
which this passage comes—he says that an episode in Stratford, when
Anne was to Shakespeare as Venus to Adonis, gave rise in later years,
in London, to a second passion, even more destructive and incomprehensible than the first.

The association of 'woman's invisible weapon' with 'some goad
of the flesh', and the phrase 'darkening even his own understanding
of himself', suggest a very old Christian ethical doctrine, in which
every sin is understood to be a reenactment of man's original sin
as it is described in Scripture, Adam yielding to woman's invisible
weapon, the rational soul yielding to some goad of the flesh. Stephen
himself later echoes the *Catechism* of his day when he refers to
Anne's seduction of Will as 'the original sin that darkened his understanding, weakened his will and left in him a strong inclination
to evil' (212.14). We may understand from this that Shakespeare's
life in Stratford was 'primal'. Its sins were 'original', and the spiritual
events of London were dark shadows of their Stratford antetypes.

Life in London was 'rich', producing an art of 'surfeit'. With
an allusion that has escaped most readers of this episode, Stephen
stresses the spiritually and psychologically debilitating nature of
Shakespeare's sojourn in London: 'Twenty years he dallied there
between conjugal love and its chaste delights and scortatory love
and its foul pleasures' (201.29–31). The allusion is to be the title of
a work by Emanuel Swedenborg translated into English in 1794 as
*Swedenborg's Delights of Wisdom concerning Conjugial Love: after
which follow the pleasures of Insanity concerning Scortatory Love.*
Swedenborg's opposition of wisdom and insanity informs the meaning of Stephen's two cities in the psychological and spiritual life of
Shakespeare—or of any artist—more profoundly than do the accidents of the poet's sex life. The 'insanity' of London is the anti-
materialistic 'madness' which Joyce defended in the Blake essay,
but which he also associated with the imagination's destruction of
experience, natural wisdom, memory, and the senses in the process
of contemplating the truth of its own being. Conversely, of course,
'wisdom' accepts the sensory experience of time and space in its
contemplation of the truth of the visible world. The 'like fate'
which awaited Shakespeare in the experience of the last sonnets

[22] The 1961 text prints *life* for *like*.

was a recapitulation of the Stratford cycle of seduction, impotence, and betrayal. While it was a spiritual and psychological experience of 'real life' it owed its shape and significance to the primal events in Stratford, which, like Dublin, is 'virgin' in contrast to corrupt and fallen London and Paris.

From the whirlpool of the two rages, a transition to the imagery of *Hamlet* occurs to Stephen, as he thinks of the porches of his hearers' ears:

> The soul has been before stricken mortally, a poison poured in the porch of a sleeping ear. But those who are done to death in sleep cannot know the manner of their quell unless their Creator endow their souls with that knowledge in the life to come. The poisoning and the beast with two backs that urged it king Hamlet's ghost could not know of were he not endowed with knowledge by his creator. That is why the speech (his lean unlovely English) is always turned elsewhere, backward. (196.39)

The analogy between God the Creator and the artist as creator is here made explicit. As God can endow his creatures with knowledge in the afterlife, so Shakespeare informs the ghost with his own knowledge, turning his speech backward to the pristine realm of experience, to Stratford. Continuing with his account of Shakespeare as the ghost, Stephen says,

> He goes back, weary of the creation he has piled up to hide him from himself, an old dog licking an old sore. But, because loss is his gain, he passes on toward eternity in undiminished personality, untaught by the wisdom he has written or by the laws he has revealed. His beaver is up. He is a ghost, a shadow now, the wind by Elsinore's rocks or what you will, the sea's voice, a voice heard only in the heart of him who is the substance of his shadow, the son consubstantial with the father. (197.8)

Shakespeare is the ghost in several senses. He is a fictional ghost of his own creation and a metaphorical 'ghost' in his retirement back to Stratford after a long absence and change of manners. But 'going back' also means going back beyond Stratford 'on towards eternity', where Shakespeare becomes presumably a third kind of ghost, less fictional and metaphorical than the other two. In this sense, as the ghost of a man, he is untaught by the wisdom he has written or by the laws he has revealed. His motive has been psychological and spiritual, an attempt 'to hide him from himself' that was fueled by the enormous creative force of his London 'madness'. But since the temporal experience of the artist's senses, even to the mortal wounding of his soul, are those 'present things' to which in his creative imagination he bends, he has revealed, despite himself, the truths of drama and poetry. As the person of the creator he exists only as the ghost in the eternal world of the play; but his consubstantial son lives forever as Hamlet. The 'facts of life' of which Stratford is the symbol in Stephen's thought are not just the stuff of literary realism, the kind of cosmopolitan social detail that the artist can find anywhere. They are the events that shape the essential forms of his soul, embodying the essential 'wisdom' and 'laws' of birth, death, seduction, betrayal, avarice, and reconciling filial and grandfilial love. By imaginatively returning in London to the facts of Stratford, Shakespeare's art recreates the primal myth of human life. The son of his soul was created in London to immortalize the name of the dead son of his body in Stratford.

Conjugal Love

Stephen's interest in Shakespeare's life is that of a brother poet, not a literary critic. The critic's aim is to understand and appreciate the work of art, but Stephen attempts to comprehend the process by which the intense imagination transmutes transitory human experience into the immortal events of art. From his point of view, Russell and John Eglinton in turning away from the facts of Shakespeare's life deny the realities of their own. Russell quotes the famous epigram of the aesthete from *Axel*: 'As for living, our servants can do that for us, Villiers de l'Isle has said. Peeping and prying into greenroom gossip of the day, the poet's drinking, the poet's debts, we have *King Lear*: and it is immortal' (189.15). He speaks for the critic when he insists that in contrast to the plays the private life of the poet is of interest to schoolboys (185.20) and the parish clerk (189.13), but Stephen refutes him on the spot, albeit silently.

In one of his wittiest interior monologues, Joyce has Stephen associate Russell's remark with a bit of greenroom gossip in his own life: his debt of a pound to Russell. At first he denies to himself that he owes Æ the money, rationalizing that it was borrowed by another person because in the intervening five months the molecules in his body have changed. But then he recalls the Aristotelian doctrine of the soul in *de anima*: 'But I, entelechy, form of forms, am I by memory because under everchanging forms' (189.39). His memory recalls those former 'I's', adding them up to 'I': 'I, I and I. I'. Accepting the consequences of his reasoning, he owns up to the debt: 'A. E. I. O. U.' Right on the page before us a poet's private debt becomes a work of art, and in the process Joyce gives us the psychological rationale: knowledge of the debt is preserved through the welter of subsequent experience by memory, and becomes an attribute of the artist's soul. The artistic self-consciousness of which this fictional moment is born reminds us of a fact more significant than Stephen's memory of the debt: Joyce's memory of it. Where, one is tempted to ask, would *Ulysses* be if Joyce had had a servant to live his life for him?

When John Eglinton denies the literary importance of Shakespeare's father and wife, Stephen interprets it as a denial of Eglinton's own family life and sexuality. He recalls stories of the elder Magee, an icon of rough country vitality, who embarrassed his elegant son on his visits to the library. With the delicate wit that characterizes Joyce's portrait of Eglinton, the narrator ironically echoes Eglinton's praise of Falstaff, who was not a family man ('I feel that the *fat* knight is his supreme creation'), by saying of Eglinton, '*Lean*, he lay back' (206.36).[23] This hint that Eglinton admires the imagined character who is his own opposite conforms to the general satire of the librarians: they are ill equipped to be men of letters because their own lives are too circumscribed to comprehend the laws and wisdom revealed by art. They see no need to interest themselves in the meaner details of Shakespeare's life when they will not admit such events into their own, denying the connexion between life and art that is the basis of Stephen's and Joyce's aesthetics of the classical temper. Joyce's satire on this prissiness in 'The Holy Office' was directed at its effect on contemporary literature, but Stephen's concern is deeper and more personal in 'Scylla Charybdis'. Half-consciously he seeks a new pattern for his own life that will carry him beyond the roles of Katharsis-Purgative and Leviathan in the poem, where he stands 'Self-doomed,/ Unfellowed, friendless and alone' (*CW*, 152), to a more productive absence from the scene of his youth and a nearer conformity to the life of Shakespeare.

[23] My italics.

Stephen, therefore, holds up not just his interlocutors' lives for comparison with Shakespeare's, but also his own. From Magee the elder his thoughts move to Kinch the elder and to the meeting with his father at the dock on returning from Paris to his mother's deathbed. Fathers are inevitably separated from their sons, 'sundered by a bodily shame' (207.35). 'What links them in nature?' he asks, 'an instant of blind rut' (208.4). Paternity, which 'may be a legal fiction', is not an easy subject for him. '*Amor matris*, subjective and objective genitive', by contrast, 'may be the only true thing in life' (207.27), and in the first three episodes it has been of greater concern to Stephen in his mummer's mask of a mourning Hamlet than has paternity. Now he is breaking new ground, 'battling against hopelessness' (207.9) and wondering uncertainly, 'What the hell are you driving at? I know. Shut up. Blast you! I have reasons' (207.31). Psychologically, it is a breakthrough for him to discover that paternity 'is a mystical estate, an apostolic succession, from only begetter to only begotten' (207.21) for it shows him the way to his own paternity, actual and aesthetic. *Amor matris* is a reciprocal bodily and emotional relationship between mother and child, which he could experience only as a son. But paternity, not the madonna, is the mystery on which the Church and (in Stephen's theolologicophilolological aesthetic) art is founded (207.24).

The most ruthlessly revealed respect in which Stephen considers the young librarians to deny life is in their sexuality. Mr Best, who has the thing that according to Blake's *Note-Book* women require in men, 'the lineaments of gratified desire', reminds Stephen of the wellpleased pleasers of the women of Paris (191.26 and 42.34). He is envious of Best's good looks, willing to give his 'five wits for youth's proud livery he pranks in'. This allusion to Shakespeare's sonnets leads Stephen to imagine Best as the youth to whom the poet gave his love and his mistress: 'There be many mo. Take her for me. In pairing time' (199.7). But he is 'tame essence of Wilde' in his innocent fascination with the literature of corruption. John Eglinton, on the other hand, is a stern puritan who believes you cannot eat your cake and have it—and he has his. Anticipating Mulligan's outrageous mockery of the librarians as masturbators, Stephen more discreetly and more wittily thinks, 'They fingerponder nightly each his variorum edition of *The Taming of the Shrew*'. In contrast to the rich sexuality of Shakespeare's art and to Stephen's recon-

struction of the poet's life, they are 'unwed, unfancied, ware of wiles'
(213.38).

Not that Stephen's situation is much better. Most of the pound
Æ lent him he spent 'in Georgina Johnson's bed', for he has, like
Katharsis-Purgative, been 'Bringing to tavern and to brothel / The
mind of witty Aristotle' (CW, 149). Mulligan's accusation of finding Stephen 'at his summer residence in upper Mecklenburgh street
. . . deep in the study of the Summa contra Gentiles in the company
of two gonorrheal ladies, Fresh Nelly and Rosalie, the coalquay
whore' (214.27) is more malicious than untrue. Stephen would
have it otherwise. In 'Proteus' for example, he feels a vague but
powerful longing, aroused by remembering a girl he had seen looking into Hodges Figgis' window the preceding Monday, 'Touch me.
Soft eyes. Soft soft hand. I am lonely here. O, touch me soon now'
(49.4). He doesn't know who she is or what he wants her to be.
His fantasy, like Joyce's erotic imagination in those days, wavers
between the elegant literary lady and the 'pickmeup'. His speculation
about her includes, too, 'those curse of God stays' which Joyce disparaged in letters to Nora in the summer of 1904. 'Why do you
wear those cursed things?' he complained.[24] Five years later, recalling the time before he met her, Joyce wrote, 'I was a strange lonely
boy, walking about by myself at night and thinking that some day a
girl would love me. But I never could speak to the girls I used to
meet at houses. Their false manners checked me at once. Then you
came to me'.[25] In precisely this lonely anticipation of love, Stephen
asks himself, as he finishes speaking of Anne Hathaway's tumbling
Shakespeare in a cornfield, 'And my turn? When? Come!' (191.19).
'Wait to be wooed and won. Ay, meacock. Who will woo you?'
(210.17).

Having known the pleasures of scortatory love, he wants now
the chaste delights of conjugal love, not the empty obscenities of a
Buck Mulligan or Katharsis-Purgative. Philosophically, too, nothing
would be gained by exchanging the formless spiritual essences of
Russell for Mulligan's soulless essences of form. Mulligan's witty
brain easily gives birth in the last few minutes of the dialogue to a
parody of Burns's 'John Anderson', a burlesque of Everyman, a
parody of Yeats's 'Baile and Aillinn', a denigration of the Abbey

---

[24] Letters, II, 51.
[25] Letters, II, 236–237.

Theatre, cynical advice to Stephen about flattering Lady Gregory, and a recollection of the nuisance Stephen committed at a rehearsal in the Camden Hall, all couched in such terms of endearment as 'you inquisitional drunken jew jesuit!' If his friendship with Mulligan had shown promise at one time of developing into a strong emotional attachment, it is not now to be. Stephen has resolved to leave the tower and to make no concessions. In 'Proteus' he thinks of Mulligan, 'staunch friend, a brother soul: Wilde's love that dare not speak its name. He now will leave me. And the blame? As I am. As I am. All or not at all' (49.22). Not long before, Stephen had broken with an even better friend. At the beginning of 'Scylla and Charybdis' he thinks of Cranly, 'My soul's youth I gave him, night by night' (185.2), using words similar to ones that Joyce wrote about Byrne in a letter to Nora the summer they met: 'When I was younger I had a friend to whom I gave myself freely—in a way more than I give to you and in a way less. He was Irish, that is to say, he was false to me'.[26] In Joyce's life as in Stephen's, a new stage was being prepared through the break with the great friends of his youth.

The final breach with Mulligan is not to be sudden or dramatic. The idea occurs to Stephen at the end of the chapter when he stands aside to let Bloom pass: 'Part. The moment is now' (217.24), but he knows that he will only meet himself again, like Maeterlinck's Socrates and Judas, who find wherever they go the occasion for wisdom or betrayal (213.14–17). In the general symbolism of the whole book, Bloom's passing between Stephen and Mulligan is significant. In the literary and aesthetic terms of 'Scylla and Charybdis' it is less so. Bloom does not hold with the optimistic element of Stephen's 'deeper insight'. As would Mulligan, he 'dissented tacitly from Stephen's views on the eternal affirmation of the spirit of man in literature' (666.34). His errand in the library is the epitome of ordinary business—to trace an advertisement from a newspaper. Both he and Mulligan stop in the adjoining museum first, to observe the statue of Venus. But their attentions are drawn to opposite ends of the goddess. Mulligan celebrates her divinity's power to enkindle life, 'the Greek mouth that has never been twisted in prayer' (201.5), while Bloom satisfies his curiosity on a point of the physiological conveniences of divinity, whether the gods have rectums (176.37–38). Something of the essential character of the two

[26] *Letters*, II, 50.

men is revealed in their differing attitudes, despite their both being to the Scyllan side of Stephen. Anything less than the power of pagan divinity to overcome human limitations is subject to Mulligan's mockery, whereas the intense activity of Bloom's curiosity is centred on a human point of reference.

It is the human reference point in Shakespeare's art, by means of which the whole world of his creation can be traced back to its beginnings in Stratford, that has taught Stephen the value of his own humanity. Mulligan mocks the human condition, Russell and the others deny its reality. Stephen at the end is closer to Bloom, who embodies it. Half-consciously he associates Bloom with the man he dreamed of the night before, but as he walks out of the library into the daylight of Kildare street there are no other birds of omen, only the reconciling smoke from *Cymbeline*, rising out of two chimneys across the way: 'from wide earth an altar'. In words reminiscent of John Dowland's, which Joyce later quoted to Nora, 'O strive not to be excellent in woe',[27] Stephen thinks he will 'cease to strive'. What he in space and time has been and is to become will be the pattern of his art. This quiet note of reconciliation, like the intellectual struggle which preceded it, is convincing because Joyce has done in 'Scylla and Charybdis' what Stephen has learned he must do. He has reconciled the truth of the imagination to the truth of 'these present things', the actualities of his own life, in affirmation of *det gaadefulde jordliv*.

Only one event has been omitted, the crucial one, through which Joyce himself moved on 16 June 1904, from being a son toward his ineluctable paternity. Nora, the virgin to whom he spoke in Nassau street a few days before, is at most a fantasy in *Ulysses*. Of another Nora there is much more in Molly Bloom, the wife of Joyce's other self, the man whom after Bloomsday Stephen is to become. But that becoming, that finding 'in the world without as actual what was in his world within as possible' (213.13), remains in the immortality of Joyce's art only a possibility for Stephen, who lives forever as the consubstantial son. Like Hamlet, he is 'reading the book of himself' (187.11), and like Shakespeare will presumably continue to 'walk through' himself, 'meeting robbers, ghosts, giants, old men, young men, wives, widows, brothers-in-love' (213.19). But when he meets himself as husband and father,

[27] *Letters*, II, 259.

Stephen is still a lonely boy. There is no name in *Ulysses* for the one who is to change him. The way has been prepared. Her lover awaits. But her only name is Nora: 'O Nora! Nora! Nora! I am speaking now to the girl I loved, who has red-brown hair and sauntered over to me and took me so easily into her arms and made me a man'.[28]

[28] *Letters*, II, 233.

WANDERING ROCKS

Clive Hart

After the mind-stuff of 'Scylla and Charybdis', with its indoor
setting, we pass to the open-air physical world of the city. While
the contrast is obvious, there is also a sense of continuity. As Mr
Kellogg points out,[1] Joyce felt it important to hold to the now, the
here, as the essential 'classical' basis from which all flights of artistic
imagination might begin. 'Wandering Rocks', following immediately
on Stephen's theorizing, is Joyce's most direct, most complete celebration of Dublin, demonstrating succinctly his conception of the
importance of physical reality, meticulously documented, as the soil
from which fictions may best grow.

Joyce was by temperament an urban man. However he might
celebrate, in *Finnegans Wake*, the delights of river and mountain,
field and flower, these were projections of fantasy, metaphors of the
artistic imagination the tenor of which was always life as he knew
it in the urban environment. While Joyce might not feel at home,
in the ordinary sense, in Dublin, it was there that he felt in touch
with the real world. It was there, too, whether in fact or in fancy,
that he could best express and develop his fundamentally ambivalent
relationship with reality. Throughout his life Joyce was troubled by
the contradictory needs to be at once accepted and rejected, to partake and to be banished. His putting himself at a physical distance

[1] See previous essay.

from the city while totally immersing himself in it in imagination was only the most obvious of the means he used to deal with that ambivalence (revealed elsewhere in Richard's to-have-and-have-not relationship with Bertha and in Stephen's aesthetic ideal of dominance *in absentia*).

In one's relationship with a city one may simultaneously belong and be alone. Joyce, very much the loner, rejected the values of the Dubliners while feeling both that he belonged to Dublin and that Dublin 'belonged to him'. The strength of his desire mentally to possess the city can hardly be over-estimated. His at times almost sentimental cultivation of his memory of streets and shops, sounds and smells, attested by many visitors to the Joycean apartments on the Continent (apartments which were never allowed to attain the comfort and status of 'home'), is indicative of the importance that he attached not only to his urban, physical roots in the general sense, but also to intimate, conscious awareness of those roots in exact, undistorted, documentary detail. He asked his friends and relatives to send him tram tickets, newspapers, portable scraps of urban life. Having used these to construct a sound documentary foundation, he felt free to make organic modifications dictated by the shaping forces of the artistic conception. In accepting and expressing the documentary reality of the city, Joyce was belonging; in recreating it with modifications for his art, he was exercizing his will over it, making it his own.

If Joyce's relationship with the city had been merely the expression of a personal ambivalence, it might be considered a purely autobiographical matter of no concern to the literary critic. It is, however, an element of fundamental importance in the structure and meaning of *Ulysses*, a book singularly unsuited to the rigours of the old New Criticism. Mr Kenner has recently explored with great insight some of the artistic considerations that may have led Joyce to evoke the Dublin of 1904 in such detail. Sensing a parallel with archaeological attitudes to Homer's Troy, he speaks of *Ulysses* as a 'book . . . made not of mere sonorous words which neither hurt nor nourish, but of cups and saucers, chairs and tables, sticks and stones'.[2] Joyce had said, with allowable hyperbole, that he wanted *Ulysses* to be a documentary source from which Dublin, if

[2] Hugh Kenner, 'Homer's Sticks and Stones', *JJQ*, VI, 4 (Summer 1969), 298.

destroyed, might be recreated.[3] In saying so, he was shoring up physical fragments against the potential ruin of total imaginative disembodiment, but it was more than a private problem for the artist: it was one of the central creative issues around which he constructed his novel.

Neither Bloom nor Stephen belongs, wholly and vitally, to this meticulously evoked city environment. *Ulysses* gives clear expression, among other things, to that common twentieth-century theme, modern man's difficulty in integrating the disparate inner and outer worlds, worlds of experience which will not cohere, and which remain intractable to the end. Neither in their relations with the urban world, nor in relation to each other, are Stephen and Bloom able to achieve and sustain an adequate synthesis of inner and outer. In this predicament they are not, of course, alone. In the Dublin of *Ulysses*, aspiration is rarely matched by achievement, perception fails to confirm intuition, actions do not lead to expected results, hopes remain velleities. Despite the many pleas for the contrary view, it seems to me that this is true throughout Bloomsday, and that nothing much has happened by the end of the book. The situation has, perhaps, been clarified for both men, but the problems remain, and life, it seems, will carry on in much the same fashion on 17 June 1904. Hopes are, of course, continually raised by congruences that are ultimately seen to be false. The relevance of Shakespearean themes to both Stephen and Bloom, rising to a symbolic climax in the well-known moment when they both see the head of Shakespeare in the mirror in 'Circe', points to a relationship but leads to no true meeting of minds. The amusing erroneous calculations about their relative ages in 'Ithaca' provide an ironic comment on the emptiness of any attempt at harmony. The search for unity is, it seems, a failure.

Perhaps more important is the struggle within each to achieve some resolution of the tensions between inner and outer worlds of experience. In this respect Stephen is repeatedly reminded that he is not free to work out his spiritual problems *in vacuo*, that his 'throb . . . within' is matched by a 'throb . . . without' (242.13). Haines speaks of his mind's having lost its balance; 'You should see him . . . when his body loses its balance', replies Mulligan (249.1). Stephen's self-involvement is repeatedly countered by enforced con-

---

[3] Budgen, p. 69.

frontation with the physical world, the meeting with Dilly being a
still more acute reminder than is the violent scene of the assault by
Private Carr. Earlier in the day Stephen has evoked painful and vivid
memories of his family and of his mother's death, but, while vivid,
those memories are later seen to lack something of reality. Stephen's
'bowl of bitter waters' (9.33), his imaginative transmutation of the
image of Dublin bay, his recall of the prayers for the dying, are
powerful in the context of 'Telemachus':

> In a dream, silently, she had come to him, her wasted body
> within its loose graveclothes giving off an odour of wax and rose-
> wood, her breath bent over him with mute secret words, a faint
> odour of wetted ashes.
> Her glazing eyes, staring out of death, to shake and bend my
> soul. On me alone. The ghostcandle to light her agony. Ghostly
> light on the tortured face. Her hoarse loud breath rattling in
> horror, while all prayed on their knees. Her eyes on me to strike me
> down. *Liliata rutilantium te confessorum turma circumdet: iubi-*
> *lantium te virginum chorus excipiat.*
> Ghoul! Chewer of corpses!
> No mother. Let me be and let me live. (10.15)

In the afternoon this is given a different perspective, shown to
be too remote from the depressing reality of the Dedalus family
situation to be of any real value in defining Stephen's position for
him. In 'Wandering Rocks' he uses to himself a similar diction, a
similar imagery, but these are now clearly placed in their remote
gothic self-indulgence by the shabby but still hopeful context of
external reality:

> He took the coverless book from her hand. Chardenal's French
> primer.
> —What did you buy that for? he asked. To learn French?
> She nodded, reddening and closing tight her lips.
> Show no surprise. Quite natural.
> —Here, Stephen said. It's all right. Mind Maggy doesn't pawn
> it on you. I suppose all my books are gone.
> —Some, Dilly said. We had to.
> She is drowning. Agenbite. Save her. Agenbite. All against us.
> She will drown me with her, eyes and hair. Lank coils of seaweed
> hair around me, my heart, my soul. Salt green death.
> We.
> Agenbite of inwit. Inwit's agenbite.
> Misery! Misery! (243.19)

While physical reality for Stephen is most directly represented by the presence of other human beings, for Bloom that reality is not only other people, but also the inanimate physical world which Stephen avoids. 'I do not like that other world she wrote. No more do I. Plenty to see and hear and feel yet' (115.5). Bloom goes on to think 'Feel live warm beings near you. . . . Warm beds: warm full-blooded life' and life, for Bloom, means above all Molly. But it also means 'cups and saucers, chairs and tables, sticks and stones'. Apart from the central problem of his alienation from Molly, Bloom is endemically an outsider, scorned and rejected, or at best tolerated, by his fellow Dubliners. The physical reality of the city, however recalcitrant, is a lesser enemy. Here, in the world of 'phenomenon', Bloom is safer, more sure of himself. Like Odysseus, he is barnacle-encrusted and brinesoaked, but, again like Odysseus, he survives the buffetings of inanimate matter. Indeed, it is often his relationship with the gritty physical universe that provides potential salvation from personal attack. He is skilful at handling matter, and enjoys his relationship with it. His ebullience, his enthusiasm, his optimism, find their best expression in his practical-minded attitude to day-to-day urban activity. He is never happier than when engaged in constructive physical work or in planning imaginary civic improvements, such as running a tramline down the North Circular road. While no doubt much of Bloom's concern for recurrent trivia may properly be thought of as an escape from serious moral and psychological issues, the presence of a world against which one can knock one's sconce is vitally important to him.

The outer world of Dublin, dialectically opposed to the inner worlds of the protagonists, is rooted in the real, historical circumstances in which Joyce himself lived, a world of physical reality which the reader must also get to know (if only at second hand) in order fully to understand the meaning of much of the book. As Richard Kain, Joseph Prescott, R. M. Adams, and others, have pointed out, Joyce's fictional Dublin is often identical with the real Dublin of 1904. Where that reality is explicitly recreated in the book it may be treated in the same way as one treats any other fictional, imagined world—Dickens's London, Faulkner's Jefferson, Lawrence's Sydney. Often, however, *Ulysses* is far from explicit and the reader finds that he must go in search of further documentary facts with which to supplement Joyce's account. There is a deliberate blurring of the distinction between fiction and reality, and the wider the reader's knowledge of the latter, the more meaningful the former becomes.

Nowhere is greater use made of documentary reality than in 'Wandering Rocks' which provides both a composite portrait of most of the book's minor characters and a panoramic view of Dublin itself. It is a relatively static moment in which the major issues, fully stated in the earlier chapters, are succinctly restated before, in 'Sirens', Joyce begins to develop them towards resolution. Since there is very little action in 'Wandering Rocks', Joyce can give his readers time to look around them and observe the setting in which he has placed the earlier events. He does not, however, allow his readers to relax but adopts, on the contrary, the persona of a harsh and awkward narrator whose difficult personality is the most salient thing about the chapter. The physical world which Bloom handles with such natural ease is capable of living an organic life of its own. In so far as it is merely a conglomeration of discrete physical phenomena, Dublin belongs to Bloom as much as to any man; in so far as those phenomena cohere in a greater unity, Bloom belongs to it.

Odysseus was able to choose between the alternative dangers of Scylla and Charybdis and the wandering rocks. Joyce makes his readers and characters negotiate both. In navigating his way through this tricky chapter the reader, at risk as much as Odysseus or Telemachus, crosses from one conceptual extreme to the other as, in physical imagination, he passes from the north of the city to the south, and from Christ to Caesar. The outermost of the chapter's nineteen sections present, in Conmee and the Viceroy, personifications of 'a Roman and a British flag', hoisted in uneasy peace over Ireland. Joyce's mockery of their twin domination, while both biting and amusing, is a relatively simple piece of social commentary. Of greater importance is what goes on between the extremes. Neither Bloom, who is at the centre (section 10), nor Stephen, who appears on both sides of Bloom (sections 6 and 13), sees or is aware of the Roman and British representatives. Their problems cannot be expressed in such simple terms. Nor are we concerned, here, with the confrontations of the two men and their fellow citizens. Even their interactions with their physical circumstances are minimal. Although Stephen is conscious, if in no great detail, of the 'very large and wonderful' world which 'keeps famous time' (242.19), he has not yet reached the point at which he can involve himself in it. Bloom, by contrast, is shown in this chapter less conscious of his surroundings than at almost any other point in the book. Both he and Stephen have retreated into themselves, Stephen to confront his guilt, Bloom to confront his sexual longings. In Bloom's case, in particular, the tension between inner and outer has been drawn to an extreme. He and the city are less at one here than at any other time. He is not seen walking, speculating, or looking. His only contact is with an atypical dealer[4] and he is entirely unconcerned, for the moment, with external reality. It almost seems as if this climactic presentation of the urban world were irrelevant to him. Bloom has withdrawn to the centre in every sense: at the city's physical centre, and at the central point of the novel, he is brought to full awareness of the nub of his psychic and bodily concerns. In the city's sanctum, the undercover porn-shop, *Sweets of Sin* is produced from behind the curtain, like the ark of the tabernacle. Bloom has, in a sense, reached his goal, has found what he is looking for, and he is virtually the only person in the chapter to do so. But, equally, the reader is made acutely aware of the vast distance that separates centre from surface. Reintegration will be difficult.[5]

Sweets of Sin was the goal of the outward journey. There is still the return to be negotiated, the return to contact with physical circumstances and to mastery of the urban consciousness. Here, in 'Wandering Rocks', we are given our one general view of the peripheral world with which Bloom now seeks to be reunited. It is, of course, a human world, an abrasive and self-contradictory society. But it is also a physical entity, made up of the streets, buildings, corners, objects, on which so much stress is laid throughout the chapter. This is the same city as had swallowed, and tried to digest, the Bloom of 'Lestrygonians'. There, however, we saw only its alimentary tract, whereas here we see the whole creature, whose lineaments are traced by the pattern of its veins and arteries.[6] Although Bloom is not directly concerned with the events of the chapter, we read here of the things with which he involves himself when he is free of his

[4] From whom he rents—not buys—*Sweets of Sin*. See the entry in the budget: '1 Renewal fee for book 0. 1. 0' (711.20).

[5] For further comment on the concept of the centre in this chapter see Leo Knuth, 'A Bathymetric Reading of Joyce's *Ulysses*, Chapter X', *JJQ*, IX, 4 (Summer 1972), 405–422.

[6] According to Joyce's *schema*, 'blood' is the organ of the chapter.

personal distress. He normally occupies his thoughts with destitute families, maimed beggars, tramlines, commerce, mechanical gadgets, advertising, and civic organization generally. While Bloom could certainly never administer a city, the new Bloomusalem or any other, his views on these matters are worthy of attention. Although discouraged by his fellow Dubliners from being one, it is as burgher that Bloom would be most effective and most comfortable.

In contrast to the fluent, uninterrupted narrative of 'Scylla and Charybdis', 'Wandering Rocks' seems at first to be singularly disjointed and fragmented. Nevertheless, here also there is structural unity, and in defining that unity we define Bloom's circumstances.

The narrative manner of each of the sections is apparently simple, lucid, self-contained, unencumbered by allusion or linguistic complexity. The simplicity is, however, an illusion, a trap for the naive reader. This is, indeed, a chapter full of traps for everyone, readers and characters alike. Things are not what they seem, and most of the characters are a prey to illusion or frustration. For them the city is continually disappointing and evasive. Artifoni and young Dignam miss their trams; Kernan misses the cavalcade; a statue imperiously bids halt; a telephone rings rudely; an invitation to a boxing match is out of date; a pot on a range is deceptively promising. But above all it is the reader who undertakes the dangerous imaginative journey, in emulation of the Argosy. Diligent scrutiny enables him to emerge unscathed, or almost so. Only his tail is lightly nipped by the few riddles which remain unsolved.

Bloom's sanguine nature and Stephen's indifference have both led us to take the physical city rather for granted. For the past nine chapters we have grown familiar with Dublin. Joyce's habit of naming places and things without explanation or description, as if he were writing for fellow-citizens, has given us such a sense of belonging that we are able to move easily in our imagined urban landscape. Now, however, for the first time, the city begins to assert itself. It is by no means as tractable as we had thought.

In many chapters of *Ulysses* Joyce creates a single and distinctive narrative consciousness, and despite the fragmentation this is as true of 'Wandering Rocks' as of any other. With the reduction of Bloom and Stephen to everyday proportions, neither more nor less important, for the moment, than any other Dubliners, we grow aware of the presence of a *spiritus loci*. The consciousness which presents 'Wandering Rocks' is in a sense that of Dublin itself, and the spirit is endowed with a distinctive personality. While 'Wandering Rocks' uses a number of narrative tones and points of view, from the careful patronizing of Conmee to the tired journalistic penny-a-line on which the brilliant variations of the coda are based, these all share a special kind of non-interpretative objectivity. But the objectivity is a disingenuous fraud, a deliberate trap. The narrator makes no assumptions, provides no comment. While almost everything that he says is, strictly speaking, true, there are many lies of omission, the narrator failing to provide essential connective information which we accordingly have to extrapolate for ourselves. Nearly everything is presented as if seen for the first time. 'A onelegged sailor' in Conmee's section (219.8) is still 'A onelegged sailor' (not 'The onelegged sailor') when he reappears in section 3 (225.15). The narrator pretends to be innocent of self-knowledge. A similar kind of disingenuous simplicity is found elsewhere when the avoidance of congruence in dealing with the sailor is matched in reverse by the inclusion of many unexpected and false congruences. The reader is continually in danger of making wrong assumptions. According to Frank Budgen, while Joyce was working on the chapter, he 'bought . . . a game called "Labyrinth", which he played every evening for a time with his daughter Lucia. As a result of winning or losing at the game he was enabled to catalogue six main errors of judgment into which one might fall in choosing a right, left or centre way out of the maze'.[7] There are many kinds of trap into which the reader of 'Wandering Rocks' is likely to fall, and while I have been unable to reconstruct Joyce's 'six main errors of judgment', I think it is possible to distinguish four types: explicit cross-references (including both true and false congruences), implicit cross-references, linguistic and nomenclatural ambiguities, and apparent errors.

Some of the traps depend upon an interplay between the topography of Dublin and the narrator's use of language, while others are almost purely linguistic. Language being so dominant a feature of the chapter, an examination of the narrator's verbal consciousness must precede any detailed scrutiny of the traps. Reading this chapter is like walking in the maze of a city's streets. One finds oneself continually taking wrong turnings, being caught in dead ends, having to retrace

[7] Budgen, p. 125.

one's steps. Common spatial expressions often have more than one
potential meaning. The girl in Thornton's bends 'archly' (228.7);
although politically impotent, John Howard Parnell is able to 'translate' a bishop (248.22). Often, as here, the appropriate sense is clear
enough, but the reader needs to be vigilant. The first words of the
chapter set the tone and warn of the dangers to come: 'The superior,
the very reverend John Conmee S.J.' 'The superior' contains, for
the unprepared reader, a small but significant potentiality for error.
It could be either noun or adjective. While the primary sense is
nounal (Conmee was Superior of the Jesuits in Gardiner street),
adjectival 'superior', forming a semi-antithesis to 'interior' in the next
line, is very fitting in at least two senses: the man's consciousness of
his spiritual pre-eminence is reflected in his elevated physical position
on the presbytery steps. (Conmee's route is also the most northerly
in the chapter—superior in a cartographic sense.) A similar problem
arises with the first verb: 'reset his smooth watch'. Thus far one
might read 'reset' as 'adjusted the time of'; it is only when one reads
further—'in his interior pocket'—that one becomes aware of the
primary meaning: 'replaced'. This narrator is omnipresent, and very
much in charge. He is remote, 'behind or beyond' his handiwork, but
by no means indifferent. He reports, but rarely condescends to explain, conceals and reveals according to whim, and both we and the
characters suffer from his totalitarian dominance.

Although not everyone is seen from the inside, no one in the
chapter is free from possible exposure without warning. In 'Wandering Rocks' we listen to a greater number and variety of interior
monologues than anywhere else in Ulysses, the character of the
monologues and the contexts in which they are placed often creating
in the reader a sense of unease. The urban mind which reveals these
things to us is capable of a great deal of malice, of straightfaced
Schadenfreude. Conmee's section begins in a manner carefully but
awkwardly suspended midway between interior monologue in the
strict sense and conventional second-hand reportage. 'What was that
boy's name again? Dignam, yes. Vere dignum et justum est. Brother
Swan was the person to see' (219.4). The past tense, 'was', prevents
our establishing a really intimate relationship with the monologue.
We overhear Conmee from a mockingly respectful distance as the
narrator parodies the priest: he mediates between the reader and
Conmee just as Conmee mediates between God and man. As the

Roman Catholic Church interprets the Scriptures for its flock, so the
narrator uses style to interpret the Church.

Not until section 5 do we again directly penetrate a mind, and
this time it is a mind of an entirely different stamp. One tiny snatch,
three words, is all we ever hear of Boylan's thoughts on Bloomsday:
'A young pullet' (228.1). It is enough. Boylan, a caricature, never
thinks, we are to suppose, in other terms. His comment about the
blond girl in Thornton's is matched, a few lines later, by the girl's
response to him: 'got up regardless, with his tie a bit crooked'. Such
minuscule scraps of interior monologue serve to emphasize the narrator's dominant, privileged position and his playful but also ruthless
handling of the characters. Although the blond girl blushes, she gives,
in her thoughts, as good as she gets. With her, as with Molly, Boylan,
who thinks himself the conquering hero, ultimately makes himself an
object of derision. That, at least, is the view of things imposed on us
by the narrator. Throughout most of *Ulysses*, up to 'Wandering
Rocks', the interior monologue has served not only to enrich our
knowledge of the inner lives of the characters, but also, as a consequence, to increase our compassion for them. Knowledge brings understanding, and understanding, pity. Now, however, the interior
monologue is made to serve other, harsher purposes, as it is turned
on and off at carefully selected moments.

The same sort of thing is done in reverse in section 9. Here a
further snatch of monologue, one sentence only, is sufficient to make
a crucial distinction between our responses to the superficially similar
Lenehan and M'Coy. M'Coy's implicit dissociation from Lenehan's
story about Molly, and our sympathetic response to M'Coy's mixture
of care for Bloom and fear that he might suffer, or have suffered, a
similar marital fate, is prepared for by his thoughtful disposal of the
banana peel as he waits in Temple Bar: 'Fellow might damn easy get
a nasty fall there coming along tight in the dark' (233.20). This is
Bloomian solicitude, in a slightly lower register. In Bloom's diction,
M'Coy's 'damn easy' would be 'easily', and the prudent abstainer
would very likely have omitted the qualifying 'tight', but the awareness of the needs of others is the same. Above all, however, the
snatch of monologue emphasizes that the angle of vision, the selection of detail, the degree of compassion, are firmly controlled. The
carefully cultivated air of neutrality is a sham. The Lenehan we know
from *Dubliners* and from other evidence in *Ulysses* is not only a

waster but, at least to a limited degree, an object of pity; if we could hear his thoughts in 'Wandering Rocks' he might very well arouse in us as much compassion as does M'Coy.

The proliferation of interior monologue, even when continued for long enough to do justice to personality, serves once again to lessen the reader's emotional involvement by treating so many people alike and spreading the attention in differing directions. We overhear Stephen and Bloom from well-established narrative positions, but Bloom, though more intense, is perhaps less interesting in this chapter than is Mr Kernan (another alternative Bloom) who is very fully characterized. Molly appears only in the flesh (a part of it), but Miss Dunne, a possible substitute for Martha (the possible substitute for Molly), is presented both physically and mentally. Although she is hardly attractive, our admission to her thoughts about Boylan emphasizes once more his failure to dominate the personalities of the women who serve him with their bodies. Miss Dunne's mind is more like Gerty's than it is like Molly's, and the narrator's choice of object for exposure further controls the degree and application of our compassion.

The final passage of monologue, the comparatively extended portrait of Master Patrick Dignam, is a succinct example of the new use of the method. Master Dignam is hardly more attractive than is Miss Dunne. His childish sorrow and puzzlement arouse our pity, in a general sense, but although we listen to his thoughts, we are not really admitted into the inner reaches of a personality, as we are when Stephen and Bloom contemplate the effects of death on their lives. Master Dignam's world is full of other people and of physical objects, but it does not contain much of himself: as a person he hardly seems to exist. Bloom, in this chapter, is all centre, personality in action; Master Dignam is all periphery, responding to a succession of stimuli. The child tries to create a centre for himself: 'Death, that is. Pa is dead. My father is dead' (251.38). He is searching for understanding, but not only for understanding: he is trying to feel, to make the statements emotionally meaningful to himself. The attempt is a failure; he has yet to develop a personal centre and must content himself for the time being with his peripheral relationship to the phenomenal world. The inverse correspondence of Dignam's situation and that of Stephen is stressed by Simon Dedalus's expostulation a quarter of an hour earlier, when talking to Dilly: 'Wouldn't care

if I was stretched out stiff. He's dead. The man upstairs is dead'
(238.16).

The narrator's failure to 'explain' is nowhere more obvious than
in the interpolations from section to section. These provide the simplest class of disparate, juxtaposed, unexplained facts of which the
reader must make what he can. That the interpolations indicate, in
the first place, simultaneities of action soon becomes clear enough.
Virtually everyone passes unscathed through this first *rite de passage*.
But while one quickly understands the spatio-temporal relationships
involved, the causal relationships between the interpolations and
their contexts are sometimes less easily found, and in searching for
them one learns still more about the temper of the narrative mind
which is at work. In most cases the interpolations appear to arise
from processes of association that are macrocosmic equivalents of the
processes seen in action in the interior monologues of individual
characters. As in the case of the characters, the associations are
definitive of personality. The mind of this city is both mechanical
and maliciously ironic. It chooses to define itself openly by means of
physical relationships which are usually visual and observable in
present time. What holds the city together is not a common conceptual basis, but the web of connexions which may be formed
within the texture of its surfaces. Nor is there anything here of the
paralysis of *Dubliners*; the city's mentality is mercurial and unpre-
dictable. At the end of this essay I have listed the interpolations in
sequence, with explanations for their causal relations, as I understand
them.

The 'trap' created by the interpolations leads to another. It is
easy to assume that the explicit cross-references are the only important structural links in an otherwise impressionistic chapter. 'Wandering Rocks' is in fact full of verbal echoes and thematic connexions
which are, so to speak, potential interpolations to be made by the
reader himself. Failure to see these relationships necessarily leads to
faulty judgments and emphases. Easy conclusions, reached on the
assumption that within each section all is lucid and linear, are shown
to need modification as we grow aware of the correspondences which
everywhere reveal that the narrator has ironic *arrières pensées* about
any proposition. Many of the correspondences are, like the interpolations, synchronic, and consultation of the chart in Appendix B will

make them easier to perceive. While Father Conmee is happily dreaming of the 'joybells . . . ringing in Gay Malahide' (223.16), the joyless 'Barang!' of the lacquey's bell is heard in Dillon's auction rooms (237.15); as he thinks, in gracious prose, of the 'listless lady, no more young' (223.26) who 'walked alone the shore of lough Ennel', the demented, vicariously litigious and far from listless elderly female leaves the Four Courts, to walk along the quays of the Liffey; while he is reading the *Pater noster*, Boody is bitterly saying 'Our father who art not in heaven' (227.3). Here are a few more of the scores of examples: Boylan, the theatrical entrepreneur, looks into the shopgirl's blouse while Miss Dunne, Lenehan, and M'Coy all look at the poster of Marie Kendall, the music-hall artist (all of these people being closely associated by the action of the chapter); Lenehan's hands mould 'ample curves of air' (234.36) while Bloom reads how Raoul's *'hands felt for the opulent curves . . .'* (236.13); while Conmee 'gravely' blesses Lynch and Kitty, Ned Lambert ('blast your soul', 231.40), Ben Dollard ('God eternally curse your soul', 244.29), and Tom Kernan ('He's as like it as damn it. . . . Damn like him', 240.21) are all cursing; as Artifoni is telling Stephen how he once believed that *'il mondo è una bestia'* (228.22), Bloom is showered with sexual warmth, 'cowing his flesh' (236.22); Kernan thinks of Dollard's 'Masterly rendition' (241.14) just as Dollard himself sings a note and asks 'Not too dusty? What?' (245.5), while at the same time Stephen is watching old Russell in his shop: 'Dust webbed the window and the showtrays. Dust darkened the toiling fingers with their vulture nails. Dust slept on dull coils of bronze and silver . . .' (241.24).

Requiring still closer scrutiny are the diachronic cross-references. While in order to watch the synchronisms of the action we have imaginatively to raise ourselves to a God's-eye viewpoint, looking down on to the city as on to a map, in order to apprehend the diachronic motifs we need to become still more God-like and enter the Eternal Now from which we may watch all events at all times happening 'simultaneously'. From this vantage point we observe the ironies of the 'boiled shirt affair' (226.21, 234.4),[8] and of the association of Conmee's 'listless lady' with the 'listlessly lolling', unladylike Miss Dunne (223.26, 229.24). We see possibilities of corruption in the application of the word 'queenly' both to Mrs M'Guinness and

[8] First pointed out to me by Leo Knuth.

to the seductress of *Sweets of Sin* (220.36, 236.18), and we heed the
implication of mechanical emptiness in Conmee's relations with the
three small boys who had 'sixeyed' (220.16) him a few minutes before Rochford's machine 'ogled them: six' (229.16). Among other
cross-references are the ironic association of the 'sunnywinking leaves'
(219.19) which shade Conmee, and the frocktails of the ceremoni-
ously dressed Mr Kernan, which 'winked in bright sunshine'
(240.25); and the use of the adverbs 'incredulously' (232.14) and
'credulously' (252.26) in connexion with the elderly female—words
which, although etymologically antithetical, are made by the context
to appear semantically indistinguishable.

Nomenclatural ambiguities provide a kind of trap for the avoidance of which one needs detailed knowledge of the city's history and
topography. One of the most common forms taken by this kind of
ambiguity is the narrator's habit of renaming things already referred
to in other and sometimes more usual terms. Carlisle bridge (240.8)
is the same as O'Connell bridge (235.34); Dan Lowry's musichall
(232.37) is the Empire musichall (233.1) under an older name; the
'council chamber of saint Mary's abbey' (230.15) is 'the old Chapterhouse of saint Mary's abbey' (245.8). This device is brought to a
climax in the final section in which the Viceroy is given a different
title by most of the Dubliners who view his progress through the city
streets. A variation is the narrator's use of archaic and forgotten
names for familiar places: 'Mud Island' (222.8) is an old name for
the dumping ground which has now become Fairview Park; 'Dame
gate' (253.13), long since gone, was in the old east wall of the city,
about where the southern end of Parliament street is now.

The device works in reverse when the same term is used for
distinct objects and events. The reverend Nicholas Dudley, Curate in
Charge of saint Agatha's church north William street (222.3), has
nothing to do with the Viceroy, the Earl of Dudley; Mr Bloom the
dentist (250.14) does not know Mr Leopold Bloom; Dignam's court
(220.28) is in an area of the city far too wealthy to interest the
Dignam family. Lambert and O'Molloy, who have just been talking
in 'Mary's abbey' (the building, 230.15), come forth 'slowly into
Mary's abbey' (the street, 231.8). Once again a warning about this
kind of thing is included in the opening paragraphs of the chapter,
when Conmee muses 'Dignam, yes. Vere *dignum et justum est*'
(219.4). Conmee's pun on the opening words of various mass pref-

aces may perhaps conceal a second level of meaning for the reader. The words are usually translated as 'Truly it is fitting and just'; as Mr Bloom might say about the whole of 'Wandering Rocks', 'See? it all works out' (154.19). (A variant of the Dignam motif recurs later in Conmee's section, when he thinks of the French verb *moutonner:* 'A homely and just word,' 224.7.)

Apparent errors introduce the most difficult and also perhaps the most controversial kind of reader trap. It has sometimes been suggested that Joyce worked discrepancies into the physical actions and descriptions of 'Wandering Rocks', that the chapter is a demonstration of Stephen's dictum about the artist's errors being 'portals of discovery' (190.22) and that the unwary reader will not realize that he has been deceived unless he compares the statements in the text with the facts of the Dublin of reality. While this is in some respects true, it is not, I believe, true in the sense in which it is commonly assumed to be. On the surface of 'Wandering Rocks' there are a great many statements which appear to be erroneous, but on closer examination almost all of these are resolvable in one way or another. Two sorts of possible 'error' need to be distinguished: those that are illusory and attributable to misstatements by the characters or to the deviousness of the narrator; and those others, fewer in number, that remain after the illusions have been dispelled. The illusions have long been the subject of commentary: Father Conmee is walking in Clongowes fields in memory only; Parnell's brother is playing chess in the DBC, not in Mary's abbey; Mrs M'Guinness's 'fine carriage' (220.34) is a reference to her gait, not to a vehicle which she owns. While most of the apparent errors can be shown to be illusory in this way, a few unresolved discrepancies invite attention as portals of artistic discovery opened by Joyce in the surface of the real world of the Dublin of 1904.

While I believe that Joyce wanted as close a match as possible, a seamless join, between the fictional and factual parts of his book, he had, of course, to change some of the facts in order to accommodate his fiction. He did not, nevertheless, change only the essentials, but enriched Bloomsday with many further alterations such as the shift of the date of the viceregal cavalcade, which had in fact taken place on 31 May 1904.[9] Close scrutiny of these changes is especially important in 'Wandering Rocks', with its emphasis on physical real-

[9] *Surface and Symbol,* p. 218.

ity. Joyce took the utmost pains over the physical details, even causing the throwaway, Elijah, to move at a speed which, according to
the Dublin Port and Docks Board,[10] is consistent with the probable
rate of flow of the Liffey two and a half hours after high tide on that
June day. When first relating the chapter to the real city, the reader
finds that a number of passages which he had hitherto assumed to be
examples of straightforward documentary reporting contain what he
is now led to think of as concealed 'errors'. Young Dignam expects
to find a Sandymount tram in Nassau street, whereas the Sandymount tram ran along Great Brunswick street, to the north of Trinity; Ned Lambert speaks of clearing the sacks away from the windows
of Mary's abbey, whereas the chapterhouse is a semi-basement without windows. Further information shows the narrator once again
to have been disingenuous, to have been toying with the reader who
has learned a little about Dublin but is still insufficiently informed.
There was a second Sandymount tramline, known as the 'Sandymount (Haddington Road)' line, which ran along Nassau street;[11]
the chapterhouse once had windows, which had been bricked up
by 1904 but whose outline would be visible in Love's photographs.[12]
While it is therefore very dangerous to refer to errors in 'Wandering
Rocks', I nevertheless list here six factual anomalies at least one of
which seems pointless and may be due to inadvertence, while the
others in various ways enrich the fictional texture.

In section 3 Joyce writes of 'MacConnell's corner' (225.15).
MacConnell's pharmacy was the last house in Lower Dorset street
before the junction with Eccles street. This building was not, however, on the corner, which was occupied by No. 1 Eccles street. If
there is any point in this change it escapes me, and I believe the
error to have arisen from Joyce's having used Thom's, whose list
of street numbers and occupiers could have led him to think that the
pharmacy was on the corner. The next error is of greater substance.
In section 6 the narrator says 'By the stern stone hand of Grattan,
bidding halt, an Inchicore tram unloaded straggling Highland soldiers of a band' (228.29). A casual glance is sufficient to show that

[10] Telephonic communication, August 1970.
[11] Information from Mr William Birney, of Dublin, an expert on the history
of the Dublin trams.
[12] D. A. Chart, *The History of Dublin*, London, 1907, pp. 276–277: 'In the
east wall may be traced three lancet-shaped windows, splayed inwards; one of
which, a fine example of the earliest lancet style, is in good preservation'.

the familiar statue of Grattan in College Green is of bronze, not stone. The stony command of 'halt' is perhaps an accurate reflexion of the psychological implications of the moment, while 'stone' is of course consistent with the theme of the wandering rocks. It may also remind both Stephen and the reader of Moses, the tables of the law, the one-handled adulterer, and the plum-stones.

The third 'error' seems designed, like the reference to 'Dame gate', to deepen the historical perspective. Toward the end of the Mary's abbey section we read that Lambert 'followed his guest to the outlet and then whirled his lath away among the pillars' (231.6). The chapterhouse contains no pillars, nor does there appear to have been anything of that kind, in 1904, in Meetinghouse lane, into which Lambert and O'Molloy have just emerged. While the word may perhaps be meant to apply to the 'piled seedbags' (230.34) the casual mention of the pillars would seem, in the first place, to be a reference to the ghostly columns of the fine, large abbey of which there remains only a small and gloomy vaulted room almost engulfed by the graceless structures of modern commerce.

A further error not explicable in terms of the external reality of 1904 occurs in section 17, when Farrell is seen frowning 'at Elijah's name announced on the Metropolitan Hall' (250.8). Taken literally this would indicate that Farrell was possessed of exceptionally keen eyesight, since the Metropolitan Hall was in Abbey street, on the other side of the river. There probably is indeed some implication of unusual powers or perhaps even of clairvoyance as Farrell stares, in the last section, 'across the carriages at the head of Mr M. E. Solomons in the window of the Austro-Hungarian viceconsulate' (254.24) which is several hundred yards away. What he is looking at in section 17, however, is probably the Merrion Hall, one block to his right, which we may suppose to have been wrongly identified in his demented brain. Even his sighting of Mr Solomons may be an illusion, since, according to Thom's, the viceconsulate moved from Nassau street to an outlying address at some time between 25 October 1903 and 25 October 1904.

In section 19 there are two amusing intentional changes in Dublin topography. When describing the cavalcade's progress down Ormond quay, the journalist-narrator says 'From its sluice in Wood quay wall under Tom Devan's office Poddle river hung out in fealty a tongue of liquid sewage' (252.27). As Richard Ellmann has pointed out,[13] Tom Devin, a friend of the Joyce family, had been demoted from his post on the city administration to the office of the Corporation Cleansing Department, 15–16 Wood quay. Poddle river emerges, however, from a sluice in the wall of Wellington quay, not Wood quay, nor has it ever in its history flowed under Wood quay.[14] Joyce was seeking a more powerful image of unified sewage.

The last intentional error is one of the most obvious of all, and one to cause any Dubliner's eyebrows to rise. The cavalcade, having passed out of the city centre, moves southwest toward the Mirus Bazaar, and in so doing it crosses the 'Royal Canal' (254.37). The narrator has his canals mixed: the Royal Canal is the one to the north of the city; this is the Grand Canal. It is as unthinkable that Joyce should have made such a mistake as that a Londoner should confuse the Edgware and Old Kent Roads, or a New Yorker, Lexington and Park Avenues. To the Viceroy all things are royal; the canal is instantly renamed in his honour, and a hint of structural circularity is introduced as we recall that Conmee had crossed the (real) Royal Canal in the first section of the chapter.

Time and place are the real unifiers of 'Wandering Rocks'. According to Frank Budgen, 'Joyce wrote the *Wandering Rocks* with a map of Dublin before him on which were traced in red ink the paths of the Earl of Dudley and Father Conmee. He calculated to a minute the time necessary for his characters to cover a given distance of the city'.[15] I have already indicated some of the ways in which the spatio-temporal facts add to our understanding of the chapter. With so many things going on at once we may also ask whether the timing of the events contains distortions or impossibilities, either real or illusory, similar to those that are so common among the spatial descriptions. The chart, reproduced in Appendix B, is an attempt to show what is happening, minute by minute, throughout the period of the chapter. Before I embarked on this study three results seemed possible: (1) the spatial and temporal interrelationships might prove to have been worked out in realistically exact fashion; (2) they might be sufficiently exact to suggest

[13] *Letters*, II, 66n.
[14] I am indebted to Mr John Garvin, Dublin City Commissioner, for information about the history of the Poddle.
[15] Budgen, pp. 124–125.

that Joyce intended such a result, but the timing might prove to have been botched in the execution (highly possible, even probable, given Joyce's notorious arithmetical weakness); (3) the relationships, or at least some of them, might prove to be so wildly impossible as to indicate an antirealistic intention.

Joyce provides just enough temporal information. Assuming that Conmee's watch is correct, the time is precisely stated at the beginning ('Five to three', 219.3). A terminus *ad quem* may also be found if we pass on into 'Sirens', with which 'Wandering Rocks' overlaps, and listen to the clock striking four (or, rather, five to four: 'Pub clock five minutes fast', thinks Bloom, 173.2). One further precise time is given, in 'Penelope', when Molly remembers that she threw the coin to the sailor at '¼ after 3' (747.31).[16] Although in the course of the chapter the narrator has three other opportunities to state the exact time, he withholds the information with his usual malice: when Boylan looks at his watch and decides that his gift to Molly should be sent at once, we are not allowed to see the dial; M'Coy answers Lenehan's inquiry with a vague 'After three' (233.16); in section 19 John Henry Menton stares at the cavalcade while 'holding a fat gold hunter watch not looked at in his fat left hand not feeling it' (253.29). The interpolations, indicating simultaneities, are nevertheless sufficiently numerous to allow one to assign fairly specific times, based on normal rates of walking and talking.

Partly as an amusement, and partly with the serious purpose of testing the extent of Joyce's realism, I undertook, on foot in Dublin, a literal form of 'practical criticism', timing the various routes taken by the characters, and also gathering information about the frequency of trams,[17] the normal speed of a cavalcade, etc. (I have assumed that the Dedaluses live where John Joyce's family lived in June 1904: 7, St Peter's Terrace, Cabra.) The results of the calculations based on these investigations are shown in the chart, which makes clear that 'Wandering Rocks' is constructed so as to be, in terms of timing, realistically exact (or at any rate very nearly so). There is, here, no intentional distorting, no grotesquerie, no 'fractured surface', of the kind to be found in 'Cyclops' and 'Ithaca'.

---

[16] Leo Knuth pointed this out to me after I had drawn up the chart. It was pleasing to see that the time fitted the scheme which I had already constructed on indirect evidence.

[17] Five-minute intervals, on the Dollymount line.

The characters move at rates consistent with physical life in Dublin in 1904. While occasionally Joyce hurries things a little (Simon has to walk rather briskly from Dillon's auctionrooms to 'Reddy and Daughter's'), simple realism is the basis of all the action.

A reader trap involving time is to be found in the ninth section (Lenehan and M'Coy). Lenehan pops into Lynam's to check on the starting price for Sceptre. The Gold Cup, due to start at three o'clock, Greenwich Mean Time, was in fact run shortly after three. The reader must remember, however, that as clocks in Dublin were set to 'Dunsink Time', twenty-five minutes behind GMT, M'Coy's 'After three' (about 3.13, Dunsink time, according to my chart) corresponds to about 3.38 at Ascot. The race has already been run; Sceptre has lost. This is not an oversight on Joyce's part. Before the development of wireless, race results were sent by telegram, and *post factum* bets could still be placed before the information was received. On Bloomsday the telegram is expected in Dublin at 4 P.M., Dunsink Time (265.11). In 'Ithaca' we learn of Bloom's plan to set up a private wireless telegraph which will beat the system by sending 'the result of a national equine handicap . . . won by an outsider at odds of 50 to 1 at 3 hr. 8 m. p.m. at Ascot (Greenwich time) the message being received and available for betting purposes in Dublin at 2.59 p.m. (Dunsink time)' (717.28).

Bloom, adrift on the swell of his sexual imagination, and Stephen, trapped in the dust of the burial earth, are surrounded by the working parts of a physical and social machine of great intricacy. Later in the book Joyce will play games with the documentary realities of space and time, but in 'Wandering Rocks' he gives us the high point of precision and clarity of line. The chapter, standing midway between the two halves of the book, is both a culmination of the first and a preparation for the second. In the first half Joyce has created a solid foundation from which to launch the later flights of verbal art that begin with 'Sirens'. By now we know enough of the 'facts' to be able to keep our bearings and never to lose sight, above all, of Bloom, the real flesh and blood man in a real brick and concrete city. The significance of the city, for Bloom and for the reader, is ambiguous. 'Wandering Rocks' celebrates its solidity, its shapeliness, its liveliness, its organic nature; it also, however, emphasizes its malice, its treachery, its shabbiness.

While re-emergence from fantasy into the real world may be Bloom's future salvation, the journey will be far from easy.

The city's malice is nevertheless no more than a reflection of the inadequacies of the protagonists. It not only surrounds Stephen and Bloom: it also acts out for them their needs, fantasies, and faults of character. Those needs, fantasies, and faults, explicitly dramatized in the expressionism of 'Circe', are here implicitly reflected in events of which Stephen and Bloom remain unconscious. In its structure 'Wandering Rocks' bears some relationship to 'Circe'. Each consists of a sequence of more or less separate scenes, linked in both cases by verbal and thematic associations which are to some degree independent of space and time. In contrast to 'Circe', where most of the associations are explicit, those of 'Wandering Rocks' are usually implicit, obscure, and perceivable only after careful scrutiny. But in making himself fully aware of the structural associations, the reader builds up, in imagination, a texture not unlike a daytime equivalent of the later phantasmagoria. The verbal texture of 'Wandering Rocks' is highly complex, being denser in cross-correspondence, motif development, and rhythmic variation than that of any chapter that precedes it, while Stephen and Bloom are here more directly involved with their central spiritual and emotional problems than they are at almost any other time before or after the nighttown scenes. On the surface, the minor characters live independent lives, with a minimum of interaction; in terms of the book's total organization, and in the mind of the thinking city, they nevertheless unconsciously co-operate to dramatize the mental states of the protagonists. Conmee, the Dedalus girls, Simon, and in a sense young Patrick Dignam, act out charades which demonstrate Stephen's needs and difficulties. Boylan, Miss Dunne, Lenehan, M'Coy, and, once again, young Master Dignam (a surrogate for Rudy) are among the principal dramatizers of Bloom's problems. The relationships between these disparate bits of dramatization serve to show how intricate are the patterns of urban life, while the narrator's malice is a reflection of the inadequate personal relationships of the principals. By solving their problems, Bloom and Stephen will grow to be in command of the system; when no longer threatened by their fantasies they will be free of spiritual and emotional danger from Conmee, Boylan, Simon, Miss Dunne. When Bloom and

Stephen are fully in command of their own lives the priestly unc-
tuousness, the entrepreneur's lasciviousness, will no longer seem to
be the most salient characteristics of the society. Not until then
will they dominate the webs of urban association and be able, with
truth, to say: 'Dublin belongs to me'.

*   *   *

APPENDIX A: THE INTERPOLATIONS

I do not understand the reasons for some of the interpolations. The
following complete list of the thirty-one uses of the device is accompanied by comments in which I offer the simplest explanations of
those which I believe I do understand:

TEXT	COMMENT
1. Father Conmee smiled and nodded and smiled and walked along Mountjoy square east. Mr Denis J. Maginni, professor of dancing, &c., in silk hat, slate frockcoat with silk facings, white kerchief tie, tight lavender trousers, canary gloves and pointed patent boots, walking with grave deportment most respectfully took the curbstone as he passed lady Maxwell at the corner of Dignam's court. (220.22)	Ironic physical contrast: Conmee is attending to the affairs of the Dignam family; Maginni is walking past the inanimate Dignam court. Neither is especially involved in 'Dignam'. Parallelism: Conmee, smiling, is eager to make himself agreeable. Maginni is associated with the art of self-advertisement ('Lestrygonians', 153.34).
2. —It's very close, the constable said. Corny Kelleher sped a silent jet of hayjuice arching	Ironic physical contrast: Kelleher is concerned with death, Molly with life. Parallelism: Bloom's law of falling bodies.

TEXT	COMMENT
from his mouth while a generous white arm from a window in Eccles street flung forth a coin. (225.8)	The constable's words are ambiguous (reader trap).

3. He swung himself violently forward past Katey and Boody Dedalus, halted and growled:
—*home and beauty.*
J. J. O'Molloy's white careworn face was told that Mr Lambert was in the warehouse with a visitor. (225.20)

Both the sailor and J. J. O'Molloy are begging. There is an ironic contrast between the sailor's song and the tales of insurrection being told in Mary's abbey.

4. —Did you put in the books? Boody asked.
Maggy at the range rammed down a greyish mass beneath bubbling suds twice with her potstick and wiped her brow.
—They wouldn't give anything on them, she said.
Father Conmee walked through Clongowes fields, his thinsocked ankles tickled by stubble.
—Where did you try? Boody asked.
—M'Guinness's.
Boody stamped her foot and threw her satchel on the table.
—Bad cess to her big face! she cried. (226.9)

The books are, of course, Stephen's.
Conmee's opinion of Mrs M'-Guinness (220.34) contrasts with Boody's.

TEXT	COMMENT
5. —Peasoup, Maggy said. —Where did you get it? Katey asked. —Sister Mary Patrick, Maggy said. The lacquey rang his bell. —Barang! (226.28)	At this moment Simon, standing outside the auction room, is sneering: '—The little nuns! Nice little things! O, sure they wouldn't do anything! O, sure they wouldn't really! Is it little sister Monica!' (239.10). Cf. 'Peasoup' and 'saucy' (238.8).
6. —Our father who art not in heaven. Maggy, pouring yellow soup in Katey's bowl, exclaimed: —Boody! For shame! A skiff, a crumpled throwaway, Elijah is coming, rode lightly down the Liffey, under Loopline bridge, shooting the rapids where water chafed around the bridgepiers, sailing eastward past hulls and anchorchains, between the Customhouse old dock and George's quay. (227.3)	An association of Our Father, Elijah, need, and potential salvation.
7. —Can you send them by tram? Now? A darkbacked figure under Merchants' arch scanned books on the hawker's car. (227.26)	Both Boylan and Bloom, seeking presents for Molly, find immediate sexual stimulation.
8. The disk shot down the groove, wobbled a while, ceased and ogled them: six.	Two machines are functioning. Rochford hopes to sell his to Boylan, Miss Dunne's employer.

TEXT	COMMENT
Miss Dunne clicked on the keyboard:	Miss Dunne is concerned with ogling.
—16 June 1904. (229.15)	

9.   —16 June 1904.
Five tallwhitehatted sand-
wichmen between Mony-
peny's corner and the slab
where Wolfe Tone's statue
was not, eeled themselves
turning H.E.L.Y.'S and
plodded back as they had
come.

Two advertising agencies are at
work. In 'Lestrygonians' Bloom
momentarily thinks that the
sandwich-board men are employed by Boylan, rather than
by B. M'Glade, advertising
agent, of 108 Middle Abbey
street: 'Boyl: no: M'Glade's
men' (154.30). Cf. also Bloom's
'Smart girls writing something
catch the eye' (154.33).

Then she stared at the
large poster of Marie Kendall, charming soubrette,
and, listlessly lolling, scrib-
bled on the jotter sixteens
and capital esses. (229.18)

10.   In the still faint light he
moved about, tapping with
his lath the piled seedbags
and points of vantage on the
floor.

Charles Stewart Parnell and
Silken Thomas arouse memories
of recent and early Irish history.
J. H. Parnell is scrutinizing
points of vantage on his chess-
board.

From a long face a beard
and gaze hung on a chess-
board. (230.33)

11.   —The reverend Hugh C.
Love, Rathcoffey. Present
address: Saint Michael's,
Sallins. Nice young chap he
is. He's writing a book about
the Fitzgeralds he told me.
He's well up in history,
faith.

Conmee has just remembered
the clouds over Rathcoffey.
There is an ironic association
here with the idea of love.

TEXT	COMMENT
The young woman with slow care detached from her light skirt a clinging twig. (231.12)	

12.   He slid it into the left slot for them. It shot down the groove, wobbled a while, ceased, ogling them: six.

    Lawyers of the past, haughty, pleading, beheld pass from the consolidated taxing office to Nisi Prius court Richie Goulding carrying the costbag of Goulding, Collis and Ward and heard rustling from the admiralty division of king's bench to the court of appeal an elderly female with false teeth smiling incredulously and a black silk skirt of great amplitude. (232.7)

?

13.   While he waited in Temple bar M'Coy dodged a banana peel with gentle pushes of his toe from the path to the gutter. Fellow might damn easy get a nasty fall there coming along tight in the dark.

    The gates of the drive opened wide to give egress to the viceregal cavalcade.

    —Even money, Lenehan said returning. (233.18)

Horses provide the obvious link, while the connexion between 'Sceptre' and the Viceroy is a hint at the powerlessness of British rule in Ireland.

TEXT	COMMENT
14. Master Patrick Aloysius Dignam came out of Mangan's, late Fehrenbach's, carrying a pound and a half of porksteaks. —There was a big spread out at Glencree reformatory, Lenehan said eagerly. The annual dinner you know. Boiled shirt affair. (234.1)	The contrast in the quality of the foodstuffs is linked to the ironic similarity of the reformatory and the O'Brien Institute, to which Master Dignam will be going.
15. —I know, M'Coy broke in. My missus sang there once. —Did she? Lenehan said. A card *Unfurnished Apartments* reappeared on the windowsash of number 7 Eccles street. (234.8)	The tale is, of course, about Molly. Both she and Lenehan are preparing to meet Boylan.

16. Onions of his breath came across the counter out of his ruined mouth. He bent to make a bundle of the other books, hugged them against his unbuttoned waistcoat and bore them off behind the dingy curtain.
    On O'Connell bridge many persons observed the grave deportment and gay apparel of Mr Denis J. Maginni, professor of dancing &c.
    Mr Bloom, alone, looked at the titles. *Fair Tyrants* by James Lovebirch. Know the kind that is. Had it? Yes. (235.30)
	Dublin, from both the inside and the outside. Contrast: 'many', 'alone'.

TEXT	COMMENT
17. Young! Young! An elderly female, no more young, left the building of the courts of chancery, king's bench, exchequer and common pleas, having heard in the lord chancellor's court the case in lunacy of Potterton, in the admiralty division the summons, exparte motion, of the owners of the Lady Cairns versus the owners of the barque Mona, in the court of appeal reservation of judgment in the case of Harvey versus the Ocean Accident and Guarantee Corporation. (236.28)	The illusion of Bloom's sexual imagination, compared to the reality of the Dublin in which he lives.
18. —Barang! Bang of the lastlap bell spurred the halfmile wheelmen to their sprint. J. A. Jackson, W. E. Wylie, A. Munro and H. T. Gahan, their stretched necks wagging, negotiated the curve by the College Library. (237.15)	This is the 'last lap' for the Dedalus household. The Library may remind one of the earlier attempts to pawn Stephen's books.
19. —You got some, Dilly said, looking in his eyes. —How do you know that? Mr Dedalus asked, his tongue in his cheek. Mr Kernan, pleased with the order he had booked, walked boldly along James's street. (237.39)	Both men have been drinking. Leo Knuth points out a subtler reason: Mr Dedalus has his tongue in his cheek, while Tom Kernan had lost a part of his in 'Grace'. Molly remembers the incident (773.27). Kernan has made money; Mr Dedalus is presumed to have borrowed five shillings.

TEXT

COMMENT

20. —Here, Mr Dedalus said,
handing her two pennies.
Get a glass of milk for yourself and a bun or a some-
thing. I'll be home shortly.

He put the other coins in
his pocket and started to
walk on.

The viceregal cavalcade
passed, greeted by obsequi-
ous policemen, out of Park-
gate.

—I'm sure you have an-
other shilling, Dilly said.
(238.42)

Wealth and poverty? Cf. the relationship between the obsequi-
ous policemen and their father-
figure, the Viceroy, and that between Dilly and Simon.

21. Saw him looking at my
frockcoat. Dress does it.
Nothing like a dressy ap-
pearance. Bowls them over.

—Hello, Simon, Father
Cowley said. How are
things?

—Hello, Bob, old man,
Mr Dedalus answered stop-
ping.

Mr Kernan halted and
preened himself before the
sloping mirror of Peter Kennedy, hairdresser. (239.37)

Both Simon and Kernan halt.
Simon is about to comment on
Dollard's dress.

22. Aham! Must dress the
character for those fellows.
Knight of the road. Gentleman. And now, Mr Crim-
mins, may we have the honour of your custom again,

The crumpled throwaway, representing Bloom, contrasts with
the dressy Kernan. Sir John
Rogerson's quay may arouse associations of the importing of
tea. The quay and tea are both

TEXT	COMMENT
sir. The cup that cheers but not inebriates, as the old saying has it.	important elements in 'Lotuseaters'.

North wall and sir John Rogerson's quay, with hulls and anchorchains, sailing westward, sailed by a skiff, a crumpled throwaway, rocked on the ferrywash, Elijah is coming.

Mr Kernan glanced in farewell at his image. (240.10)

23. Outside the Dublin Distillers Company's stores an outside car without fare or jarvey stood, the reins knotted to the wheel. Damn dangerous thing. Some Tipperary bosthoon endangering the lives of the citizens. Runaway horse.

Comment: Mr Breen is shortly to be almost run over by the cavalcade.

Denis Breen with his tomes, weary of having waited an hour in John Henry Menton's office, led his wife over O'Connell bridge, bound for the office of Messrs Collis and Ward. (240.35)

24. Orient and immortal wheat standing from everlasting to everlasting.

Two old women fresh

Comment: Stephen's quotation from Traherne (which is in the famous passage about childhood) had been suggested to him, in 'Pro-

TEXT	COMMENT
from their whiff of the briny trudged through Irishtown along London bridge road, one with a sanded umbrella, one with a midwife's bag in which eleven cockles rolled. (242.5)	teus', by the sight of the two old women.

25. I might find here one of my pawned schoolprizes. *Stephano Dedalo, alumno optimo, palmam ferenti.*

Father Conmee, having read his little hours, walked through the hamlet of Donnycarney, murmuring vespers. (242.31)

Comment: Conmee had been rector of Clongowes.

26. —And how is that *basso profondo,* Benjamin? Father Cowley asked.

Cashel Boyle O'Connor Fitzmaurice Tisdall Farrell, murmuring, glassyeyed, strode past the Kildare street club.

Ben Dollard frowned and, making suddenly a chanter's mouth, gave forth a deep note. (244.38)

Comment: ?

27. —That'll do, Father Cowley said, nodding also.

The reverend Hugh C. Love walked from the old Chapterhouse of saint Mary's abbey past James and Charles Kennedy's, rectifiers, attended by Geral-

Comment: The group on the quay, discussing Love, are unaware that he is walking very close by. Love is, of course, Cowley's landlord.

TEXT COMMENT

dines tall and personable, towards the Tholsel beyond
the Ford of Hurdles.

Ben Dollard with a heavy
list towards the shopfronts
led them forward, his joyful
fingers in the air. (245.7)

28. He signed to the waiting   The cavalcade had left the vice-
jarvey who chucked at the   regal lodge; one horse leaves the
reins and set on towards   castle.
Lord Edward street.

Bronze by gold, Miss Ken-
nedy's head by Miss Douce's
head, appeared above the
crossblind of the Ormond
hotel. (246.5)

29. —There's Jimmy Henry,   Whatever may be Boylan's rea-
Mr Power said, just heading   son for waylaying Bob Doran,
for Kavanagh's.   it is not in order to raise money

—Righto, Martin Cun-   for a destitute family.
ningham said. Here goes.

Outside *la Maison Claire*
Blazes Boylan waylaid Jack
Mooney's brother-in-law,
humpy, tight, making for
the liberties.

John Wyse Nolan fell
back with Mr Power, while
Martin Cunningham took
the elbow of a dapper little
man in a shower of hail suit
who walked uncertainly with
hasty steps past Micky Anderson's watches. (246.30)

30. Haines opened his new-   Leo Knuth points out that the
bought book.   one-legged sailor's body has lost

TEXT

—I'm sorry, he said. Shakespeare is the happy huntingground of all minds that have lost their balance.

The onelegged sailor growled at the area of 14 Nelson street:

—England expects . . .

Buck Mulligan's primrose waistcoat shook gaily to his laughter.

—You should see him, he said, when his body loses its balance. Wandering Ængus I call him. (248.33)

31.   He tasted a spoonful from the creamy cone of his cup.

—This is real Irish cream I take it, he said with forbearance. I don't want to be imposed on.

Elijah, skiff, light crumpled throwaway, sailed eastward by flanks of ships and trawlers, amid an archipelago of corks, beyond new Wapping street past Benson's ferry, and by the threemasted schooner *Rosevean* from Bridgwater with bricks. (249.30)

COMMENT

its balance. 'England expects' may also be read, in this context, as 'Haines expects'.

At 18.33 Haines is called the 'seas' ruler'.

?

APPENDIX B: THE CHART

I believe that all of the movements shown in the chart are both possible and natural, and that all of the simultaneities and other factual indications of the chapter are fully and accurately represented. Although it is, of course, possible to vary the timing of some of the events by a minute or two without altering the basic layout, I am convinced, after many attempts to find alternatives, that the main sequences of 'Wandering Rocks' can be arranged in no other way, that in all important respects the spatio-temporal pattern of the chapter is fully determined.

While much of the information given here is easily predictable, some of the movements extend our knowledge of the characters in ways which, though consistent with what we already know, are perhaps less easy to foresee. Boylan, who has plenty of time to spare, strolls up Grafton street with a lazy rather than a jaunty walk; O'Molloy, scrounging for money and unsure of himself, hesitates for a few minutes before entering the abbey; Lenehan and M'Coy, who also have time to spare (since Lenehan at least is waiting for the his meeting with Boylan at 4.00), stay chatting by the Liffey for some twenty minutes after we leave them; Farrell strides out very briskly indeed, while Richie Goulding is in no hurry to get anywhere.

It is, of course, possible that I have overlooked some other way of arranging things which would allow of major adjustments, but anyone contemplating the construction of an alternative scheme should be aware that the interrelationships present some very tricky problems. The chart was drawn up in the following way. First, the events of each of the sections were enacted in Dublin (often with several repetitions) and the mean times noted. Conmee's pleasant stroll and Kernan's strut were among the sections that caused no difficulties, but my attempts to simulate the movements of a one-legged sailor aroused the suspicious attention of a garda, and I fully expected the same thing to occur when I hobbled like the two old women from London bridge road.[18] While for some of the sections, considered independently, the timings are indeterminate, for others it is possible to measure the probable elapsed period with a fair

---

[18] On one of these occasions progress was halted while the Presidential motorcade passed through the city centre. Mr De Valera drove out after luncheon from the old viceregal lodge, on his way to inaugurate the Horseshow in Ballsbridge, accompanied by motorcycle outriders, firmly seated in their saddles.

degree of accuracy. Each of the timed sequences was set out, minute by minute (but, except for Conmee's section, without initial reference to a time of day) on a strip of paper corresponding to one of the columns in the finished chart. The moments represented by the interpolations were then marked on the slips in red, and an attempt was made to arrange the columns so that the interpolations would correspond throughout. At this stage it became apparent that certain initial assumptions had to be modified, and in particular that, in keeping with the spirit of the chapter, some things had to be allowed to occur at a more leisurely rate than the minimum time might suggest. It became necessary, also, to refine and qualify the idea of simultaneity represented by the interpolations. When quotations from another section refer to unique events there is no problem: the moment indicated by the side glance, in interpolation 21, at the meeting of Simon Dedalus and Bob Cowley (239.39), must be precisely the same as that of the meeting itself, stated in the same words in section 14 (243.33). A question arises, however, with quotations, or approximate quotations, which refer to events having imprecise temporal extension. Is the statement prefiguring Bloom's presence at the bookstall—'A darkbacked figure under Merchants' arch scanned books on the hawker's car' (227.27)—an exact temporal marker referring to the moment, similarly described, at which Lenehan and M'Coy see him there in section 9 (233.27), or may it be taken to refer to some other moment during the total period of Bloom's scrutiny of the books? My chart reveals that the moments represented by the two passages cannot, in fact, be the same; the moment of the interpolation is the earlier by several minutes. While in some analogous cases (e.g., John Howard Parnell in the DBC, interpolation 10) a precise synchronism is possible, it is evident that the narrator does not use verbatim repetition as a structural equivalent of strict simultaneity. The temporal relationships of 'Wandering Rocks' are determined by the nature of the physical events rather than by the texture of the words.

The arrangement of the chart is not, of course, dependent in any essential way on my activities with a stopwatch in Dublin. One may achieve the same results, as Joyce himself did, by working with a map, a ruler, and a knowledge of local conditions, such as street gradients. My practical approach merely provides more direct confirmation of Joyce's fundamentally realist intentions.

SIRENS

Jackson I. Cope

A musical episode was easy to place in Dublin, for Dublin is, or was, a musical town, with a particular passion for vocal music. A few Dubliners of the older generation meet in the lounge of the Ormond Hotel and a couple of songs . . . constitute the entertainment. No writer with any respect for probability would dare to make the same thing happen in London.[1]

So observed Frank Budgen. Simon Dedalus sings of past love, his fine tenor whiskey-cracked. Lydia Douce's garter vibrates to the fantasies of future love, *sonnez la cloche*. Between the two, Boylan jingles toward his assignation with Molly Bloom. And Molly is a Dublin diva: so song draws love into the web of time at the critical hour of four.

Even the sea sings in the 'Sirens' chapter. Songs are sung, remembered, multiplied; in a musical book of full-bodied singers and parodists this chapter alone mirrors the musical expertise of James Joyce, alone echoes the lonely song of the past which Gabriel Conroy heard from the disembodied tones of Aunt Julia Morkan and the hoarse tenor of Bartell D'Arcy as his wife stood like a wraith of beauty at the head of the stairs. And to this chapter alone Joyce attributes a musical 'technic' with the much-disputed phrase 'fuga

---

[1] Budgen, p. 137. Cf. R. M. Kain, *Fabulous Voyager: James Joyce's 'Ulysses'*, rev. ed., New York, 1959; *The Sacred River*, London, 1949, pp. 29–48 for other early statements on *Ulysses'* Irish sounds.

per canonem'.[2] Nor should we overlook the irony of the less-than-literal scenic designation of the schema: 'the concert room'. 'Sirens' is to *Ulysses* just what Bloom designates it: 'Shira Shirim'—Song of Songs (729.4).

The overture of fragmented phrasings from the main body of the chapter boldly announces a drastic shift in stylistic technique, all the more marked for coming upon the heels of the meticulous narration of 'Wandering Rocks'.[3] Even Joyce's most ardent supporters were puzzled and alarmed. Ezra Pound had corrected Bloom's bad manners in defecating before the public of the *Little Review* in 1918, but he covered his embarrassment with commercial cant. It was only in reacting to 'Sirens' that he openly questioned Joyce's aesthetic judgment. He softened the impact upon both their sensibilities by joking,[4] but here was where the busy *Lector benevolens* let his doubt show us exasperation. When Pound's opinion was reinforced by Harriet Weaver, Joyce responded characteristically; his best defence always was to be offended:

> You write that the last episode sent seems to you to show a weakening or diffusion of some sort. Since the receipt of your letter I have read this chapter again several times. It took me five months to write it. . . . Mr. Pound wrote to me rather hastily in disapproval but I think that his disapproval is based on grounds which are not legitimate. . . . The word *scorching* has a peculiar significance for my superstitious mind . . . each successive episode, deal-

---

[2] Gilbert, pp. 240ff., offered a defence of the schema designation. Lawrence L. Levin, 'The Sirens Episode as Music', *JJQ*, III (1965), 12–24, argues carefully for 'fugal' structure, and Zack Bowen, 'The Bronzegold Sirensong: A Musical Analysis of the Sirens Episode in *Ulysses*' in *Literary Monographs I* ed. Eric Rothstein and Thomas Dunseath, Madison, Wis., 1967, pp. 245–298, has made a thorough musical analysis to which I am heavily indebted for explanations of musical and plot counterpointing. Vernon Hall, Jr., 'Joyce's Use of Da Ponte and Mozart's *Don Giovanni*', *PMLA*, LXVI (1951), 78–84 was a careful pioneering of some aspects of this counterpointing. It is worth noting that the 'Sirens' occupies four pages in the song listings of Hodgart and Worthington (*Song in the Works of James Joyce*, New York, 1959) a total approached only by the lengthy 'Circe'.

[3] Cf. the observations of Sultan, pp. 24–25, 222.

[4] 'The peri-o-perip-o-periodico-parapatetico-periodopathetico—I dont-off-the-markgetical structure of yr. first or peremier para-petitec-graph....you have once again gone "down where the asparagus grows" and gone down as far as the lector most bloody benevolens can be expected to respire' (10 June 1919) in Forrest Read, *Pound/Joyce*, London and New York, 1967, p. 157. For the corrections of 'Calypso', see pp. 301–2.

ing with some province of artistic culture (rhetoric or music or dialectic), leaves behind it a burnt up field. Since I wrote the *Sirens* I find it impossible to listen to music of any kind. . . .[5]

The question posed by the chapter, in view of its dramatic shift in style, is the import of that shift and style: what does the music of 'Sirens' tell us about *Ulysses*?

To begin to answer, one must pose an anterior question: who are the Sirens? Lydia Douce and Mina Kennedy receive scant attention from Bloom. They can be our nominees only if Blazes Boylan, 'conquering hero,' is the ironic Ulysses so intent upon his quest for Penelope's bed that he is deaf to the vibrations on Lydia Douce's thigh. Molly, Stuart Gilbert reminded us, is a manifestation of the Great Mother, Gaia-Tellus, and her symbol of symbols is the rose.[6] When one remembers that Euripides (*Helena*, 167–173) made the Sirens daughters to Gaia and notices the rose bouncing on Lydia's breast, one is tempted to see Boylan evading the surrogate temptation for the real, flirtation foregone that adultery may be accomplished. But the irony is pointless unless Boylan triumphs in his conquest of Penelope's chastity, and Bloom is pointedly honoured as 'the unconquered hero'.

Is the siren-song, then, perhaps that of Simon Dedalus who sings of 'love and war', of memory and treachery? Certainly Simon's singing draws larger drafts upon Bloom's psyche than Lydia's garter does upon that of either Bloom or Boylan.[7] But the danger of succumbing to barren self-pity has been tested in 'Lotuseaters', with Bloom's romanticizing of *dolce far niente* and an aura of *Nada* centring upon the pleasantly quiescent phallic flower of the imaginary bath; has been tested again in 'Hades' with his projection of suicide fantasies from father to son under the pressure of converging losses as Boylan, Rudy, and Virag all appear with sudden immediacy in his memory: 'No more pain. Wake no more. Nobody owns' (97.9).

We must return for the identity of the Sirens once again to the centre, to Molly. 'Là ci darem' is Molly's song, pulling Boylan

[5] *Letters*, I, 128–129 (20 July 1919).

[6] Cf. Barbara Seward, *The Symbolic Rose*, New York, 1960, p. 208.

[7] Sultan, pp. 228–231, points out how Bloom evades the internal temptations at the Ormond, losing enthusiasm for the literary seduction of Martha Clifford and refusing to join the three old male singers, 'widower, bachelor and priest' (although Cowly is *not* a priest, in fact) in lives of unmarried 'loneliness, barrenness, hopelessness'.

to her past the longing Lydia. As he leaves the Ormond, 'Bloom heard a jing, a little sound. He's off. Light sob of breath Bloom sighed on the silent bluehued flowers. Jingling. He's gone' (268.1). Early in the chapter (contrasting with his avoidance of Boylan at the close of 'Lestrygonians') Bloom, sighting Boylan's 'jauntingcar', decides to 'Follow. Risk it' (264.2) and thus arrives at the Ormond bar. But now he resists the temptation to follow further. Molly is, throughout *Ulysses*, all: at the beginning Calypso, at the ending Penelope. And Bloom is able to return to her in that character of the waiting and faithful wife because Bloom here recognizes that she is also the Siren, recognizes that hers is the siren-song tempting Boylan, that his own impulse to interfere in their affair is a siren-song that would destroy them all. Bound to mastication with Richie Goulding, he resists.[8] When he first found Boylan's letter on the hallfloor Bloom's 'quick heart slowed at once' (61.36). When he took Molly her morning tea after delivering it, he could not keep himself from lingering, from asking to know what he knew: 'In the act of going he stayed to straighten the bedspread.—Who was the letter from? he asked'. (63.27). But he refrains from allowing this knowledge to project the past into disaster. 'Draw near', sang the Sirens to Ulysses, 'For we know all that the Argives and Trojans suffered on the broad plain of Troy . . . and we have foreknowledge of all that is going to happen on this fruitful earth' (*Odyssey* XII; 187–191). It is this Odyssean turn from determinism, the refusal to accept even his own foreknowledge which marks the 'Sirens' as the turning point in *Ulysses*.[9]

In her own way, Molly appreciates the strength of Bloom's wisdom. The vibrations of her bed, of Boylan's jingling jauntingcar, of their past, all reverberate throughout Bloom's painful stop at the Ormond Hotel. But they are set by him into a context of nature and the natural in humankind: 'Jingle jaunty. Too late. She longed to go. That's why Woman. As easy stop the sea. Yes: all is lost' (273.3). Molly, in the night, thinking back on the same experience, also places it in a natural context, but one that implicitly approves of

[8] Bowen, 'Bronzegold Sirensong', p. 272, observes that Bloom's recollection of Molly's song when they first met makes her role 'that of Siren as she extends through "Waiting" a musical promise of good things to come'.

[9] The rejection of the temptation of knowledge in the *Odyssey* is associated with broader pre-Hellenic traditions, including the Edenic temptation in Gabriel Germain, *Essai sur les Origines de certains Thèmes Odysséens et sur la Genèse de l'Odyssée*, Paris, 1954, pp. 382–390.

Bloom's restraint at the expense of Boylan's passion for possession: 'stupid husbands jealousy why cant we all remain friends over it instead of quarrelling . . . the man never even casts a 2nd thought on the husband or wife either its the woman he wants and gets her what else were we given all those desires for' (777.6). The 'yes' and the 'sea' of Bloom's meditation upon Molly foreshadow her own recollections, of course, in the closing pages of *Ulysses*, and the congruence of their submission to nature's benevolent tyranny of love is underlined by Molly's acknowledgment that the vibrant affinities are real. At the close it is not the stallion-like Boylan but Bloom with whom she feels at one: 'yes that was why I liked him because I saw he understood or felt what a woman is' (782.19).

But how to reconcile this victory in Molly's psyche of Bloom *patiens* with the 'all is lost' defeatism of Bloom's resignation? Only Stanley Sultan has clearly recognized that in the course of 'Sirens' Bloom contemplates defeat, defection, remonstrance, to reject them in light of a new hope. If all nature is predestined to cyclic repetitions, these may include personal renewals: 'No son. Rudy. Too late now. Or if not? If not? If still? He bore no hate. Hate. Love. Those are names. Rudy. Soon I am old' (285.5). Bloom's confidence in the vigorous choice between these names is seen to be attested and tested when he gives the citizen a courageous lecture on 'Universal love': 'Love, says Bloom. I mean the opposite of hatred' (333.14).

If we turn to the beginning of 'Sirens' we can see the same pattern of renewal for Bloom in another formulation. Whatever we may say about the musical model for the prelude, we can recognize Leopold Bloom's domination of its fragments through their repeated echoes and metamorphoses of his name and thoughts and through the flatulent epitaph with which he concludes both prelude and chapter ('pfrwritt. Done'). Moreover, it is Bloom's mood of regretful nostalgia for the lost paradise of love that sounds dominantly over the harsher ringing, junglings, crowings, and crashings of the prelude phrases: 'Blue bloom. . . . Longindying call. . . . Sweetheart, goodbye! . . . All is lost now. . . . When first he saw. Alas! . . . I feel so sad. . . . So lonely blooming. . . . All gone. All Fallen. . . . Last rose Castille of summer left bloom I feel so sad. . . . Done' (256.7). Yet the last word of the prelude is, like the last word of *Ulysses*, affirmative, redirectional: 'Begin!'

It points out that the first phrase of the prelude, 'Bronze by gold', is also the first phrase of the post-prelude narrative, and so invites us to see a structural circularity, a *Finnegans Wake* in little within the peculiar form of 'Sirens'. But if Bloom is dominant in the prelude, 'Begin' must also be the admonitory reaction to 'done', a promise of the patience by which the 'unconquered hero' makes adversity the instrument for love's recovery. 'Begin' is a signature upon Bloom's action. And it is the external authority of Joyce himself that encourages us to seek here a turning-point in *Ulysses*, a new beginning. It comes in the letter to Budgen written more than a year after 'Sirens' had appeared serially in the *Little Review*, when he was in the midst of work upon 'Circe':

> Last night I thought of an *Entr'acte* for Ulysses in middle of book after 9th episode *Scylla & Charybdis*. Short . . . like a pause in the action of a play.[10]

A pause between the acts, a mid-point, was to be followed by 'Sirens', a shift into a radically different stylistic mode to begin the second phase of the progress by which Bloom and *Ulysses* move from Molly's initial negative 'Mn' (56.25) to her final 'Yes' (783.14).

Boylan is the Homeric suitor. But the *Odyssey* is being retold as a split narrative: since Joyce's Telemachus doesn't know that he is starting his search from his father's house, Mulligan must be invented as the son's image of the false occupant of Stephen's psychic home. The equation is simplified by the manipulative, aggressive correspondences between the two men: Boylan is to Bloom what Mulligan is to Stephen: 'Usurper'. And, like Bloom in the Ormond Hotel, Stephen articulates this identification of personal and mythic roles as Mulligan, false priest, false prophet, false messenger, sings the first siren song of *Ulysses*:

> A voice, sweettoned and sustained, called to him from the sea. . . . It called again. A sleek brown head, a seal's, far out on the water, round.
> Usurper. (23.21)

This may serve to remind us of the obvious in a new dimension: if 'Sirens' is a musical culmination it is also the episode, along with Bloom's meditative 'Lotuseaters', most inundated by water in a novels that begins with a view of the sea and closes with a recollection

---

[10] *Letters*, I, 149 (24 October 1920).

of it. But in that earlier episode Bloom had succumbed to the womb of the bath house, his phallus limp under the impact of Boylan's psychic presence. It was the vision of himself floating like the chap in the dead sea, languid.

But now the drowning are Dubliners, Simon Dedalus and the others whom Bloom watches and listens to from a new vantage of decision: 'They pined in depth of ocean shadow, gold by the beerpull, bronze by maraschino, thoughtful all two' (269.29). The shunned sirens stand by while Simon and his cronies are discoursing in fantasy upon the charms of Molly Bloom and Boylan is following her siren song 'là ci darem'. Plato perhaps began the metaphor of subaqueous life in the *Phaedo* (Steph. 109) when he described man's existence being 'just as if a creature who was at the bottom of the sea were to fancy that he was on the surface of the water, and that the sea was the heaven through which he saw the sun and the other stars'. But Joyce certainly gave it continuity: 'Men, he said . . . are like deep-sea fish, swimming in water that is mysteriously irradiated with light from above the surface but unable to rise to the surface to see'.[11]

Bloom's departure from the Ormond is poignant with the realization that Boylan has irrevocably gone, that the 'heaving embon' of Lydia was not directed to him ('Ha. Lidwell. For him then not for'), that the Croppy Boy's death of which Dedalus sings, all of life's losses, in fact, are a 'Very sad thing. But had to be'. 'I feel so lonely Bloom' (286.28; 287.4) he sighs at leaving. But this is a heroic loneliness. 'By rose, by satiny bosom, by the fondling hand, by slops, by empties, . . . past . . . bronze and faint gold in deepseashadow, went Bloom' (287.1). He has left the drowned Dubliners behind. And as he leaves we hear the firm 'Tap. Tap. Tap' of the Blind Stripling, that flawless pianist whose blindness echoes Stephen's experiment in closing his eyes and, tapping his ashplant before him, walking 'into eternity along Sandymount Strand' (37.21) and anticipates Stephen's playing at Bella Cohen's piano.[12]

This presence is one more indication of Bloom's emergence as the father (he has, of course, earlier aided the blind boy as he will

[11] Marvin Magalaner and Richard M. Kain, *Joyce: The Man, the Work, and the Reputation*, New York, 1956, p. 175.

[12] For Stephen and the Blind Stripling, see J. Mitchell Morse, 'Joyce and the Blind Stripling', *Modern Language Notes*, LXXI (1956), 497–501.

later aid Stephen) and Dedalus's deafness to the rhythms of life. When Simon's songs had begun, he sat at the piano. But 'The keys, obedient, rose higher, told, faltered, confoooed, oonfuood. Up ctage strode Father Cowley.—Here Simon, I'll accompany you, he said. Get up' (272.1). The superficies of sorrow focus upon Bloom and his temporary loss to Boylan, but the deeper tones tell us that Simon Dedalus is drowning, faltering, losing that Stephen toward whom Bloom is now moving. Let us remember a detail usually misread because read univocally. 'Under the sandwichbell lay on a bier of bread one last, one lonely, last sardine of summer. Bloom alone' (289.12). A stroke of black humour, coordinating the imagery from *Martha*, the sea motif, Bloom's isolation, all in the used-up, late-afternoon naturalism of the depiction. An image of Bloom cuckolded and cut off. But to replace it in context is to see it as the funeral of the consubstantial father singing of war and death amidst reminders of that Stephen to whom Bloom draws nearer as Simon mourns his own ichthyic life:

> —Shout! Ben Dollard shouted, pouring, Sing out!
> —'lldo! cried Father Cowley.
> Rrrrrr.
> I feel I want . . .
> Tap. Tap. Tap. Tap. Tap.
> —Very, Mr Dedalus said, staring hard at a headless sardine.
> Under the sandwichbell lay on a bier of bread one last, one lonely, last sardine of summer. Bloom alone.
> —Very, he stared. The lower register, for choice. (289.6)

'Bloom alone'—but Bloom has left, moving now toward the destiny no one had predicted but the narrator, surfacing from the Ormond, past the Sirens, hydrophile, undrowned.

The action of 'Sirens' is split to an extraordinary degree even for *Ulysses*. It begins not with a psyche but a place: the Sirens' island, that Ormond bar, the container into which so many life streams are being drawn. And it is a place without Bloom, one toward which he is not even moving at the opening, if he nonetheless later chooses to enter it. When he does so, in pursuit of Boylan, he becomes for the first time intentionally what he has been all along, in fact: an observer. Here is the first irony. The narrative describes the activities of others—Douce and Kennedy, Lenehan and Boylan, Simon Dedalus, Dollard and Cowley, Richie Goulding —being heard and seen by Bloom but without his interaction at the *point du départ* for his new active role in the novel's economy. The second irony is that as Bloom becomes determined to act upon his own insights the reader is able to assume a superior vantage-point for the first time, enabled by the mythic narrator to see Bloom's wisdom within the perspective of its local limitations and ultimate validation. In no book is speaker decorum so important, because Joyce has minatured in *Ulysses* that mode of perception in which a grain of sand may be the key to the universe if rightly fitted into the puzzle of the structure; every stone is a keystone. Or it may be only a grain of sand to the mind's eye. To illustrate, Stephen drunk mumbles about 'The lords of the moon, Theosophos told me, an orange-fiery shipload from planet Alpha of the lunar chain, would not assume the etheric doubles and these were therefore incarnated by the ruby-coloured egos from the second constellation' (416.30); memories of Blavatsky's spirits under the influence. But a moment earlier the narrator had once again brought life out of the waste land as the brutal oxen 'murderers of the sun' tramp to the 'dead sea' only to be metempsychosed into Milly, the Virgin, the life-giver who 'after a myriad metamorphoses of symbol' shows as 'Alpha, a ruby and triangled sign upon the forehead of Taurus' (414.24–41). The same motifs can be nonsense from the lips of Dubliners, half-formed hopes from a Bloom, promises of the future from that hovering consciousness of the myth of life whom we can only inadequately call 'the narrator'.

It is this interplay of vision and venality that we must read as we read 'Sirens'. And since the least conscious characters are the observed of the observed observer Bloom, we can break the narrative into several blocks dominated by their activities doubly reacted upon.

The first of these finds the Misses Douce and Kennedy alone in the bar except for the brief 'imperthnthn' delivery of their tea by the boy of the boots. Douce, gazing at the viceregal cortege through the shadowing crossblind thinks herself admired by a toff in a coach and both seamlessly continues the action from 'Wandering Rocks' and introduces the theme of those 'frightful idiots' men, ogling in lust. The continuity from 'Wandering Rocks' allows a 'separate' interaction, here as in the earlier chapter, allows Bloom and Boylan

and the Dedalus group all to be moving with independent simultaneity toward the Ormond—and Bloom's march is the first recorded.

The counterpointing is double. 'O wept! Aren't men frightful
idiots?' gloats the eager Douce, while the less sirene and open Kennedy 'with sadness' repeats the lesson the Misses Morkan's Lily had
learned at a younger age: 'It's them has the fine times' (258.1–7).
It is in direct conjunction with this exchange of eager and bitter
clichés that Bloom's approach is first remarked:

> A man.
> Bloowho went by by Moulang's pipes, bearing in his breast the
> sweets of sin, by Wine's antiques in memory bearing sweet sinful
> words, by Carroll's dusky battered plate, for Raoul. (258.8)

Everything is working. One notices the pipes bearing pride of first
place here and the recurrence when Simon Dedalus's first action
upon entering the bar is to fill his pipe, a point we will return to
later. But, of course, what we notice of importance is Bloom's
arrival as the archetype of furtive lasciviousness called up by the
barmaids, made farcical by the pun upon 'breast', then all inverted
into yet another not-quite repressed reminder of Boylan and Molly
by the delayed tag line from *Sweets of Sin*: '*All the dollarbills her
husband gave her were spent in the stores on wondrous gowns and
costliest frillies. For him! For Raoul!*' (236.8). The narrator poises
indecisively with us over Bloom seen hiding sexual luxury in the
secret heart and Bloom as castrate cuckold when Joyce interposes
the interrogative which is also the momentarily valid identification:
'Bloowho'. The boy brings the tea, grossly casts his own impertinent
fantasies across the gross fantasies of Lydia Douce still at the window
watching her supposedly conquered swell ('What is it? . . . Your
beau, is it?') and leaves—to the narrator's decisive identification:
'Bloom'. Decisive, yes. But what is the decision? Bloowho?

The barmaids' chatter continues and arrives at the 'old fogey' in
Boyd's, the chemist's, whereupon the narrator injects another inter-
rogatory: 'But Bloom?' It associates Bloom with the repulsive and
repulsed 'hideous old wretch' and simultaneously questions the
validity of the judgment. 'Here he was', Miss Douce pursues her
recollection, 'ruffling her nosewings. Hufa! Hufa!'

> —O! shrieking, Miss Kennedy cried. Will you ever forget his
> goggle eye?

Miss Douce chimed in in deep bronze laughter, shouting:
—And your other eye!
Bloowhose dark eye read Aaron Figatner's name.

. . . .

By went his eyes. The sweets of sin.

. . . .

—O greasy eyes! Imagine being married to a man like that,
she cried. With his bit of beard!

. . . .

Married to Bloom, to greaseaseabloom.
—O saints above! Miss Douce said, sighed over her jumping
rose.

. . . .

By Cantwell's offices roved Greaseabloom. (259.33)

The spatial directives on Bloom's progress separate him literally
from the bar, the bit of beard assures us that the girls have not leapt
from the narrative of one old fogey to another. The narrator has
placed Bloom as fantasy and fact, walking toward the Ormond while
speculating upon the rectums of 'Bassi's blessed virgins', and placed
him not in the vision but in the psychic typology of Lydia Douce.
If this makes Bloom another fogey, the symbolic rose and 'married'
make Molly another Lydia. The narrator is a master of ironies,
ubiquitously present to point out the unconscious in other people's
jokes. So Lydia's hysterical 'greasy eyes' can be converted by him
through the mechanism of musical prolongation into a reminder
that Leopold is 'greaseaseabloom', that strong sailor upon the sea of
life rounding home toward Ithaca, toward Molly, 'Married to Bloom.
Greaseaseabloom'. Hydrophile, 'Mr Bloom crossed bridge of Yessex'
(261.42) as the second block of action in the Ormond begins: the
arrival of Simon Dedalus.

Dedalus arrives seeking George Lidwell, Lenehan arrives seeking
Blazes Boylan, and Bloom arrives to watch Boylan. The action is
light, preparative. Where paths crossed in 'Wandering Rocks',
themes are crossing here. The section is dominated by tumescence—
a sort of group masturbation which makes 'Nausicaa' thematically
inevitable. Simon flirts with Douce; Lenehan, put down by Kennedy
ignoring his flirtations, is brought up by Douce again ('Miss Douce
reached high to take a flagon, stretching her satin arm, her bust,

that all but burst, so high. —O! O! jerked Lenehan, gasping at each
stretch' (265.20), and all issues as Lenehan and Boylan are gratified
by the climactic music of teasing Douce's garter: 'Sonnez! Smack.
. . . La cloche'. It is the rhythm of everyone's (Lydia's, Lenehan's,
Bloom's) vicarious participation in Boylan's imminent ecstasy. This
is brutally reinforced by the heavy repetition of that word of Molly's
surrender to Bloom, 'Yes':

> But a long threatening comes at last, they say. Yes, yes.
>   Yes. He fingered shreds of hair, her maidenhair. . . .
> (261.35)

And it is brutally underlined by the accented dancing of the rose
upon Lydia's breast and the refrain heard from the room beyond which marks Boylan's safe passage by the little siren Lydia
on his way to Molly, and also marks Bloom's imminent loss:
'— . . . Sweetheart, goodbye!' (267.8).[18] The intertwined frustration of Bloom and Douce is carried on as she, under the dominance
of Boylan, sings snatches from 'The Shade of Palm' about a Molly-
figure, 'Idolores, queen of the eastern seas'.

But beneath the rhythm of fantasies roused by Boylan's appearance emerges the act of reversal by which Bloom, fleeing the memory
and person of Boylan to this point, wills a new course of action:

> For Raoul. He eyed and saw afar on Essex bridge a gay hat riding
> on a jauntingcar. . . . Jingling on supple rubbers it jaunted from
> the bridge to Ormond quay. Follow. Risk it. (263.40)

So Bloom seduces Richie Goulding into the Ormond, vaguely
hoping to frustrate Boylan, changes his mind, and allows Boylan to
leave to Simon Dedalus's sad music. Bloom hears a music of his own:
'Bloom heard a jing, a little sound. He's off. Light sob of breath
Bloom sighed. . . . Jingling. He's gone' (268.1).

As Boylan leaves, Ben Dollard and Father Cowley enter and,
having heard Simon Dedalus playing, demand a song. The latter
demurs but, just at the moment of Bloom's melancholy realization
of the jingling music of the conqueror's march, Dedalus succumbs:
'—Love and war, Ben, Mr Dedalus said. God be with old times'

---

[18] Bowen, 'Bronzegold Sirensong', p. 254: 'As Boylan approaches the bar
the opening strains of "Goodbye, Sweetheart, Goodbye" are heard. His stay in
the Ormond will end with the conclusion of this song, which is being played,
presumably by Simon Dedalus, during the entirety of Boylan's brief visit to the
bar'.

(268.4). Douce's gaze after the departed Boylan, 'Douce's brave eyes, unregarded, . . . Pensive (who knows?). . . . She drew down pensive (why did he go so quick when I?)' (268.6) merges with Bloom's as all again are momentarily immersed in 'slow cool dim seagreen sliding depth of shadow, *eau de Nil*' (268.12).

The Dubliners recall the old concert for which Bloom supplied Ben Dollard with formal clothes, long ago, hint at Molly's reputation ('—Daughter of the regiment', 269.30), and sing while Bloom and Goulding eat.

But 'love and war' is a dichotomy heavily charged by Bloom's public defiance of the citizen in Barney Kiernan's to which we have alluded: 'Love, says Bloom. I mean the opposite of hatred'. Bloom too remembers Dollard's tight trousers at that earlier concert:

> Night he ran round to us to borrow a dress suit. . . . Trousers tight as a drum on him. . . . Molly did laugh when he went out. Threw herself back across the bed, screaming, kicking. With all his belongings on show. . . . Well, of course, that's what gives him the base barreltone. (270.32)

Molly at this hour meets Dollard's match in Boylan ('I never in all my life felt anyone had one the size of that'). But she adjusts this experience by immediately realizing that 'Poldy has more spunk in him' (742.33).

Dollard of the mythic phallus, 'bassooned attack, booming over bombarding chords' upon a love song, appropriate to the burning image of Boylan: '—*When love absorbs my ardent soul . . .*' (270.5).[14] The stallion, the aggressive cock ('One rapped on a door, . . . did he knock Paul de Kock, with a loud proud knocker, with a cock carracarracarra cock. Cockcock', 282.35), Boylan fails in love: 'War! War! cried Father Cowley. You're the warrior' (270.8). Love songs are not war songs. So, for all of Boylan's temporary ascendancy as the 'conquering hero', Dollard's inability to sing the lover's part[15]

[14] Joyce's word-play here is associated with other passages in Fritz Senn's modest 'Quoint a quincidence', *JJQ*, VII (1970), 210–217.

[15] Bowen, 'Bronzegold Sirensong', pp. 257–258 explains that the duet is for a lover who should be a tenor and a warrior who, like Dollard, is a bass. Frederick Sternfeld points out that *Don Giovanni* 'has a . . . distinguishing characteristic that is important for *Ulysses*, that its hero is a bass—a departure from the accepted eighteenth-century pattern' ('Poetry and Music—Joyce's *Ulysses*' in *Sound and Poetry* ed. Northrop Frye, New York, 1957, pp. 49–50). He views this as an indication of Bloom's relative weakness, but in drawing yet another analogy between Dollard and Boylan it would seem designed to discredit the latter rather than Bloom.

foreshadows the failure of both phallic warriors. 'Sure, you'd burst the tympanum of her ear, man, Mr Dedalus said . . . with an organ like yours' (270.13).

And it is Dedalus himself and Bloom who are left to counter-point one another in a love song (which, by the way, identifies the small detail of their simultaneous interest in pipes as a prelude in miniature echoing the technique of the large prelude). Dedalus is urged to sing the aria from *Martha* and draws attention to the identifying props which unite him to Bloom, and the blind stripling to Stephen: 'Mr Dedalus laid his pipe to rest beside the tuningfork and, sitting, touched the obedient keys'. But in self-derogation (by the speaker) and self-identification (by the narrator) he does so saying 'Ah, sure my dancing days are done, Ben . . . Well . . .' The attitude is that of Bloom toward paternity: 'Too late now. Or if not? If not? If still?' As Simon plays, however, 'The keys, obedient, rose higher, told, faltered, confessed, confused. Up stage strode Father Cowley. —Here, Simon, I'll accompany you' (272.1). Too late, indeed: the paternal pianist's fingers falter upon the keys under the silent criticism of the stripling's tuning-fork. And Bloom listens, appreciating Cowley's playing ('way he sits into it, like one together, mutual understanding'), the piano's tune ('Sounds better than last time I heard. Tuned probably'), and Dedalus's confusion. The action and symbols seem to draw Bloom toward Simon, Simon toward Stephen, only to deny their identity, seem to pose the same question as the narrator: 'Bloowho?'

To answer we must observe the building of a new masturbatory pattern, a new vicarious tumescence within this block of action. But where the earlier rhythm was physical, bridging an arc of desire between Lydia's bosom and thigh, this one is metaphoric. It begins in images of physical love under the impulse of Bloom's thinking about musicians and arriving, always, at the rhythm of Boylan by way of the 'jiggedy jiggedy' association of a conductor's legs:

> Only the harp. . . . Girl touched it. Poop of a lovely. . . .
> Cool hands. Ben Howth, the rhododendrons. We are their harps.
> I. He. Old. Young. (271.18)

Where the music of the garter was made upon the flesh, now the flesh is made instrumental in a different way. In the pause between Dedalus's and Cowley's playing, Richie Goulding offers Bloom a whistled rendition of *Tutto è sciolto*[16] which picks up a rising pattern with sexual undertones, as well as nostalgia, carried by the imagery of birds in flight:

> Richie cocked his lips apout. A low incipient note. . . . A thrush. A throstle. His breath, birdsweet. . . . All lost now. Mournful he whistled. Fall, surrender, lost. (272.33)

But the surrender and the rush of flight, fall and rise, are all one in Bloom's final turning of these observations upon his own situation and Molly's, upon the initial stimulus, Boylan: 'Touch water. Jingle jaunty. . . . That's why. Woman. As easy stop the sea. Yes: all is lost' (273.2). 'Yes'. Molly's word again appears in the tumescent phase of the narrator's rhythm and in Bloom's sense of being swept away by life's sea of sexuality. Drowned. Old. His dancing days done. But he has crossed Yessex Bridge. And Simon Dedalus will be the sustainer of that crossing. At first, as Simon sings the love song, all seems explained by the cry of flesh to flesh (*sonnez la cloche*). Bloom snaps his rubber band, acknowledges a pseudo-scientific truth: 'Tenors get women by the score. Increase their flow' (274.12). Simon sings on and almost proves it as the tumescent play of images rise in Bloom's mind:

> Bloom. Flood of warm jimjam lickitup secretness flowed to flow in music out, in desire, dark to lick flow, invading. . . . To pour o'er sluices pouring gushes. (274.35)

But then the song climaxes 'in a cry of passion dominant . . . with deepening yet with rising chords of harmony' which sing '—Co-me thou lost one':

> It soared, a bird, it held its flight, a swift pure cry, . . . soaring high, high resplendent, aflame, crowned, high in the effulgence symbolistic, high, of the ethereal bosom, high, of the high vast irradiation everywhere all soaring all around about the all, the endlessnessnessness. . . . (275.40)

The comic tumescence bursts this time, though, not upon the thigh but upon the fulfilment of singer and auditor: 'Co-me. . . . To me! Siopold'.

For all of the irreverent mockery of Bloom's pathetic situation, and the skilful exploitation of the vocabularies of motion (Lydia)

---

[16] For bearings of the lyric upon the action see Bowen, 'Bronzegold Sirensong', pp. 263–265.

and music (Dedalus) to describe the inner movement of fantasy, the fusion of Simon Dedalus and Leopold Bloom here invites one to look for another action beyond the masturbatory allegory. Later in this case study of mysterious paternity, after all, one has to confront the fusion of 'Blephen Stoom'.

This is the moment of passing on, Simon's best moment, Bloom's 'beginning' toward his paternal destiny. If we allow the joke to have its poetry, we meet Joyce's precedent patterns of aspiration in the birdflight, disembodied, soaring.

Gabriel Conroy had listened to his Aunt Julia and felt that 'To follow the voice, without looking at the singer's face, was to feel and share the excitement of swift and secure flight'. The failure at the piano, the outbursts against Stephen, Goulding, Mulligan, the brutality exercized upon Dilly in 'Wandering Rocks' all indicate that Simon Dedalus's dancing days are, indeed, done. And yet his voice carries us 'high in the effulgence symbolistic', and we do well to hear the echoes answering art.

Simon here, as Aunt Julia in 'The Dead', becomes a soaring voice when faceless, beyond Bloom's view. Beyond consubstantiality, even substantiality, beyond the face of Julia or Simon, beyond the thigh of Lydia or the phallus of Boylan there remains the myth of art's power, its hold upon the future: *Et ignotas animum dimittit in artes*, Joyce offered as epigraph to A *Portrait*, allowing us to read on *naturamque novat*. When Stephen consummates this myth it is in a realization of his name, his paternity: 'a hawklike man flying sunward above the sea . . . a symbol of the artist forging anew . . . a new soaring impalpable imperishable being' (AP, 170).

Dedalus that was is giving way to Dedalus that will be, Simon bowing out 'high in the effulgence symbolistic' to allow Icarus to *become* Dedalus; but offering to the new father Bloom the idiom by which Stephen can be trained to transcend himself, to soar— music, the sound of the past, unfamiliar, not consubstantial, transcendent as the 'mystery of paternity'. The mythic inversion is transacted: Simon becomes an Icarus, drowned in the temptations; Lapwing Stephen is assured the potential of a Dedalian flight beyond the net of pride. Leopold Bloom has become the mediator of the mystery by which mythic fate can be averted. Stephen will later lie in the street unconscious and become fused with little Rudy. Here

Bloom accepts paternity from a drowned Simon Dedalus: met-him-pike-hoses.

We might note a minor measure of concinnity here where Bloom, Simon, and Stephen are being drawn more closely into conjunction than anywhere else in *Ulysses*. After the admiring applause for Dedalus's rendition, Ben Dollard says: 'Seven days in jail . . . on bread and water. Then you'd sing, Simon, like a garden thrush' (276.31). Simon Dedalus has sacrificed his voice to drink, almost literally drowned himself in the belly-god Dubliner's way. Stephen Dedalus has also sacrificed his voice, but as an act of rejection of that material well-being with which his third father, Almidano Artifoni (does that lovely Italian name conceal a saxon pun?) tempts him: *Anch'io ho avuto di queste idee, . . . mi sono convinto che il mondo è una bestia. È peccato. Perchè la sua voce . . . sarebbe un cespite di rendita, via. Invece, Lei si sacrifica* (228.21).

Having received the 'apostolic succession' of paternity, Bloom will move from the Ormond toward his meeting with Stephen at the National Maternity Hospital, toward his pedagogical session with Stephen in the kitchen of 7 Eccles street ('catechism personal', 'catechism impersonal' the schema informs us). And it is in the next action block of 'Sirens' or, rather, in Bloom's reactions to it, that we learn the nature of the future lesson through the omniscient observation of a narrator whose world is a myriad metamorphosis of symbols.

Simon's singing is admired; Richie Goulding reminisces upon Simon's powers to Bloom; Tom Kernan struts into the Ormond; George Lidwell, Solic., strokes Lydia Douce's arm; the deaf waiter brings Bloom pen and ink with which he writes a naughty letter to Martha Clifford, covering it as job-hunting before Richie Goulding's uninterested inquiry; Lydia flirts with Lidwell by offering him the listen of a conch-shell from her seaside vacation; Ben Dollard sings 'The Croppy Boy', and is getting a good deal too much appreciation from 'Tomgin Kernan' as Bloom detaches himself from the situation and leaves the Ormond—not, of course, without a 'Thanks, that was heavenly' (286.29) wished silently toward Lydia whose hand on the beerpull gently touching had quietly completed the masturbation cycle of the Ormond (286.18). Like all third comings, Lydia's repetition of the earlier, tenser versions of desire is muted, foreshortened, as is the whole action; because now it is time to repeat actions, never changing, and yet to let the tutorial voice come forward to interpret them. Bloom does so. The narrator does more.

While Simon's singing is being praised by Goulding, Bloom is idly playing at cat's cradle with an elastic band and marvelling at the power of music to bring harmony out of discord. He has heard Dedalus's characteristic venom against 'the Goulding faction' of the family in the funeral carriage (88.18), and now thinks 'Brothers-in-law: relations. We never speak as we pass. . . . The nights Si sang. The human voice, two tiny silky cords. Wonderful, more than all the others' (277.9). 'Vibrations'. And with this train of thought 'Bloom ungyved his crisscrossed hands and . . . plucked the slender catgut thong. He drew and plucked. It buzzed, it twanged' (277.15). Vibrations, indeed, echoing Lydia's elastic garter: *Sonnez la cloche!* It is sufficient to remind Bloom of those other hands, those other thighs which are even now beginning the duet of seduction from *Don Giovanni* 'Là ci darem la mano':

> Thou lost one. All songs on that theme. Yet more Bloom stretched his string. Cruel it seems. Let people get fond of each other: lure them on. Then tear asunder. . . . Gone. They sing. Forgotten. I too. And one day she with. Leave her: get tired. Suffer then. Snivel. Big Spanishy eyes goggling. . . . He stretched more, more. Are you not happy in your? Twang. It snapped.
> Jingle into Dorset Street. (277.23)

The song is ended, a broken chord. The stream of life has passed him; all of the past ends like all songs on the note of the lost one, forgotten. 'I too'. It is very Homeric. In *The Poetics* Aristotle had observed this. 'Recognition', he said, is stimulated when things seen and heard recall for us events that have had an emotional signifi-cance, as 'in the story of Alcinous where Odysseus hears the lyre player and, reminded of his past fortunes, weeps' (1455a). And like Odysseus's, Bloom's mood of defeat and loss is momentary. It is about to be placed in the perspective that redeems all history and enables the unconquered voyager to return home safely to wife and son.

Bloom reacts to his psychic low immediately by a stratagem of safe vengeance, a sublimation even more pathetic ('Bore this', he admits) than the vicarious fulfilment of Lenehan upon Lydia's

smackwarm thigh: he begins a letter in response to his partner in
literary adultery, Martha (Bowen and others have commented upon
the irony that the lost Martha of Simon's song is, psychologically,
Molly and that her loss initiates the fantasy of a Martha whom
Bloom wishes were Molly). Engaged in this furtive game (in which
the self-image of the knowing cuckold can be displaced by that of
the secret conqueror), Bloom catches up only snatches of Goulding's
running conversation, to which he can key his outward responses in
polite clichés of noncommunication while using them as stimuli to
his stream of consciousness. It is the return of a technique perhaps
learned from Dujardin and which has been essentially abandoned
in *Ulysses* since the *tour-de-force* of Bloom's meeting with M'Coy
in 'Lotuseaters'. But Bloom's inner stream is now at one of the
significant points of fusion with, and correction of, that of Stephen
Dedalus.

> —Grandest number in the whole opera, Goulding said.
> —It is, Bloom said.
> Numbers it is. All music when you come to think. Two multi-
> plied by two divided by half is twice one. Vibrations: chords those
> are. . . . Musemathematics. And you think you're listening to the
> ethereal. But suppose you said it like: Martha, seven times nine
> minus x is thirtyfive thousand. Fall quite flat. It's on account of the
> sounds it is. (278.14)

Bloom has come down from the heights of the 'ethereal bosom'
to which Simon's song had transported him. The inevitable rational-
ism of the scientistic mind is exerting its gravity. But Bloom's solutions are not reductive. If the vibrations are reducible to chords,
equations, they are oral, made from 'two tiny silky cords. Wonderful,
more than all the others'.

Hours earlier on Sandymount Strand the image had been
Stephen's, tying him into the nightmare of history, a strangling consubstantial umbilical: 'The cords of all link back, strandentwining
cable of all flesh' (38.1). In 'Proteus', come 'to read, seaspawn and
seawrack', Stephen's 'boots crush crackling wrack and shells' (37.3,
11). We are reminded that in 'Nestor' Stephen's associational pattern had bound shells with a collection of Stuart coins kept by
Deasy and, thence, with the deathmask in which history confronts
the young teacher: 'Stephen's embarrassed hand moved over the
shells heaped in the cold stone mortar . . . dead treasure, hollow

shells' (29.36). This nightmare sense of a dead past haunts Stephen's walk along the beach: poor mariners appear as 'Human shells' (41.10), a drowned man is recollected as swept along with 'silly shells' (50.6), Stephen's rotting teeth are mere 'Shells' (50.35). It is in this context of despair that Stephen envisions history as a throttling universal umbilical which he would escape could he return to origins, to 'naked Eve' whose 'Belly without blemish' stood from 'everlasting to everlasting' because 'She had no navel' (38.6). The umbilical cords suggest telephonic cords, and Stephen's ironic joke is to call across the cords of modern communication a plea of primitivism. 'Hello. Kinch here. Put me on to Edenville. Aleph, alpha: nought, nought one'. It is the world of Eve without a navel, of that mythic unity before history began, the state of God before the courage of creation, of the artist as existential coward, of man retreating into the myth of the Urmother's womb. Mulligan, of course, had hailed the sea as the 'great sweet mother' (5.9), and this association leads Stephen to define his dilemma in metaphoric narrative.[17] Mulligan has recently rescued a man from drowning, and Stephen questions his own fears in contrast: 'I would want to. I would try. I am not a strong swimmer. . . . Do you see the tide flowing quickly in on all sides, sheeting the lows of sand quickly, shell-cocoacoloured? If I had land under my feet. I want his life still to be his, mine to be mine' (45.37).

Stephen's dilemma is insoluble. Wanting the private ahistoricity of the unbifurcated paradise, a world static from everlasting to ever-lasting, he still finds that he must shuffle on the shells of that history (seawrack) which threatens him with limitation, with a heritage at one end and death at the other. He would want to save the drowning man if he could do it without commitment, each retain-ing their separate identity untouched. It is the Stephen who meets his sister Dilly at the bookstall, recognizes her need, his own, and retreats into the image of his mother's death which he has carried from the first pages of Ulysses: 'She is drowning. Agenbite. Save her. . . . She will drown me with her, eyes and hair. Lank coils of seaweed hair around me, my heart, my soul. Salt green death' (243.27).

---

[17] I attempted to place this metaphoric action within a broader context, in 'The Rhythmic Gesture: Image and Aesthetic in Joyce's Ulysses', ELH, XXIX (1962), 67–89 and to define its resonances from Hebraic and pseudo-Hebraic sources in 'Ulysses: Joyce's Kabbalah', JJQ, VII (1969), 93–113.

But Stephen's attention is diverted to a gypsy woman trudging down the beach, and he senses that if 'Loose sand and shell-grit crusted her bare feet', too, nonetheless, she has 'Tides, myriad-islanded, within her, blood not mine, *oinopa ponton*, a winedark sea. Behold the handmaid of the moon' (47.37). This passing stranger incarnates the two halves of Stephen's impossible dichotomy: she struggles the straitened route of history with her path across the seawrack, but has the freedom of the sea within her. Like Eve, she is the source from which the tides originate, creatrix and servant alike of the forms of the past. Stephen's misconception is only in his retreat from this double existence under the stress of his alienation. Perhaps it is the fearful female image which persuades him to miss his own cue about the interaction of past and present, micro- and macrocosmic seas, because in explicating *Hamlet* Stephen will incarnate the sea again: 'the sea's voice, a voice heard only in the heart of him who is the substance of his shadow, the son consubstantial with the father' (197.13).[18] In any case, what Stephen has missed, Bloom is now ready to discover as father and son move toward recognition.

Blood and heart as the voice of the sea reemerge in the 'Sirens', an episode threaded with casual images drawn from the sea, as well as those more crucial ones we have noticed: the barmaids with 'moist' hands, with 'wet' and 'coral' lips, Simon Dedalus singing 'to a dusty seascape', the bar become a 'reef', the 'oceansong' Lydia hums. And the narrator binds the imminent action more decisively to Stephen's seaside meditations of the morning when Bloom not only catches up the association of numbers, cords, and communication, but does so in a context which echoes Eve and 'Edenville'. The refrain 'all is lost now' runs through Simon's ballad, of course, and is echoed in the 'All gone. All fallen' of 'The Croppy Boy'. A tailor is drawn in only that the narrator may tell us his shop is at 'number five Eden quay' (279.36).

And the missing symbol of Stephen's sense of the past as dead and deadly has been waiting as a muted but central prop from the opening pages of 'Sirens': 'Miss Douce halfstood to see her skin askance in the barmirror gildedlettered where hock and claret glasses shimmered and in their midst a shell' (259.3). As Bloom finishes his letter to Martha his imagination returns too actively to Boylan

---

[18] 'Consubstantial' in this passage is the result of an argument which has made the 'son' an aesthetic work produced by the 'old father, old artificer'.

and Molly in a momentary silence ('Walk now. Enough. . . . Wish they'd sing more. Keep my mind off', 280.29) and he tries to get the attention of the deaf waiter[19] Pat in order to leave for his appointment at Barney Kiernan's.

Pat's deaf delay, however, exposes Bloom to that banal scene which his commentary will convert into the wisdom of *Ulysses*. Lidwell has coyly wooed Lydia ('Miss Douce withdrew her satiny arm, reproachful, pleased', 277.35), who is still quite full of her holiday and brings the seashell into action:

> She had a gorgeous, simply gorgeous, time. And look at the lovely shell she brought.
> To the end of the bar to him she bore lightly the spiked and winding seahorn that he, George Lidwell, solicitor, might hear.
> —Listen! she bade him. (281.2)

Holding it to his ear, Lidwell 'heard'. This last reminding us of the human vocal cords, 'Wonderful, more than all the others'. And it is juxtaposed to a single 'Tap', reminder of the perfect ear of the blind stripling. The shell sings, counterpart to the wonderful human voice, while Bloom and, more distantly and mysteriously, the blind stripling hear its song. Lidwell, Douce, and Kennedy now listen alternately.

> Bloom through the bardoor saw a shell held at their ears. He heard more faintly that that they heard, each for herself alone, then each for other, hearing the plash of waves, loudly, a silent roar. . . .
> The sea they think they hear. Singing. A roar. The blood is it. Souse in the ear sometimes. Well, it's a sea. Corpuscle islands.
> Wonderful really. (281.16)[20]

[19] There are antipodal monosyllabic movements in this episode of musically expanded vocables. One is that of Pat the deaf waiter ('Pat is a waiter who waits while you wait. Hee hee hee hee. He waits while you wait. Hee hee. A waiter is he', . . . 280.36). The other is the approaching sound of the Blind Stripling: 'Tap. Tap. Tap'. The former is unmoved, 'waiting', because he can hear nothing. The latter is inexorably moving because he can hear all, see nothing. Both are stigmatized by limitations to emphasize that Bloom is the narrator's image for one who lives both in and beyond the bondage of sense.

[20] The Buffalo manuscript (Spielberg, V. A. 5 p. 35, third unnumbered page) nicely tunes us to Joyce's purposes in revision: 'The sea they think they hear. singing and a roar. The blood it is. singing in the ear sometimes. Blood is a sea, sea with purple islands'. Two observations: first, the alteration from 'it is' to 'is it' harmonizes with Bloom's usual tentativeness concerning scientific explanations of the phenomena; second, 'souse' substituted for 'singing' suggests the two-way action, the interplay, between the outer sea and the inner. The

Bloom in 'Lestrygonians' had given a shudder of unconscious agreement to the signatures of death which Stephen had read in the shells and seawrack on the strand. In serio-comic consonance with the micro-macrocosmic interdependencies of the novel's symbols and theme, Bloom projected his intestinal strains into the vast image of a dying universe: 'Gasballs spinning about, crossing each other, passing. Same old dingdong always. Gas, then solid, then world, then cold, then dead shell drifting around' (167.13). Here the shell is a universal history of dead forms. But in listening to the listeners at the Ormond Bar, Bloom is drawn through the conch shell to articulate a realization not shared by Stephen. Stephen seeks only to free himself from the cords to his past, with which timidity makes him feel strangled, while Bloom sees that the past is always being made alive through the third ear of the microcosm. The shell waits, holding its message from the past ('Akasic' memories: 143.30). The sea within vivifies the greater sea without, recapitulating its 'singing'. And when Stephen ultimately learns to view the relationship of micro- and macrocosm in this way, learns that the past is not a dead hand upon the present if the present breathes life into the past, he awakens from the nightmare view of history. It will be Bloom who will instruct him, and the instruction will come, inevitably, as song: 'What was Stephen's auditive sensation? He heard in a profound ancient male unfamiliar melody the accumulation of the past' (689.21).

When the conch shell is laid aside, Bloom determines to leave the Ormond, and does so to the strains of Ben Dollard singing 'The Croppy Boy', that song of the young betrayed by those two masters Stephen resists, 'The imperial British state . . . and the holy Roman catholic and apostolic church' (20.34).[21] In signalling the waiter,

blood can sound within the shell, but the shell also makes an internal music ring within the ear.

[21] Bowen, 'Bronzegold Sirensong', pp. 283–291, analyzes in detail the interplay of the song's words with Bloom's reactions and associations. We observed above Dollard's symbolic fitness for the warrior's part rather than the lover's in 'Love and War'. Bowen observes the similar significance of 'The Croppy Boy' which 'is about particularly Irish things: betrayal, religion, sentimentality, and war. This is the song the boys want to hear and the things about which their lives revolve. "*Qui sdegno*", a song of peace, is voted down in favour of the inherently militant' (283). Sternfeld, 'Poetry and Music', argues that the Croppy Boy is an avatar of Stephen Dedalus, as is the Blind Stripling (pp. 26–31).

paying his bill, and taking leave of Richie Goulding, Bloom's thoughts (interspersed not only with the phrases of the song but the sounds of the final phases of Boylan's journey to and arrival at 7 Eccles street) wander to Dollard's fall into drink and bankruptcy and placement in a home for indigents. At the moment of his betrayal's consummation his thoughts (encouraged by the song) are upon decline and death: 'Ruin them. Wreck their lives. Then build them cubicles to end their days in. Hushaby. Lullaby. Die, dog. Little dog, die' (283.29). In a moment he flashes back to the grey rat at Dignam's burial ('Chap in the mortuary. . . . Wonder where that rat is by now' 284.7) and then rises again to memories of better days with Molly, only to sigh wistfully in unison with Dollard's song: 'All gone. All fallen' (285.1).[22]

'I alone am left of my name and race', sings Dollard in the role of the Croppy Boy, and Bloom picks it up: 'I too, last my race'. But it is just here that the second turn toward active paternity, a *vita nuova* occurs. If Bloom's symbolic acceptance of a paternal role with Stephen has been signalled in the rising arc of the 'Siopold' fusion, it is this song of war and death and loss which brings him to react with love and sex and hope for another kind of paternity: 'No son. Rudy. Too late now. Or if not? If not? If still? He bore no hate. . . . Rudy. Soon I am old' (285.5). The juxtapositions of womb and tomb throughout *Ulysses* are too frequent to want re-capitulation. But usually they have moved across the natural cycle of decline ('Extraordinary the interest they take in a corpse. Glad to see us go we give them such trouble coming', 87.16). In this in-stance there is a dramatic reversal as recollections of death inspire a hope for renewed and new life. It is just here that the impulse for Bloom's unwonted breakfast request is born. He goes to rest this night to a litany of 'roc's auk's egg in the night of the bed of all the auks of the rocs' (737.25), leaving Molly to marvel that 'he never did a thing like that before as ask to get his breakfast in bed with a couple of eggs' (738.1). The eggs will be fertile; the pun has been prepared in this moment of decision when, having symbolically

---

[22] Little ironies are made to counter every sympathetic engagement. Bloom's recollection of a bosomy Molly at the opera 'Hypnotised, listening' to his ac-count of Spinoza (284.36), is an illusion burst for the reader by Molly's ex-planation of her apparent 'hypnosis': her period had unexpectedly come upon her in that exposed public position (769.9).

won Stephen, Bloom discovers what Molly knows: 'Poldy has more spunk in him' (742.33).[23]

Confirmation of Bloom's renewed sexual hope arises as his attention immediately turns full upon Miss Douce for the first time. Though he thinks her probably a virgin, his fantasies and the narrator's metaphors nevertheless come together upon birth. Dollard's song warns the Croppy Boy that he has but 'One hour's time to live', and again Bloom's associations reverse the course of nature from death to life: 'Poor Mrs Purefoy. Hope she's over. Because their wombs'. The narrator catches up the word as he describes Lydia: 'A liquid womb of woman eyeball gazed. . . . Heartbeats her breath: breath that is life' (286.7). But it is Molly, not the surrogate, in whose womb the manchild must come to rest (737.12). So Bloom leaves the bar to walk another arc of the long circle home, accompanied by the sounds of the Ormond drinking, the stripling's tapping, his own farting epitaph upon the old world of Irish sentiment and sterility which he has left behind 'in deepseashadow'.

But as he does, he realizes something most necessary if the renewal of the past lies in melody, song, the human voice, most necessary if 'Love's Old Sweet Song' is once again to be his own with Molly: 'Play on her. Lip blow. Body of white women, a flute alive. Blow gentle. Loud. Three holes all women. . . . With look to look: songs without words' (285.32). Sex like the 'Sirens', is the song of songs awakening all to life.

To return to the question posed at the beginning of this discussion, let us ask again what the music of 'Sirens' tells us about *Ulysses*. As we have seen in detail, *Ulysses* changes in every respect with this chapter. Joyce thought of it as opening a second half of the novel; Bloom reverses his psychic direction from passive to active; the symbolic construct of the sea and the shell is metamorphosed from the hopeless dichotomy it constitutes for Stephen into Bloom's song of union; Pound and others quite rightly recognized a drastic shift in stylistic technique. The style ceases to be traditional, if complexly counterpointed, narrative and becomes seriously imitative of the chapter's 'art', which is 'music'.

[23] Sultan, pp. 412–422, comments upon the miraculous connotations of the roc's egg and associates it with the breakfast eggs as an unspecified symbol of conjugal renewal.

Indeed, if stylistic experiment will mark the entirety of the last half of *Ulysses*, in only 'Sirens' and 'Oxen of the Sun', with its embryonic development, does Joyce consistently translate into stylistic techniques the 'art' of the chapter; elsewhere he is content with allusive relationships. In both cases, the style itself becomes symbolic of the total action. Both, because the two are complementary. Common consent can be asserted upon only one point: *Ulysses* is about fathers and sons, a search (successful or unsuccessful) for paternity. Had Josie Breen not told Bloom of Mina Purefoy's labour pangs, Bloom would not have arrived at the lying-in hospital and become Stephen's paternalistic protector. The physical birth in the background indirectly gives birth to their relationship and to that vision of Rudy rising from the fallen Stephen which conforms to the spiritual mystery of paternity. And that mystery is consummated in the ancient male melody that frees Stephen of his fear of communion with the past, with history, personal and public, with the other. Song and birth are face and obverse of one another. And so it is proper that, in 'Sirens', song should awaken Bloom to yet another paternity, that imitated in 'Oxen of the Sun'—the consubstantial paternity possible if it is not too late to beget once more upon Molly, to play once more upon the body of woman, 'flute alive. . . . songs without words'.

'Sirens' is the chapter in which the possibility of renewed communion is recognized and, as the final word of the prelude promises, the movement toward that renewal is begun. What has been separate starts toward convergence: Stephen and humanity, Bloom and Molly. The much-argued musical form of the prelude can be viewed as the first symbol of this convergence in the chapter: the fragments at the beginning are disparate, without meaning, if underscored by a sense of Bloom's presence. But as Bloom emerges toward himself and a recognition of his inevitable paternal role ('kismet. Fate', 289.26), as he moves toward a new harmony, those fragments are drawn together into a cohesive pattern in which we comprehend precisely the coherence of inner and outer music, of that music of the blood which sounds as a sea ever renewed in a shell, or as an Hebraic melody chanted from father to son, or in the silence of love.

CYCLOPS

David Hayman

More even than 'Sirens' in which perception is rendered as liquified sound, 'Cyclops' is the 'mixed media' chapter. In it Joyce purposefully mixes diurnal and nocturnal modes, juxtaposing a conventional direct narrative voice and a jumble of mocking asides, the spoken and the printed word. The action of this chapter ironically suggests a symposium on Christian love. Set in a low pub at a lively hour it focusses on the behaviour of frustrated men, impelled by jealousy, pride, greed, and thirst, portrayed with muted rage and hilarity by a social reject, who, in another epoch would have been a professional story teller and satirist, a man respected and feared by Irish kings. Among the factors influencing Joyce's strategy are the time of day, the seduction of Molly, the need to phase out the Bloomish consciousness, and the Homeric parallel. The result is a complexly mimetic unit where, for the first time, we are deprived both of Bloom's voice and of an objective narrator.

In order to find out what occurred in Barney Kiernan's at 5 P.M. on 16 June, the reader is transported at an unspecified hour to an unnamed pub where he listens silently to the porterous voice of an insistent and self-assertive clown, whose character and station are almost as important as the tale he tells and slants. A drifter, without family or function, the narrator has, one suspects, turned his hand to many jobs and failed at all of them. Having no real enthusiasms, loyalties, or scruples, he now lives from thirst to thirst. Apparently he is personable enough to enjoy the respect of the backbiters who surround him, but perhaps he is tolerated for fear of his sharp tongue and satirical wit. A bitter gnome, he prudently bows to power, attacks only the impotent, priding himself on his 'inside' information rather than on his capacities or achievements. His professional relationship to authority (see old Troy) and his dubious social position as a dun make him especially cautious and explain his disengagement from the citizen's violence. But, for all his airs, he has no real influence and less courage. The cruel gossip he delights in comes from other duns and process servers or from the sort of person who lives at the City Arms hotel. Repeatedly, he betrays his ignorance and his sources, limiting himself for the most part to hearsay and opinion. It follows that Molly's infidelity comes to him as an insight and that even Bloom has access to more facts about men like Cunningham and Power. Blind to his own viciousness, he criticizes the harmless Bob Doran for his marriage and maundering, the citizen for his hypocrisy and excesses, Joe Hynes for his impecuniousness, the Breens for their pretences gone sour, and above all Bloom. A thorough-going opportunist, he can forget his anti-Semitism to work for an unlicensed Jewish grocer against the wiles of a boghopping swindler.

The narrator's opinions, though petty and distorted, are important. Like his lower-class Dublin jargon, they reflect those of the mob he personifies and, thanks to Joyce's technique, they influence our own reactions. As eavesdroppers on a Dublin day, we develop a thirst for his gossip, a grudging respect for his reliability, and a taste for his wit. His language conveys directly, and we experience vicariously the quality of his thirst, his painful urination, his almost physical distaste for weakness in others, and the prejudices conditioned by his calling. (He hates dogs as biters of process servers; he likes men who treat; he fears violence that brings notoriety.) Those he scorns are caricatured mercilessly, but like all good caricatures, his portraits are disturbingly right. His Bloom is a verbose 'lardy face' whose virility is in question and whose wife has 'a back on her like a ballalley' (305.38–40). He insists on repeating the canvasser's circumlocutions and the verbal ticks which we recognize as a sure sign of embarrassment. Given our sense of Bloom's native wit and our sympathy with him at this moment, we may in 'Cyclops' discount as ignorant or prejudiced a remark borne out later during 'Eumaeus':

'I declare to my antimacassar if you took up a straw from the bloody floor and if you said to Bloom: *Look at, Bloom. Do you see that straw? That's a straw.* Declare to my aunt he'd talk about it for an hour so he would and talk steady' (316.35). Thanks to our bias and to the ring of truth beneath the hyperboles, we know that our hero is battling lesser men in the pub and that, while he shows his intelligence to his own disadvantage, his is the noblest role. Since the narrator records what he sees as well as what he suspects, Bloom emerges from this chapter guiltless of all offence; for, ultimately, though we laugh at the dun's expression, we share relatively few of his attitudes.

Since Bloom in 'Cyclops' is more seen than seeing, our eyes are drawn first to the dramatic context and especially to the behaviour and habits of the monster-in-residence. Already swelled with the fluids of dropsy, alternately goaded on and restrained by the others, the citizen swells further with rage and drink as the chapter progresses. His behaviour toward Bloom both follows and reverses that of Homer's giant. Seeing the Jew as an uninvited guest in Ireland, he nevertheless invites him into the pub where he unhospitably attacks him, reacting to what he reads as challenges to his authority. A man craving sycophants, he is angered by Bloom's argumentativeness and frustrated by a shift in the balance of opinion. Indignant when Bloom fails to treat out of his 'winnings', he falls victim to a blind rage. A failure of sight and insight causes him to miss his mark in more ways than one when he throws the biscuit tin after the departing stranger, for with this act he reveals the extent to which, as the narrator puts it, 'the mighty' have 'fallen' (292.27).

Like the narrator (and possibly Alf Bergan), the citizen is a figure we have not met before. Inverting Homer, Joyce makes him nameless. If the narrator is a projection of a fringe decorum based on values not held by the reader, the citizen represents a belligerent, self-pitying nationalism, generated by a hypocritical and self-serving morality. In terms of his role, the action is a swelling and a false release: the unsatisfactory ejaculation of a tired old man. In relation to this development, the ex-shotputting citizen is a cosmi-comic figure. Like Homer's demi-god and volcano, he overshadows the rest of the book's action. He has challenged Bloom's manhood, made manifest his rootlessness, and complicated his return. The final challenge and its response constitute, as in the *Odyssey*, the prelude to,

rather than the climax of, the hero's difficulties. Before Bloom can
return to Molly, he is obliged to pay for this facile and doubtful victory by initiating himself into his own inner mysteries.

Since the citizen dominates and, in a sense, makes the scene
as the stentorian voice of a past-praising Irish present, since he is
available for more of the chapter than Bloom himself though for
less than the narrator or Joe Hynes, we may ask who and what he is
and even from what he derives. Richard Ellmann has described
Joyce's model, Michael Cusack, as a man of 'middle height' with
'extremely broad shoulders' given to wearing 'a broad-brimmed hat'
and 'knee breeches' and dedicated to the revival of Irish sports. An
outspoken traditionalist he was virulently anti-everything-English.[1]
When Joyce met him in his decline, he must have already lost the
humour and vigour needed to enter a pub shouting 'I'm Citizen
Cusack from the Parish of Carron in the Barony of Burren in the
County of Clare, you Protestant dog!'[2] In *Sentimental Education*
there is another 'revolutionary' who calls himself 'Citizen'. Flaubert's
Regimbart spends his time in cafes soaking up drinks and pompously
spouting political opinions designed to stimulate the revolution of
1848, an uprising that Flaubert characterizes as a bitter farce. Citizen
Regimbart, far from being the harbinger of future glory, is a pathetic
and hypocritical ghost whose wife supports him by making dresses
for the rich. The people who come to pass the time with him treat
him as an amusing and inconsequent blowhard. Joyce may have
combined Cusack and Regimbart in his anonymous citizen. There
is yet another dimension. Magnified and distorted by the narrator,
inflated by the asides, the citizen becomes a grotesque giant of the
pantomime tradition against whom Joyce pits the puny hero and the
pathetic clown, Bloom. Finally, even if we see the citizen as a self-
parody, we eagerly seize on the details that heighten his individuality
and render him less general. This tension between the formula and
its embodiment makes the chapter more interesting as a border
area: for Joyce has only begun imposing boldly stated literary conventions on an elaborately realistic matrix.

Disregarding for the moment the stylistic trappings, we see the
citizen dramatically, less as the ineffectual monster of pride than as
a pitiful ruin, an aborted promise, a harmless biscuit eater like his

[1] Ellmann, p. 62n.
[2] *Ibid.*

companion Garryowen, who 'won't eat' Bloom or anyone else. His gruff humour, the clublike atmosphere of adulation and exclusion he encourages, his pose as the whimsical monarch in his court, his appeals to baser instincts, all suggest weakness rather than strength. His true condition is best described by the dun:

> Gob, he's not as green as he's cabbagelooking. Arsing around from one pub to another, leaving it to your own honour, with old Giltrap's dog and getting fed up by the ratepayers and corporators. Entertainment for man and beast. (312.37)

Since none of the drinks go on his account, he is in fact no host but many times the guest. Unlike the antisocial Cyclops, he craves company, and if he enjoys a good laugh or sneer at another's expense, there is a hint of self-mockery in the opening exchange with Hynes in which both men parody a ritual of recognition.[3] Much of the time he is playing the part to an audience used to his postures and delighted (or bored) to see him all 'wind and piss like a tanyard cat' (328.13). They play along when he sardonically toasts Parnell's *Irish Independent* for deserting its founder's principles. They know that the Gaelic which he reserves for the dog or uses in curses to ornament his speech is an affectation. Can he really speak a language few of them can understand? A 'Fenian' living on his past, he is said to be in bad odour for 'grabbing the holding of an evicted tenant' (328.18), and Joe Hynes has to tell Alf Bergan, 'There's the man . . . that made the Gaelic sports revival. . . . The man that got away James Stephens. The champion of all Ireland at putting the sixteen pound shot' (316.20).

Grotesque chauvinism makes him a joke, a lunatic has-been who must be humoured or gently nudged toward sanity and whose fixations inhibit free discussion. If he is not always wrong, he is never original or stimulating. The only serious problem that interests him, hoof and mouth disease, is more adequately attacked by the anti-Semitic Orangeman, Deasy. Significantly, Hynes, the one man who comes specifically to see him, gets little satisfaction when he raises

[3] Phillip Herring, ed., *Joyce's 'Ulysses' Notesheets in the British Museum*, Charlottesville, Va., 1972, 'Cyclops' 1, lines 73–82 (p. 83). In his notes to this chapter Joyce lists a long series of questions, answers, and gestures which he credits to the Ribbonmen, an Irish terrorist group. Chances are the Ribbonmen no longer existed in 1904.

the question that prompted his visit. When John Wyse Nolan reports to the citizen on the 'caucus meeting [to] decide about the Irish language' (324.30), a meeting at which precisely nothing took place, he responds with embarrassingly inappropriate enthusiasm. Since his actual concerns are so trivial as to be pathetic, his life is one long self-deluding frustration watered by the porter or stout that has ruined his health. His references to James Stephens and to Kevin Egan, which recall Stephen's bitterly sympathetic reflections on forgotten valour in 'Proteus', may lead us to ask which is better, exile or an embattled, outdated, and unrewarded activism.

Under the circumstances, Bloom's appearance, which signals the beginning of the action, promises diversion much as Ulysses' arrival must have eased the boredom of Polyphemus. By calling the stranger into the pub, the Fenian is at once acting like a host and asking for a quarrel; for Bloom is in his eyes a helpless symbol of the alien establishment. We may be sure that there have been other brushes and that the citizen knows who Bloom is if not what his opinions are. If nothing else, he believes him to be a freemason.

The tension builds subtly but predictably. Unwilling to fight but holding to his rational positions with a notable lack of humour (Poldy serious is Poldy dull as we learn in 'Eumaeus'), Bloom persists in countering the citizen's positions with his random knowledge or undercutting crude witticisms, like the allusion to a hanged man's erection, with ponderous 'scientific' explanations. Though he stands virtually alone, the citizen is goaded on by the trickster Lenehan, whose jealousy and suspicions stimulate the old man's thirst and help focus his rage. But even the peacemakers, Nolan, O'Molloy, and Cunningham, feed the flames they try to quench, pander to the patriot's prejudices, while riling him further with provocatively moderate statements. Everything comes to a head during Bloom's second absence, in a scene during which, baffled at being ignored and upstaged by the establishment toffs, the citizen questions the outsider's virility before identifying him with the Wandering Jew:

—O, by God, says Ned, you should have seen Bloom before that son of his that died was born. I met him one day in the south city markets buying a tin of Neave's food six weeks before the wife was delivered.
—*En ventre sa mere*, says J. J.
—Do you call that a man? says the citizen.

—I wonder did he ever put it out of sight, says Joe.
—Well, there were two children born anyhow, says Jack Power.
—And who does he suspect? says the citizen.
Gob, there's many a true word spoken in jest. One of those
mixed middlings he is. Lying up in the hotel Pisser was telling me
once a month with headache like a totty with her courses. (338.5)

Completing the citizen's train of thought and adding up his own
second-hand information, the I-narrator easily identifies Bloom and
Breen as 'mixed middlings'. It is already too late for peacemaking
when Cunningham pompously adds the inevitable corollary to
Bloom's plea for brotherly love, a plea for 'Charity to the neighbour'
(338.24) for whom he and his friends 'cannot wait'. The citizen's
vitriolic 'Ahasuerus I call him' (338.27), is muted, but his anger is
doubtless sharpened by Ned Lambert's order for drinks, four drinks
only, for Cunningham, Crofton, Power, and himself. The supreme
slight is to buy but half a round. Thirsty still, the narrator pointedly
looks 'round to see who the happy thought would strike' (341.5)
when the stigmatized Bloom bursts in, supposedly loaded down with
his winnings from the Gold Cup. What moment could be less oppor-
tune? Drunk, thirsty, insulted, suspicious, and frustrated by the
others' refusal to respond to his accusation: 'Don't tell anyone. . . .
It's a secret' (341.19), the citizen rushes, cursing in Irish, to the door
where he hurls his parting insult—a cheer! Since this is a portrait of
comic frustration, the narrator is right to label it clowning. In the
inverted world of Irish public-house values, Bloom has violated the
cardinal rule of hospitality. He has failed to treat his hosts. This is
the opposite of Ulysses' sin of befuddling and maiming his inhospita-
ble host, but the result is analogous: blindness and misdirected rage.
The clown of excess has been foiled by the vulnerable fool and even
the explosion has aborted in the paralytic atmosphere of a world in
inanition.
Everyman and noman, the complete individual and the comic
convention, Bloom is the active centre of the action in 'Cyclops' and
its passive focus. To achieve this effect Joyce first built the particu-
larized individual and then gradually, beginning with 'Aeolus' diminished his role. The process culminates in the reversal of his consciousness in 'Circe', but 'Cyclops' finds him in a medial position, at once
a sympathetic character and an object of ridicule. The action of the
chapter is the perfect correlative for this stage in his development, or

rather exposure. Having come to Barney Kiernan's pub on an errand of mercy, he is drawn against his will into conversation with the 'citizen'. Taunted and teased unmercifully at a time when he is particularly distraught over Molly's behaviour, he consistently turns the other cheek, speaking for peace and reason in a den of violent fools. Emboldened by his need to forget, he tries to justify the English to Irish nationalists; remaining sober as the citizen gets progressively drunker and more violent, he makes shift to conceal his despair. As an outspoken representative of charity, love, common sense, sobriety, and prudence, the outsider has precipitated resentment, suspicion, and violence. But we are not only concerned with what happens to him and what he does but also with what is done to him or because of his presence: what, in short, his presence does to the atmosphere of this place at this time.

Anti-Semitism may be a major crux (others are nationalism, culture, and virility). Taking his Jewishness for granted, Bloom has not felt obliged to identify with or defend Jews, for he has not been forced to accept exclusion. Indeed he has frequently been uncomfortable with his own diluted Jewishness. As Joyce puts it in his notes, he 'hates the jew in the jew'.[4] Prior to 'Cyclops' he has felt only veiled anti-Semitism and oblique denigration. His position in 'Cyclops' is therefore in tension with that of an alienated Stephen in 'Nestor'. There, the reluctant Irish Catholic is challenged to defend the Catholic Irish against an Orangeman with whom he is not completely in disaccord. Curiously, Bloom's defence of English discipline ('. . . isn't discipline the same everywhere? I mean wouldn't it be the same here if you put force against force?', 329.30), sounds very much like Stephen's defence of Jewish business methods in 'Nestor'. Whereas Stephen is defending an underdog with whom he unconsciously identifies, Bloom is speaking up for and identifying with the master nation, exposing himself as a weak emblem of hated power. His act is equally ambiguous, though, under the circumstances, apparently more courageous. Unlike Stephen, some force drives him further, toward real courage, toward identifying the Irish and the Jews and eventually defending himself as a Jew. (In 'Circe' Stephen needs to be drunk and half demented to articulate a muddled rejection of all such ties. The two scenes are naturally, if ironically, parallel.)

[4] *Ibid.*, 'Cyclops' 10, line 11 (p. 119).

What prompts Bloom to push his points so vigorously in the face of such obvious and unequal opposition? Even if we accept his genuine sense of fairness and his concern for the suffering, we may still ask what makes this prudent man uphold his Jewishness in a conversation with obvious anti-Semites? One probable, if partial, answer is that he cannot help himself, given his preoccupation with Molly and Boylan. What begins as a conversation designed to sublimate his real concerns ends with a demonstration of his ability to defend himself against unreasonable prejudice. A key paragraph is the following:

—Robbed, says he. Plundered. Insulted. Persecuted. *Taking what belongs to us by right. At this very moment,* says he, putting up his fist, sold by auction off *in Morocco* like slaves or cattles. (332.36) [my italics]

We know what is being taken by whom 'at this very moment'. We also know that Morocco and things Moorish are invariably associated with Molly. Bloom has 'blown his cool' while trying to sublimate a real distress. Molly means more to him than nation or race. No wonder, as the narrator recalls, 'he collapses all of a sudden, twisting around all the opposite, as limp as a wet rag' (333.6). Under the circumstances, how ambiguous and yet how admirable is his reply to Alf, 'Love . . . I mean the opposite of hatred' (333.14). He has in fact turned the other cheek. Compulsion has led him blundering to courage. Circumspection tells him to hold his peace until the moment when he is driven to reveal his public identity, reassert his Jewishness, and along with it to declare, however clumsily, his pride. It is perhaps a supreme irony that Bloom is finally driven to play the citizen's game, naming famous ancestors.

The end of 'Cyclops' marks Bloom's first step toward the possible recovery of his self-possession and manhood, to say nothing of his return to Molly's man-warmed bed. But the public act for which the citizen has provided the necessary stimulus is also a comic act, characterized by the usual bumbling and misinformation. Bloom upsets his friends almost as much as his enemies when he speaks of Christ's father and then his 'uncle'. Ultimately, he satisfies only himself (and the reader in pursuit of analogies). Though perhaps it cannot be said to well up from or assuage his deepest distress, this clumsy, prudent, heroic action marks the moment when being a Jew in Dublin ceases to disturb him. When he begins to accept himself, and, in a more profound sense, discover hidden roots, he can also begin to reconsider his relationship to Molly. Perhaps the point is that two simultaneous orgasms have released the man in him. Or to put it differently, the declaration of his alien identity and the usurpation of his marital rights coincide to eliminate his dread of such occurrences, and provide some of the psychic energy for 'Circe'.

'Cyclops' has a full spectrum of well-delineated characters whose behaviour constitutes the ground against which Bloom and the citizen work out a confrontation generated by pride and despair. Each of these minor figures has a dual dramatic function. By ratifying at least one of the citizen's prejudices and generally humouring him, each contributes to the anti-Semitic tension. On the other hand, none of them fully or to the same degree shares the old man's enthusiasms and almost all of them at some point say something in Bloom's favour, counter the citizen's views or try to calm him down. As a result none of this faint-hearted crew is guilty of outrage though each in his own way contributes to the chaos. As the following *dramatis personae* indicates, Joyce has carefully arranged and timed the entrances to accent the drama of estrangement and self-assertion. Most of the characters are introduced in pairs, and the more responsible (Lenehan excepted) make their entrances only after the stage has been set and Bloom has been exposed to the citizen for eighteen pages. By their number and power they gradually tip the scales in Bloom's favour:

The I-narrator: a dun, 'collector of bad and doubtful debts'. (292)
Joe Hynes: a newspaper reporter, who has just been paid. (292)
The citizen: a minor Fenian and ex-athlete, now a dropsical sponge pretending to be working for the cause. (295)
Alf Bergan: an employee at the subsheriff's office. (298)
Bob Doran: an insignificant clerk out on his yearly bender. (298)
Leopold Bloom: a canvasser for the *Weekly Freeman*. (302)
J. J. O'Molloy: a lawyer on the skids. (320)
Ned Lambert: a merchant in seed and grain. (320)
John Wyse Nolan: a journalist whose wife runs an Irish farm dairy. (324)
Lenehan: a sponge and tout who may have a job on the racing sheet. (324)
Martin Cunningham: a civil servant at the castle. (336)

Jack Power: a police department employee. (336)
Crofton: 'pensioner out of the collector general's, an orangeman'. (336)

Not included in this list are four figures mentioned in the prologue: Old Troy, the policeman; a sweep whose mock-erotic violence almost turns the narrator into a cyclops; the unlicensed grocer Moses Herzog and his foxy antagonist, Michael Geraghty, whose behaviour inverts the action of the chapter. Also omitted is Denis Breen, who never enters the pub, though his presence is felt in the argument. We may see him as a surrogate for Bloom, another sort of outcast: the unhappy moonstruck victim of a practical joke committed in all likelihood by Alf Bergan (160.3). The sweep's phallic stick and aborted violence, Herzog's Jewish identity, the sly trickery of Geraghty and the folly of Breen overshadow the whole chapter.

Since most of the characters are familiar to us from *Dubliners* and/or earlier chapters of *Ulysses*, we are able to supply dramatic shading omitted by the myopic narrator. The chronically impecunious Joe Hynes, perhaps the most genuine Fenian in the group, has already shown his mettle in 'Ivy Day in the Committee Room' by defending the opposition candidate and reciting a moving if mediocre tribute to Parnell. We have seen him briefly as a barely competent reporter in 'Hades', where Bloom has to help him list the mourners. Later, in 'Aeolus', Bloom tells him to collect his pay and thus enables him to treat the sponges in Kiernan's instead of repaying his debt of 'three bob' (119.33). If he is relatively gentle with Bloom, who has proved a lenient creditor and a helpful colleague, he does not defend him before the others, whom he joins in suspecting Bloom's motives and doubting his virility. Still, motivated by a mixture of concern for Bloom and respect for the old man, he acts unsuccessfully to restrain the citizen in his moment of blind rage.

By contrast to Hynes, who has attained temporary respectability and affluence and who functions as an active character oscillating between the two camps, Bob Doran is completely passive and temporarily both a comic outsider and an emblem of the place. Perhaps his marriage to Polly Mooney after the events described in 'A Boarding House' has ruined his life, perhaps not. We know him only as an ineffectual and gentle sort, a minor clerk who finds solace in the periodic bender, the classic victim of social illness and Irish paralysis.

In 'Lotuseaters' he figures as M'Coy's companion at the moment when both men learned of Dignam's death, a fact which makes his maudlin effusiveness in 'Cyclops' all the more comic and pathetic.

Lenehan occupies a special place, for he functions as a complement and foil to Boylan just as Lynch extends the role of Mulligan. Even before he enters 'Cyclops', Lenehan figures with Mulligan as a Dublin streetsinger (307.3) in an aside which bridges the age gap and joins the two comic couples. His role as clownish drifter and sponge, if it needs restatement after 'Two Gallants', is constantly reiterated in *Ulysses*, where he quips his way into the newspaper office, cadges drinks from Stephen, Boylan, and Nolan and even turns up at the Holles Street hospital. Still, while the reader of *Ulysses* may guess that he suffers some remorse and resents the kicks he is bound to receive, he is unlikely to associate him with the cadging Corley of 'Eumaeus'. Ebullient in the early chapters, where he touts the phallic horse, Sceptre, and makes dull quips or pretends to a continental gloss, Lenehan turns up with John Wyse Nolan halfway through 'Cyclops' in mourning for a lost race and concerned that he has lost face with the well-heeled Boylan. (We suspect that Joyce is hinting at a latent homosexuality in Lenehan similar to that of Mulligan, a tendency expressed very differently in Bloom's and Stephen's relationship with each other and with their male rivals.) Rather than affront Bloom, he accuses him behind his back (of winning where others have lost) and thus maliciously polarizes the tension bringing on the final explosion in which, like a true Mephisto, he takes no part. A weak man, he exhibits the jealousy, slyness, and treachery of a Lynch, with whose role in 'Circe' his behaviour in 'Cyclops' is consonant.

Martin Cunningham, Jack Power, and the orangeman Crofton have little more than walk-on parts in 'Cyclops', where they save Bloom in the name of the state against which the citizen strikes out. (It is fitting that the old man attacks nothing but Bloom in the presence of these minor functionaries.) Since all three have been characterized earlier (Crofton in 'Ivy Day' and tangentially in 'Grace', Cunningham and Power in 'Grace', 'Hades', and 'Wandering Rocks'), they are brought in only so that they may act in character as civilized or 'siphilized' men reacting to fanaticism which they recognize as more than simple anti-Semitism. If they take Bloom's part, it is only to keep from identifying with the citizen's hysterical behaviour and at that only after they have with pompous witticisms cleared themselves of philo-Semitism or Bloomitis. Such luke-warm protectors combine the function of the legal defence staff and the indifferent but just gods (and point ahead to the role of Kelleher in 'Circe'). Of the three, only Cunningham, as leader, has a role to play, but, together, they clothe Bloom in a cloak of non-nationalistic respectability before spiriting him away from the terrible encounter.

More central to the dramatic action of 'Cyclops' are three characters developed exclusively in *Ulysses*: Lambert, O'Molloy, and Nolan. In 'Proteus', 'York's false scion', Lambert Simnel, is associated with the oft-repeated allusion to the Irish as 'All kings' sons' and a further allusion to Ireland as a 'Paradise of pretenders' (45.26, 29). The Simnel allusion might pass unnoticed, but we are urged to link him with Ned Lambert by a reference in 'Hades' which identifies the fastidious character who has turned his coat (literally) with the embodiment of futile pretence. Bloom reflects on the contents of a hawker's barrow, 'Simnel cakes those are, struck together: cakes for the dead. Dogbiscuits. . . . Mr Kernan and Ned Lambert followed . . .' (100.37). Lambert is a man whose relations with power enable him to trade on influence he himself lacks, the prince who may come into power when 'Old Chatterton, the vice-chancellor . . . his granduncle or his greatgranduncle' dies (124.11). Appropriately, he is introduced in a 'Cyclops' aside as 'the prince and heir of the noble line of Lambert' (320.2). A reasonable man, he is knowledgeable in the history of Dublin and Ireland.[5] Two acts and an omission characterize his role in 'Cyclops'. He speaks out only briefly against the belief that outsiders will save the Irish cause (330); he takes no part in the attempt to restore the citizen to order at the end of the chapter when, along with J. J. O'Molloy, he is 'paralysed with the laughing' (343.34). At no time, despite his presumed reasonableness, his tolerance, and his friendship for Bloom, does he intervene in the argument. No wonder this genial drinking companion and uncommitted friend finds his last echo in Stephen's cryptic allusion to the 'suine scions of the house of Lambert' (569.11). He is a true son of the old sow, a sensitive man of inaction, an echo of James Duffy in 'A Painful Case'.

Ned Lambert is a dealer in seed, unmarried and isolated; J. J.

---

[5] It is no coincidence that in 'Wandering Rocks' Lambert is linked to the aborted rebellion of Silken Thomas.

O'Molloy is a cultivated and witty failure given to gambling: 'Cleverest fellow at the junior bar he used to be' (125.2), says a knowledgeable Bloom. He spends his day chasing Lambert hoping to get 'a leg over the stile' (320.16) and tries to keep up appearances by maintaining a polished but humble manner. Though broke and begging, he treats lesser men to cigarettes and drink. His forte in both 'Aeolus' and 'Cyclops' is the quip that goes unnoticed. Though he is responsible for introducing in his mild and oblique way an anti-Semitic topic, the Canada Swindle case in which a Jew has bilked other Jews, his manner is resented. Characteristically, his serious legal opinion on Breen's case is neither heard nor understood. The narrator claims that he is 'doing the toff' when, with a typically opaque allusion, he accuses the citizen of ignoring the facts:

> So J. J. puts in a word doing the toff about one story was good till you heard another and blinking facts and the Nelson policy putting your blind eye to the telescope and drawing up a bill of attainder to impeach a nation and Bloom trying to back him up moderation and botheration and their colonies and their civilisation. (325.1)

One thinks of Bloom, who agrees without understanding, but more especially of Stephen in similar circumstances, a more promising voice of incomprehensible reason: 'a darkness shining in brightness which brightness could not comprehend' (28.16). In fact, by virtue of his secret jargon, his private wit, and his faded condition, O'Molloy is Stephen's surrogate on the threshold of the night, humane and hopeless, incapable of diverting the conversation, paralyzed in the moment for action. If Bloom's unconscious mind accepts O'Molloy as a defence attorney in 'Circe' (463.64), it is a measure of the little man's silent admiration rather than of the lawyer's virtue.

John Wyse Nolan is a journalist[6] whose wife runs the Irish farm dairy and whose conservationist sympathies qualify him for the fictive role of Irish forester in one of the asides later in 'Circe'. A knowledge that Bloom is contributing to the support of Dignam's widow probably determines his treatment of him in 'Cyclops'. If Nolan's behaviour is puzzling, his motives are clear enough. He is genuinely interested in the nationalist cause but too fairminded to prefer the citizen's mindless fanaticism to Bloom's frequently flabby maunderings. He has come from a rather inconclusive meeting on the Irish

---

[6] *Surface and Symbol*, p. 58.

language and probably feels the irrelevance of that cause and the inadequacy of its supporters. It is clear from 'Wandering Rocks' that the position he respects is one worthy of Martin Cunningham (246.48) to whom he is generally subservient. Though his companion is the clownish Lenehan, he himself stands for reason between the embattled camps. If he goads Bloom into his defence of tolerance and love, his reaction to the heartfelt outburst is one of surprised respect: 'Well . . . isn't that what we're told? Love your neighbours' (333.22). The narrator blocks out the details of his defence, but his allusion to Bloom's Sinn Fein sympathies tips the scales for the embattled outsider and underscores the citizen's failure to do anything comparable. It makes little difference here whether or not Bloom actually did give Griffith an idea. (We wonder why Bloom himself makes no mention of it in his private thoughts.) What matters is that the Jew has managed to win at least one dedicated supporter, that he is not completely alone in the den of nonsense.

Along with the narrator and the citizen, there is one other character who figures in no other chapter, the fun-loving jokester, little Alf Bergan. This embodiment of Irish laughter and mockery is guilty of only one minor sin, the introduction of Breen's madness and inadequacy as a topic of pub conversation, an act that leads by a devious route to the revelation of Bloom's vulnerability. If Nolan stands for reason and moderation, Bergan stands for humour in moderation. He is a witty rogue who seldom exceeds the bounds of decency, a foil for other clowns who frequently do (see Punch Costello), a man free from the malice, cowardice, false *bonhomie* of Lenehan and Lynch. Lacking the dedication of Hynes and the vice of Doran, eager only for the light laugh, he joins Hynes and surpasses him in trying to restrain the giant of rage: 'hanging on to his elbow' as he waddles out to throw his biscuit tin toward the sun in its decline.

Among the *personae* of this chapter, Bergan, Doran, Lenehan, and Breen contribute most to the impression that the context is farcical and the community a group of drifters, drunks, lunatics, clowns, and sponges. The impression is delusory; the humour is in the eye of the I-observer and most of the characters are solid enough citizens. Stripped of its asides and narrated objectively, the action would be funny and pathetic and perhaps dull, but certainly not hilarious. However, building inevitably toward a broadly comic if not an orgasmic, climax, it contrasts with the muted developments and unaccented endings of the earlier sequences. The point is that we are entering a realm of more rather than less conventionally controlled presentation. If the day has been filled with 'real' people seriously engaged by a world that screens them from their deeper human concerns, the night relaxes that engagement in order to mime the internal conflicts, expose the roots of identity, and, most important, to reorient and reintegrate the chief *personae*. The cosmic-psychic drama exposes us to the disruptive and explosive but relatively predictable and rigid conventions of farce.[7]

Though the action described in 'Cyclops' has taken place at about 5 P.M., darkness prevails in the pub on all levels. It is a dark place, anger and violence darken the air, prejudice darkens the minds of men, drink befuddles their brains. Without warning, Joyce turns to subjective (even myopic) anecdotal narrative, a primitive form with an honourable lineage in Irish literary and public circles.[8] The delightfully spiteful narrator, who makes no attempt to cover up his fringe morality and his unacceptable profession, draws us into his confidence and into the pub universe, disarms us with wit and verbal vigour. By his very presence he obviates the need for the conventional narrator and the possibility of recording anyone else's thought. He manages to combine the roles of chronicler, commentator, companion, and clown while determining the mode of our apprehension, and epitomizing in his person a lower Dublin (and hence universal) milieu.

Perforce, his is a functionally forked tongue. If his own descriptive and evaluative remarks are in lower-class dialect and cant, he records the characters' words, as might an objective literary narrator, in a variety of voices. However false his opinions, his eye, his ear, and his memory rival those of the artist or the camera. Furthermore, the

---

[7] For an account of the thematic use of farce in *Ulysses* see my 'Forms of Folly in Joyce: a Study of Clowning in *Ulysses*', *ELH*, XXXIV (June 1967), 260–283.

[8] See Barrington's *Personal Sketches of His Own Times*, which features popular anecdotes of Irish social life in the eighteenth century; George Moore's *Hail and Farewell* with its sketches of the Dublin literary scene; and of course Oliver St. John Gogarty's 'gossipaceous' books. To this list we should prefix the work of another Irishman, Sir Richard Steele, whose mimetic strategies parallel Joyce's. Above all Joyce makes use of living models, the born story tellers one finds in any Irish pub. He delights in the Irishman's ability to spin a yarn filled with circumstantial detail and garnished with wit.

very consistency and coherence of his attitude, his enjoyment of language, his relative detachment, and the fact that his biases and condition lead him to tar everybody (whom he thinks inferior) with the same brush, make his extravagant opinions frequently compelling.

Just as there is a tension within the narrative persona, there is a clear tension between our informed reading of the events and our enjoyment of the biased presentation, between the delightful if disturbing surface and the human experience it conveys. We laugh in full awareness that we are being manipulated, but our laughter is frequently tinged with regret and misgiving, if not distaste. In the following passage, for example, the sentiments are crude enough to make even an anti-Semite twinge, though, as often happens, the rhetoric of rejection permits a free enjoyment of the rhetorical process itself:

> Courthouse my eye and your pockets hanging down with gold
> and silver. Mean bloody scut. Stand us a drink itself. Devil a sweet
> fear! There's a jew for you! All for number one. Cute as a shithouse
> rat. Hundred to five. (341.11)

This staccato utterance, the narrator's *cri de coeur* (the 'your' and the implied present tense are crucial), appropriately recalls the stichomythia of Greek old comedy. The possibility that Bloom has money he won't spend on treats is an occasion for comic outrage far in excess of its stimulus, for the narrator was at the time drinking his second pint. (Unless, of course, we assume that a present thirst elicits retrospective rage.) The whole statement is belied by our knowledge of Bloom's honest impecuniosity and unstinting charity, a knowledge that undercuts and in a sense doubles the humour of the speaker's overstatement.

Paralleling and punctuating the citizen's swelling mood, the narrator's rage underscores the socially acceptable reason for his own indignation: (present) thirst rather than hate. It belies basic discontent, hopeless frustration, and the absence of real values. In this context, words, conventional gestures of rage, mockery, and scorn, become action:

> But begob I was just lowering the heel of the pint when I saw
> the citizen getting up to waddle to the door, puffing and blowing
> with the dropsy and he cursing the curse of Cromwell on him, bell,
> book and candle in Irish, spitting and spatting out of him and Joe

and little Alf round him like a leprechaun trying to peacify him.
(341.41)

We are suddenly made aware through this remarkably precise but clearly hyperbolic description that the citizen is physically an unworthy opponent even for Bloom.[9] The effect is, of course, not pity for the bloated old ruin but amusement at his ineffectual progress. The narrator's position again undercuts his statement. He was unmoved but diverted by the episode, preoccupied with his own drink, truly for 'number one'. If the whole sentence recounts a continuous action, the details render it comically discordant, affecting us as might a keystone cops sequence. The comedy is clearly in the mockery, in words like 'waddle', 'puffing and blowing', and the slangy 'peacify', and in the image of Alf as a 'leprechaun'.

But there is another element. A theatrical distance is gained by the narrator's self-placement. If at times he has identified with the ranter, sharing, if nothing else, his thirst, at this moment he is the coolest of observers of the hot action, the least charitable. Every presentation of disorder *presupposes* an equivalent sense of order and coherence. By exposing an impromptu eruption of folly, the speaker *imposes* on it a sort of sanity and order and *asserts*, for the benefit of his silent audience, the priorities of order. To this effect he tardily apostrophizes the irate citizen in whose presence he hardly dares open his mouth:

> Arrah, sit down on the parliamentary side of your arse for Christ' sake and don't be making a public exhibition of yourself. Jesus, there's always some bloody clown or other kicking up a bloody murder about bloody nothing. (342.9)

For all the absurdity of the moment, we are not immersed in folly when a speaker can reflect on the legal consequence of a violent action in the midst of an excited reenactment:

> Gob, if he got that lottery ticket [the biscuit tin] on the side of his poll he'd remember the gold cup, he would so, but begob the citizen would have been lagged for assault and battery and Joe for aiding and abetting. (345.7)

Clearly, loyalty to reason and accuracy outweighs even prejudice, while love of a good story and lively malice outweigh loyalty to any

---

[9] A parallel circumstance differently treated is Gerty MacDowell's limping exit in 'Nausicaa'.

cause. Similarly, the speaker's inactivity at the scene of the action makes him doubly active in his recounting, while his gifts as a mimic give him a reliability almost equal to that of the impersonal (and seemingly invisible) narrator of the early chapters. In fact, this last aspect of his art is what most softens the transition from an objective to a subjective perspective, from day to night: this aspect plus the highly individuated accent of his speech. For the monologue mediates between the stream of consciousness and its absence, between the narrator of the earlier chapters and the force behind the innovations in the later ones.

Joyce has invented a speaker with powers of organization far beyond those of the ordinary teller of tales. Yet, through the engrossing texture of his account, with some help from the asides which distract us from the narrative improbabilities and the proliferating details, he has managed to make the account seem natural and uncontrived. It is only after a close inspection of the apparent chaos that we discover how carefully entrances are controlled, distance is adjusted, motifs are alternated, and how characters are made to contribute both to the action and to the spectrums of attitudes and social position.

In a fairly typical five-page section of the narrative (300–305), the speaker continues or introduces at least fourteen different and more or less clearly distinguishable topics. While discreetly advancing the action, these artfully interwoven elements help contribute to our sense of a social gathering characterized by random activity. (1) *Bloom's* presence is the first topic introduced on page 300. (His behaviour, culminating in a spurious unmasking, may be thought of as a developing motif.) Called earlier 'the prudent member' he is alluded to here as 'that bloody freemason' by the citizen disturbed by his alien presence outside the pub. The citizen's remark drops into the void, displaced by Alf's discussion of hanging and the 'Bundle of whisps' of 'hangmen's letters' which he takes from his pocket.[10] We recall Stephen's *dio boia* (213.23) and see the 'hang-

[10] Joyce has introduced the letter motif in 'Telemachus' with 'the mailboat clearing the harbour mouth' (5.11). See also Bannon's card from Westmeath, Deasy's hoof-and-mouth letter, and Stephen's telegram. These are complemented by the letters from Milly, Boylan, and Martha Clifford, and old Virag-Bloom's suicide note.

man' god as the spirit of this popular place.[11] (2) *Violence* as a symptom of social evil is translated into a mode of behaviour only at the end of the chapter, but the violent subjects which constitute the cyclops' nourishment proliferate in the opening pages. By contrast, as the atmosphere becomes explosive, the conversation, thanks to Bloom's intervention, turns increasingly on morality, religion and ethics. (3) Bob Doran's intrusive question refers us back to the topics introduced earlier when Alf Bergan exploded into the pub: *madness* and *Breen.* (4) Doran's maundering leads the narrator to underscore the little drunkard's symbolic and sympathetic function as an illustration of the *effects of alcohol*: 'Bob's a queer chap when the porter's up in him'. In the inverted world, 'harmless' drunkenness and gambling are almost virtues, sobriety is close to vice. The pathetic Doran, like the improvident Dignam, helps characterize the pub's role in the seventh city. (Repeated and otherwise counterproductive intrusions reenforce an implied Dignam-Doran relationship which parallels the Breen-Bloom coupling.) (5) It is Alf who introduces the topic of *Dignam's death*, the cause of Bloom's visit to the pub. (6) The seemingly arbitrary shift to Dignam advances the motif structure by introducing the topic of *ghosts*, emblems of the unquiet past, and providing the occasion for the ghost interlude after which we return to earlier topics (1,2): *Bloom* enters the group and a *hangman's letter* is read and discussed. (7) By refusing to accept a drink (but accepting a phallic cigar) Bloom violates the pub decorum reintroducing the topic of *treating*. During the discussion of capital punishment, Bloom is associated with the (8) *dog Garryowen* (a projection of age, irrationality, and looming violence), for whom the narrator has an understandable professional dislike. (The speaker's professional isolation, second only, one would think, to the hangman's, is a covert motif in this chapter, one that helps explain his ambivalent stance and shifting distance.) (9) An allusion to the hanged man's erection introduces the topic of *virility* associated here with love-futility-death. (10) It also gives Bloom,

[11] Since 'Kiernan's hobby was the collection of exhibits connected with crime', the pub was decorated with such items as 'counterfeit coins (which he nailed to his counter), weapons that had been used in murders, a piece of rope which had bound the Sheares brothers, the glass of the hangman who hanged them, and other hangmen's glasses' (Gilbert, p. 258). While omitting the specifics, Joyce manages to convey the spirit of the place and its grisly associations.

who, according to Joyce's notes, is 'excited wants to say many things',[12] a chance to reveal his *intellectual superiority* thus challenging the citizen's position and affronting the others' ignorance. (11) The great man's knee-jerk response is to underscore Bloom's alien status and his own superiority by discoursing on *Irish history*, (12) *British injustice*, and (13) *'new Ireland'* or *social and political improvement*, topics about which he would blather indefinitely were it not for Bloom's argumentativeness. (14) The developing exchange, a dull *battle of wits* or rather a battle of dull wits, will culminate in what Joyce calls in his notes a 'cursing duel'.[13]

It is, of course, difficult if not impossible and perhaps even wrong to label all of the topics or limit their implications. But this approximation of the bare bones should point up Joyce's method of juggling themes and controlling the action through the narrative persona, while sustaining interest through a device comparable to conventional novelistic unresolved action. (Conversation, like subvocal thought, often has this quality.) The reader, like the projected listener, is befuddled, puzzled but intrigued and entertained by the richness of the surface. He is also encouraged, if not conditioned, to attend, however subliminally, to the various trends and to organize them within the developing structure. In opposition to the inconclusive and generally unconcluded talk in 'Aeolus', the topic-laden narrative of 'Cyclops' leads (on the naturalistic level at least) to the inevitable catastrophe, a false resolution. So does the apparently random entry pattern of the minor characters, each with his particular position and preoccupations, each more or less ignorant of what has preceded his arrival, and each altering by his presence the balance of power and the tone of the discussion. If its explosive ending places the chapter in opposition to all the earlier chapters that remain open, the narrative action (as opposed to the asides) discreetly contributes to the process of the book by extending already established themes, furthering the central action and the dialectic of the chapter styles, while filling one and perhaps two temporal slots.

Before proceeding to a treatment of the time and place-annulling asides, we should attend briefly to the question of the locus and time of the I-narration. What little evidence we have concerning

---

[12] Herring, *Joyce's 'Ulysses' Notesheets*, 'Cyclops' 5, line 2 (p. 100).
[13] *Ibid.*, 'Cyclops' 5, line 8 (p. 100).

this event is found in three porterous passages which might otherwise escape our attention:

1. Ah! Ow! Don't be talking! I was blue mouldy for the want of that pint. Declare to God I could hear it hit the pit of my stomach with a click. (298.27)

2. Didn't I tell you? As true as I'm drinking this porter if he was at his last gasp he'd try to downface you that dying was living. (329.32)

3. Goodbye Ireland I'm going to Gort. So I just went round to the back of the yard to pumpship and begob (hundred shillings to five) while I was letting off my (*Throwaway* twenty to) letting off my load gob says I to myself I knew he was uneasy in his (two pints off of Joe and one in Slattery's off) in his mind to get off the mark to (hundred shillings is five quid) and when they were in the (dark horse) Pisser Burke was telling me card party and letting on the child was sick (gob, must have done about a gallon) flabbyarse, of a wife speaking down the tube *she's better* or *she's* (ow!) all a plan so he could vamoose with the pool if he won or (Jesus, full up I was) trading without a licence (ow!) Ireland my nation says he (hoik! phthook!) never be up to those bloody (there's the last of it) Jerusalem (ah!) cuckoos. (335.25)

The famous gonorrheal micturition (3) is ambiguously connected to the action of the I-narrative. Virtually a microcosm for the entire chapter, it imitates both the development of the action and the fragmentation achieved by the asides. But its exact status is puzzling unless we realize that we are witnessing two parallel activities artfully mingled: the urination that intervenes between Lenehan's attack and Nolan's defence, and a second urination that takes place drinks later in an unnamed pub. The key to this is in the parenthetical asides. The exclamations of pain and satisfaction are disturbingly immediate, but their indeterminate temporality needs the matter of fact 'there's the last of it' to confirm the dual time. The reader has been drawn gradually into the context of the moment, sharing not only the experience of micturition but the immediate unpleasantness of the spit, before he can fully appreciate the ambiguity of his and the narrator's situation. Retrospectively, he may see the opening commonplace ('Goodbye Ireland I'm going to Gort') as an early clue.

Such hints help us reconstruct a bit of the secondary context and to explain the strategy of the chapter as it relates to the stylistic development of the book. Since it is doubtful that the speaker is addressing the words in parentheses to himself, we must assume that the unnamed treater-listener has also gone off to 'pumpship' and that the words are meant to do more than interrupt the narration and lower the speaker further in our eyes while momentarily linking him to us on a sensual level. (Thanks to the lapses in the narrative, the repetitions, the sense of physical strain, we experience his painful urination vicariously.) The narrator has had time to visit at least one pub after Kiernan's and probably more, time enough to swallow as many as eight pints of free porter ('gob, must have done about a gallon'), even if we allow for hyperbole. He has probably told the tale at least once before and he is retelling it now in the hope of shaming another dupe into buying drinks. We watch him recover a fumble, cutting short his catalogue of treats and treaters to return to his attack on Bloom, showing that he too is 'uneasy in his . . . mind to get off the mark'. The hour is late, possibly later than the final 'cuckoo' of 'Nausicaa', or 9 P.M.

The first of the three passages cited above is the only other moment in 'Cyclops' when we experience a direct sensual connexion with the speaker. Like the urination paragraph, it may simultaneously convey two distinct but identical events. The exclamations that open it can be more than signs of a recollected sensation so immediate that it must be expressed in the present tense. They may also refer to a present experience, the most recently purchased pint. Less obviously, the 'Ah! Ow!' foreshadow the '(ow!) . . . (ow!) . . . (ah!)' of the urination, where the order is significantly reversed. The second of our three citations is more conclusive. Here the use of direct address may be ambiguous, a mere rhetorical tick, but the act of swearing by a drink in the present tense illuminates the whole chapter. Taken together, these passages justify 'Cyclops' as a night chapter and help explain the radical departure implicit in the use of the burlesque asides.

The asides belong to a nocturnal decorum generated by a single impulse if not a single persona, a resourceful clown of many masks, a figure apparently poles apart from the self-effacing narrator. This figure may be thought of as an *arranger*, a nameless and whimsical-seeming authorial projection whose presence is first strongly felt in 'Aeolus', where he starts usurping the prerogatives of the objective narrator by interjecting the frequently intrusive mock-headlines.[14] To 'Scylla and Charybdis', 'Wandering Rocks', and 'Sirens', he contributes less obvious but more whimsical effects.[15] Finally, in 'Cyclops', where his prime effects are juxtaposed as asides to the predictable voice of the outcast narrator, he comes into his own, obliging us to equate his presence with the diminution of lucidity, the assertion of the unconscious and instinctual side of experience, the inexplicable realm of darkness through which light ultimately shines darkly. Unlike the I-narrative, which, for all its irreverence and hyperbole, conveys a continuous and evolving action and, with astonishing concision, suggests much more, the asides are usually at variance with the meaningful content of the chapter. Still, by obeying the law of unpredictability, the basic principle of farce, they mimic the factice chaos of the after-hours spree, helping to turn the barroom brawl into a metaphor for the disorder of melting minds which accompanies the decline of the sun. Since the tale is being reenacted during the 'present time' of 'Cyclops', the asides, by pointing up the tension between the two times and the two lights, coordinate the complementary modes of 'Oxen of the Sun' and 'Cyclops'.

If most of the asides are irreverently intrusive, taking off from, rather than clarifying the action, over a third of them (eleven in all), contain specifics relevant, if not essential, to the plot. Several are straight enough to belong to the daylight world of journalistic pop-culture (see the boxing match on page 318 and the execution sequence on pages 306–310).[16] One passage from the narrative proper could qualify as an aside (see the Alaki's visit on page 334) while at least one other might belong to both worlds. Further, though there is indeed quite a range of styles and subjects treated in the asides, none of them exceeds the probable rhetorical and intellectual

[14] Joyce has prepared us for this intrusive presence by introducing curiously ambiguous passages as early as 'Telemachus', varying his techniques in the first six chapters, and insisting on abrupt and disconcerting transitions. But it is only here that we face a presence that the reader cannot naturalize.

[15] Ultimately, we might attribute to him the very chapter shifts, inexplicable naturalistically and only partly related to the Odyssey parallels.

[16] A similar mixing and blending can, of course, be seen elsewhere in the book, as for example in 'Aeolus' where the headlines occasionally belong to the action.

level of the crowd in the pub. We may group them all conveniently under a handful of categories that are both subliterary and non-personal,[17] as opposed to the highly literary, wittily cultivated and individualized voices in 'Oxen of the Sun'. Given the context in which Bloom passes for a well-informed and literate man, journalistic flummery, the Irish literary revival, romance revival, folklore, and religious pastiches suffice to cast crazy lights on the action. The adequacy of this tactic is perhaps best illustrated by the ease with which Joyce inserts what appears to be a literal transcription of the journalistic parody into the narrative texture without calling undue attention to his use of virtually identical techniques in the execution aside. We must conclude that the disparity between the continuous and the discontinuous elements in the chapter is both real and only apparent, that incoherence and irreverence are in complex ways yoked to reverence and a respect for forms and even for human values. This is also true of the obvious satirical content, since satire always implies respect for some sort of reason and a positive if implicit order.

There is throughout the chapter a discreet blending and mixing of the levels of presentation, but at certain points the interaction is transparently obvious. The description of the Keogh-Bennett match, a paradigm for the English-Irish conflict, is suggestive of the pagan-christian conflicts of Roman times. Since both conflicts are projected by the pub-group in which Bloom appears as a mock-serious Christ, the remarkably undistorted account functions at once as a satirical allusion to present commitments and a sign equating two historical moments. Rhetorically pandering to brutal tastes, it is set off against the Irish patriots' savage verbal attacks on British brutality. More, we must see this mock-war in the light of Stephen's view that the boys on the playing field in 'Nestor' are expressing the bloody tendencies of a nightmarish history. This bit of reportage, which could just as well have been cited verbatim by the I-narrator, is at one end of a spectrum stretching roughly to the vision of Bloom-Elijah's ascent, an aside which makes no pretence of being logical or time-bound but which, while seeming out of time altogether, links us ironically to the daily cycle and the sun's trajectory, to the infinite return, and to planetary motion, the dimensions in short of 'Ithaca'. On the

---

[17] See Appendix to this chapter.

other hand, the acceptability of the boxing-match as rhetoric and history also places it on an axis linking narrational time and the temporal lapses of the asides.

A few examples should suffice both to illustrate further this interaction and to point up the role and range of the asides. A passage in legalese inflates the significance of the Herzog-Geraghty affair while giving us names and other details missing from the narrator's irreverent account. It apparently operates much as do the catechism responses in 'Ithaca', but since the language is unalloyed legal jargon, however inappropriate to its object, we should think also of the Bennett-Keogh aside. Like most of the informative asides, these two give us information we could do without. But their effect is to telescope the rhetorical distance. The arranger's sixth utterance illustrates another tactic. Delivered in nineteenth-century archaic or romance revival diction (a debased foreshadowing of the Malory pastiche in 'Oxen of the Sun'), it is a good example of the mirror technique by which the arranger introduces humour even where the action is not intrinsically funny. (I quote both the aside and the complementary paragraph):

> And lo, as they quaffed their cup of joy, a godlike messenger came swiftly in, radiant as the eye of heaven, a comely youth, and behind him there passed an elder of noble gait and countenance, bearing the sacred scrolls of law, and with him his lady wife, a dame of peerless lineage, fairest of her race.
>
> Little Alf Bergan popped in round the door and hid behind Barney's snug, squeezed up with the laughing, and who was sitting up there in the corner that I hadn't seen snoring drunk, blind to the world, only Bob Doran. I didn't know what was up and Alf kept making signs out of the door. And begob what was it only that bloody old pantaloon Denis Breen in his bath slippers with two bloody big books tucked under his oxter and the wife hotfoot after him, unfortunate wretched woman trotting like a poodle. I thought Alf would split. (298.30)

The stilted prose of the aside, though incongruous, is funny largely in terms of the referents which, exceptionally, it precedes. It functions as well to point up Breen's role and the Breen-Bloom parallel, by focussing on Breen's traditional role as pantaloon, the *Commedia del'Arte* model for Shylock, and by echoing the preceding aside, in which Bloom's name appears for the first time:

—I saw him before I met you, says I, sloping around by Pill lane and Greek street with his cod's eye counting up all the guts of the fish.

Who comes through Michan's land, bedight in sable armour? O'Bloom, the son of Rory: it is he. Impervious to fear is Rory's son: he of the prudent soul. (297.36)

Here the inverse strategy applies; the informative aside mirrors the narrator's passage. It is fitting that the styles are strikingly similar since both sets of paired passages deal with wandering comic outsiders.

There is little in the earlier chapters to compare with the verbal extravagance of the second aside with its catalogue of improbable flora and fauna (salt-water fish for St Michan's nonexistent streams and exotic trees for its missing forests). Such exuberance is in keeping with the arranger's freedom from the daytime controls. Still, it is accompanied by formal checks more rigid than anything not related to the arranger's role. Each aside is locked securely in its own particular mode of mockery, with its own inner consistency and predictability; each is a closed structure; each is a completed action, a statement, or simply a self-contained rhetorical unit.

The most remarkable, however, is the execution aside (306–310). At first glance this four-and-a-half page narrative burlesque seems little more than a delightful irrelevance, a rollicking satirical spoof. It is among the loosest passages in the book, larded with worn-out verbiage, expanded by a Rabelaisian catalogue. But it is also, as the following sentence will show, a model of its kind, pointed, varied, and relatively concise, with significant links to other chapters:

A posse of Dublin Metropolitan police superintended by the Chief Commissioner *in person maintained order* in *the vast throng* for whom the York Street brass and reed band *whiled away the intervening time by admirably rendering* on their *blackdraped instruments* the *matchless melody endeared to us from the cradle* by Speranza's *plaintive muse*. (306.35; my italics.)

Such tired language comments at once on journalistic prose, pub discussions, and public morality. As do the actions described elsewhere, it also suggests the farcical excesses of the pantomime. So closely controlled are the rhetorical connectives, so meaningless are the flourishes, that we are on the verge of chaos while still in sight

of stylistic norms. This aside points us toward at least three parallels:
the freely mannered pastiches of 'Oxen of the Sun' where the original
style is generally more scrupulously imitated; the terse 'factual' and
objective prose of the 'Circe' stage directions which describe pantomime extravagance; and the limp Sancho-Panzesque narrative style
in 'Eumaeus', where the voice is Bloom's but the thoughts are those
of a supercilious mocker similar to the persona behind the masks in
'Cyclops'. The latter parallel helps illustrate how free the arranger
can be with both his material and the naturalistic context. No one,
not even Bloom, speaks or writes such circumlocutory prose:

> All the same Bloom (properly so dubbed) was rather surprised
> at their memories for in nine cases out of ten it was a case of tar-
> barrels, and not singly but in their thousands, and then complete
> oblivion because it was twenty odd years. Highly unlikely, of course,
> there was even a shadow of truth in the stories and, even supposing,
> he thought a return highly inadvisable, all things considered.
> (649.11)

The reader of these sentences, like the reader of the 'Cyclops' sentence cited above, is engaged and delighted by the process of not-
telling, the prose of antinarration which Samuel Beckett has since
perfected and applied to the service of negation. In short, his role
as perceiver has been reversed despite the fact that he can still catch
and retain allusions to other parts of the action. His mind is forced
to relax, but he remains tensed for clues and allusions, suspended between joy and concern.

The execution aside, full as it is of goodies and irrelevancies,
has a number of functions. First, it provides a pattern and materials
for the martyrdom of Bloom in 'Circe', a fact that illustrates once
more the freedom of the arranger from the limits of a naturalistic
decorum and the characters' minds. Second, it interacts with other
parodies. Third, as one of the few narrative sequences in the book,
complete in the Aristotelian sense of having beginning, middle, and
end, it mocks the very idea of completion. At the same time, it in-
trudes upon and breaks the rhythm of another narrative sequence
whose coherence is delightfully marred by the practice of inserting
asides. Fourth, it is a testing ground for technics that are at once
incongruously joined and harmoniously attuned to the spirit of mockery. Finally, it toys gravely with the conflicting moralities of the
nationalists and the imperialists living under the Edwardian um-

brella. All of this is quite apart from any intention to parody the *Odyssey* or a ritual execution or to suggest the quality of outrage present in the hangman's letter, in the nationalistic argument, or in the Police Gazette item inspected by Hynes.

It is axiomatic in *Ulysses* that the principles of unity and control are most in evidence precisely at the point where comic diffuseness takes over. In 'Cyclops' we have a narrative with obvious development and resolution, to say nothing of a dramatic frame. If the asides are characterized by their variety and their framebreaking propensity, and by the fact that they variously disrupt, mesh with, reflect, neutralize, and invade the narrative, undercutting, refocussing, and reenforcing the irreverence of the narrator, they are also consistent with the farcical forms appropriate to the night and most particularly with that native form, the Dublin Christmas pantomime.

Like the pantomime, this chapter has a simple plot based on a popular model which it distorts: Ulysses' encounter with the Cyclops, a trickster tale which was already treated farcically in classical times (see, for example, the only extant satyr play, Euripedes' *Cyclops*).[18] The prime tactic of the pantomime is not the elaboration upon a burlesqued model (children's tales or nursery rhymes, folktales, literary bywords, etc.) but the obfuscation of its dramatic development. If the means are often trivial, the goal is after all only mindless frivolity and rollicking farce. Not only is the main plot line broadly humourous and irreverent; it is also repeatedly interrupted by irrelevant if entertaining skits or songs, vaudeville or musichall routines. Even the resolution comes as just one more elaborate side-effect in a loose-jointed entertainment rather than as the inevitable and satisfying conclusion. Characteristically, the end takes the form of a transformation scene artificially engineered to punctuate and reconcile the jumbled tendencies. The transformation scene may well be just another piece of spectacle, radically different in conception from either the skits or the body of the action, something

---

[18] James Atherton has brilliantly described the pantomime element in *Finnegans Wake* and the tradition that Joyce was exploiting ('*Finnegans Wake:* "The Gist of the Pantomime" ', *Accent*, XV, Winter 1956, 14–16.) In 'Forms of Folly in Joyce: A Study of Clowning in *Ulysses*', (n. 7 above), I have dealt with some aspects of the pantomime in *Ulysses* where it contributes to the thematic content and formal texture of the evening chapters. A good recent study of the pantomime is *Harlequin in His Element*, by David Mayer, Cambridge, Mass., 1969.

akin on a farcical range to the conclusion of comedy or the *deus ex machina* ending of some classical tragedies. The point is that the pantomime was, and still is for many Dubliners, a popular form, more than the equal of the music that informs 'Sirens', a sort of public language to which the clientele of Kiernan's pub might respond directly. It is also a form appropriate to the dual temporality of 'Cyclops', and to the evening hours in general; for it dislocates conventional perception and imposes a logic of calculated incoherence, a secret order roughly analogous to that of dreams and the subconscious.

I shall not dwell on the numerous references in *Ulysses* to the pantomime and even to the Gaiety Theatre for which Bloom failed to write a 'topical song . . . entitled *If Brian Boru could but come back and see old Dublin now*, commissioned by Michael Gunn' in 1893 (678.26). We may note that all three protagonists refer to pantomime skits, actors, and characters several times, and that, like everything else in *Ulysses*, such references are more than window dressing or topical allusion. They constitute an important thematic strand and perhaps provide a clue to Joyce's method in the later chapters. To support this view, we have several notes under the heading 'Cyclops': one alludes to an Irish pantomime dealing with Brian Boru and Finn MacCool, both of whom figure importantly in *Finnegans Wake*; two others refer to the pub tale of how the Irish soldier Buckley shot a Russian general during the Crimean war. This tale, a favourite of Joyce's father, was to become in *Finnegans Wake* a televised skit of the pantomime variety inserted in a riotous public-house chapter.[19] A final allusion was appended to the partial first draft of 'Circe' as the last item of a schema: 'Transformation Scene'. Doubtless Joyce associated both of these chapters with the pantomime.

How does the pantomime format inform 'Cyclops'? First, the main plot, true to convention, gives a mock-heroic dimension to a heroic tale. The device of the first-person narrator telling the tale in low jargon from an outsider's antiheroic perspective is a good prose analogue for the theatrical burlesque which draws its raw materials from literature, recast in stage dialect. The tale of Cyclops, like those of Nausicaa and Circe, is consistent with the sort of sub-

---

[19] Herring, *Joyce's 'Ulysses' Notesheets*, 'Cyclops' 1, line 39 (p. 82), and 'Cyclops' 5, line 65 (p. 102).

jects treated in the pantomime. It is doubtless no accident that these three Homeric analogies are among the most clearly stated and broadly burlesqued in the book.

The asides, too, have a pantomime function in the chapter. Timed and spaced irregularly and designed to vary the prose texture, they function as equivalents for the frequent scene breaks in the pantomime itself. The execution aside, for example, is a perfect skit, complete with comic song and mock sentiment, while the forester's wedding is a fine bit of pageantry. Many of the shorter asides could be treated chorally or mimed. But none of this should be taken too literally since the arranger, as surrogate producer and star performer, has created literary analogues for the form.

The two tactics, aside and I-narration, are reconciled in a transformation scene (similar to the vision of Rudy at the end of 'Circe') which resolves the episode into transcendental mirth:

> When lo, there came about them all a great brightness and they beheld the chariot wherein He stood ascend to heaven. . . . And they beheld Him even Him, ben Bloom Elijah, amid clouds of angels ascend to the glory of brightness at an angle of fortyfive degrees over Donohoe's in Little Green Street like a shot off a shovel. (345.22)

Bloom, as the westering sun, is properly elevated and deflated in this passage which briefly unites the method of the asides with the voice of the narrator. The last six words provide a break in the decorum equivalent to a wink from a pantomime angel still clad in the full glory of his transformation scene robes.

The farcical, which is most clearly embodied in Joyce's adaptation of pantomime conventions, overshadows but does not cancel out the serious or the simply comic dimension of 'Cyclops'. Bloom's grave encounter with overt hostility, his self-mastery and potential self-discovery help complicate the attitudes generated by this chapter since they are tensed against the multivalent irreverence of narration and asides. Similarly, the on-going development of the action, seen through the narrator's rhetoric and despite his attitudes and purposes, is tensed against the jangle of effects designed to break both rhythm and frame, imposing a factice chaos on the rather static environment. Finally, the dual temporality with its implications of dual mental sets is internally tensed and arched between 'Cyclops' and 'Oxen of the Sun', telescoping and expanding the evening sequences.

No metaphor will suffice to describe Joyce's accomplishment here, but perhaps an image from the *Symposium* will serve to underscore the thrust of the chapter. It is one of the most unlikely rogues of the day, a veritable Mulligan of a man, Alcibiades, who in one of the most brilliant of Plato's extended metaphors compares Socrates to a little clay Silenus: 'they're modelled with pipes or flutes in their hands, and when you open them down the middle there are little figures of gods inside'.[20] We may apply this metaphor to the understanding of the more outrageously farcical of Joyce's chapters which do indeed hide the gods within their grotesque bellies. Here the voice of dissolution is indeed the voice of a deeper and hitherto unrecognized order, the very spirit of reason within the dialectic of this novelistic universe.

*   *   *

APPENDIX: CATALOGUE OF THE ASIDES

In the following list, I have tried to suggest the range of possibilities and the fundamental coherence of the asides, most of which parody nineteenth-century adaptations of earlier styles. (In his notes Joyce describes some of his technics for 'Cyclops' as 'exaggeration of things previously given: [Superlatives]' and 'longwinded simile'.[21]) My descriptive categories are meant to be suggestive approximations. The asterisked items contain information about the main action:

292.31–293.16	*Herzog—legalese or language of contracts (not deformed)
293.38–294.32	heroic setting—Irish revival
294.35–295.32	same
296.5–297.27	hero described—irished Rabelais or simply hyperbolic Irish revival (heroic)
297.39–41	*Bloom—romance revival
298.30–34	*Bergan and the Breens—romance revival or 19th century Homeric

[20] *Plato: Collected Dialogues*, ed. Edith Hamilton and Huntington Cairns, New York, 1963, p. 566.

[21] Herring, *Joyce's 'Ulysses' Notesheets*, 'Cyclops' 2, lines 18, 20 (p. 86).

299.30–300.12	*Terry serves Alf—as above but broader
301.13–302.13	Dignam's ghost—theosophical
302.14–16	lament for Dignam (see also 303.10–11)—Irish revival
304.16–19	executioner—gothic revival
304.37–305.9	*hanged man's erection—medical journalese
306.23–310.38	the execution—human interest and public affairs journalese, high style (cf. burlesque on 334)
311.34–312.32	Garryowen's curse—cultural reportage
313.35–314.8	*Doran to Bloom—polite novelese
315.21–25	Black Liz—nursery rhyme
315.39–316.19	parliamentary—Hansard
316.39–317.5	Gaelic sports meeting—public reportage
318.29–319.19	*Bennett-Keogh match—sports reportage (not deformed)
319.37–320.3	*Molly and O'Molloy—romance revival
322.34–323.28	*law court—legal language mixed with epic and romance revival plus comic Irish reference
324.32–40	*Nolan's entrance—romance revival
325.22–26	*Lenehan drinks—Irish revival (heroic)
327.1–36	the wooded wedding—social reportage
329.23–29	on British corporal punishment—parody of the Apostles' Creed (provenance ambiguous)
331.39–332.28	the handkerchief—documented description, Irish archaeology
333.27–37	on love—graffiti
336.21–337.33	entry of Bloom's 'friends'—renaissance revival (?)
338.39–240.42	blessing the precincts—religious reportage
341.28–40	the cab-ship—epic revival
342.37–343.28	Bloom's departure ceremony—state visit reportage (cf. execution aside on 306 and burlesque on 334)
344.3–345.6	the seismic shock—scientific reportage
345.22–32	Bloom's theophany—Old Testament

NAUSICAA

Fritz Senn

The last scene of the preceding chapter transfigured Leopold Bloom and projected him skyward at a specified and ballistically advantageous angle. The ascendant curve is continued into the first part of 'Nausicaa', which gratifyingly exalts Bloom, at least as viewed from the favourable angle of one observer, from a particularly one-eyed, romanticized perspective. The observer, Gerty MacDowell, herself intently watched by Bloom, is in turn portrayed at her spectacular best, with fulsome touches and lavish colours. In addition, both she and Bloom are emotionally and physiologically exalted. 'Nausicaa' is a chapter of culminations, of aspirations and high expectations, of sky-gazing and firework-gazing, of ecstatic flights and raised limbs.

The sustained flight, in 'Nausicaa' as in 'Cyclops', owes much to the elevation of its language. Its heights are rhetorical. Stripped of its metaphorical props, the flight becomes no more than fleeing. The escape from the citizen's rage transforms itself into a mysterious embrace, with Bloom, lingering lovingly in a soft world slowly losing its harsh contours, seeking refuge and comfort for his afflictions in illusory fulfilment.

Like all ballistic curves, those described in 'Nausicaa' contain a rise, a climax, a descent, and an abrupt return to the ground. The movement is paralleled in such details as the rockets of the bazaar

fireworks, a ball thrown and kicked, a stick flung away, and a bat
flying to and fro. Within the human body, the movement corresponds to the surge of blood which animates Gerty's cheeks with
quaint blushes or a 'telltale flush' (349.16), implicitly contributing
to the underlying genital tumescence.

'branded as the lowest of the low' (354.25)

The protagonists' rise to unprecedented heights is counterpointed,
conspicuously enough, by a converse movement of which the
reader, who inevitably depreciates the various altitudes according to
his own scale, is very much aware and to which Gerty MacDowell
herself carefully closes her eyes. The parabola of the flight is a parable
of frustration and loneliness. In the setting of all-embracing love,
Bloom resorts to the most isolated form of sexual gratification, an
event made more poignant by his realization that a more vital and
more mutually fulfilling embrace has recently been staged at home.
Gerty too has been thwarted, by the loss of the attentions of her
boy, who has, of late, been distracted by an entirely different kind
of 'exhibition' (349.31, 352.7); and she is out to gain attention elsewhere. The way in which the two work off their disappointments
would have found little sympathy in any culture that produces these
frustrations, and none at all in the Ireland of 1904. Masturbation
is a sin in the Catholic context, and its essential sterility made it an
offence in the Judaic code. We can translate the term into more
contemporary condemnatory terms, such as 'self-deception' and
'escapism'.

In Gerty's and Bloom's brief coming together, there is no coition
(they do not go together, co-ire); both merely linger in relative
proximity, within visual range, and then continue on their lonely
ways, Gerty on hers, moreover, with a limp. There is no consummation, no physical touch (only, we are told, 'consummate tact', and
even that is used to 'pass . . . off' something unpleasant; 363.24),
no verbal contact. Fewer words are spoken in 'Nausicaa' than in the
other chapters (except the basically silent 'Proteus' and 'Penelope').
Two monologues, one indirect, one direct, the one before, the other
after, are its suitable expression. The cheap satisfaction is brought
out in a style of cheap fiction, lacking vitality, incapable of communication.

'Nausicaa' then is a profitable chapter for the critic who may rise to the occasion and comment, with Cyclopean assurance, on the multiple inadequacies displayed by the two lovers, treating them, according to his inclination, with benign condescension or downright contempt. 'Nausicaa' yields ample illustration for the marriage counsellor, the preacher, or the moral guide. The moralistic attitude first manifested itself in public through the activities of the Society for the Prevention of Vice, which instituted legal proceedings in 1920, thus stopping the book's first flight in serial publication and bringing it abruptly down to court. Sentences similar to that pronounced in the Court of Special Sessions in New York, in 1921, have been reiterated since, with some relevant fashionable modifications: nowadays the author is generally enlisted on the right side; he is in fact represented as implicitly adding his voice to those expressing righteous disapprobation of his characters.

'Look at it other way round' (380.28)

There is no intrinsic necessity to restrict one's views to censorious glances from superior vantage points. These may even blind us to some of the chapter's scintillating delights. One of the potential moral effects of *Ulysses* is that it can condition us, more than any previous novel, to suspend or, at any rate, postpone the moralizing tendency that consists in dispensing blame and credit, in favour of a series of constant readjustments and a fluctuating awareness of the complexity of motivation. 'Nausicaa' at least enables us, besides the pleasures of judicial evaluation, to experience sympathy and to arrive at the kind of intricate understanding that makes the attitude of forgiveness (cf. 358.17) just as pointless as its opposite.

In the imperfect world of Dublin, 1904, the imperfect solution that the two characters allow themselves to be driven to, passively reactive rather than passionately active, does have some advantages. There is relief from various tensions, relief from the conflicts of aggression and prejudice, as in Barney Kiernan's, and relief also from the depressing squalor of the Dignams' household. Bloom's foreignness, usually a cause of trouble, stands him in good stead in 'Nausicaa', heightened as it is by some spurious effects. There is compensation for recent setbacks. Bloom knows one has to be 'Thankful for small mercies' (368.21). For the moment he feels young again. At the end of the day, the encounter is listed positively as having been accompanied by 'pleasant reflection' (722), and there have been few enough such moments. Substitute satisfactions are better than no satisfactions at all, and Bloom, for one, appreciates the benefits to be derived from the momentary shutting off of unpleasant aspects of reality: 'Glad I didn't know it when she was on show' (368.4).

Throughout, *Ulysses* interfuses reality with illusion, and in some parts the validity of the distinction is even challenged (it seems to have disappeared entirely in *Finnegans Wake*). 'Nausicaa' varies the theme in its own manner, ringing the changes on the mind's inventiveness in superimposing satisfactions of which reality is acutely devoid. Illusion, partly 'optical illusion' (376.26), is one way of 'smoothing over life's tiny troubles' (347.25). Without some tempering from the imagination, reality might well become unbearable. Belief in 'intercessory power' (356.32) or in the curative and beautifying power of advertised goods performs such tempering functions, and so does art. To afford illusory gratifications is one of the legitimate functions of fiction, of highbrow literature no less than of Gerty's favourite reading matter.

Some techniques for putting up with bothersome situations and creating compensatory patterns are compulsorily learned in our childhood: 'Tommy Caffrey could never be got to take his castor oil unless it was Cissy Caffrey that held his nose and promised him the scatty heel of the loaf of brown bread with golden syrup on' (346.36). That sets the tone for 'Nausicaa', similarly coated with syrupy 'sweetness' (360.23). When baby Boardman is deprived of his ball, his frustration is dealt with by two other mechanisms prominent in the chapter, titillation and the conjuring up of fictitious scenes from a life far higher than one's own, rendered in stylized form: 'And she tickled tiny tot's two cheeks to make him forget and played here's the lord mayor, here's his two horses, here's his gingerbread carriage and here he walks in, chinchopper, chinchopper, chinchopper chin' (353.12).

Such escape mechanisms, basically aimed at diverting attention from disagreeable aspects of reality, also have some positive value. Bloom at least meets a being who, by virtue of whatever distorting projections, seems to accept him and to desire him. Something approaching love does, after all, take place, and a kind of rapport is established: 'Still it was a kind of language between us' (372.35). The lack of communication in *Ulysses* is perhaps less surprising than the occasional occurrence of *some* imperfect communication. Gerty, injured and slighted, presents herself to her best advantage for one short span, at the proper distance, with just the right degree of illumination to increase her glamour (which is what the advice she gets from the fashion page amounts to). Even after the release of tension and after the effects of the stage setting have worn off, Bloom is capable of sympathizing with her. 'Poor girl' is one of his first thoughts. Nor does he appear to be any more depressed or guilt-ridden than we know him to have been previously.

The pathetic climax of the two chance lovers resembles Bloom's confrontation with the citizen, an earlier blend of conviction, tumescent courage, irritation, and pulpit sentimentality, where Bloom is sublimely exalted as well as ridiculously abased—and there it would be equally hard to place him, or the events, conclusively on any evaluative scale.

After Bloom's precipitate proclamation of the gospel of love, he does in fact embark on a tour of love in its varieties. The visit to the Dignams is an act of charity; romantic love culminates in 'Nausicaa' (which is steeped in colours of loveliness, including even the 'lovely' dog Garryowen); the depths of sexuality are charted in 'Circe'; paternal love comes into its own from 'Oxen of the Sun' to 'Ithaca'. At the same time these pursuits are also patently motivated by an unwillingness to face domestic realities. As against any normative ideals, Bloom's performances fall short. Still, in his encounter with Gerty he comes within visible distance of his own definition of love as 'the opposite of hatred'. The abortive message that Bloom writes into the sand and effaces immediately, 'I . . . AM. A.' (381), happens to contain, besides himself, the Latin root *ama-*, love, no doubt outside his own consciousness and yet somehow 'done half by design' (382.2), indicative more of a wish, unfulfilled like the rest of them, than an achievement. In one respect Bloom attains the Christian aim of forgiving his most recent persecutor, the citizen: 'Look at it other way round. Not so bad then. Perhaps not to hurt he meant' (380.28).

'matters feminine' (346.15)

With the 'Nausicaa' chapter we enter, for the first time, a predominantly female world. So far Stephen and Bloom have moved in a masculine environment. No single woman was present in 'Cyclops', except for glimpses of wretched Mrs Breen as the servant of her master (who, through the postcard 'U.P.: up', is treated to his own rise and fall). Now we are immersed in the soft cadences of feminine fiction, with three girls in the foreground dominating a triad of young males, reducing Bloom to the role of a spectator. Gerty's is the first feminine mind that is unfolded before us at any length. Before that the reader was favoured with a few parenthetical flashes of the minds of the seductive barmaids in 'Sirens', who also provide flirtatious distractions for careworn Dubliners. Miss Douce even performs an exhibitionistic set piece for two ogling males.

An earlier mild prefiguration of Gerty MacDowell is the Miss Dunne of 'Wandering Rocks'. Her brief succession of thoughts include 'mystery', 'love', and envious comments on the pictorial exhibitionism of a star of the Dublin stage, named Marie (Kendall), 'holding up her bit of a skirt'. She considers the fascinated stare of men and a 'concertina skirt' for herself (229.28). Like Gerty, she has a secret in her drawer (cf. 442.18), she hopes (as Gerty 'wishes') 'to goodness' (229.30, 357.18, 361.1), and she uses the tumescent word 'swells'. Her employer, Blazes Boylan, generally better off than Bloom, is at the same moment viewing the charms of another blushing girl, while anticipating the more palpable charms of Molly.

The oblique characterization of Gerty MacDowell is the first extended delineation of a female psyche. From now on, the book moves through several female phases. The Virgin, Joyce's 'symbol' for 'Nausicaa', is succeeded by the Mother and the Whore in the next two chapters—three archetypal manifestations of the Feminine. In 'Penelope', Molly's fullness encompasses them all. On a smaller scale, the three girls in 'Nausicaa' play all these roles, being virginal but having maternal responsibilities in 'Nausicaa', and scortatory duties in 'Circe'.

'the gathering twilight' (363.30)

The immersion in this female world coincides with the oncoming of night. Gerty appears in twilight; at the end of the chapter darkness has descended. Bloom estimates the time by such signs as the waning of the light and the appearance of the mailboat. The sun set in Dublin at 8.27 p.m. on 16 June 1904 (as indicated in *Thom's Directory*), and lighting up time for cyclists (376.16) was fixed at

9 hours 17 minutes, as the *Evening Telegraph*, sold in the streets at Sandymount a little before that time, told its readers.[1]

In most mythological representations, and in the grammatical gender of Indo-European languages, the night is female. The darker half of *Ulysses* is ushered in by Gerty and closed by Molly's ruminations in her bedroom; at the end the faint incipient lustre of approaching dawn, and the remembered swelling memory of a scene steeped in the sunlight of Gibraltar and of Howth, herald a new turning toward the sun. Immediately after 'Nausicaa', in the first word of the next chapter, 'Deshil',[2] there is another metaphorical turning toward sun and son.

The second, larger part of *Ulysses* extends between opposite poles of womanhood: young, immature Gerty, lame and incomplete (she is only accorded half a chapter), and ripe, fullblown Molly. Bloomsnight is structured symmetrically, enclosed at each end by female outpourings, fluid, subjective, with orgasmic climaxes. These are accompanied by male counterparts, arranged concentrically— Bloom's sober reflective attempt at a reasoned view in 'Nausicaa' is set off against the rationalized pseudoscientific and objective inventory of 'Ithaca', both down-to-earth, disillusioned stocktakings. Both chapters end, similarly, with Bloom's falling asleep and with a transition into dream language, a dissolution of narrative as masculine control gives way to uninterrupted, associative strings of words and memories (382, 737). In the *Odyssey* too, the isle of the Phaeacians is closest to Ithaca and the last stop on the return journey.

Tucked between enveloping folds of femininity, the meeting, interacting, parting of Bloom and Stephen are circumveloped by a darkness that both does and does not comprehend them. They are thus 'wombed in sin darkness' (38.10). The image of an enfolding womb within which the most significant action takes place is more than a convenient analogy. Regression into uterine security is at the core of infantile notions of illusory escape, as in 'Nausicaa'; the same local anatomical habitation is necessary for the more positive interpretations concentrating on birth and rebirth or for Stephen's concept of a creative womb of the imagination. A womb is

---

[1] *Evening Telegraph*, Thursday, 16 June 1904, p. 2, column 4.

[2] P. W. Joyce, in *A Social History of Ancient Ireland*, Dublin, 1920, has a chapter on 'Turning "Deisol", or Sunwise' (vol. I, p. 301). The word *deisol* or, in modern spelling, *deiseal, deisil*, is pronounced 'deshil'.

included in the word 'wombfruit' at the beginning of the 'Oxen of the Sun' chapter (383.4), whose organ is the womb. The last page of 'Ithaca', which is symmetrically opposite and in which Bloom disappears, contains a corresponding image: 'the manchild in the womb' (737.13).

There is an uterine quality to the darkness of the night of 16–17 June, enfolded in a female texture, and stretching from the metaphorical all-including embrace that sets the scene in 'Nausicaa' (with an early glance at dear old Howth) all the way to the remembered real, carnal embrace on Howth Head.

'a story behind it' (355.25)

Gerty MacDowell is the latest avatar of the temptress in Joyce's fiction. Her first incarnation is as Polly Mooney in 'The Boarding House', who exposes herself to a male viewer, at night, against a backdrop of candles. She first emerges in a scene full of social pretence and cliché, e.g., 'the *artistes* would oblige' at one of the 'reunions'. She is both naively innocent and cunningly knowing; her song mentions 'sham'. She is explicitly referred to as 'a little perverse madonna' (D, 62–63). Her grammar, like Gerty's, is imperfect, but what, says Mr Doran—and it could have been said by Gerty or one of her authoresses—, 'would grammar matter if he really loved her?' (D, 66). Polly and Gerty know how to cry in front of a mirror (D, 68; 351.17). And Polly 'knew she was being watched' (D, 63). Her seduction, however, has graver consequences. Mr Doran considers vainly and irrationally escape by flight through the roof but is brought down to reality by the confederate forces of familial and social gravity, and by Cyclopean threats. Bloom, at any rate, is more prudent than Polly's victim, who by the time of *Ulysses* has further declined to a wretched state. A handshake briefly unites the two in 'Cyclops', with the I-narrator putting them in the same category: 'Shake hands, brother. You're a rogue and I'm another' (313.33).

A *Portrait* presents its own gallery of temptresses, leading up to the vision in Chapter 4 and the villanelle of Chapter 5. The girl who meets Stephen's gaze on the strand connects two otherwise separate strands of sensual eroticism and mariolatric images of purity. The similarity between this twilight scene and the portrait of Gerty MacDowell in *Ulysses* has often been remarked upon. The stage setting in both contains the beach, the dusk, the sea, weedgrown rocks, the display of thighs, pictorial representation, and elevated vocabulary. The mind is turned to higher things. The universe and the world are freely brought to bear on the situation, Stephen relating to 'the heavenly bodies, . . . the earth, . . . some new world' (AP, 172), while Gerty can be just as liberal with the evocation of 'worlds' (351.14, 357.41, etc.). There is neither physical contact nor any spoken word to break the spell. It takes the next section— Chapter 5 of A Portrait, part 2 of 'Nausicaa'—to re-establish more realistic proportions.

'Same style of beauty' (380.31)

To realize just how much the 'Nausicaa' chapter metamorphoses elements of Stephen's ecstasy on the beach in A Portrait, it is worth collating a few images and phrases. Almost every item, for example, of the catalogue that describes the impression made on Stephen by the bird-girl has been re-used. Both girls are alone, gazing into the distant sea, aware of being watched, and in both cases there is mention of waist, bosom, hair, face, softness, drawers, skirts, slenderness, touch, shame, etc. Some specific transpositions are amusing. The 'magic' changing the girl into the likeness of a seabird is at work in 'Nausicaa' too, in the 'magic lure' (364.22) in Gerty's eyes. The sea-bird may have become a 'canary bird' (359.5), but Bloom himself thinks of 'seabirds' (380.11). The girl's legs are 'delicate'; delicacy is one of Gerty's strong points, extending to her hands (348.32), her flush (349.16—flushes are part of the scenery in the Portrait too, p. 172), and the 'pink' creeping into her pretty cheek (356.10). Since 'from everything in the least indelicate her finebred nature instinctively recoiled' (364.32), she would be peeved to know that Bloom callously awards the palm of delicacy to her rival: 'That squinty one is delicate' (368.6). The ivory of the bird-girl's thighs is part of Gerty's make-up: 'ivorylike purity' (348.19). The term 'slateblue' contains Gerty's favourite colour, but Bloom uses 'on the slate' (375.36) in quite another context. The 'ringdove' (362.34) associated with Gerty's defiant voice may be compared to the 'dove-like' bosom of Stephen's vision, or to her skirts, which are 'dove-tailed'. The 'worship' of Stephen's eyes has its counterpart in Bloom's 'dark eyes . . . literally worshipping at her shrine' (361.41). The 'faint flame' that trembled on the cheek of the girl in A *Portrait* is re-lit as a 'warm flush . . . surging and flaming into her [Gerty's] cheeks' (356.17). Even the precious word 'fashioned', which is used for the trail of seaweed in the earlier scene, seems to have been transferred from the literary tradition to the marketplace—to the ambit of 'Dame Fashion', one of Gerty's patron saints, whose call she follows as a 'votary' (350.8), just as Stephen devoted himself to Art.

A more detailed list of such transferences would include the cry uttered by both Stephen and Gerty at their respective raptures, a trembling of limbs, a phrase like 'the palest rose' (AP, 172), which becomes 'waxen pallor' in conjunction with 'rosebud mouth' (348.19). Gerty's climax could be called, as Stephen's in fact is, 'an outburst of profane joy' (AP, 171). Etymologically, 'profane' means 'outside the temple' (Lat. *fanum* = fane), which is exactly where the action on Sandymount strand takes place, literally near 'that simple fane beside the waves' (354.6).

It is, above all, one of Stephen's choicest terms, 'radiant' (see AP, 169 and 'radiance', *passim*, in the aesthetic theory) which, together with another thematic word of A *Portrait*, is now applied to Gerty MacDowell's showy appearance: 'a radiant little vision' (360.22). The 'pure radiance' of the Virgin (346.8) is one of many links.

The two visions are made up of the same touches, sometimes with a marked drop in tone and connotation. The purple tinge, noticeable in A *Portrait*, but not easily appreciated with critical nicety, has now been applied much more strongly. One's impressions of the earlier scene will now be readjusted; in the comic exaggerations of 'Nausicaa' some traits in A *Portrait* are seen in a different light. The two episodes reflect on each other. In a sense, 'Nausicaa' continues the familiar technique of A *Portrait*, the repetition of an earlier event in a rearrangement, with a change of tone and a new slant (often amounting to a disillusionment) brought about, very often, by a reshuffling of the same verbal material with some additional twists of phraseology. The reading experience is characterized by shifts of perspective (one of the structural devices of *Ulysses*), which should also make us wary of singling out any one of the stages in the process of cognition, however convincing, as the decisive one.

'with careful hand recomposed' (370.9)

We know that Joyce, while working on *Ulysses*, met a live incarnation of whoever had inspired the event that had been turned into the vocational epiphany on the beach in Chapter 4 of *A Portrait*. Late in 1918, in Zürich, Joyce saw and addressed a girl, Martha (or Marthe) Fleischmann, bearing a name which itself contained an alluring tangle of Ulyssean motifs, and embarked upon a liaison which was mainly an affair of looks and letters (at least until its climax, a final rendezvous of, presumably, more daring enterprise, shrouded—for us—in appropriate obscurity, but illuminated—for the participants—by candles specially and ritualistically provided; fittingly, the episode has been reported by a painter, Joyce's friend Frank Budgen, in whose studio the meeting took place).[3]

Whether acting on impulse or imitating Bloom's epistolary precedent, Joyce sent his Martha some letters and one postcard (this, addressed from 'Odysseus' to 'Nausicaa', is now lost;[4] as it happens, Gerty received one 'silly postcard', 362.39)—documents of a *Schwärmerei* which prove that the Swiss seductress reinforced some of the attractions that were to be attributed to Gerty Mac-Dowell. The affair, with a strong element of 'studied attitude' (355.26) on Joyce's part, no doubt also contained its serious involvement. The letters allow us some rare glimpses into that mysterious process of distillation which turns living experience into distanced art. The situation already has about it an air of a laboratory experiment arranged with a view to literary exploitation. In real life Joyce could adopt fictional roles by comparing himself outright with Dante or Shakespeare, while playing a provincial Romeo or Tristan.

Again it is fascinating to watch Joyce using, to express private feelings for the kinetic purpose of evoking an emotional response, the same turns of phrase (though in French and German) and the same images that served him, not too much later, for the hilarious parodies of 'Nausicaa'. He did not of course use the letters (which were out of his hands and whose preservation is accidental) as he might use the actual text of previously published

[3] Ellmann, p. 462; Frank Budgen, *Myselves When Young*, London, 1970, pp. 189–194.

[4] Heinrich Straumann, in *Letters*, II, pp. 430–431.

works. All we can say with certainty is that concepts and analogies that were in his mind in 1918 to 1919, and which were used for practical purposes, recur in the chapter that was drafted a few months later.[5] The artist is in full control of his material, which seems to be more than we can claim of the lover and correspondent.

In the first letter, of December 1918,[6] Joyce gives voice to his frustration at not seeing Martha, whose name he does not yet know. His first visual impressions include her big hat, similar to the one that Gerty takes off with striking effect, and, in more detail, 'la mollesse des traits réguliers et la douceur des yeux'. The charm of Gerty's eyes is general all over 'Nausicaa', and her 'sweetness' is tied to her whole vision (360.23), but the softness of her face is explicitly noted: 'her softlyfeatured face' (348.40). Joyce goes on to remark how he thought Martha was a jewess, an illusion, but an endeavour to make life conform to fictional patterns. In the fictional refashioning, the inversion of racial roles corresponds to the shifting of the sentimentality to the female partner. In his letter, Joyce then adduces the symbolism that is central for much of his writing, and in particular for 'Nausicaa' and 'Oxen of the Sun': 'Jesus Christ a pris son corps humain: dans le ventre d'une femme juive'. Molly, at least, will be turned into a half-jewess.

Joyce confesses to giving in to 'une espèce de fascination'. Bloom is 'fascinated by a loveliness that made him gaze' (361.15). The letter also conjures up the evening scene, 'un soir brumeux'. Martha has given a sign ('. . . vous m'avez fait un signe'), and so does Gerty on page 367. Joyce hints at Byronic repercussions in his life: '. . . je suis un pauvre chercheur dans ce monde, . . . j'ai vécu et péché et créé . . .'. The same instances of a dissolute but creative life figure in Stephen's visionary repertoire (AP, 172), and, accordingly, Gerty projects that Bloom 'had erred and sinned and wandered' (367.15).

In this long first letter, with its odd confessional urge, Joyce

[5] A. Walton Litz, The Art of James Joyce, London, 1961, writes that 'Nausicaa, begun in Zürich in the autumn of 1919, was finished in Trieste early in 1920' (p. 144).

[6] Letters, II, pp. 431–432. These and other parallels between Joyce's letters to Martha Fleischmann and phrases in 'Nausicaa' were pointed out in my review of Richard Ellmann's edition of the Letters in Neue Zürcher Zeitung (Zürich), 26 February 1967. Other biographical sources are to be found in the unpublished letters to Nora of 1909.

slightly rejuvenates himself to establish a parallel with the great writers. He uses the imagery of an entry into the night: 'C'est l'âge que Dante a eu quand il est entré dans la nuit de son être'. A few lines later Joyce even refers to the infantile retreat into the darkness of the womb, so basic to the nocturnal chapters in *Ulysses*: '. . . je m'en irai, un jour, n'ayant rien compris, dans l'obscurité qui nous a enfantés tous'. Joyce is paraphrasing Stephen's 'darkness shining in brightness which brightness could not comprehend' (28.16), as well as 'wombed in sin darkness . . . made not begotten' (38.10)—subtleties that must necessarily have been lost on a somewhat puzzled Martha Fleischmann whose preferred reading is reported to have been sentimental novels. Joyce calls Martha 'gracious' and 'rêveuse', and both gracefulness and dreaminess are among Gerty's attributes.

In another letter (9 December 1918) Joyce compares Martha's suffering, brought on by illness, to his own: 'moi, j'ai souffert aussi'. Gerty wonders if Bloom too 'had suffered' (358.9). In the last extant letter Joyce switches over to languishing phrases in German. He describes Martha's face: '. . . Dein Gesicht, aber so blass, so müde und so traurig!' This air of sadness suits Gerty's complexion too: her 'sad downcast eyes' (349.20), for example, and in another passage: '. . . that tired feeling. The waxen pallor of her face . . .' (348.19). In a last imaginative flight Joyce soars to Gertyan heights of imagery and emotion, kitsching that note of romantic rapture to sweet perfection, though (in *this* case no doubt unwittingly) marring the effect by a grammatical lapse:

> Durch die Nacht der Bitterkeit meiner Seele fielen die Küsse Deiner Lippen über meinen Herz—weich wie Rosenblätter, sanft wie Tau.

We don't know where Joyce's tongue was when he wrote those cadences. After the enchantment was over, at any rate, the dewy softness acquired a different quality. In 'Nausicaa' the rapturous burst, 'O so soft, sweet, soft', is followed by 'all melted away dewily' (367.4–5). And the dew that covers Sandymount strand is more matter of fact: 'Dew falling. Bad for you, dear, to sit on that stone. Brings on white fluxions' (376.29).

The litany of the Blessed Virgin is the source for Joyce's parting address to Martha Fleischmann: 'O rosa mistica, ora pro me!' Translated into the novel, it becomes '. . . pray for us, mystical rose' (356.27), and again '*Ora pro nobis*' (358.22).

These letters show that Joyce did not have to look very far for the psychological material he was to deal with, his own *personae* proved a rich quarry. The attitudes of the pining adorer contributed more to the 'Nausicaa' chapter than the adored girl herself. Joyce's introspective acumen and capacity to see himself from a distance must have been remarkable. An element of spite, consequence of almost inevitable frustration, may have been at play too in the malicious reversal of roles: the sentimentality and doubtful taste and the languishing are projected on to the girl. Bloom (roughly of the age of Joyce when 'Nausicaa' was being written in 1919 to 1920) appears detached and down to earth. It remains one of the mysteries of literary creation how the internal set-up that could produce such dewy epistolary prose could be transmuted, by processes of displacement and transference, into the comic portraits of Gerty MacDowell and Mr Leopold Bloom.

'Must have the stage setting' (370.14)

It is appropriate that Gerty's portrait is made up of strokes found elsewhere in life and fiction (Joyce's and others'). Make-up is her medium. Gerty's plumes are borrowed ones, so much so that some readers deny her any individual character. She is composed of traits assembled in a technique of collage and montage, in keeping with the chapter's art, painting.

However, Gerty MacDowell is not wholly dependent on her models. The coda of the 'Wandering Rocks' chapter introduces her in a revelatory vignette which condenses her component traits and limitations, excepting only the posing and the artificial embellishment:

> Passing by Roger Greene's office and Dollard's big red printing house Gerty MacDowell, carrying the Catesby's cork lino letters for her father who was laid up, knew by the style it was the lord and lady lieutenant but she couldn't see what Her Excellency had on because the tram and Spring's big yellow furniture van had to stop in front of her on account of its being the lord lieutenant. (252.39)

Joyce exposes Gerty's preoccupation with appearance, dress, and position and her attempt to take a vicarious part in Her Excellency's excellency. The sentence has a tenseness about it which we shall notice again in 'Nausicaa'. Its rhythm, combining a supple pace with a halting awkwardness, suggests Gerty's limp, while the imagery includes three strong primary colours. The little episode is a frustrated vision into which reality crudely interferes. The style exemplifies in a lower key the tone that characterizes Gerty. We learn, indeed, that it is possible to know 'by the style'.

'Wandering Rocks' emphasizes location in space, and Gerty's meticulously specified location indirectly reveals one of her roles, even if this is frustratingly out of the uninformed reader's range of vision. Some special knowledge of Dublin is required, in keeping with the labyrinthine technique:[7] between Roger Greene's office (referred to in 'Nausicaa' as the site of a slightly voyeuristic scene—372.3), at no. 11 Wellington quay, and Dollard's big red[8] printing house, at nos. 2, 3, 4, and 5 Wellington quay, she must have passed, at nos. 8 and 9, the firm of Ceppi, Peter and Sons, picture frame and looking glass factory, and statuary manufacturers, as they are officially listed.[9] They might well furnish some of the stage property for 'Nausicaa': pictures, looking glass, and statuary. Bloom, who follows in Gerty's footsteps a few minutes later, notices that Messrs Ceppi deal in statuary: '. . . by Ceppi's virgins, bright of their oils' (260.37).[10] On her first appearance Gerty is thus tacitly juxtaposed with the Virgin Mary displayed in a shop window, done in bright oils. The bright colours will return in 'Nausicaa', where, in her new position on the rocks of Sandymount, she is set off against the Virgin Mary, whose Litany is part of the background.

'accidentally on purpose' (359.33)

It so happens that the sentence that first announces Gerty contains just two verbs in its main clause, 'knew' and 'couldn't see'. This may give a perverse twist to the first words of the Virgin Mary when confronted with the Angel of the Lord and his announcement.

---

[7] 'Symbolic Juxtaposition' in *JJQ*, V, 3 (Spring 1968), 276–278.

[8] The same words mean erection to Molly: that 'big red brute of a thing' (742.3).

[9] For example in *Thom's Official Directory* for the year 1905, Alex. Thom & Co., Dublin, 1905, p. 1667.

[10] Bloom is carrying the *Sweets of Sin*, to complete the missing traits in Gerty's presentation: seduction and cliché language. There is another inversion of roles here: it is Gerty who appears occupied with solid, down-to-earth matter, Catesby's cork lino, meant for the ordinary home, while Bloom is after illusory wish-fulfilment through the written word.

She said: 'How shall this be, *seeing* I *know* not a man?' (Luke, 1:34).[11] The only other words uttered by the Virgin are quoted verbatim in 'Nausicaa', at 358.12

Coincidence may play into Joyce's sacerdotal hands, but it is no coincidence that the operative words 'see' and 'know', with their negations, are prominent in 'Nausicaa', often in close conjunction. For example, '. . . Gerty could see by her looking as black as thunder . . . and they both knew that she was something aloof, . . . and there was somebody else too that knew it and saw it . . .' (363.1–6); '. . . so she said she could see from where she was . . . and she knew he could be trusted . . . there was no one to see only him . . . because she knew about the passion of men like that. . .' (365.25, 30, 36, 39), etc. The chapter is, in one sense, a variation on the subject of seeing (with numerous synonyms) and knowing. In the biblical sense there is no knowledge in the encounter. Cognition and vision blend and are both interdependent and complementary. Both Bloom and Gerty see things without knowing and know about what they cannot see. The reader in turn knows more than he sees. Even a limitation of one's perception ('See her as she is spoil all', 370.14) or of one's knowledge ('Glad I didn't know . . . ', 368.4) may at times prove to be an advantage.

Earlier in the day, on the same beach, Stephen contemplated the relation between knowledge and the ineluctable modality of the visible: 'thought through my eyes' (37.2), and went on to conduct an experiment by closing his eyes. Indirectly the closing of the eyes also introduces the visually oriented 'Nausicaa' chapter, at least etymologically. The initial 'mysterious' embrace (346.2) suggests mystery, originally a form of gaining knowledge without the senses. The word derives from Greek *myo*, to close (said of the eyes). Bloom links the word 'mystery' with perception in darkness: '. . . into a cellar where it's dark. Mysterious thing too' (374.35). Cognition through vision is connected with Aristotelian 'diaphane' in 'Proteus', the sensual leering in 'Nausicaa' with transparent stockings.

The precedent of the Virgin's own words does not necessarily justify the prevalence of seeing and knowing in Gerty's chapter. Even so it is worth noticing that the phrases singled out as examples

[11] The Douay version does not use 'seeing', but another favourite word of Gerty's: *because* I know not man'. See p. 301.

of the bad grammar of Polly Mooney, the perverse little madonna and forerunner of Gerty, are 'I seen' and 'If I had've known' (D, 66). In *Ulysses* she is known for 'exposing her person' (303.6) and to be 'open to all comers', which suggests an irreverent equivalent for a 'refuge of sinners' (358.22).

'singular devotion' (356.26)

Gerty MacDowell's apposition with the Virgin Mary is transparent enough. In the nearby Star of the Sea church, the Litany of the Blessed Virgin is recited, blending with the main narrative. Stuart Gilbert pointed out that the Abbey of Howth, suggested by the references to Howth Head (especially at the beginning, 346.4), was dedicated to the Blessed Virgin.[12] Sandymount itself is situated in the parish of St Mary. Some of the Virgin's appellations have been assimilated to the description of Gerty's exterior. Her face is noted for its 'ivorylike purity' (348.19), her heart is worth its 'weight in gold' (355.12)—gold and ivory had already acquired liturgical overtones in *A Portrait*. The Virgin is undefiled, Gerty's soul 'unsullied' (367.11). Physically Gerty remains virginally untouched, while some of Mary's spiritual attributes are also translated into physical terms: she is 'full of grace', her figure and face being 'graceful' (348.14, 365.36). Joyce conceives of her as wearing 'immaculate' stockings: 'there wasn't a brack on them' (360.10); 'brack' is Gaelic for speck or stain.

Some of the epithets in the Litany can be related to Gerty, and not only in scathing irony, but, like everything else, with perspectival modification. Stylistically, of course, the immutable appellations of the Virgin are not far removed from the stereotypes of cliché. Gerty is, for the time being, 'most powerful', and as we are told expressly at 367.13, she is 'merciful' (354.27). For practical and not entirely irrelevant purposes, she proves a refuge for one sinner and a 'comfortress' for at least one of the 'afflicted' (358.22), a momentary 'haven of refuge' (358.25) for Bloom who has 'erred and sinned and wandered' (367.15). If judged by the same Catholic view, of course, the refuge he finds is in sin itself. But he finds relief and forgiveness and pardon, like the faithful at the retreat (Bloom's tarrying is another form of retreat). He belongs to the 'toilers for their daily

---

[12] Gilbert, p. 281.

bread', with 'careworn hearts' (356.27, 28). As a 'child of Mary' (364.7) Gerty would be pledged to imitate the example of the Virgin as best she could in daily life. Weighed in the balance of orthodoxy, her actual conduct would not rate very high, but in Bloom's valuation it may do. Evaluation is a tricky matter, liable to error and modification: 'Remember about the mistake in the valuation' (377.39).

The Annunciation is explicitly referred to by way of the remembered words of the priest in the confession box. He seems to apply the Virgin's words of submission, 'be it done unto me according to Thy Word', rather obliquely to the idea of obeying 'the voice of nature' (358.42, 38), himself establishing a somewhat mundane parallel. Gerty's thoughts immediately turn to the priest and his home, which features 'a canary bird' (359.5). Buck Mulligan, joking joiner of the holy and the ribald, has prepared us for the Holy Family, whose 'father's a bird' (19.4); Léo Taxil's dialogue about 'le pigeon' (41.15) has similarly prepared us for another bird in 'Nausicaa', for this bird, revealed as a cuckoo.[13] The cuckoo's ninefold cry reverberates blasphemously up toward the Holy Ghost as well as downward to Bloom's domestic situation. At the end of the chapter the clock speaks with a columbine tongue, it 'cooed' (382.26). Gerty's own words, as she says that she can throw her 'cap at who I like' (being thus blessed among women), ring out 'more musical than the cooing of the ringdove' (362.33).

In the vision of A Portrait, 'a wild angel had appeared' (AP, 172); in 'Nausicaa' a bird, a bat, and a dark stranger appear, while there is inversion in the phrase 'Dark devilish appearance' (369.17). Bloom, when he considers writing a 'message' (381.30), comes linguistically close to being an angel (angelos = messenger). His message reveals him to be lonely and disappointed, though his confession remains unfinished: 'I . . . AM. A'. Whether we substitute '. . . a cuckold', '. . . a naughty boy', '. . . alone', or whatever, we bear in mind his earthly fichue position, in marked contrast to the more divine overtones contained in the 'A'. It suggests an incomplete half of the Christ of the Revelation (who is A and O, beginning and end). There is a faint adumbration of a Jehovean

[13] Also heralded by Buck Mulligan, at 212.35; it is Mulligan too who has introduced masturbation as a major theme connected with literature.

I AM THAT I AM; or, through another tangential extrapolation, we may be reminded of how, when told about the woman taken in adultery, Jesus 'stooped down, and with his finger wrote on the ground, as though he heard them not' (John, 8:6). Bloom, who 'stooped' and 'gently vexed the thick sand' (381.18, 28), is often motivated by not wanting to hear about a woman taken in adultery.

Such potential divine flutters may be left in limbo or accepted in addition to the direct references to the Annunciation. At whichever elevation we prefer to place the essence of the sterile encounter between Bloom (pitiful human being set off against godlike potentialities) and Gerty, the following chapter contains the real birth of a real son, discussion of the 'utterance of the Word' (422.42), and countless theological allusions. As the Annunciation promises, the 'fruit of thy womb' (Luke, 1:42) will be blessed and come to life, in the thrice repeated 'wombfruit' at the beginning of 'Oxen of the Sun'.

'Suppose there's some connection' (374.33)

Joyce creates, and invites us to treat, his chapters almost as individuals, with distinct idiosyncrasies and with affinities for each other. 'Nausicaa' has some special bonds. It is certainly paired off against the preceding chapter, 'Cyclops', after whose noisy brawling and brute force it appears soothing and quiet. Both are climactic chapters, dealing with sentiment and passion. The men in 'Cyclops' are concerned with politics, chauvinism, war, rebellion, execution, punishment, fighting (finding a female counterpart, too, in the three girls' malicious bickerings; the twins in 'Nausicaa' are already engaged in strife about the power and possession of castle and ball). The girls in 'Nausicaa' dream of love and marriage. Bloom's involvement is significant, he inclines to making love (in 'Nausicaa' his participation is voluntary and deliberate) rather than to making war (the entanglement in Barney Kiernan's comes about mainly by accident and imprudence).

In either case views are dimmed by prejudice, combined with hatred or with romantic notions. Stereotypes have replaced judgment and discrimination, attitudes to life fall into ready-made categories. The protagonists see what they have been conditioned to find and remain blind to the rest. Eyes are important, their use in 'Nausicaa' ranging all the way from candid glances to blindness: 'Thinks I'm a tree, so blind' (377.30). Identities are mistaken. In fact, Gerty's mind is almost incapable of recognizing an identity. There is a pre-existing classification to which phenomena have to conform, and she, herself, seems predetermined: '. . . she was more a Giltrap than a MacDowell' (348.13). Bloom cannot be appreciated for what he is, becoming a dark, handsome foreigner with all the trappings of the mysterious stranger of popular fiction. For Gerty, he consists of projections. Even noses are categorized in advance: '. . . but she could not see whether he had an aquiline nose or a slightly *retroussé* from where he was sitting' (357.37). The citizen's categories were different, but similarly fixed.

There are many oblique views. Edy Boardman, who has a squint, can be acutely and unpleasantly perceptive. Spite, in fact, usually makes the observer more sharp-sighted, and even Gerty grows one-sidedly keen-eyed when it comes to criticizing her rivals, even if she never attains the terseness of the Narrator in 'Cyclops'.

Soon after Bloom's entry, the conversation in Barney Kiernan's pub veers round to 'ruling passion' and erection (304), which are suitably associated with death and execution. Bloom sets himself up as an expert and is parodied as a 'scientist' (one who knows). In both chapters Bloom is exalted and humiliated. In his defiant outburst he is seen as 'an almanac picture' (333.3), anticipating the one that Gerty keeps in an intimate place: 'the grocer's christmas almanac the picture of halcyon days . . .' (355.21). His act is presented as a rise ('Old lardyface standing up . . .') and a fall ('then he collapses all of a sudden'), followed by detumescent imagery: '. . . as limp as a wet rag' (333.4–8). The subsequent persiflage of the propagation of universal love thematically features our heroine: 'Gerty MacDowell loves the boy that has the bicycle' (333.28). The whole of 'Nausicaa' could be taken as an extension of this parodic sketch.

The style of Gerty's part could easily have found a place as one of the Cyclopean parodies.[14] The opening caress of the summer evening, which had begun 'to fold the world in its mysterious em-

---

[14] One passage from such a parody, indiscriminately scattering loveliness over the scenery, anticipates the style of the first part of 'Nausicaa': 'Lovely maidens sit in close proximity to the roots of the lovely trees singing the most lovely songs while they play with all kinds of lovely objects . . .' (294.7).

brace' (346.2), is lifted from such a parody, the Execution scene:
'The hero folded her willowy form in a loving embrace' (309.33),[15]
a sentence proclaiming the literary execution of Gerty MacDowell,
to which loving care is devoted in 'Nausicaa'.

Bloom's exit from the Cyclops' den is followed by the one explicit naming of the Blessed Virgin in the citizen's benediction:
'The blessing of God and Mary and Patrick on you' (333.41). In
accordance with the theme of violence, the Virgin Mary is perverted,
in the imperialist's creed, into an instrument of brutal force and
suppression: 'born of the fighting navy' (329.25). In clear contrast,
the Virgin offers her friendly protection to all who need it (356.33),
while 'the fighting navy . . . keeps our foes at bay' (328.36). Gerty,
of course, is connected with the navy through her clothes, wearing
a 'navy threequarter skirt' (350.14). In Joyce's view, even the I-narrator's favourite expletive is etymologically derived from the Virgin
('by our Lady'),[16] so that 'bloody' conveniently takes care both of the
sanguinary aspect and the blasphemy, the I-narrator of 'Cyclops'
reversing the manner of the implied narrator of 'Nausicaa', choosing
a register that is too low and vulgar as against one that is too elevated.

In 'Cyclops', Throwaway is announced as the winner of the
race, and the outsider Bloom suffers innocently for a causal connexion for which he is not responsible. His hasty flight is clothed
in the glory of Elijah's ascension, 'clothed upon', 'raiment' and 'fair
as the moon' (345) all pointing forward to the next chapter, which
celebrates the coming of this Elijah as a throwing away of seed on
Sandymount strand, an onanistic waste of the potential needed for
the continuation of the race.

Both chapters have a bi-polar structure, in 'Cyclops', as an
alternating sequence of rudely clashing passages (fit expression of
political strife and conflict), in 'Nausicaa', in evident antithetical
symmetry. Even the motif of the change of name and address is continued into 'Nausicaa': 'Might be a false name however like my
and the address Dolphin's barn a blind' (372.36).

[15] Even the willow returns in 'Nausicaa': 'Weeping willow' (377.32).

[16] Joyce writes about the use of 'bloody' to Grant Richards: '. . . it is strange
that he should object more strongly to a profane use of the Virgin than to a
profane use of the name of God' (5 May 1906, Letters, II, 134). Stuart Gilbert,
perhaps prompted by Joyce, refers to it as 'Our Lady's adjective' (p. 255).

'Because it's arranged' (374.6)

Both Cyclopean war and Nausicaan love were among the chords struck in the 'Sirens' chapter, notably in the song *Love and War*, the stanzas of which are confused by Dollard and mused upon by Bloom (270.5, 8, 31). 'The Croppy Boy' prepares us for rebellion and execution, the aria from *Martha* for Gerty's lure. The opening words of the latter set off a corresponding 'endearing flow' (273.34), and the culminating '*Come!*' with its soaring imagery and orgiastic tension (275–276), anticipates events and emotions in 'Nausicaa', which is after all a visual restaging of temptations manifested as aural charms in 'Sirens'.

Bloom's voyeuristic inclination was first exposed in the 'Lotus-eaters' chapter, with its varied possibilities of escape from reality. One vicarious satisfaction is the adoration of Martha Clifford, who corresponds with a Bloom she does not know and who likes a name he doesn't have. Like Gerty, she goes in for thinking (77.40), is interested in perfume, has difficulties with her vocabulary,[17] and inadvertently blows up a disturbing word into a 'world' (77.37), equalling the hyperbolic generosity with which Gerty, of whom everyone 'thought the world' (355.17),[18] verbally handles whole worlds of experience. Bloom lumps the two girls together on page 368, and Joyce's affair with Martha Fleischmann provides a cluster of extraneous links.

The chemist's assorted 'ointments', 'alabaster lilypots', and 'lotions' toward the end of 'Lotuseaters' (84), all recurring in 'Nausicaa', might furnish the cosmetic ingredients for Gerty's make-up. Her florid expressions, the 'embroidered floral design' of her present (359.2) and of the chapter's style are a kind of 'language of flowers', like the one Bloom makes up after reading Martha's letter (78). Almost two pages (374–375) may be seen as a recall of events and motifs introduced in 'Lotuseaters'. Bloom even remembers that

[17] Both mistake singular forms for plural ones: 'my patience are exhausted' (78.8); 'the perfume of those incense' (357.25).

[18] '. . . those iron jelloids . . . had done her a world of good' (348.15); 'she would give worlds to be in the privacy of her own familiar chamber' (351.14 —it might be simpler just to leave and go to her chamber); 'She would have given worlds to know what it was' (357.40); 'Dearer than the whole world would she be to him' (364.25); 'the only man in all the world for her' (365.4). Joyce is also parodying his own macrocosmic aspirations in writing *Ulysses*.

he has forgotten the lotion. It is Gerty, moreover, who with a Wildean touch literally approximates to the *Lotophagoi:* 'often she wondered why you couldn't eat something poetical like violets or roses' (352.20). The 'organ' of 'Lotuseaters', the genitals, becomes covertly central to 'Nausicaa', Bloom's limpness being foreshadowed in the limp and languid floating flower with which the earlier chapter closes.

The 'Proteus' chapter shares its setting, near Leahy's terrace, with 'Nausicaa'. Stephen, too, changes from one pose to another, but with him it is an intentional arrangement, while Gerty is determined by attitudes that she does not recognize *as* attitudes. Stephen's imitations are volitional, skilful re-creations, recalls of pretences and disguises. His thoughts are evoked in their vivid wayward fluctuations, with unique freshness and originality, at least in their startling combinations. The collage of his thoughts is conscious. Gerty, ineluctably visible, specializes in thinking too. She is 'lost in thought' or, soon afterwards, 'wrapt in thought' (354.27): this is precise; thinking for her is a becoming pose, to be used like drapery. As against the immediate contents of Stephen's thinking in 'Proteus', for Gerty 'thinking' is often an intransitive verb (see 354.18, etc.), an attitude familiar from so many paintings. She too tries her hand at 'reading' non-verbal phenomena: 'the story of a haunting sorrow was written on his face' (357.39), but this is hardly to be equated with trying to read the signatures of all things (Bloom comes closer to it in 'All these rocks with lines and scars and letters', 381.34). She would not dream of bringing anything or anyone 'beyond the veil' (48.36). No protean flux is caught in the sequence of essentially static pictures that constitute the first part of 'Nausicaa'.

'there for a certain purpose' (355.29)

'Nausicaa' also looks forward to the next chapter. Its close, with the three times threefold call of 'Cuckoo', leads directly into the evocation of Helios, with its three paragraphs of three sentences each. Nine is, of course, a significant number for the chapter of Birth. Holles street is associated by Bloom with the once-attentive nurse Callan (373.12; 385.27), who, along with Gerty, figures in the brief list of women attracted to Bloom on 16 June (722.28). The crime inveighed against in 'Oxen of the Sun' has been committed in 'Nausicaa'. Bloom becomes, in Joyce's comments, what he has just

wasted—sperm.[19] At the other end of the sterility-fertility axis, the
'A' which Bloom attributed to himself in his writing in the sand,
reappears as 'Alpha, a ruby and triangled sign upon the forehead of
Taurus' (414.40).

Of all the pastiches of the 'Oxen of the Sun' chapter, the
Dickensian paragraph on pages 420–421 comes closest to the style
of Gerty's meditations. It abounds in emotional adjectives ('brave
woman', 'loving eyes', 'her pretty head', etc.). Gerty's adolescent
sentimentalities are carried over into motherhood. The mother, like
Gerty, 'reclines', but with 'motherlight in her eyes'. The mysterious
embrace, when domesticized, is transformed into 'lawful embraces'.
Gerty has set the tone for 'a nice snug and cosy little homely house'
(352.31), complete with tall husband and brekky and all the rest,
the details being lovingly filled in by the eulogy of father Purefoy.
Through his association with Catesby's cork lino, Gerty's father
suggests the comforts of the ideal home ('always bright and cheery
in the home', 355.9), while his drinking and gout reveal the actuality.

'That's where Molly can knock spots off them' (373.22)
Gerty and Molly Bloom, Nausicaa and Penelope, have some traits
in common, and Molly is ubiquitous in Bloom's half of the chapter.
Superstition, ignorance, and faulty grammar are common to both
of them, as is a splendid inconsistency. Both begin their menstrual
cycle. They set great store by their appearance and their clothes;
they thrive on admiration; their thoughts circle around men. Bloom
is able to assess this last aspect shrewdly, and his condensation 'he,
he and he' (371.9) summarizes one salient aspect both of Gerty's gush
and of the gyrations of Molly's monologue. The scale is always reduced in the younger girl, who can muster fewer males than Molly.
Her slim graceful figure and somewhat anaemic nature contrast
with Molly's amplitude. Gerty looks away into the distance, or up
at the sky, while Molly is earthy, even tellurian, stained, and, on the
whole, horizontal. Gerty is only half reclined. Molly's coarseness
expresses itself with gusto, even though there is a prudish streak
in her too, but Gerty's finebred nature instinctively recoils from
everything in the least indelicate.

For all that, their thinking and their language are often very

[19] 'Bloom is the spermatozoon, the hospital the womb . . .' (*Letters*, I,
140).

similar. Compare Gerty's '. . . those cyclists showing off what they hadn't got' (358.15) with Molly's '. . . she didnt make much secret of what she hadnt' (750.22). They can be equally catty about members of their own sex and would feel contempt for each other. In many ways the style of 'Penelope' is prefigured in 'Nausicaa', many of the sentences of which string together without pause or punctuation,[20] and with the same lack of subordination:

> . . . but those iron jelloids she had been taking of late had done her a world of good much better than the Widow Welch's female pills and she was much better of those discharges she used to get and that tired feeling. (348.15–18)

This could be translated, with few changes, into the rhetoric of the last chapter. Gerty's diction (assuming that this would be her own) is characterized by one of the cardinal words of 'Penelope', 'because',[21] which she uses abundantly and usually without any causal function: 'But this was altogether different from a thing like that because there was all the difference because she could almost feel him draw her face to his and the first quick hot touch of his handsome lips' (366.4).

Molly, though attached to her own form of sentimentality, would not, however, be caught in Gerty's artificialities, having generally a good sense of what is spurious about others. She makes fun of euphemisms, prefers 'a few simple words' to phrases from 'the ladies letterwriter' (758), and Bloom remembers that she 'twigged at once' that the man Bloom thought goodlooking 'had a false arm' (372.1). She has a sharp eye for pretence, circumlocution, and evasive euphemisms. Her 'Lord couldnt he say bottom right out and have done with it' (741.6) contrasts with the ripple of thrilled queasiness which even a diluted 'beetoteetom' causes in Gerty (353.20).

'perfect proportions' (350.32)

At a first glance the chapter (it is one of glances) appears bipartite, with distinctly contrasting, complementary halves. Gerty's outlook is

---

[20] Note that the sentence which introduces Gerty on pp. 252–253 has little punctuation in its first part and none in its second.

[21] 'Penelope's four cardinal points being the female breasts, arse, womb and cunt, expressed by the words *because, bottom, . . . woman, yes*' (*Letters*, I, 170).

characterized by self-inflated infatuations beyond critical questioning, by hyperbole, self-deception, and a basically timid selectivity.
There is an upward tendency in the first half, with altitudes as diverse
as the promontory of Howth, a castle built of sand, amatory and
social aspirations and pretensions, glances at the flying fireworks, at
the Blessed Sacrament raised in the benediction service, at a view
high up offered by Gerty. The imagery is lofty, and an accumulation
of heights such as 'queenly *hauteur*, . . . higharched instep, . . . a
gentlewoman of high degree, . . . how to be tall increase your height'
are to be found in the space of a few lines (348.31–349.9). Language
is correspondingly exalted, as though it too had to be kept from
touching base ground.

In Bloom's section, eyes, with language, are kept nearer the
ground, over which Bloom bends, and on which he writes. He is
very aware of the rocks they are sitting on as part of his present
reality: 'Bad for you, dear, to sit on that stone. Brings on white
fluxions' (376.30). His monologue is interspersed with the customary
objectifying qualifiers, 'but', 'all the same', 'on the other hand', 'look
at it other way round'. Where Gerty is unthinkingly posing, he does
a lot of his usual 'supposing'. His mind is, of course, revealed to us
after the orgasmic release, when he is again in control of his emotions. The effect is a sobering down, a reduction of things to their
everyday dimension.

The boundless generalities of Gerty's wishful reveries become
concrete trifles. The 'infinite store of mercy', noted in Gerty's eyes
(367.13), becomes more manageable in Bloom's gratitude for 'small
mercies' (368.21). The chapter is structured by such contrasts, as
when the sweet and homely cosiness of connubial life imagined in
the first section is set against Bloom's *précis*: '. . . till they settle
down to potwalloping and papa's pants will soon fit Willy and
fuller's earth for the baby when they hold him out to do ah ah'
(373.4). The earthiness is unmistakable, and it is the 'settling *down*'
that is typical of the second half of 'Nausicaa'. It is exemplified in
the baby's 'ah ah', so different from the high-pitched 'O!s' that go
before (367.1) or from the evasive terms that are used for similar
bodily processes of Baby Boardman. Again, we may compare the
various perfections that adorn Gerty—showing off 'her slim graceful
figure to perfection.' (350.16), her 'perfect proportions' (350.32),
her rosebud mouth, 'Greekly perfect' (348.21),—with Bloom's aside

that a 'defect is ten times worse in a woman' (368.3). The first half presents a rich palette of colours, especially blue but with liberal daubs of scarlet, crimson, rose, coralpink, etc., against which the second half appears grey, and Bloom 'off colour' (372.29).

'a kind of language between us' (372.35)

Despite numerous contrasts of that kind, the chapter is not the simple dichotomized structure it appears to be at first blush (it is a chapter of blushes too). Not all the colours are reserved for the first half, but those toward the end of the chapter are less visualized, more abstractly thought about (376.23). Not all the ups are scattered over the first half. Bloom too looks up at rockets, at the stars and the moon, if with a weary mind. Conversely, Gerty's section has its downs, the 'fallen women' (364.34) and the 'fine tumble' she wishes on Cissy Caffrey (359.34) (significantly to dethrone her from the elevation of 'her high crooked French heels'). Most poignantly, her own accident occurred 'coming *down* Dalkey hill' (364.21—not, of course, Gerty's italics). The general pattern, then, is mirrored as a succession of smaller movements within either section, so that each part potentially contains the whole.

The two halves are also intricately dovetailed, separated by a definite break and yet joined by a gliding transition. When Gerty's gush gives way to dewy melting, there follows a quiet paragraph which temporarily blends Bloom and Gerty. Both seem painted by the same painter's brush, and he 'coloured like a girl' (367.8). Even Bloom's physical position becomes identical with hers: 'He was leaning back against the rock behind. Leopold Bloom (for it is he) . . .' (367.8). His identity is revealed for the first time (in a novelistic fashion reminiscent of 348.8), and he is judged by the morality appropriate to this kind of literature. But there is a drop in tone, and one sentence—'At it again?'—reaches down to Bloom's half. The accustomed pitch is immediately resumed and Bloom is stylistically approximated to Gerty: 'A fair unsullied soul had called to him and, wretch that he was, how had he answered?'

The opposite occurs in the next long paragraph, describing Gerty's farewell greeting, in which she briefly touches the ground of typically Bloomesque prose: 'Wonder if he's too far to' (367.27), one bit of direct inner monologue, with the typical trailing off. But she at once rises again, literally and stylistically: 'She rose. . . . She

drew herself up to her full height . . .', and prepares her exit. Her
actual movements bring her in touch with the earth, and her walk
is expressed in the plainest possible language, without artificial
embellishment: 'Slowly without looking back she went down the
uneven strand . . .'. Only when she sublimates the awkwardness of
her gait into a stylized pose is there a last, short-lived ascent: 'She
walked with a certain quiet dignity characteristic of her . . .', but
by now the line of vision is clearly directed at her feet and Bloom's
sudden realization plunks the narrative down with a final jolt: 'Tight
boots? No. She's lame! O!' Even the 'O' conveys a fall. From now
on the language jogs along in relatively short, halting steps.

The transition has been prepared for in another interlacing
counter-movement. In spite of appearances, the forced deportment
of Gerty's style has been felt as essentially lame all along, and correspondingly the limping procession of Bloom's thoughts emerges
as basically more dignified.

'it was all things combined' (372.31)

Nor is Bloom's half all of a piece. Though it would have to be read
aloud with a level voice, it has its ups and downs. Even the narrative is lifted from Bloom's perspective at some points, notably when
a 'lost long candle [wandering] up the sky' (379.6) raises the point of
view and brings about a sweeping motion of the camera for a survey
ranging from the streets of Sandymount across the bay to Howth
Head, re-personified, as in the opening shot (346.4). The style, too,
is raised and broadened, reverting to the novelette manner, with
pretty pictures and a touch of Thomas Moore's glow-worm, until
the lighthouse of Kish far away, winking at Mr Bloom, brings the
perspective, along with the tone of the tale, back to Bloom's level.
For one paragraph the narrative has risen above Bloom's head, in a
'tryst' (379.10) that is also stylistic.

The first postorgasmic rocket, at 372.22, also widens the perspective to take in the party of girls and children in the distance,
resulting in a quickening of Bloom's pulse and a little climactic
flutter 'Will she? Watch! Watch! See!' imitative of the central outburst of the chapter and, in its wording and rhythm, echoing the
morning scene outside the Grosvenor hotel (74.27).

With Bloom's dozing off at the end, the style shifts again, to
become unpunctuated associative alogical dream language (382.13).

Afterwards the narrative splits up into three parallel strands, separated by the voice of the cuckoo clock, a temporal divider for an action going on in three different places. A short Bloom passage is followed by an evenly descriptive bit relating to the priest's house, before a last jerk brings the tone back to Gerty's more homely vein and a style that virtually closes the embrace indicated in the opening lines of the chapter.

'Her high notes and her low notes' (374.30)

'Nausicaa' is technically complex, numerous discordant ruptures disturbing the basic division into two main parts. Not even the style of Gerty's half is as monotonous or uniform as critics have assumed. Like 'Cyclops' and 'Oxen of the Sun', 'Nausicaa' is a compendium of moods and styles, though the spectrum is narrower. Apart from flat descriptive passages, baby talk, a sermon, a recipe, and other variants, there is Gerty's own palette, of which it may be useful to distinguish such sub-categories as:

'LUXURIANT CLUSTERS' (349.15)

—the sweetly romantic passages that we usually consider the trade mark of the first half of 'Nausicaa'. 'Mayhap it was this, the love that might have been, that lent to her softlyfeatured face at whiles a look, tense with suppressed meaning, that imparted a strange yearning tendency to the beautiful eyes, a charm few could resist' (348.39). Their features are precious, elevated diction, pretentious and threadbare metaphors, ample adornment. Few nouns lack decorative epithets: 'There was an innate refinement, a languid queenly *hauteur*, . . . her delicate hands and higharched instep . . .' (348.30). Such lines cannot simply be read aloud, they have to be declaimed.

'ENDEARING WAYS' (346.22)

—a more homely sentimental vein, with less variety in its imagery, but full of feeling: '. . . he would give his dear little wifey a good hearty hug and gaze for a moment deep down into her eyes' (352.34).

'SUMPTUOUS CONFECTION' (351.24)

—the fashion page of the women's magazine: 'She wore a coquettish little love of a hat . . .' (350.16).

'MADAME VERA VERITY' (349.4)

—the column of practical advice: 'Then there was blushing scientifically cured' (349.8).

'PERSUASIVE POWER' (346.39)

—advertisement slogans: 'the fabric that caresses the skin' (366.27).

'LITTLE TIFFS' (348.27)

—more straightforward girlish thoughts that often move at a brisk pace with a touch of vicious directness: '. . . irritable little gnat she was' (360.37).

'UNMENTIONABLES' (347.24)

—at times Gerty's voice drops to evasive vagueness when an unpalatable or unladylike subject is bypassed in the flattest way, with phrases like 'when there for a certain purpose', 'that thing must be coming', 'without all that other', 'the other thing', 'a thing like that'.

Such styles and tones and other variants that we might mention could be arranged in a kind of hierarchy. The most conspicuous effusions of (what Gerty would consider) poetical (and we condescendingly classify as) kitsch occur as high points in the narrative rather than as a continual performance. It is difficult to remain in the upper register throughout.

'Keep that thing up for hours' (374.22)

Stylistically, and psychologically, there is a strenuous attempt to sustain that high tone together with repeated failures 'to keep it up' (those words are also implied by Bloom's recall of the song about Mary who 'lost the pin of her drawers', 368.38, thematically in tune). The different stylistic elevations are juxtaposed in free and surprising discords, with comic drops and new flights. The tone keeps changing within a limited range so that the chapter is one of those characterized by the marvellously attuned wrong note. The ups and downs can be seen as sequences of tumescence and detumescence, pathos and bathos, or inflations and deflations (Bloom remembers blown-up phrases from 'Aeolus', 'moonlight silver effulgence'—

370.17; 'Nausicaa', like 'Aeolus', depends on airy distensions; Gerty's
figure is composed of rhetorical ones).

Some of the shifts in the exposition illustrate this (significantly,
'Nausicaa' is the only chapter that has an exposition). The opening
description of the *dramatis personae*, not ostensibly lofty, still aims
at a stately pace and is clearly literary: 'The three girl friends were
seated on the rocks, enjoying the evening air which was fresh but
not too chilly' (346.11). Somewhere around the middle the tone
flops; 'seated' does not quite match the conversational 'but not too
chilly'; the implied situational contexts jar, if only slightly (another
change from the clashing strong contrasts in 'Cyclops'). Some readjustments will occur later in the reading, when the epithet 'girl
friends' will be undercut by the give and talk of girlish gall and by
Edy Boardman's speaking 'none too amiably' (347.41). Even if an
identical phrase is repeated, such as 'on the rocks', it can assume a
baser meaning: 'when we were on the rocks in Holles street', Bloom
remembers (369.39). This sense can retrospectively obtain in the
opening scene too. Gerty's life is on the rocks.

While the strained-after grace of the sentence quoted above is
not, perhaps, decisively marred, there is nevertheless a chill. A bit
of fresh air, real air, has interfered with the air of refinement. All
through the chapter, natural or common things, like 'stones and bits
of wood', or else parts of the physical (not figurative) body ('. . . but
it was only the end of her nose', 351.31) have a way of breaking the
spell.

After 'chilly', the effort to elevate the diction is evident in redundancy: 'Many a time and oft were they wont . . .'. A tiny drop
follows, 'to come there', and a gentle rise, 'to that favourite nook',
and another descent into a more homely strain, 'to have a cosy
chat', then a spurring of the poetic impulse: 'beside the sparkling
waves . . .'. But after this sparkle we are in for a trivialized tumble—
'. . . to discuss matters feminine'. And so the chapter stumbles
forward and tension mounts, the stylistic heights grow dizzier, and
the ecstatic flights correspondingly longer. Toward the centre the
sentences swell and punctuation decreases (every comma or period
is, after all, a stop to fetch breath and a brief touching of the ground),
until we reach the magnificent sweep of the climax and are ready for
the final descent and the last drop.

'Just changes when you're on the track' (368.39)

The stylistic metamorphoses, some rapid, others gliding, need not be interpreted as merely vertical shifts. The language could be recorded on a sort of oscillogram, but it would not be simple to articulate the discernment of modes of language which we believe we can grasp intuitively. The flexibility of the style, with its odd traverses and sudden bounds, contrasts pointedly with Gerty Mac-Dowell's inflexible fixedness and her unconscious and tacit acceptance of the several poses of which the styles are the outward and visible form. The constant re-focussing obliges the reader to sharpen his sense of the disparities (some inherently comical) and the perpetual clashes between illusory disguises and chilly reality. Each new attitude is apt to invalidate the previous one. But even within one given stylistic level, the metaphors often jostle each other incongruously: 'that vile decoction which has ruined so many hearths and homes had cast its shadow over her childhood days . . .' (354.18). And Gerty is able to move unconcernedly from the 'scorn immeasurable' that emanates from her eyes, to 'one look of measured scorn', on the same page (362.17, 41; the more liberal, unmeasured quantity, by the way, is reserved for the female rival).

Scenic changes implicit in the stylistic and metaphorical potential of this chapter's language will be taken literally in 'Circe', where they are grotesquely staged. Stylistic guises adapted to the current themes are, of course, the distinctive mark of *Ulysses*; in the later chapters the method is intensified by formal intricacy, and the adaptability of the style, corresponding to the mercurial assumption of expedient roles, may perhaps be understood as a reflection of Odyssean tactics. Odysseus is known for his versatility: he cunningly suits his language, form of address, and guise to the immediate purpose and has on occasion recourse to impersonation (at times divine agencies help along with a touch of transfiguration). When he appears to Nausicaa from the bushes, he is in fact quickly considering alternative approaches to win her over and decides on sweet words and the pretence that she is a goddess, queen, or bride.[22] (Gerty's presumptions are similar.)

---

[22] *Odyssey*, VI, 141–185.

To change one's voice according to the situation is common to Odysseus and to *Ulysses*, whose true hero is language. The language of the book is *polytropos*: ingenious, resourceful, resilient, of many turns—wiles or tropes.[23]

At the same time, the style chosen for Gerty's parts (and within the framework of her own ambitions), the cliché and the shopsoiled charms of stereotyped fiction or commercial slickness, is manifestly unable to characterize anything outside itself. It reflects only its own vacuity, it hardly illuminates or communicates, its glitter is narcissistic, its essence is self-gratification.

'all put on before third person' (374.13)

Montage helps Joyce to convey both the interior landscape of Gerty's mind and her environment. The question is whether the various items fit together. To the reader's delight, they do not. Gerty's fashions and styles do not do what articles of clothing should do—they do not 'match' (which is one of the thematic words: 'with caps to match', 346.22; 'to match that chenille', 350.19; 'blue to match', 366.15; 'As God made them He matched them', 373.32). Thematic references to fashion are highly appropriate. Fashion is a matter of putting something on, of a careful array of different elements to create a type, its success depending on taste and discernment. It is also changeable. Fashion and cosmetics serve to touch up the appearance, and Gerty's appearance is put together from many little touches. We are privileged to experience her charms along with the means by which she will achieve them: 'Her hands were of finely veined alabaster with tapering fingers and as white[24] as lemon juice and queen of ointments could make them' (348.21).

We are also treated to a close-up of Gerty's mind and, simultaneously, are made aware of the forces that helped to shape it. The first half of the chapter is a novelette conveying the de-formation of Gerty MacDowell: what she is and what made her what she is. The kind of writing here parodied would lead to that kind of thinking,

---

[23] Fritz Senn, 'Book of Many Turns', *JJQ*, X, 1 (Fall 1972), 29–46.

[24] The whiteness of Gerty's hands, and the 'snowy slender arms' (366.37) may also owe something to Homer's Nausicaa: '*Nausikaa leukolenos*' (*Odyssey*, VI, 101), 'Nausikaa of the white arms', as Butcher and Lang translate it (p. 95). A number of Gerty's traits can be traced back to Homer.

which, in turn, if it could articulate itself, would produce that kind of culture. In one way, Gerty is indistinguishable from the forces that determine her. That through such a mélange of set pieces and trash, she does emerge as a person in her own right, however limited, is a triumph of indirect characterization.

'piquant tilt' (353.27)

Part of the humour of the paradoxically slanted episode may result from reading certain phrases as though they belonged to a context different from the apparent one. Each verbal unit seems to belong to a number of situational frameworks, just as the whole of *Ulysses* can be viewed within naturalistic, psychological, symbolic, Homeric, and numerous other contexts. Some of the turns language takes are inversely appropriate. Gerty is introduced as 'in very truth as fair a specimen of winsome Irish girlhood as one could wish to see' (348.10). She is precisely such a *specimen*, by definition something selected as typical of its class, by etymology something to look at, something in fact that one might be content to see, as Bloom is, wishing for little other contact. There *is* 'suppressed meaning' in her look (348.41), she has 'raised the devil' in Bloom (360.30). The 'studied attitude' of the lady in the almanac picture (355.26) epiphanizes Gerty's own posing and describes a scenic principle of the 'Nausicaa' chapter. Not only does Gerty wrap herself 'in thought', she is really 'lost in thought' (348.10). It seems appropriate to offer 'A penny for [her] thoughts' (360.40).

By expressing unmitigated disdain for the cliché, for *kitsch*, and for a victim like Gerty MacDowell (or Bloom's inept endeavours), we also, of course, are adopting a Gertyan pose, pretending to remain perpetually above their inefficacious lure. But the lure affects us too, on and off. Romantic *kitsch* in 'Nausicaa' (or in 'Sirens') also serves to embody the motif of seductiveness, to which most readers are not wholly immune. There is a fascination about that glamour too, an appeal that we hesitate to acknowledge. In fact, clichés could not have become popular but for some inherent charm, however cheap. The *Portrait* expressed this lure in all its elusive complexity. That Joyce (like the best of us) was attracted to *kitsch*, in music, in painting, and in literature is fairly obvious but less relevant than the skill with which he knew how to work on our susceptibilities, seducing us and at the same time allowing us to laugh about the tricks that are being used. Our laughter sometimes becomes a bit ostentatious and the clichés in which *we* give voice to distaste for the literary cliché testify to the intricacies of structure and tone, and, finally, to the complexity of response that is closely tied up with human motivation—difficult to trace and even more elusive of evaluation.

The axis along which we might measure our own attraction or repulsion is only one among the many subtly graduated scales that make up the network of multiple foci that is *Ulysses*. There is a protean quality about 'Nausicaa' too. Its simple outlines and the even-textured appearance are deceptive. The surface alone reveals itself as jagged as the uneven strand, 'stones and bits of wood . . . and slippy seaweed' (367.37)—full of ups and downs. For *this* relief, too, much thanks.

THE OXEN
OF THE SUN

J. S. Atherton

This chapter is an exercise in imitative form. Joyce is trying to make words reproduce objects and processes. The reader is confronted in the three opening paragraphs with an example of this technique employed for the traditional purpose of setting the place. The three paragraphs, each with threefold repetition, form a verbal equivalent for Homer's island of Trinacria, literally 'Three headlands' or, as it is described in Lamb's *Adventures of Ulysses*, 'having three promontories jutting into the sea'.[1]

Perhaps Joyce deliberately made the opening difficult to understand in order to warn his readers that what follows requires careful reading. The first word 'Deshil' is a pun in Gaelic, being a phonetic rendering of *deiseal, deisil*, which, when used by itself, means 'May it be right!' or 'May it go well!' and is thus very suitable to begin a difficult task. It also means 'Going to the right', or going in a clockwise or sunwise direction—the opposite to the widdershins used by witches—and so the natural and lucky way to proceed. The second word, 'Holles', refers to Holles Street; and the third word is Latin for 'Let us go'. So the whole combines 'Let it be right!' and 'Let us go south to Holles street'. The second triple repetition is an invocation

---

[1] Lamb, *The Adventures of Ulysses*, chapter 3. Joyce uses the spelling *Trinacria*, which Lamb presumably took from Vergil, not the usual transliteration *Thrinacia*.

to the sungod Helios, owner of the sacred oxen and here personified by Sir Andrew Horne who was, in 1904, in charge of the hospital in Holles street, and whose conveniently phallic surname allowed Joyce to use him as a fertility symbol. The third paragraph, 'Hoopsa, boysaboy, hoopsa!' is, as Stuart Gilbert pointed out, 'the triumphant cry of the midwife as, elevating the new-born, she acclaims its sex'.[2] There may be also a triumphant cry from Joyce that the language is being made to perform tricks like jumping through hoops; there is certainly a statement that the whole thing is to go in circles, there being, according to Joyce, 'nine circles of development (enclosed between the headpiece and tailpiece of opposite chaos)'.[3]

The rest of the chapter develops at length Joyce's experiment in presenting verbal equivalents for reality by means of the well-known attempt to parallel the growth of a child in the womb using passages illustrating the development of English prose from Anglo-Saxon to modern times. Joyce's letter to Frank Budgen, in which he described this while he was engaged on it, has often been reproduced, but it is so relevant to my purpose that I must quote it in full:

Am working hard at *Oxen of the Sun*, the idea being the crime committed against fecundity by sterilizing the act of coition. Scene, lying-in hospital. Technique: a nineparted episode without divisions introduced by a Sallustian-Tacitean prelude (the unfertilized ovum), then by way of earliest English alliterative and monosyllabic and Anglo-Saxon ('Before born the babe had bliss. Within the womb he won worship'. [Gilbert notes at this point that 'Readers will notice differences from the final version in *Ulysses*'.] 'Bloom dull dreamy heard: in held hat stony staring') then by way of Mandeville ('there came forth a scholar of medicine that men clepen etc') then Malory's *Morte d'Arthur* ('but that franklin Lenehan was prompt ever to pour them so that at the least way mirth should not lack'), then the Elizabethan chronicle style ('about that present time young Stephen filled all cups'), then a passage solemn as of Milton, Taylor, Hooker, followed by a choppy Latin-gossipy bit, style of Burton-Browne, then a passage Bunyanesque ('the reason was that in the way he fell in with a certain whore whose name she said is Bird in the hand') after a diarystyle bit Pepys-Evelyn ('Bloom sitting snug with a party of wags, among them Dixon jun., Ja. Lynch, Doc. Madden and Stephen D. for a languor he had before and was now better, he having dreamed tonight a strange fancy and Mistress Purefoy there to be delivered, poor body, two days past her time and the midwives hard put to it,

[2] Gilbert, p. 291.
[3] *Letters*, III, 16.

God send her quick issue') and so on through Defoe-Swift and Steele-Addison-Sterne and Landor-Pater-Newman until it ends in a frightful jumble of Pidgin English, nigger English, Cockney, Irish, Bowery slang and broken doggerel. This progression is also linked back at each part subtly with some foregoing episode of the day and, besides this, with the natural stages of development in the embryo and the periods of faunal evolution in general. The double-thudding Anglo-Saxon motive recurs from time to time ('Loth to move from Horne's house') to give the sense of the hoofs of oxen. Bloom is the spermatozoon, the hospital the womb, the nurse the ovum, Stephen the embryo.[4]

As appears from this letter, there are at least five processes going on in addition to the customary development of plot and portrayal of characters one expects in a novel:

1. A series of imitations showing the development of English.
2. A continuation of Joyce's Homeric parallels.
3. A treatment of the growth of the human foetus.
4. An outline of 'faunal evolution'.
5. A linking with earlier parts of *Ulysses*.

The first of these is the most surprising and was Joyce's chief concern, as it has been that of his critics. It gave him scope for the flair for mimicry that Gogarty and Stanislaus agreed in admiring,[5] and the 'prodigious memory' that Frank Budgen declared had 'by heart whole pages of Flaubert, Newman, de Quincey, A. J. Balfour and of many others'.[6]

One would expect however that, even with a prodigious memory, anyone attempting such a task would need some guidebooks. Stanislaus Joyce is on record as saying that while writing this chapter his brother studied Saintsbury's *History of English Prose Rhythm*.[7] It is evident from a study of the text that he also used the little anthology by W. Peacock in the World's Classics series, *English Prose: Mandeville to Ruskin*, published in 1903 and reprinted frequently since with the same pagination. He may have used other anthologies, and probably consulted the complete texts of some writers, but all that is known of his Trieste working library is a list

---

[4] *Letters*, I, 139–140.

[5] Stanislaus Joyce, *My Brother's Keeper*, London, 1958, p. 104: O. St John Gogarty, *It Isn't that Time of Year at All*, quoted in R. E. Scholes and R. M. Kain, eds., *The Workshop of Daedalus*, Evanston, Ill., 1965, p. 211.

[6] Budgen, p. 181.

[7] Ellmann, p. 489.

of the books on one of his shelves—'Shelf 3'.[8] The rest of the inventory has not survived. It seems probable, from internal evidence, that Joyce consulted the volumes of the *New English Dictionary* (*OED*) which were then available (i.e. up to about the end of *T*).

Joyce's usual method of composition was to make many notes, write a short first version, and then rewrite and expand. Many of his notebooks and early versions have survived, and the relevant ones have now been published.[9]

The section following the invocation and beginning 'Universally that person's acumen . . .' (383.9) represents, as Joyce said, 'the unfertilized ovum'. Again there is an attempt at producing a verbal equivalent for an object, the convoluted sentences enclosing a central core corresponding to the layers within the cell. It also represents chaos before creation. When the overlapping layers are unwound the meaning appears as: 'Every wise man knows that it is our duty to reproduce our species. The Celts have therefore always honoured the study of medicine and provided laudable care for pregnant women'. This is presented in four paragraphs corresponding to the fourfold division of the cell, with the alien-seeming element 'Before born babe bliss had. Within womb won he worship' (384.31) doing duty as the literal presentation of the centriole by which the cell will be fertilized as well as introducing the oxen-of-the-sun motif. Reference to 'the O'Shiels' and so on establishes the Irish background alongside Homeric Trinacria. The passage is undoubtedly original and ingenious; it suffers however from one unpardonable fault—it is boring.

The next passages are much more readable. We enter the first month of pregnancy with 'Some man that wayfaring was' (385.3) which describes Bloom arriving at the hospital door and being invited in by nurse Callan. The style is derived from that version of Anglo-Saxon which George Saintsbury produced in his *History of English Prose Rhythm*. Partly to show what Anglo-Saxon rhythms were like, partly to prove his dubious theory that any intelligent English reader could read Anglo-Saxon, Saintsbury translated his specimen texts into a very odd jargon. Joyce chose one typical sentence of this to represent the instant of fertilization. It is Saintsbury's

---

[8] Ellmann, pp. 794–795.
[9] Phillip F. Herring, ed., *Joyce's 'Ulysses' Notesheets in the British Museum*, Charlottesville, Va., 1972, pp. 162ff.

version of a line from Aelfric's *Homilies* in which Aelfric quotes
the Centurion's remark in Matthew, 8:8: 'Lord I am not worthy
that thou shouldst enter under my roof'. Aelfric has: 'Drihten, ne
som ic wyrde þaet þu innfare under mine ðecene', which Saintsbury
renders: 'Lord, not am I worthy that thou infare under my thatch'.[10]
In Joyce's hands this became 'that he would rathe infare under her
thatch' (385.19), with the thatch representing both the hospital
roof and—as Partridge and other lexicographers of slang will confirm
—the female genitalia. Modelled on Saintsbury's half-translated examples, the paragraphs have an amusingly Anglo-Saxon flavour. Joyce
would know, from his study of Saintsbury, if not before, that allitera-
tion was a feature of Anglo-Saxon verse not prose; but it helped to
produce the effect he wanted and tied up with the 'double-thudding'
motive of the oxen. The diction is meticulously controlled. No words
of Romance origin are admitted—not even those that were used in
Anglo-Saxon. Obsolete words of Anglo-Saxon origin, such as 'thole'
(385.8) to bear with patience, 'swire' (385.15) neck, and 'grameful'
(385.33) sorrowful, are displayed at fairly regular intervals to garnish
the antique flavour. One such word, 'twey', has been misprinted as
'they' (385.10, first occurrence) in the new Random House edition.
An imitation antique, 'bellycrab' (385.42) for cancer of the bowels,
may be a result of Joyce's reading in Saintsbury about Bishop Reg-
inald Pecock, whose style is imitated from Saintsbury's versions[11]
in the paragraph beginning 'The man that was come into the
house . . .' (386.9) along with various other old English passages.

   On the narrative level, Bloom has arrived at the hospital, met
nurse Callan (here called a nun because 'nurse' is French in origin)
and been told that the Doctor O'Hare he asked about died at 'yule'[12]
which is surprising since 'childermas' (385.42), 28th December, the
Feast of the Holy Innocents, so obviously fits the theme of the
chapter. The thunderstorm, 'levin leaping' (385.16), is threatening
God's anger. The progress of geological time is brought in with
mention of 'over land and seafloor' (385.24). We are at a period
when life is developing in the seas. Any reader who had not been
warned that Joyce was bringing in references to 'faunal evolution in
general' would overlook this, but it is typical of the subordinate

---

[10] Saintsbury, *History of English Prose Rhythm*, London, 1912, pp. 64–66.
[11] *Ibid.*, p. 62.
[12] Buffalo Joyce MSS, V.B.12.a.

position this theme occupies in the chapter. The embryology is equally sketchy. The word 'breastbone' (385.19) seems to have been used deliberately, and it has been said that it refers to the development of the breastbone in the embryo. If so it is completely out of place here for, according to Joyce's own embryological chart,[13] this bone appears in the seventh month of gestation. A transcript of the words on this chart is given in the appendix to this essay.

The short paragraph beginning 'Therefore, everyman . . .' (386.5) is modelled on two passages. The first is a speech at the beginning of *Everyman* which says, with words modified from 'take good heed to the ending', 'look to that last end' (386.5). Joyce's version sounds more genuinely antique to the nonspecialist than does the original. The rest of the paragraph is a Joycean version of Job, I:21, 'for as he came naked forth . . .', carefully adapted to its new context.

The paragraphs beginning 'And whiles they spake' (386.23) are, as Joyce said, 'in the style of Mandeville'. The early versions, now at Buffalo,[14] seem to be free composition modelled on the Mandeville, and neighbouring, passages in Saintsbury with few direct quotations but precise reproduction of the rhythm. Joyce then seems to have turned to Peacock's little anthology and collected extracts—a phrase or a single word that struck him as interesting—on sheets of foolscap paper. He then rewrote his first version adding some of his new material and crossing out the notes in coloured pencil as he used them. This process was sometimes repeated as often as fourteen times, each version being longer than the one before it.

The additions he used from Peacock begin, in Peacock, with the word 'sithen' (386.27) from Peacock's page 4, line 2. The third line on this page has 'he was full of cautels and of subtle deceits' which went into *Ulysses* as 'he was a man of cautels and a subtle' (386.36). On the fifth line is 'no man could devise a fairer ne stronger' which provided Joyce with 'no wight could devise a fuller ne richer' (387.12). Mandeville's word 'man' was too modern for Joyce, but surprisingly his word 'delectably', from about the middle

<hr/>

[13] British Museum, Add. MS 49975. Another, less complete version is the Cornell Joyce Collection item 58. The BM MSS include pages of notes from Peacock and elsewhere used in this and other chapters.

[14] Buffalo Joyce MSS V.A.11–13.

of the same page, was used (388.9) in spite of its modern appearance. From the next page in Peacock, Joyce took 'any of the tother' (388.1) and 'apertly' (387.29), and continued in the same way through most of the book, wherever he found the manner interesting or the words intriguing. Sometimes Peacock explained words in footnotes, and this usually drew Joyce's attention. The ones explained for pages 4 and 5 are 'sithen', 'cautels', and 'apertly'—all three used by Joyce. Another example of a word that Joyce found in a footnote is 'aventryd' which Peacock explained as 'couched' when it occurred in a passage on his page 9 from Malory's 'Of Balin and Balan'. Joyce seized on the apparent *ventre* in the middle of the word and wrote: 'her name is puissant who aventried the dear corse of our Agenbuyer' (391.24). The word looks remarkably at home in a passage with a strong flavour of Jeremy Taylor, and the *OED's* derivation of this word from O.F. *afeutrer*, to set a spear in the part of a saddle specially prepared and felted for it, must have added to Joyce's delight.

It would be tedious to list all of Joyce's borrowings from Peacock but I will add a few more to show how they were used. From the same page 9 on which 'aventryd' appeared Joyce selected 'that hight Naram' on line 5 and 'a passing good man of his body' on line 6. These were written in the margin of Joyce's rough manuscript as 'that hight Lenehan' (387.42) and 'a passing good man of his lustiness' (388.10), with signs to show where they were to be included on the next rewriting of the chapter. He was not particularly careful to use words from passages belonging to the author he was imitating. One phrase 'some unaccountable muskin' (402.21) Joyce must have found in Peacock's extract from Cowper's essay 'On Conversation', since the only other sources are the *Connoisseur* for 1756, in which it originally appeared, and the fifteenth volume of Southey's edition of Cowper's *Works*. Joyce uses it in a paragraph of 'Steele-Addison-Sterne'.

Various other features of these paragraphs need attention. In addition to the story and the stylistic development, the account of the evolution of animal life goes on. Monsters, or at least one 'horrible and dreadful dragon' (386.16), have risen out of the primeval sea, and the 'fecund wheat kidneys' (387.20) have linked the passage with 'some foregoing episode of the day', in this case Bloom's break-

fast. Hundreds of details of this kind have been discussed and tab-
ulated in an article by A. M. Klein.[15] Anyone following in Klein's
steps must be grateful to him, and it must be remembered that he
wrote before Joyce's MSS were available. Unfortunately he tried
to explain everything in terms of Joyce's letter to Budgen with an
undue reverence for Joyce's tropes and a complete lack of humour.
Joyce uses the details he inserts more light-heartedly than Klein
could believe and produces effects funnier than Klein realized.

When Mandeville's 'Hideous and horrible dragon' from Saintsbury suddenly appears as the 'horrible and dreadful dragon' (386.31)
of a bee which stung Bloom there is an obvious element of farce.
When Joyce describes the hops with which Guinness, and other less
relevant brews, are flavoured as 'serpents [taught] to entwine themselves up on long sticks' (387.22) he may, as Klein says, intend us
to think 'of course, [of] the winged reptiles (the pterodactyls)' [16]
for they represent a feature of faunal development appropriate at
this stage. But when one finds that Klein can see only the pterodactyls and not the hops one begins to question his interpretation.
Furthermore the knives being used here have handles made 'of the
horns of buffalos and stags' (387.8). The word *buffalo* does not
occur in English until 1588, two centuries too late for Mandeville's
Travels, and the animal itself is geological ages from pterodactyls; although biologically it is a member of the ox family and so entitled
to trample anywhere in this chapter, its presence seems uncalled for.
Indeed I find it impossible to reduce Joyce's details to a consistent
pattern.

This may, of course, be simply the result of my own lack of
perception. One detail that puzzled me for a long time was the
presence of 'the unicorn' and 'saint Foutinus his engines' (389.33, 36)
in a passage supposed to correspond to the second month of gestation in which, according to Joyce's chart, the embryo is sexless. But
'Saint Foutinus', whose name is obviously derived from *foutre* as a
patron saint of the sexual organs, is, like the unicorn, imaginary.
They are therefore literary renderings of non-existent sexual organs,
and thus suitable for the second month. Joyce inserts many such
almost private jokes into his text.

    [15] A. M. Klein, 'The Oxen of the Sun', *Here and Now* (Toronto), I (Jan.
1949), 28–48.
    [16] *Ibid.*, p. 29.

Joyce wrote to Budgen that he used 'Elizabethan chronicle style: About that present time young Stephen filled all cups' (391.3). As the chronicles vary so much it is doubtful if there is any such style. Saintsbury speaks of 'the wash and counterwash of different eddies and tides of influence',[17] but gives no illustrative passages. Joyce produced a paragraph full of tides and eddies, mostly un-Elizabethan and far from the style of the chronicles. He quotes Blake, Yeats, Dante, St Bernard—or whoever it was who wrote the *Memorare*—and even Léo Taxil,[18] who provides a link with Proteus (41.14). There are some suggestions of Elizabethan English in the first part of the paragraph: 'mo', 'prudenter', 'quod he' (391.4, 8), alongside the Middle English 'Agenbuyer' (391.25) and 'aventried' from Malory, all combining to make this one of the most linguistically mixed paragraphs in the chapter. Joyce is writing a transitional paragraph to mark the passage from the second to the third month of pregnancy. The word 'fraction' (391.10), which means the breaking of bread in the Eucharist, may be partly intended to show this.

The third month and the Elizabethan style begin with 'Hereupon Punch Costello . . .' (392.4), the month being indicated by the song: '*The first three months . . .*' (392.7). In *Time and Western Man* Wyndham Lewis frequently claimed that *Ulysses* was an imitation of the style of Thomas Nashe, and at first sight this paragraph is one bit of evidence in support of this—perhaps the only one. But there were other Tudor writers besides Nashe who indulged in flyting, and although the rhythm here is not unlike that of Nashe in an all-out attack on Gabriel Harvey, the vocabulary is not Nashe's at all. Skelton, whose poem 'To Mistress Margery Wentworth' is quoted at the end of the paragraph ('flower of quiet, margerain gentle', 392.23), used 'chode' and 'embraided' (392.16) meaning to upbraid and taunt. Spenser was the only Elizabethan to revive the Chaucerian word 'gasteful' for terrifying, but otherwise the diction is reasonably sixteenth century.

Lenehan and Dixon are teasing Stephen about his supposed love affairs. They mention 'a curious rite of wedlock . . . as the priests use in Madagascar island' (392.39), and Joycean scholars have failed to find any such rites. Joyce made them name Madagascar

---

[17] Saintsbury, *History of English Prose Rhythm*, p. 115.
[18] See M. Magalaner, *Time of Apprenticeship*, London and New York, 1959, pp. 50ff.

because it is wrong but sounds exotic and impressive. He had read
the sentence in the article in the eleventh edition of the *Encyclopaedia Britannica*: 'There are no priests, properly so called, in Madagascar'. He had read Ernest Crawley's *The Mystic Rose* which says
that 'defloration of the bride by priests' was a custom among the
Eskimos of Greenland. The students have the wrong island. Lenehan
and Dixon have to be wrong, to be liars like Penelope's suitors.
Stephen also loses stature in this chapter. In the section for the
second month he claimed that his money had been earned 'for a
song which he writ' (391.15) instead of by the humdrum task of
teaching. He is not even above borrowing a joke from Mulligan:
'who stealeth from the poor lendeth to the Lord' (390.24; 23.7).

The anthem '*Ut novetur sexus . . .*' (393.1), which makes blasphemous play with the hymn *Pange Lingua*, indicates that sex,
according to Joyce's chart, first appears in the third month. Various
other devices appear, such as links with the library scene in 'life ran
very high in those days' (393.16; 204.20) and 'secondbest bed'
(393.24; 203.24). The sentence beginning 'An exquisite dulcet
epithalame' (393.7) suggests Sir Thomas Browne in whose style
the entire second half of the paragraph is written. Distortions of a
verse from St John's Gospel, a prayer from the Mass: '*Orate, Fratres*'
(393.24), the 'Reproaches' from the Mass for Good Friday, and
passages from the Authorised Version of *Deuteronomy* precede this.
The 'Reproaches' addressed to 'Clan Milly' (393.30) refer in the
first place to Molly Bloom; but the polysemantic technique allows
Joyce to bring in Stephen's mother and a personification of Ireland.
There is a tragic overtone of regret at the loss of faith and innocence,
and for estrangement from motherland and mother. As Gilbert says,
'Stephen for a moment likens his country to his dead mother'.[19]
Then, typically, Joyce jumps from tragedy to farce. His caricature
of Sir Thomas Browne's style is one of his funniest passages, striking
what Simon Dedalus in *A Portrait* called 'an ugly likeness', but an
unmistakable one. Joyce used Saintsbury, choosing a specimen passage which is carefully marked out in scanned feet. He avoids direct
quotation except for 'Assuefaction unto anything minorates the
passion for it'[20] which he turns into 'Assuefaction minorates atroci-
ties' (394.3). The conclusion 'the whatness of our whoness hath

[19] Gilbert, p. 296.
[20] Saintsbury, *History of English Prose Rhythm*, p. 199.

fetched his whenceness' (394.23) is a joke against both Browne and Saintsbury who said that Browne was never guilty of homoeoteleuton, or having a series of words with the same ending.

Between the parodies of Browne and Bunyan is about a page which seems stylistically to be part of the 'Milton, Taylor, Hooker' passage which Joyce told Budgen came *before* the Browne passage. There is a shorter passage in the same style around 'aventried' (391.24). On the narrative level Stephen is frightened by a sudden peal of thunder and is mocked by all except Bloom who here shows his superiority to them by trying to console Stephen. But Stephen remains rebellious, using Blake's word 'Nobodaddy' (395.4) to vent his annoyance. This serves also as a link with an earlier episode (205.41) and the mention of how 'his heart shook' (394.41) tells us that we are in the fourth month when the heartbeats are first heard.

The excellent parody of Bunyan begins at 'But was young Boasthard's fear vanquished by Calmer's words?' (395.16). Bunyan is a suitable persona for pronouncing a moral judgment on the company, but the tone in most parts of the passage and the mild obscenities involved in the story of the 'whore Bird-in-the-Hand' (395.41, 396.7) obscure Joyce's serious intention. An obscurity on a less important level is produced by the four positions of 'Two-in-the-Bush' (396.3, 11) which indicate the fifth month (when the child's movements are first noticed) by a fourfold figure. Another feature of the fifth month, the first growth of hair, is indicated later by 'a cut bob' (397.14). This again is confusing, for the 'cut bob' style of wig belongs to the age of Smollett, a century later than Pepys who is supposed to be referring to it. Joyce seems to have deliberately confused his margins so as to make it impossible to produce a neat and accurate tabulation of the various details in his chapter, although this, of course, is precisely what all we critics try to do.

The Bunyan parody ends on a deeply serious note with the denunciation: 'O wretched company . . . that was the voice of the god that was in a very grievous rage that he would presently lift his arm and spill their souls for their abuses and their spillings done by them contrariwise to his word which forth to bring brenningly biddeth' (396.23). Stanley Sultan devotes several pages[21] to showing how serious he believes Joyce to be at this point. It is 'the crime committed against fecundity by sterilising the act of coition' that

[21] Sultan, pp. 281–287.

Joyce told Budgen was 'the idea' of the whole chapter. This conscientious objection to contraception appears several times in Joyce's works, but on each occasion the tone of the passage in which the condemnation occurs leaves one in doubt as to its seriousness. Perhaps the longest, certainly the most obscure, expression of Joyce's opinion is in *Finnegans Wake*, on page 585, where Humphrey is condemned for using his 'auricular of Malthus', and never wetting the tea.

The next paragraph begins with what Joyce called the 'diary-style bit Pepys-Evelyn' but there is no sign of Evelyn and the Pepys imitation is barely recognizable. Joyce's failure arises from his reliance here on Peacock who edited the Pepys extract ruthlessly; by expurgating and by beheading, curtailing and dividing sentences he produced a jerky effect quite unlike Pepys's smooth discursiveness. As an example, here is the beginning of a sentence by Pepys: 'After a little discourse of the sad news of the death of so many in the parish of the plague, forty last night, the bell always going, I back to the Exchange, where I went up and sat talking with my beauty, Mrs. Batelier, a great while . . .'. What Joyce read in Peacock's version was: 'Sad news of the death of so many in the parish of the plague, forty last night. The bell always going. This day poor Robin Shaw . . .'.[22] Joyce's version exaggerates the looseness of sentence structure produced by Peacock's mutilations, probably without realizing that the chief characteristic of Pepys's style was a careful integration of subordinate phrases and clauses into the main body of a sentence. His insertion of some scraps of the page-opening on which the sentence quoted above occurs does little to assist the likeness. They are: 'skittish' (397.20), 'stunk mightily' (396.32), and 'by and by' (396.39). The first sentence in this paragraph is tolerable Peacock-Pepys, but most unlike the real Samuel: 'So Thursday sixteenth June Patk. Dignam laid in clay of an apoplexy and after hard drought, please God, rained, a bargeman coming in by water . . .' . As the paragraph continues, the style and the details described gradually alter in period. A 'chair' and a 'fiacre' (397.8) are mentioned, and a gentleman, 'a good Williamite' wears 'a cut bob' (397.14). What has happened is that Joyce has passed on from Pepys's account of the Plague to Defoe's *The Journal of the Plague Year*, more than half a

[22] Pepys, *Diary*, V, p. 26 (26 July 1665), Peacock, *English Prose: Mandeville to Ruskin*, p. 122.

century later. The narrative gives a lively account of the arrival of Mulligan, with his friend Bannon who is fresh from Mullingar and Milly Bloom. They have passed through a rainstorm and the narrator babbles on about prophecies of fires to follow the wind and water, bringing in words which are completely anachronistic: 'Her hub' (397.39) and 'a heavybraked reel' (397.42), for example. But a whole collection of details and words out of their supposed period marks Joyce's realization of the 'queerities' (398.9) involved in imitating in 1920 an imitation made in 1722 of a style and events belonging to 1665. Embryological time, however, goes on as usual, 'her . . . chick's nails' (397.37), the 'cut bob', and 'the young quicks' (396.33) all indicating that the fifth month has been reached when, according to Joyce's chart, the hair first appears.

From 'The Plague: Predictions and Visions' in Peacock, which must have suggested the prophecies of the last paragraph, Joyce turned to the next item: Defoe's 'A Quack Doctor'. According to Budgen 'Joyce was a great admirer of Defoe. He possessed his complete works, and had read every line of them'.[23] But Peacock was a handy guidebook. The paragraph beginning 'With this came up Lenehan' succeeds remarkably well in the difficult task of imitating Defoe. It is difficult because Defoe was the master of a neutral unmannered English style, described by Saintsbury as 'ageless'. The two extracts from Defoe look like modern English in comparison with Joyce's parody; but Joyce's parody looks—for the average reader— much more like Defoe. Joyce spices his brisk sentences with unfamiliar words. Some actually come from Peacock's extracts: merry andrew—turned, of course, to 'merryandrew' (398.16), 'honest pickle', 'tester' (398.26), and the 'design of his embassy' (398.36); some, such as 'Paul's men', 'flatcaps' (398.20), and 'sackpossets' (398.23), were already obsolete in Defoe's time; others such as 'bookies' (398.19) and a 'welsher' (399.5) are Victorian. Joyce is enjoying the opportunity of writing a really 'ageless' style, which yet appears to be the essence of Defoe.

Gradually, in mid-paragraph, the style changes to that of Swift, another of Joyce's favourite authors. The phrase 'naked pockets' (399.10), which is a rendering of 'scrotum empty'—a characteristic of the embryo in the sixth month on Joyce's chart—is at about the middle of the overlap. The conversation turns to various topics to do

[23] Budgen, p. 186.

with bulls, Papal, bovine, and Irish. The words 'the hoose of the timber tongue' (399.21), in which a 'hoose' is a cough and 'timber tongue' a fungoid disease of the mouth often accompanied by a cough, occur in a passage that is recognizably in the manner of Swift.

Bulls, especially Irish and Papal ones, are discussed in a medley of Henry II and Henry VIII, the bull *Laudabiliter* of Adrian IV who was Nicholas Breakspear and here becomes 'farmer Nicholas . . . with an emerald ring in his nose' (399.33) referring, as Thornton points out, to John of Salisbury's statement that Adrian gave Henry II an emerald ring at the same time that he gave him the authority to conquer Ireland. The passage is racy and easy to read, vividly evoking the manner of Swift in A *Tale of a Tub*, with an occasional side glance at *Polite Conversation*. The smoothness was obtained only by constant polishing on Joyce's part. Some of the seemingly most spontaneous and easy phrases turn out, when one examines the early versions, to have been second or third thoughts. Even 'a portlier bull, says he, never shit on shamrock' (399.36) began with 'on a buttercup', then 'on clover' before attaining the seemingly inevitable 'shamrock'.[24]

With the entry of Mulligan, 'Our worthy acquaintance' (401.32), the style becomes a parody of Addison, whom Joyce disliked. Eugene Sheehy records that for Joyce at university Addison was 'the world's greatest hypocrite' and he 'lapsed into Chaucerian English to state that the great "Atticus" himself was "holpen nightly to his litter" '.[25] Nevertheless Joyce reproduces his style without much mockery. Banalities, such as ' 'Tis as cheap sitting as standing' (402.8) from Swift's *Polite Conversation*, and an oddity, the 'unaccountable muskin' (402.21) from Cowper, are inserted to show Addison's occasional lapses in both these directions; but the force of this is lost when one realizes that they are not Addison's own lapses. Many Addisonian features are shown: the whimsical young gentleman, Mulligan, being cast here as Will Honeycomb; the patronizing reference to 'the poorest kitchenwench no less than the opulent lady' (402.30); the long classical quotation. With his tongue in his cheek, Joyce elegantly adopts Addison's gentlemanly manner to present material so outrageously out of keeping with it as to make this one of the funniest passages in the book; the contrast between Addison's

[24] Buffalo MS V.A.12, 17.
[25] Scholes and Kain, eds., *The Workshop of Daedalus*, p. 170.

often declared intention to improve the taste and morals of the 'fair sex' and Mulligan's outspoken plan to get them all pregnant is used to accuse Addison of the hypocrisy that Joyce believed to be his salient feature.

We then move to Sterne, who is one of Joyce's favourite writers and is often mentioned in *Finnegans Wake*. The sympathetic parody of his very personal manner begins at 'Here the listener' (404.11) in a scene that illustrates 'Sterne's habit which is to show one or two central figures in sharp isolation and in mental undress, reporting every twitch of their bodies and every flicker of their mood without scruple and without haste'.[26] The passage is funnier if it is read with its source in mind. 'The questioning pose of the head', for example, ('a whole century of polite breeding had not achieved so nice a gesture', 404.16), is derived from Sterne's encounter with the donkey in *A Sentimental Journey*. Sentiment is much in evidence: 'he wiped his eye and sighed again' (405.3), as Bannon tells of the 'new coquette cap' (404.36) Bloom gave Milly. When Mulligan speaks, the tone changes to Sterne's delicately indelicate style, full of *doubles-entendres*. Lynch winds up the passage with an example of one of Sterne's favourite devices, the unfinished indecency: when 'dear Kitty' is about to name the other activity besides bathing for which nudity is 'the fittest, nay, the only garment' (405.36) she is stopped by the ringing of a bell.

Joyce did not name the models for the next paragraphs. Gilbert said that they are Goldsmith, Burke, and Sheridan, but, although there are passages imitating these writers, other styles can be detected. Dr Johnson, whose style provides an obvious target, appears at one point:

> Singular, communed the guest within himself, the wonderfully unequal faculty of metempsychosis possessed by them, that the puerperal dormitory and the dissecting theatre should be the seminaries of such frivolity, that the mere acquisition of academic titles should suffice to transform in a pinch of time these votaries of levity into exemplary practitioners of an art which most men anywise eminent have esteemed the noblest. (408.35)

The previous paragraph, which, as Gilbert said, is in the manner of Burke, contains also a number of brief quotations from Peacock's

[26] O. Elton, *A Survey of English Literature, 1730-1780*, 2 vols., London, 1912, I, 122.

extract from an essay by the Earl of Chesterfield to whom Johnson addressed the famous letter of 7 February 1755, rejecting the Earl's offer of patronage. Joyce has put two old enemies together.

Knowing that Chesterfield and Johnson are present gives added interest to the sudden appearance of Junius in the next paragraph, and explains the significance of the phrase, 'the noble lord, his patron' (409.4). Bloom has not uttered a single word aloud, but the sudden attack comes, just as the letters of Junius did, from an undiscoverable source armed with intimate knowledge of hitherto undisclosed facts. The violence of the attack has the effect of turning the satire against itself, as the historic Junius defeated his own object by a too venomous invective, and there is, of course, a funny side to it. The description of Bloom's attempt on the virtue of Mary Driscoll, and its repulse by her scrubbing-brush, gains in humour from the incongruity of the style.

News of the birth of Mrs Purefoy's baby is now given in the stately periods of Gibbon. All the features of his style are presented: 'the use of paired words', the 'system of antithetic balance', and 'that peculiar and undulating movement' in which Saintsbury found a resemblance to the Spenserian stanza.[27] The last sentence of the paragraph provides a reproduction of the famous Gibbonian sneer, when Stephen, having been asked what should be done in the event of one Siamese twin predeceasing the other, refers his questioner to the eighth chapter of St Matthew: 'What therefore God hath joined together let no man put asunder'. The variety of monstrous births provides links with 'Proteus'. Mulligan's remark about 'the agnatia of certain chinless Chinamen' (410.31), as well as providing another shape for Proteus, repeats a jibe about Eglinton made in the library (215.31) and so provides a different link. The reference to 'the seat of castigation' (411.15) reminds us that on the literal level birth has taken place, while on the literary level we are in the seventh month when birth is possible.

In the next paragraph the phrase 'his head appeared' (412.25) indicates that birth is commencing on the literary level. The style is that of the Gothic novel, for which many examples could be suggested, The Castle of Otranto being the most obvious. It ends, however, with a few brief quotations from Sheridan Le Fanu's The House

[27] Saintsbury, History of English Prose Rhythm, p. 183.

by the Churchyard, one of the four books in 'Joyce's father's library'.[28] The hidden indication of the source, 'the lonely house by the graveyard' (412.35), is a device Joyce often used in *Finnegans Wake,* toward the methods of which this chapter makes frequent approaches. The scraps of Gaelic are explained by O Hehir in his *Gaelic Lexicon for 'Finnegans Wake.'* A 'soulth' (412.18) is an apparition; a 'bullawurrus' derives from phrases meaning 'the smell of murder, the smell of earth (presage of death)'. 'Tare and ages' is an Anglo-Irish euphemism derived from 'Tears and wounds' (of Christ), and is thus a suitable imprecation on Irish history. The sentence beginning 'Tare and ages' is an amusing caricature of one of Synge's typical sentences which have a trick of undulating along to a conclusion that goes up like a rocket. These scraps of pseudo-Anglo-Irish and pseudo-Synge enliven the passage and make it appear typical of Mulligan's brighter patter.

The mood then changes as Joyce turns to a sympathetic imitation of Charles Lamb at his most sentimental. The title of Lamb's essay 'Dream Children' is the only title from Peacock's anthology that Joyce entered in his notes, and he seems to have admired the essay. The sentimentality of Bloom's reverie over his childlessness is broken, in Lamb's manner, by occasional quaint phrases, 'a goodly hunk' (413.9), 'a quiverful of compliant smiles' (413.15), and by whimsical parentheses such as 'hey, presto!' (413.5); yet, in spite of the interruptions, the rhythm of the passage is musical. Joyce obviously tries to achieve the effect described by Saintsbury as 'a perfectly achieved conglomerate . . . [but] too much broken up to achieve the highest rhythmical results'.[29] While reproducing the broken effect Joyce makes the paragraph run smoothly into the two paragraphs in De Quincey's manner, which follow it.

Saintsbury considered De Quincey one of the greatest of English prose writers. The passage that he selected to analyse, scan, and expound the merits of contains an unexpected mention of a crocodile which is not explained, and which Saintsbury, in his comments, whimsically refuses to explain, telling his readers to look up the original and find out for themselves. Joyce knew the passage before he read Saintsbury: it comes from the first section of *The English*

[28] See Atherton, *The Books at the Wake,* London, 1959, p. 110.
[29] Saintsbury, *History of English Prose Rhythm,* p. 362.

Mail-Coach which he could 'recite by the page'.[30] The 'crocodile' was the mail-coach driver whose many-caped greatcoat prevented his turning round quickly enough to see De Quincey kissing his granddaughter, Fanny. The middle-aged De Quincey, years later, thinks back into the past 'as the roses call up the sweet countenance of Fanny' accompanied in his reverie by 'a dreadful host of semi-legendary animals—griffins, dragons, basilisks, sphinxes . . .' . The ingredients of De Quincey's fantasy reappear in Joyce's paragraphs: horses, strange beasts, 'Elk and yak, the bulls of Bashan and of Babylon' (414.18). For 'the sweet countenance of Fanny' we are given 'Millicent, the young, the dear, the radiant' (414.31), and 'a mysterious writing' (414.38) reproduces the 'eternal writing' in De Quincey's passage. The reproduction of content is accompanied by a perfect imitation of De Quincey's rhythms.

Carried along by the rhythm (and perhaps it was here that Joyce learned how to make the rhythm of the Anna Livia chapter carry all its burdens of meaning in *Finnegans Wake*) come a miscellaneous clutter of all kinds of other details. Links with previous chapters look back, since this is Bloom's reverie, to incidents connected with him. The oxen motif becomes prominent and is itself linked by a quotation to the closing speech of Yeats's *Countess Cathleen*:

> *The years like great black oxen tread the world,*
> *And God the herdsman goads them on behind,*
> *And I am broken by their passing feet.*

'Huuh! Hark! Huuh! Parallax stalks behind and goads them' (414.16). Bloom's artless puzzling over an unfamiliar word has been elevated into a symbol of his enquiring mind. In the context it becomes the driving spirit behind the universe. The choice of De Quincey is appropriate to this passage: although his ornate prose is not admired today, he is one of the greatest English writers on dreams, loneliness, and introspection. 'The dream', he wrote in the first part of *Suspiria*, is 'the one great tube through which man communicates with the shadowy'. It is, in part, this 'tube' to which Joyce refers in the Bunyan

[30] *Ibid.*, p. 313. Joyce's library, now at Buffalo, contained a volume of selections from De Quincey's works, including *The English Mail-Coach* and passages from the *Suspiria*. The La Hune Catalogue, made when these books were on exhibition in Paris, notes that a bill from a Triestine bookseller, dated 23 March 1920, was found in the book, so Joyce must have bought it to use for this chapter. (La Hune Catalogue, item 429.)

passage: 'the tube Understanding' (395.26). Because De Quincey once wrote that a creative genius was distinguished by a 'power of combination bringing together from the four winds . . . what else were dust from dead men's bones', Joyce uses this passage to show his own power of combination and concludes with a most remarkable example of it as Bloom gazes at the triangle on the label of the bottle of Bass until it becomes a 'triangled sign upon the forehead of Taurus' (414.40)—combining lingam and yoni in one symbol, which itself represents the underlying symbol of the chapter, and placing it in the depths of space.

By following Saintsbury in taking Landor to be next in order in the chronicles of English prose Joyce achieved an effective change in tone. (Peacock omits Landor altogether.) Saintsbury's specimens are from *Imaginary Conversations* between classical figures. It may be to indicate his source that Joyce names at the beginning two characters to whom Landor gave title roles, 'Alcibiades, Pisistratus' (415.2). They represent two boys from Clongowes about whom Costello is asking Stephen for news. As Stephen replies that he can re-create them by his art, Joyce demonstrates that by his art he can re-create the rhythms of Landor: 'If I call them into life across the waters of Lethe will not the poor ghosts troop to my call?' (415.4). The cadence is one that Saintsbury would have been pleased to scan, and the entire paragraph succeeds in retaining the 'other harmony of prose', while suggesting the verse rhythms that it avoids with a deftness equal to Landor's. Even that 'weakness for amphibrachs' which Saintsbury deplored is used and put into comic effect with Lenehan's 'his mother an orphan' (415.15). The subject matter changes with an abruptness characteristic of Landor. Lynch rebukes Stephen for boasting of his literary powers when 'only a capful of light odes' (415.10) bears them witness. The rest talk about the Gold Cup race, and Lynch describes how he and a girl were met and blessed by Father Conmee. Here the accounts not only form links with earlier chapters but also add to our knowledge of events. Meanwhile Stephen broods over the criticism of his work. It is the only criticism of his writing to appear in *Ulysses* for, as Peter Egri remarked: 'Joyce says very little about the quality of Stephen's writing'.[31]

Criticism of his own writing is frequent. There are many passages

[31] P. Egri, 'James Joyce and Adrian Leverkühn', *Acta. Lit. Acc. Hungaricae*, VIII (1966), p. 212.

in *Finnegans Wake* condemning his earlier work, including the 'usylessly unreadable Blue Book of Eccles'. In this chapter it comes, not by direct statement, but implicitly through the formal arrangement of the prose. Paragraphs imitating the graces of ornate prose writers are followed by a paragraph parodying the most graceless individual style used by Joyce in *Ulysses*; the prose of 'Eumaeus'. Five flaccid cliché-laden sentences containing examples of what teachers call 'common errors in the use of English' are used to describe Bloom's contemplation of the Bass label. Even here Joyce has a source-book, W. B. Hodgson's *Errors in the Use of English*,[32] from which he took such solecisms as 'him being' (416.36) for 'his being', and 'individual' (416.39) for 'person'. But the self-criticism involves, as do the parodies in 'Cyclops', a criticism of modern life and modern journalism. On the naturalistic plane it shows us a Bloom who is getting very tired.

A contrasting paragraph follows, imitating a famous paragraph in Macaulay's 'Warren Hastings' which is quoted and scanned by Saintsbury and begins 'The place was worthy of such a trial'. The weighty, dignified sentences contrast significantly with the trivialities they describe, and yet the criticism may be taken in the opposite direction, to suggest that Macaulay's description gave undeserved glamour to a piece of political jobbery. Only Bloom, 'that vigilant wanderer' (418.3), can be said to emerge unscathed, and he, of course, is 'stained by the mire of an indelible dishonour'.

The next paragraph, which is in the manner of Dickens, is unusual in that Joyce seems to have tried to make sure that everyone would recognize the imitation. He uses 'Doady' (421.1, 6, 21) three times in half a page, thus betraying an unaccustomed lack of confidence. There seems to be an air of perfunctoriness about the imitation which reminds one of Stanislaus Joyce's comment: 'My brother never cared for Dickens'.[33] Joyce reveals the sentimentality and a few mannerisms such as repetition ('a weary weary while', 420.31), and he parodies Dickens's combination of humour with social criticism in the description of the pathetic attempt to gain favour by naming the child after 'the influential third cousin of Mr Purefoy in the Treasury Remembrancer's office, Dublin Castle' (421.17). But Joyce's austerities in punctuation made it difficult for him to imitate Dickens who

[32] Ellmann, p. 794.
[33] Joyce, *My Brother's Keeper*, p. 78.

relied so heavily on the semicolon and the dash, stops that Joyce abjured.

Joyce's demonstration of 'the cool silver tranquillity' (421.37) of Newman's prose exhibits the stylist *in vacuo* by eschewing narration. While believing that Newman was the greatest of English prose writers, he accepted none of his ideas. Bloom's brooding on the past develops, as he looks at Stephen, in a passage of basic Victorian rhetoric probably meant to be in the manner of Pater. There are suggestions of Thackeray and De Quincey in the passage, but the adjectives 'a brief *alert* shock' (422.13), '*thoughtful* irrigation' (422.14), and (perhaps as an equivalent for Pater's 'hard gem-like flame') 'cool *ardent* fruit' (422.19), adequately mark the passage as in the style of Pater. As Bloom looks at Stephen he thinks again of the game of bowls that he remembered at the funeral (115.19). Bloom's only athletic triumph parallels Ulysses' throwing of the stone before Alcinous. He recalls Stephen as 'a lad of four or five in linsey-woolsey' (422.20). The parenthetical quotation '*alles Vergängliche*' (422.27), 'Everything [is] transitory', suggests the final Hymn in Goethe's *Faust*, part II, the rescue of erring male mortality by the eternal feminine. Stephen and Bloom are again linked here.

The 'linseywoolsey' also links Stephen with Bloom's son who was buried in 'the little woolly jacket' (778.31). Stephen, 'the embryo', has at last reached birth; Stephen, the character, is about to lead his friends out to the nearest pub. English prose has apparently reached full growth with the style of Ruskin. This may, of course, have been suggested by the terminal passage of Peacock's *English Prose: Mandeville to Ruskin*, but Joyce once wrote that he was 'taught by Father Tommy Meagher and Ruskin',[34] in a context suggesting that Ruskin was the model set for imitation by his master at school. Joyce impishly reproduces a feature that might have displeased Father Meagher —a tendency to write sentences without finite verbs—which is noticeable in many of Ruskin's purpler patches. For example, the account of Giorgione in *Modern Painters* has: 'A wonderful piece of world. Rather, itself a world'.[35] The sentence beginning 'Quietude of custody' (422.32) is less obviously defective—but it is not the sort of sentence of which Joyce approved, although he presents it as part of the accepted model of modern literary prose.

[34] *Letters*, II, 108.
[35] Ruskin, *Modern Painters*, London, 1846, V, ix, 74.

We are then taken outside into a confusion suitably embodied by the style of Carlyle. The words 'placentation ended' (423.8) probably tell us the biological significance of these two paragraphs. Both sentence-structure and diction are mockeries of the various eccentricities, too many to detail, which Joyce observed. But Goethe himself once declared Carlyle to be 'a moral force of great significance', and Joyce has this in mind as he uses Carlyle's voice to praise the fruitful Theodore Purefoy who will be saved like the Israelites under Gideon, for his 'fleece is drenched' (423.34; Judges, 6:38). Joyce zestfully inserts rare words into the passage, such as 'cessile' (423.23) which appeared in no English dictionary until the *Supplement to the OED* was published in 1972. The French translation, which Joyce helped to compile, translates the word as 'cessile', a word which appears in no French dictionary. The passage ends with the students declaring, with oaths by Partula (424.17), the goddess who presides over childbirth, and Pertunda, who presides over the consummation of marriage, that the time is now for drinking.

We then pass to ten paragraphs that present a literary equivalent of drunkenness. The language of the 'frightful jumble' which Joyce said he used here to present chaos is even more complex than his letter to Budgen indicated. In addition to the 'Pidgin English, . . . Cockney, Irish, Bowery slang, and broken doggerel' there is French, Scottish, Yiddish, German, sixteenth-century English canting, pugilists' and motor-racing slang, together with scraps of Latin, Gaelic, mock Welsh-English. A further element, to which no critical attention has been paid, is 'Parlyaree', the strolling players' jargon mainly derived from Italian; 'Me nantee saltee' (425.7) meaning 'I haven't a penny' is one example.

The narrative contained in this outpouring of words is hard to grasp; but the effect, of being personally involved in a drunken melee and left in a state of shock, is precisely what Joyce intended. 'Significant form' can be taken no further and its success in this episode cannot be denied since it deals with an area of experience which, to quote Joyce, 'cannot be rendered sensibly by the use of wideawake language, cutanddry grammar and goahead plot'.[36]

What happens is that they all go to Burke's pub, drink two rounds at Stephen's expense, and are turned out at closing-time, Bannon and Mulligan having previously slipped away because Ban-

[36] *Letters*, III, 146.

non has suddenly recognized Bloom as Milly's father. In the pub they meet Bantam Lyons, drunk and with his moustache shaved off, who is carrying a bunch of flowers, presumably as a peace-offering to his wife. The mysterious man in the macintosh is seen and recognized as a former patient at the Richmond mental hospital. The tatters of information about him join in this passage: He 'married a maiden' (427.24) who 'Slung her hook'. The slang phrase means simply that she left him, but we know from the 'Cyclops' chapter that 'The man in the brown macintosh loves a lady that is dead' (333.32). It is so fitting that our knowledge of him should coalesce in a medium of drunken talk where ideas are imprecise and characters seem to slip and slide that he could be taken as a personification of the passage.

In the confusion, secrets slip out, as they might do in such a situation in real life. But Joyce seems to be defying the whole tradition of fiction in the account which he gives of the activities of Stephen Hand. The passage reads: 'The ruffin cly the nab of Stephen Hand as give me the jady coppaleen. He strike a telegramboy paddock wire big bug Bass to the depot. Shove him a joey and grahamise. Mare on form hot order. Guinea to a goosegog. Tell a cram, that. Gospeltrue. Criminal diversion? I think that yes. Sure thing. Land him in chokeechokee if the harman beck copped the game' (426.21). This might be rendered: The Devil take the head of Stephen Hand who gave me a tip for a bad horse. He met a telegraph-boy with a telegram to the head of the Bass stable from the racing-stable. He gave him sixpence and steamed the envelope open. It said that Bass's mare, Sceptre, was in first-class form and certain to win. That telegram was a lie but my account is Gospel-true. It was a criminal act? Certainly. It would get him into prison if the police found out.

Interpretation of this was made impossible by Stuart Gilbert, the editor of the first Odyssey Press edition in 1932. He put a full-stop between Stephen and Hand, and all subsequent editions have followed his example. That the interpretation given above is the correct one only became known when Joyce's letter to Georg Goyert was published in 1967. Joyce had explained to his German translator: 'Stephen Hand met a telegramboy who was bringing a private racing telegram from the stable of the celebrated English brewer Bass to the police depot in Dublin to a friend there to Back B's horse Sceptre for the cup. S.H. gives the boy 4 pence, opens the telegram over steam (grahamising), recloses it and sends the boy on with it, backs Sceptre to win and loses. (This really happened and his name was Stephen Hand though it was not the Gold Cup)'.[37] The introduction of an incidental character in this way is justifiable at the level of the realistic novel on the grounds that an exploit such as Stephen Hand's would be heard of only when the people in the know were drunk and even then would be disclosed in language calculated to prevent outsiders from learning the truth. In fact a modern version of the Elizabethan thieves' canting might be expected. Perhaps it is to indicate this that Joyce gives Lenehan some genuine canting—the opening line of the song, 'The ruffin cly the nab of the harmanbeck'. (The devil take the constable's head.)[38] This, of course, is not realism: 'Tell a cram, that' is the usual Lenehan style, saying in a pun that the telegram was a lie, or 'cram'.

The narrative tells us that the drinkers expelled from Burke's hear a fire-engine, and everyone except Stephen, Lynch, and Bloom rushes off to share in the excitement. Stephen invites Lynch to come with him to nighttown: 'We two, she said, will seek the kips where shady Mary is' (428.6), the parody of Rossetti's 'Blessed Damozel'

> We two, she said, will seek the groves
> Where the lady Mary is,

receiving the simple reply, 'Righto, any old time', from the impassive Lynch, who wants to know who Bloom is. Stephen's answer echoes Mr Deasy's remark about the Jews, 'Sinned against the light' (428.9, 34.3), and he goes on to equate the fire in Mount street with the end of the world and Bloom with Christ. These things are happening that the Scriptures may be fulfilled, he tells Lynch, quoting the Vulgate version of Mark, 14:49, but changing the indicative to the subjunctive. After this blasphemy, which furthers the Homeric parallel by presenting the punishment by the god, and which reinforces other parallels, Stephen and Lynch move on and Bloom follows. Passing a poster advertising an American revivalist they give their version of what his address will be like, so ending the series of

---

[37] Alan Cohn, ed., 'Joyce's Notes on the End of "Oxen of the Sun"', *JJQ*, IV, 3 (Spring 1967), 194–201.

[38] Joyce's 'Working Library' included Grose's *Classical Dictionary of the Vulgar Tongue*, 1785; but this is an expensive volume and he is unlikely to have had it in Trieste. My own opinion is that Joyce's source for all his snatches of 'canting' was J. S. Farmer's *Musa Pedestris*. This one volume contains everything of the canting songs that he ever quoted.

parodies of forms of the English language and completing the
story of the 'Oxen of the Sun' with the account of divine vengeance.

The reader is left bemused, like a person with a hangover trying
to puzzle out what really did happen the previous night. All kinds
of minor problems arise, often taking a long time to solve. Why, for
example, should Joyce print the joke spelling '2 night' (427.10) in
a passage purporting to be pure conversation? Since it is impossible
to say '2 night' except as 'tonight' this must be taken as a reminder
that what we are reading is what was written down by Joyce. He
uses figures for numbers in the same way in Molly's final soliloquy.
This may seem to be making too much of a minor joke, and indeed
the joke apart from its purpose is not particularly funny. Most of
the others are much funnier. To my mind, it is the sheer funniness
of the passage that emerges as its outstanding characteristic, even
more than the furious vitality that is the first feature to emerge from
the confusion.

The main feature of the entire passage, in spite of all the
laborious technical exercises and the occasional tedious paragraphs,
is its wit. There are few funnier passages in all literature. But it is
more important historically as an attack on the problems of written
communication. It has opened new grounds in many directions, so
many that critical opinion is only now, fifty years later, catching up
with Joyce's practice. Commenting on the chapter, Anthony Burgess
wrote: 'We two, she said, will seek the kips where shady Mary is.
We have to seek those kips ourselves before we come into the clear
light of sanity, and even then it is a drunken phantasmagoric sanity.
. . . It seems strange that we should have to go to the next chapter
to find out what has happened in this'.[39] It is even stranger that we
do not really know what has happened until we have read Joyce's
letters. In modern jargon, Joyce is exploring an interface by punching
holes of fact in fiction and using phonetically indistinguishable symbols instead of words; he is using the medium as his message. I find
myself in complete agreement with Burgess, who is an imaginative
writer of some distinction, when he goes on to add: 'And yet, of all
the episodes of Ulysses, this is one that I should most like to have
written. . . . It is an author's chapter, a dazzling and authoritative
display of what English can do. Moreover, it is a fulfilment of every
author's egotistical desire not merely to add to English literature but

[39] Anthony Burgess, Here Comes Everybody, London, 1965, p. 156.

to *enclose* what is already there'. It is also, of course, a critic's chapter. There are very few things that can be done with English that Joyce does not do in the 'Oxen of the Sun'. What the chapter calls for is a full-length book about English in the manner of *The Arcadian Rhetorike* of Abraham Fraunce, using Joyce's chapter as Fraunce used Sidney's *Arcadia*. The chapter appeals, admittedly, only to readers concerned with the technique of writing; but in an age when mass popularity is normally accepted as the criterion of value and sometimes accorded to persons who have never attempted to master any technique at all, we cannot afford to ignore or undervalue Joyce's achievement.

*　　*　　*

APPENDIX

The embryological chart for 'Oxen of the Sun'. British Museum, Add. MS 49975:

9

50cm
3500gr
tooth sockets
thigh bone nucleus
nails long
sex complete
hair 3cm dark

8

45cm 2000g
fontanelles almost shut
face younger
cheeks fuller
outer ears nails longer
testicles lower
clitoris, nipples sacral bone
caseous gloss in joints

7

fore fontanelle smaller
old face
testicles in groin
breastbone
heelbones
40cm 1500g

6

30–34cm
1000g
scrotum empty
down
skin red
head smaller
pubics
fontanelles

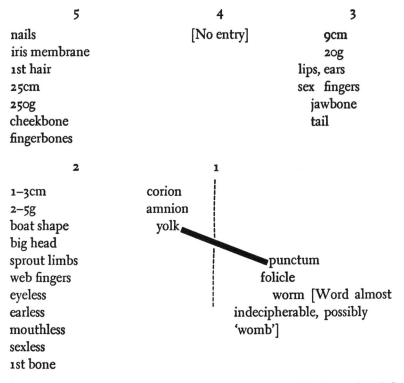

5	4	3
nails	[No entry]	9cm
iris membrane		20g
1st hair		lips, ears
25cm		sex fingers
250g		jawbone
cheekbone		tail
fingerbones		

2	1	
1–3cm	corion	
2–5g	amnion	
boat shape	yolk	
big head		punctum
sprout limbs		folicle
web fingers		worm [Word almost
eyeless		indecipherable, possibly
earless		'womb']
mouthless		
sexless		
1st bone		

[The spelling 'folicle' in 1 suggests an Italian source for these details.]

CIRCE

Hugh Kenner

When, just past the middle of the book, the reader of *Ulysses* turns from barely penetrable verbal chaos ('Pflaaaap! Not half'.) to a page laid out with reassuring typographical controls—speeches in upper- and lower-case Roman, speakers' names in small caps, narrative and description in italics—his gratitude for the *rappel à l'ordre* is apt to be mingled with astonishment at coming on what looks very like a play. But Joyce's art of slow revelation characteristically reveals itself more readily than it reveals anything else, and the ideal reader is meant at this point to reflect how thoroughly congenial is the theatre of roles and surfaces to this author's vision of things. On the first page of the book the first thing we were shown was Buck Mulligan playacting, and if Stephen Dedalus seemed to be holding himself aloof from that particular play, it was because of his immersion in a different play of his own. Mulligan who normally plays the doctor and sometimes the court jester, was playing the priest; Stephen, playing the sceptical intellect, was playing it in tattered Hamlet costume (solemn black) via the postures of a *fin de siècle* poet: Paul Verlaine, say, another sober dresser. Mulligan was not in his doctor costume but in a makeshift priest costume, a yellow dressinggown serving for chasuble. Mulligan's 'plump shadowed face and sullen oval jowl recalled a prelate, patron of arts in the middle ages' (3.33), so this is another possible role; and

on the third page of the novel he addresses Stephen by a name that
is not Stephen's, and calls him 'loveliest mummer of them all' (5.27).

Youth, for Joyce, was a trying of roles, maturity a settling into
one's role, frequently an unintended settling-in. In 'A Boarding
House' we see Bob Doran being trapped into a role which will entail many years of saying the right thing to Mrs Mooney, and from
'Cyclops', where he appears as a petulant, monosyllabic drunk, we
can gauge the strain this role entails. Joyce's way of basing characters on himself was to meditate on the ease with which, given different luck, he might have become them. He might have been Mr
Duffy in 'A Painful Case', guarded, aloof, with his Hauptmann
translation in manuscript; he might have been Gabriel Conroy in
'The Dead', with his pince-nez, his west-country wife, and his frigid
knowledgeableness. Stephen Dedalus resembles a role he actually
played, and he might have become what Stephen seems destined
to become, one more hydropsical Dublin 'character'. We see Joyce
playacting whenever a camera is trained on him: as Rimbaud, as
Mephisto, as Blind Jim, as *père de famille*; one would hardly believe
that many of his photographs are of the same man. And he *used*
roles, of course, to keep people at a manipulable distance.

More pertinently, he early grew convinced that people shape
their environment with the help of stories they know, and trap
themselves into playing parts in those stories. 'Eveline', which he
wrote when he was twenty-two, shows us a girl whose realities are
those of fiction, so much so that the utterly preposterous tale of
Frank, who says he has 'fallen on his feet' in Buenos Aires and has
a house waiting there for a bride he has come back to Dublin to
find, jibes perfectly with her starved sense of the real. Her father,
who says, 'I know these sailor chaps', fits sailors into another story
entirely, the one in which they have a girl in every port. As for
Frank, or 'Frank' (it is surely a pseudonym he is using), he understands the poor girl's fantasies well enough to insert himself into
them, and may also be conscious of employing Othello's wooing
strategies. He may even be aware of his resemblance to Ulysses,
another mariner, notorious for lies, who strode from the brine before
the innocent Nausicaa.

Stories are comforting; it is a relief for Eveline to suppose that
she is being wooed by a deliverer. And it is enhancing for Gretta
Conroy to murmer, 'I think he died for me', casting herself as Merci-

less Beaute or as a dame of chivalry, and obscuring from her imagination the fact that Michael Furey died of catching cold in the rain. Yeats in the same way conferred majesty on Maud Gonne's rabble-rousing (hurling 'the little streets upon the great') by suggesting that she had to enact her character's destiny—'and character is fate', said Heraclitus—with such opportunities as Dublin made available: 'Was there another Troy for her to burn?'

In that question we have the germ of Joyce's 'parallels', which provide roles, roles beyond those the player is aware of. Bloom is aware that his fantasies of exposing Boylan are modelled on the role of the Stone Guest in *Don Giovanni*. He is not aware, however, so far as we can tell, that such fantasies also enact the role of returning Odysseus. Joyce, however, worked from the awareness that the *Odyssey* and *Don Giovanni* have plots with the same shape, which means that many of the characters correspond, though Homer concentrates our attention on the avenger, Mozart and da Ponte on the usurper. And the plot of *Hamlet* has the same shape likewise, with attention concentrated on the absent avenger's son; and the plot of *The Count of Monte Cristo* also, a kind of demotic *Odyssey* on which Stephen Dedalus built fantasies once. It was a theme pertinent to nineteenth-century researches, this savouring of homeo-morphisms. Many myths seemed to have the same shape, many religions, many stories; *The Golden Bough* is one monument to that awareness, and the aesthetes' cult of eternal Aphrodite another. ('I am Iseult, and Helen', says Modern Beauty in Arthur Symons' poem; 'I have seen /Troy burn, and my most fondest knight lie dead'.) It follows that people who are shaping their lives by one story will be unwittingly enacting many others; it follows, too, that they may change a role for the corresponding role in some analogous plot, out of need to alter a psychic inflection, and may do this with no real discontinuity. Stephen plays Hamlet and the Outcast Bard by turns, and Joyce makes him play Telemachus unwittingly.

Roles are defined by costumes and accents, by externals: the province of the naturalistic writer. Naturalism, going through the motions of raw documentation, crawling, with its compound eyes open, across the superficies of events, would have no hope of achieving intelligible fictions did not reader and writer share the assumption that the action has a simple configuration, and a familiar one. *Madame Bovary*, so complex sentence by sentence, paragraph by

paragraph, is nonetheless simple to follow because the broad outline
of repeated seduction, complied with by the seducee out of thirst
for fulfilment, is so easy to recognize that once Rodolphe has cleared
his throat or Leon donned his jacket we know what is going on.
Flaubert, in fact, understood that his novel had exactly the shape
of the novels Emma has read, which in turn derived their shape
from Romantic fictions that were innovative once. The simpler, the
more recognizable the form, the greater diversity of detail it can
control; in Flaubert we already see the novelist moving from storytelling to studying the *effect* of stories, and cataloguing the endless
detail with which human idiosyncrasy can fill them in. Readers used
to complain that *Ulysses* has little story; about enough, say, for a
novella. That is true; but *Ulysses* does not aim to impart its story.
It takes its story for granted (and the title announces that the story
is so familiar we can find it in Homer). Its aim is to examine its
story in immediate human enactment: the working-out of the
Ulysses theme by people unaware that that is what they are working
out, but partly aware that they draw satisfaction from roles that
(reflection assures us) are variants on Homeric ones.

This wants careful stating. T. S. Eliot's famous words in *The
Dial*, for example, are less careful than they might be. 'In using the
myth', Eliot wrote, 'in manipulating a continuous parallel between
modernity and antiquity, Mr Joyce is using a method which others
must pursue after him. It has the importance of a scientific discovery'. For it was, he said, 'a way of giving shape to the panorama
of anarchy and futility which is the contemporary world'. This is
well stated, and (bating the word 'continuous') applies to the intention of Eliot's own *Waste Land*. It throws light also on another
work of which the method was finally conceived in the light of
Ulysses, Ezra Pound's *Cantos*. It is not, however, an accurate description of *Ulysses*, where we are constantly immersed in 'modernity' (1904) but receive no sense of 'antiquity' at all: nothing corresponding to the texture of Eliot's

> *A crowd flowed over London Bridge, so many*
> *I had not thought death had undone so many*

—where, in the pastiche of Dante, it is 'London Bridge' that is the
jarring note; nor to Pound's

> *Set keel to breaker, forth on the godly sea*

—which could nowise connote a departure from Dublin harbour. Joyce has little sense of the past, and never sets his imagination yearning after its echoing otherness. He takes great pleasure in grotesque present efforts to recreate the past ('*Hamlet, ou, Le Distrait: Pièce de Shakespeare*') and allows us to glimpse mighty archetypes overarching today's quotidian doings, but the density of the past is not something his readers encounter. All is surface, all is costume, as when an actor became a Shakespearean king by changing his clothes.

All is surface. All the *Ulysses* styles develop something ·that inheres in surface naturalism, the naturalism from which the book begins. This is true of the dramatic form of 'Circe'. Drama develops naturalism's externality, its linear progression in time, its refusal to ruminate and to explain. What the stage shows us is what we can see and hear. What 'Circe' shows us is what we could see and hear were everything pertinent to the goings-on translated into terms of seeing and hearing, a method already latent in the naturalism of the early chapters.

> He fitted the book roughly into his inner pocket and, stubbing his toes against the broken commode, hurried out towards the smell, stepping hastily down the stairs with a flurried stork's legs. (65.26)

This is Bloom's response, in 'Calypso', to the smell of burning kidney; in 'Circe' the kidney would have a speaking part, calling him, and a visual metamorphosis would permit us to see the stork. That is the base of the 'Circe' method. Thus:

> (*He looks round, darts forward suddenly. Through rising fog a dragon sandstrewer, travelling at caution, slews heavily down upon him, its huge red headlight winking, its trolley hissing on the wire. The motorman bangs his footgong.*)

> THE GONG

> Bang Bang Bla Bak Blud Bugg Bloo.
> (*The brake cracks violently. Bloom, raising a policeman's white-gloved hand, blunders stifflegged, out of the track. . . .*) (435.9)

Here the gong speaks, as the kidney might have, and the metaphor of Bloom's gesture becomes actual, a white glove, reversing the emphasis by which in the 'Calypso' passage a stork was implicit in his walk. That white glove is no hallucination; it inheres in the logic of the method, which is to place all figures, all analogies, all ruminations, on the plane of the visible and audible.

It follows that we can often not be sure what is 'really' going on: what a cine-camera would pick up in nighttown, or a tape recorder. Thus, at the episode's opening,

. . . *Whistles call and answer.*

THE CALLS

Wait, my love, and I'll be with you.

THE ANSWERS

Round behind the stable. (429.10)

These calls and answers seem idealized, part of a scenesetting convention. But then so does the opening description.

(*The Mabbot street entrance of nighttown, before which stretches an uncobbled tramsiding set with skeleton tracks, red and green will-o'-the-wisps and danger signals. Rows of flimsy houses with gaping doors. Rare lamps with faint rainbow fans. Round Rabaiotti's halted ice gondola stunted men and women squabble.* . . .) (429.1)

This is surely 'selected' and 'arranged' to the point of Gothic parody; a stage setting, precisely, where all is flimsy, where light is expression, where careful casting has seen to it that the shadowy men and women shall all be 'stunted'. (Surely they are an illusion; surely they are children.) They do not know, by the way, that they are serving to express Halloween grotesquerie, but then Bloom does not know that he is Ulysses. We know that Bloom is Ulysses, and we know, too, what effect the opening description of 'Circe' conveys; which means that what we know and what is 'really' there (there for a dead observer: a camera, a recorder) are somewhat different. Which means in turn, though we are apt to forget, that what seems to be happening may be subject to many small expressionist inflections, like Bloom's 'policeman's whitegloved hand', which it is misleading to call 'hallucinations'. No one is hallucinated but ourselves.

Long sections of 'Circe', of course, are most readily described as hallucinations, or at least as fantasies, by way of marking them off from the events a neutral observer would see. Thus the twenty-page section in which Bloom is tried for making improper suggestions to a scullerymaid, and the four-page section in which his dead mother appears to Stephen Dedalus, are most readily described as visions presented to Bloom and Stephen respectively. On the other hand the three pages in which Bloom is accosted by Zoe, who takes possession of his talismanic potato, are describable as 'naturalistic'. This means that a neutral observer would see and hear nothing of the trial, but would see and hear the dialogue with Zoe. However, there is no neutral observer. There is a reader (oneself) who finds the trial of Bloom, given Bloom's guilty sensuality, less surprising than the dialogue of Bloom with Zoe, given Bloom's timid prudence. And the dialogue has further touches of improbability:

(. . . *A hand slides over his left thigh.*)

ZOE

How's the nuts?

BLOOM

Off side. Curiously they are on the right. Heavier I suppose. One in a million my tailor, Mesias, says. (475.29)

It is as difficult to imagine Bloom actually saying this as it is to credit the italicized statement, a few lines later, that '*Slowly, note by note, oriental music is played*'. Clearly the reader in quest of a surface realism he can believe must pick his way very carefully, assaying every phrase with suspicion; and there will be little left when he has finished; perhaps twenty pages, out of some 170: just over 10%.

Out-and-out hallucination, irreducible naturalism, these are extremes of a continuum, extremes seldom visited. Usually we are somewhere short of one extreme. Bloom presumably thought what the page invites us to suppose he said, about the one-in-a-million disposition of his testicles, so according to the convention of an episode like 'Calypso' or 'Lestrygonians' the speech counts as naturalism though no Sony would have picked it up. On the other hand, the encounter with the watchmen which initiates the trial scene—

(. . . *Two raincaped watch approach, silent, vigilant. They murmur together.*)

THE WATCH

Bloom. Of Bloom. For Bloom. Bloom.
(*Each lays a hand on Bloom's shoulder.*)

FIRST WATCH

Caught in the act. Commit no nuisance. (453.17)

—presumably counts as hallucination though a camera would have picked up the watchmen nearby, and picked up Bloom discarding crubeen and trotter in '*a dark stalestunk corner*' where it would have been reasonable to suppose he was committing a nuisance, after which very possibly the watchmen did walk over to see.

Such gradations of reality are worth attention because early in the episode Joyce does establish, in a way calculated to catch the reader's eye, a workable convention, clearly discriminating two planes of reality, which he is then careful seldom to follow again; the reader who learns the convention at this point will be misled wholly. This is Bloom's fantasy of becoming Lord Mayor, Messiah, and martyr. We can tell exactly where it begins and ends; it is cleanly spliced in between Zoe's 'Go on. Make a stump speech out of it' (478.6) and her 'Talk away till you're black in the face' (499.9). It even observes a not unfamiliar psychological law, that fantasies, like dreams, are not referable to 'real' time, so we find it rather plausible that something very intricate could race through Bloom's mind in the pause between two sentences.[1] He was talking of

[1] 'After she achieved a self-induced trance, I explained to her that she would see a movie that she had seen years ago, that it would be very clear and vivid and that she would see it upon a signal of snapping my fingers. I made a mistake, which had to do with the realization that I had neglected to give her certain instructions, and inadvertently snapped my fingers before explaining to her about the second signal. Imagine my surprise when she immediately woke up! I felt rather provoked with myself until I noticed her amazed expression, and she said, "Why, that's the most interesting thing that ever happened to me!"

' "What happened?" I asked, not knowing quite what to expect.

' "I just saw Gone with the Wind", she replied, laughing.

' "How much of it did you see?"

' "I saw the whole thing from beginning to end. It was even better than I remembered".

'While I was still trying to figure out what had happened, she was telling me at great length about the picture. I found it hard to believe that she had really seen the whole picture, or even a small part of it, in such a short instant of time. But she convinced me by describing every detail of the opening scenes and dialogue, and continuing with vivid word-for-word reproduction as if she had just come from the theatre. Better, in fact, than if she had. It was clear that she had experienced imagery of the most vivid kind imaginable of a two-and-one-half hour picture in the time it took to snap my fingers—not between two signals; just during one snap!' Laurence Sparks, *Self-Hypnosis*, London and New York, 1962, pp. 113–114.

tobacco, and begins his 'stump speech' in the role of a workingclass agitator decrying self-destructive habits ('that weed . . . a poisoner of the ear, eye, heart, memory, will, understanding, all'). He ends it upright at the stake, burning (like a cigar) while the Daughters of Erin kneel round him with burning candles; and the final words, '*Bloom becomes mute, shrunken, carbonised*', come cheek by jowl with Zoe's 'Talk away till you're black in the face'. We may even suppose, if we want to, that this is something more than a comic coincidence, that the two planes overlapped slightly in time, and that her 'black in the face' gave his thoughts their carbonized direction. We may have recourse, in short, to the myth of the stimulus-response psychology, its comfortable 'real' world whence stimuli are emitted, its plasticized 'fantasy' world in which they are responded to. We may suppose, penumbrally, ignoring trivial inconveniences like the 'whitegloved hand', that we could go through the 'Circe' episode assigning its elements impartially to the one world or the other. We shall find we are wrong almost immediately; for on being invited to talk away till he's black in the face, Bloom adopts the role of emigrant Paddy ('*in caubeen with clay pipe stuck in the band*'), commences, 'Let me be going now, woman of the house', and concludes with allusions to his father's suicide note ('A few pastilles of aconite. The blinds drawn. A letter. Then lie back to rest'.) His last words, prolonging the suicide's role, are, 'No more. I have lived. Fare. Farewell'. To which, though clearly none of it was spoken (it is 'hallucination', or 'fantasy'), Zoe replies smartly, 'Honest? Till the next time'.

From this we may learn to trust nothing; Bloom spoke some words of disengagement, obviously, but we were not permitted to hear them. The 'naturalist' phases are not only interrupted, they are incomplete, almost whimsically so; and distorted, often subtly; and need care.

One instance is especially illustrative: the details of the payment tendered in Bella's whorehouse. The facts may be gathered from pages 556–559.

1. Bella asks about payment and Stephen hands her a banknote.

2. Lynch calls, 'Give her your blessing for me', and Stephen hands her a coin, with the words, 'Gold. She has it' (556.17).

3. Bella implies that she hasn't received 30 shillings (3 girls at 10s each). Stephen produces two crowns (the only sum that has

been unambiguously specified so far) and remarks that his sight is
somewhat troubled.

4. There is 'chattering and squabbling' about who paid for
whom.

5. Zoe folds a half sovereign into the top of her stocking.

6. Kitty clutches 'the two crowns'.

7. Bloom 'Quietly lays a half sovereign on the table . . . takes
up the poundnote' and says 'Three times ten. We're square' (558.8).
Bella ('admiringly') calls him 'a slyboots'. Bloom 'goes with the
poundnote to Stephen' and returns it to him.

8. Bloom then ('quietly') suggests that Stephen entrust him
with his remaining cash. 'Why pay more?' (559.3).

Though the evidence is scanty, and though the money swirls
round as in a short-changing trick, we can with diligence recover
the details. Up to step (6) all the money has come from Stephen;
we deduce that it consists of

a pound banknote (1), confirmed by (7)	20s.
a half sovereign (2) and (5)	10s.
two crowns (3) and (6)	10s.
Total	40s.

Two girls take the half sovereign and the two crowns; Bloom substitutes a half sovereign (10s) for the poundnote, returning the
pound to Stephen; and Bella's 'slyboots' bespeaks professional admiration for his seeing through her effort to overcharge. For clearly
Bella perceived that Stephen (who fumbled in his pocket, produced
the banknote by its corner, and handed it to her, all in one motion)
was not sure if it was a pound or half that much, and sensed that
she could extort ten shillings more. Clearly, too, Bloom takes charge
of Stephen's money because he has detected the proprietress deliberately cheating.

But Joyce allows us to take no special notice; we are even misled into supposing that a ten-shilling note is in play, when we hear
of Zoe 'folding a half sovereign into the top of her stocking' (557.18).
(And since no one could read these words till 1922, Joyce may be
banking on our being unsure whether there was such a thing as
an Irish ten-shilling note in 1904.) But only one note has entered
the transaction (1), and a pound note is later specified (7), so we

must conclude that what Zoe folded was the stockingtop, not the money, for the money was the coin preferred in step (2).

What this means is that the apparently impartial dramatic presentation conforms to Stephen's hazy sense of what is going on, not to Bloom's exact sense. Joyce could easily have made the transaction clear by specifying all the notes and coins as they were paid out. He did not, and even allowed us not to notice that he did not, because the naturalist method is ambiguous; it has tacit points of view, in this case Stephen's. Later, in the arcanum of the specifiable, in 'Ithaca' itself, a similar trick is played. The impersonal questioner says, 'Compile the budget for 16 June 1904', and the budget is promptly produced. It has been compiled, however, not by impersonal authority but as if by Bloom, for it omits what Bloom will later omit if Molly questions him: the 10s paid at the whorehouse, and the 1s he threw down later (585) to cover damage to the whorehouse lamp. Here, too, 'impersonality' has a point of view, this time Bloom's.

In short, the whole episode is phantasmagoric; the dramatic surface, with its objectivity, its naturalism, is a rhetoric throughout, and the narrative line less easy to recover than first thoughts might suppose. It is with a due sense of peril, then, that one attempts to recover the chain of bare happenings. These are: Stephen and Lynch go to the whorehouse; Zoe, a prostitute, steers Bloom there; the Madame enters, and is paid, after which Bloom takes charge of Stephen's money (but, as we learn long after—618—not of all of it; he has more halfcrowns in a different pocket); there is drunken dancing, and Stephen, scared by an hallucination, assaults the chandelier with his stick and rushes into the street; in the street he runs afoul of drunken soldiers, one of whom knocks him unconscious; and Bloom stands by him till he comes to.

There are several things to remark about this sequence. One is that toward the end of it a good many things happen; in this respect it contrasts with the episode's predecessors 'Nausicaa' and 'Oxen of the Sun', where nothing much happens at all. In 'Nausicaa' Bloom sits and gazes; in 'Oxen', people sit and yatter. The second notable thing is that on the plane of incident, what happens is the stuff of pulp fiction, not more distinguished than the plot machinations of *Ruby, Pride of the Ring*. It is bare, banal, stagy. The third is that Stephen really *is* scared by an hallucination, the only genuine hallucination in the chapter. This fact is nearly obscured by the plethora of episodes that resemble hallucinations, and are presented in an identical notation, but are, in fact, either dramatized metaphors like the whitegloved hand, or else expressionistic equivalents of states of feeling. Stephen's hallucination is one of the book's climaxes, but Joyce is a great concealer of climaxes.

A review of the evidence indicates very strongly that Stephen really is seeing things, and is frightened. When other hallucinatory interludes occur—when Bloom, for instance, goes from Lord Mayorhood to Martyrdom—no one else notices anything amiss. In this particular instance, Zoe goes right on talking, which means that the 'hallucination' articulates and extends a transient Bloomish feeling of which his observable behaviour betrays no trace. But when Stephen's mother, *'emaciated, rises stark through the floor'* (579.25) attended by *'a choir of virgins and confessors'*, Stephen, whirling amid the dancers, *'stops dead'*, Florry notices that 'He's white' (581.22), Bloom opens the window, diagnosing giddiness, and responds, 'What?' to Stephen's cry, 'Shite!' Florry's dash to get him cold water seems a response to his cry, *'Non serviam!'*, which we must apparently imagine being spoken aloud; and as for his climactic assault on the chandelier, plainly he does swing his ashplant at it, since there is verifiable damage, though not, as he supposes, a leaping out of time's livid final flame. Then *'Stephen, abandoning his ashplant, his head and arms thrown back stark, beats the ground and flees from the room past the whores at the door'* (583.16). And this too really happens, since people rush after him.

During his dialogue with the apparition he passes rapidly from role to role: the horrorstruck lay figure of melodrama ('Lemur, who are you? What bogeyman's trick is this?' 580.15), the remorseful son ('They said I killed you, mother. . . . Cancer did it, not I' 580.27), the terrified child ('Raw head and bloody bones!' 581.28), Lucifer ('*Non serviam!*' 582.14), finally Siegfried ('*Nothung!*' 583.2). The people who see him see what Queen Gertrude saw when Hamlet (III, iv) held discourse with the incorporeal air. Queen Gertrude does not see the ghost at all; Shakespeare's stage direction, 'Enter the Ghost in his Nightgown', means what Joyce's stage direction means, when it specifies that Stephen's mother rises through the floor. And Stephen is dizzy with dancing and drink, and (656.31) has not eaten for two days.

It is in the 'Circe' episode, incidentally, that we get most of our clues to another concealed climax. Stephen, we are told more than once, becomes conscious in the brothel that he has somehow hurt his hand (563.19). We may assume that the hand is not visibly damaged, since we may be sure that at the sight of blood or a bruise Bloom would be babbling sagely of disinfectants. There is no indication that he hurts it in nighttown, which suggests a trauma sufficient to mask pain for an hour or so. The likelihood is that he struck someone or something during the scuffle at the Westland Row station, and putting this likelihood together with Bloom's remark that if Stephen were to present himself at the tower he wouldn't 'get in after what occurred at Westland Row station' (619.39), we may suspect that he did something of profound importance: that he asserted himself and took a swing at Mulligan. If so, then Telemachus/Hamlet has taken arms against one usurper, even though Bloom/Ulysses leaves Blazes Boylan unscathed. That Joyce's Hamlet should become the man of action comports with the principle by which Joyce's Ulysses becomes the man of acquiescence. And if so, moreover, if indeed Stephen did punch Mulligan, and punch him hard enough to receive damage to his hand that pains him an hour or more later, then it is one of the most important incidents in the book, and, given what we know of Stephen's character, a turning-point in Stephen's life. Yet it happened (if it happened) completely offstage, in the interval between two episodes, covered moreover by emphasis on Mulligan's efforts to give Stephen the slip. We may reflect on that other critical event, Boylan's liaison with Molly Bloom, which also occurs offstage. Bloom is persuaded that it happened, which is all that matters for Bloom. Did it? We can't be sure until Molly's rumination.

One last 'naturalistic' detail. In a chapter of mutations and transformations, it is fitting that a whole stratum of the first half of the book should be transformed, and sure enough, we learn that Stephen, acutely myopic, has been without glasses all day:

> Must get glasses. Broke them yesterday. Sixteen years ago. Distance. The eye sees all flat. . . . Brain thinks. Near: far. Ineluctable modality of the visible. . . . (560.2)

'Sixteen years ago' recalls another time of broken glasses, made memorable by the pandybat of Father Dolan, whose apparition pops out of the pianola a page later. 'Ineluctable modality' recalls the 'Proteus' episode, the transactions of which with the seen world, we now realize for the first time, were conducted amid objects Stephen could barely see. He saw as much as he did because in strong sunlight the eye's iris closes down and diminishes the circles of confusion. How he saw, we may gauge from the detail in 'Telemachus', where the 'threadbare cuffedge' at a distance of, say, eight inches is sharp, while the distant sea is 'a dull green mass of liquid' (5.38), lifeless, unsparkling.

So much for what 'really' happens. Now for what 'seems' to happen, and on the page enjoys exactly the status of everything else on the page, shaping the reader's experience of what he reads and compelling him to partake at once of the episode's wild comedy and of Bloom's psychic purgation.

Our first intimation that time and space, in this episode, obey special laws occurs within eight pages, when 'a sinister figure' (436.10), at first sight no queerer than some we have already encountered, regards Bloom from under a sombrero. Bloom, if we are to believe the text, addresses him in Spanish, is asked for a password, rejoins in words of French and Gaelic, and mutters, 'Gaelic league spy'. But of course we are not to believe the text; we are to understand a metaphor for Bloom's sense of clandestine adventure. So when Bloom's dead father appears on the next page ('What you making down this place? Have you no soul?' 437.24), we seize the metaphor for his sense of guilt, expressing itself through the figure of parental disapproval. But the incident does not terminate after making this point. Rudolph Sr. continues to catechize Bloom in imperfect English; Bloom's mother appears 'in pantomime dame's stringed mobcap' (438.22), crying 'Sacred Heart of Mary, where were you at all, at all?'; we are aware that they are playing parts, the stage Jew and the stage Irishwoman, the elaborately specified costumes denoting the parts with insane thoroughness of emphasis; and that Bloom too, enacting scenes of his past and present psychic life, plays parts and is instantly recostumed as the roles mutate. Costume is role, and self is a medley of allotropic roles.

His guilt prolongs itself; his parents are superseded by Molly (439.8), a contemptuous Molly whose demand to be addressed henceforth as 'Mrs Marion' (her concert billing) corresponds to his fear that she may be henceforth linked with Boylan. Her Turkish costume comes from the dream he remembered after masturbating in 'Nausicaa', her 'opulent curves' from the *Sweets of Sin* he bought in 'Wandering Rocks' (236). These are guilty memories, and guilt next introduces the lotion for Molly he ordered but forgot to pick up, then the soap he picked up but hasn't yet paid for, then Sweny the chemist and the price of the transaction (85.16). True to the principles of 'Circe', the soap rises like a sun and speaks a couplet, and Sweny's face appears in its disc requesting 'Three and a penny' (440.28). In the 'Lotuseaters' episode, when Bloom visited the chemist, he also visited a church, and the white disc with a face superimposed on it resembles an oleograph of a consecrated host bearing the visage of Christ.

It is needless to particularize the principle further. Motifs are collected from elsewhere in the book exactly as Bloom's interior monologue has collected them in earlier sections, and tracing them to their sources we may discover the shape of the emotional field that is collecting them. The one thing that is new is the projection, the externalizing of motifs as tableaux, suitably costumed and equipped with lines to speak. Projection entails one further novelty, the zany inventiveness with which new details proliferate. Thus Molly in her Turkish costume is accompanied by a camel who takes on, in a few lines, a personality of his own.

> *The camel, lifting a foreleg, plucks from a tree a large mango fruit, offers it to his mistress, blinking, in his cloven hoof, then droops his head and, grunting, with uplifted neck, fumbles to kneel. Bloom stoops his back for leapfrog.* (440.3)

This camel, a comic detail, turns into a self-projection of Bloom's, as Bloom acknowledges in stooping '*for leapfrog*' as the camel kneels.

We now have a formula for the vitality of the 'Circe' episode. Old pieces appear in new and surprising patterns, with an episodic vividness that strikes the attention. We are likely to gather the impression that absolutely everyone and everything in the book turns up here somewhere, animated by a new and phantasmagoric life. All those pieces, so plausibly fitted for so many hundred pages, seem here to be suddenly dumped out of the frame for retesselation at what looks like random and turns out to be a transcendent kind of sense. And as the vivid visions proceed, old detail spawns new detail, defined and etched by the sharp specifying language that gives transient wisps of feeling the corporeality of Dante's journey. And

low comedy—the camel plucking the fruit—collapses the high-
falutin that might otherwise claim analogies with *Faust* or with
Flaubert's *Tentation* to the common denominator of pantomime,
the demotic *Walpurgisnacht*. For books themselves are roles, the
roles motifs play. *The Count of Monte Cristo* is the *Odyssey* on
holiday; the pantomime is the dream-vision made concrete for
children. And as *Ulysses* is the *Odyssey* transposed and rearranged,
'Circe' is *Ulysses* transposed and rearranged. We sense a vast closed
field, the western mind, within which, like pieces in a kaleidoscope,
motifs are permuted, vivid, bright, transient, for ever.

We also sense, since most of these visions are associated with
Bloom, that Bloom is being somehow transformed by their agency.
As dreams, by Freud's showing, are the protectors of sleep, so
fantasies, Joyce appears to suggest, are ministers of sanity. If Bloom
is not crushed by his guilts, his apprehensions, and his frustrations,
it is because their energies leak off into fantasy, and as 'Circe' proceeds we may follow him working out a course of psychic purgation.
He has seven principal fantasies.

1. The first element to be purged is recent sexual guilt: Gerty
MacDowell, a brief remote encounter, receives less than half a
page (442). Mrs Breen ('Josie Powell that was, prettiest deb in Dublin') has been on his mind much longer; she is a destiny that might
have been his had Molly not been his destiny, and she now occupies
some seven pages (442–449), taking his thoughts back to their days
of semi-serious flirtation. He may as well indulge such reveries, seeing what Molly has indulged with Boylan this afternoon; snatches
of *Love's Old Sweet Song* and *Là ci darem* (445) serve to inter-
twine the two indulgences.

2. Next, earlier and more diffuse sexual guilt is explored. This
episode (453–475) is triggered by the sight of the watchmen, who he
imagines will imagine that he has committed a nuisance in a dark
corner. Hence the format of the fantasy, a trial. Martha Clifford,
his correspondent, is the first complainant, Mary Driscoll, a serving-
girl to whom he once 'made a certain suggestion', is the second.
His self-abnegation before the court transforms itself into a desire
to be dominated by society ladies; this transforms itself into a
consciousness of being cuckolded; and in a second eucharist parody,
corresponding to the apparition of the soap in the previous fantasy,
a cuckoo-clock is elevated by the priests who were elevating the

host at benediction when Boylan came to Molly, while the brass bed at 7 Eccles street rings a threefold chime. Bloom is sentenced to death, but the recollection of having gone to Dignam's funeral restores a psychic balance, and the fantasy terminates.

3. Next, still in the street, he is accosted by Zoe, who appropriates his potato, and whose advances send his self-esteem oscillating toward delusions of grandeur. For over twenty pages (478–499) he scales facile heights, as Lord Mayor, lawgiver and dispenser of civic reforms, only to plunge with equal facility toward bisexuality and martyrdom. At the end of this episode he dies the death he was spared in the previous fantasy; what has died, for the purposes of this evening, is part of the timidity that has always rendered him ineffectual in practical situations. Still on the trail of Stephen, he enters the bawdy-house.

We may note that while nearly all the material in these three fantasies is drawn from Bloom's secret life, occasional details creep in that are foreign to his experience. Thus, when J. J. O'Molloy defends him in Fantasy 2, he speaks (465.5) Seymour Bushe's words, uttered in the 'Aeolus' episode (140.12) when Bloom was absent. This seems not to be a lapse on the careful author's part: it is an early instance of the mingling of Bloom's mind and Stephen's in preparation for the terminal metamorphosis of Stephen into Bloom's dead son. This is an expressionist, not a psychological chapter, and we should beware of determining too definitely which thoughts belong to whom. The next fantasy, the End of the World interlude, is perhaps an example. Though it draws mostly on material appropriate to Stephen (French phrases, Æ's jargon, the medical students' talk at the end of 'Oxen of the Sun'), at least two elements, Reuben J. Dodd and the Evangelist, are community property, and the vignette as a whole crystallizes a conversation involving everyone present. The stupidest whore in the room has attempted to make conversation—'They say the last day is coming this summer' (505.16); that is enough to precipitate the extravaganza, which need not be assigned to any particular consciousness.

4. Now that Bloom is installed in the whorehouse parlour, detachment and knowingness become *de rigueur*. Enter, therefore, Grandfather Virag, technical authority on everything from sexual appraisal to the cure of warts (511.23). His antics correspond to Bloom's effort to maintain a guiltless detachment ('This book tells

you how to act with all descriptive particulars', 514.26), the detachment which, in other circumstances, mobilizes the role of Henry Flower. Unsurprisingly, Bloom turns into Henry, cool, self-possessed, seeing to his moustache, beard, and hair (522.23). For Virag, people are animals and bodies have parts. His spirit presides over marriage manuals and Mitteleuropa psychological researches. He concludes by unscrewing his own head and emitting a sharp 'Quack!' (523.8).

5. But Bloom's new self-possession is not an equilibrium, only a temporary stasis. The entrance of Bella Cohen, massive and semimasculine whoremistress, triggers the longest of all the fantasies, the one that commences with a change of sex, drags out his most shameful masochistic and voyeurist acts and reveries, and reaches back to the inchoate desires of boyhood, to the time when he 'sacrificed to the god of the forest' (549.16)—a masturbation, apparently—after watching 'Lotty Clarke, flaxenhaired . . . through illclosed curtains, with poor papa's operaglasses'. A calf witnessed this, trees and thickets surrounded it, the recall has for context yews, nymphs, a waterfall. Bloom's sexuality (like Anna Livia Plurabelle's) has been traced to its origins, the burgeoning undifferentiated amoral world of nature. So despite the extremes of degradation through which his psyche passes in this episode, he is appeased, and prepared at its close to take charge of Stephen's fortunes. He recovers his potato from Zoe—the preservative, the Homeric *moly*—and quietly puts right Bella's cheating when the money is exchanged.

6. Sexual guilt, for the time being, is expunged. There remains one demon to be exorcised, the spectre of cuckoldry. This is brief. He is sustained by a sense of communion with Stephen, reinforced by the brief conversation about sixteen and twentytwo (563.18). A quick vignette, spliced between the giggling of whores (564) and Bloom's 'When will I hear the joke?' (568.2), brings Boylan to the premises, to hang his hat '*smartly on a peg of Bloom's antlered head*' and announce, 'I have a little private business with your wife' (565.14). Bloom is all subservience and acquiescence, not, however, in masochistic delight (that has been dissipated, for now) but in acknowledgment of the fact that he continues to accept what he accepted this afternoon. William Shakespeare, cuckold, keeps him distinguished company.

Thus ends Bloom's purgative way; the dancing follows, and Stephen's hallucination, and the mad exit, and the wrangle with the soldiers. Throughout Bloom plays the father, unafraid. He defies Bella's effort to extort another 10 shillings for the cracked lamp, (584–585), he pushes through the crowd and tries to coax Stephen away just when Private Carr is offering to bash him on the jaw (589), even tries to talk a little sense into the soldiers, intercedes with the watchmen (605) when Stephen lies prostrate, and stands guard in nighttown, when everyone else has left, over the still form. This is not the Bloom we have known, timid, prudent, guiltridden, expecting rebuff; this is (briefly) the father Stephen has never known.

7. 'Circe' ends, then, with a Transformation Scene, the climax of the pantomime.

(. . . *Against the dark wall a figure appears slowly, a fairy boy of eleven, a changeling, kidnapped, dressed in an Eton suit with glass shoes and a little bronze helmet, holding a book in his hand. He reads from right to left inaudibly, smiling, kissing the page.*)

BLOOM

(*Wonderstruck, calls inaudibly.*) Rudy! (609.19)

Rudy, (eleven now, as he would be had he lived) has nevertheless the infant corpse's '*delicate mauve face*': accepted now, transfigured. The lampshade Stephen struck was also mauve: colour of the aestheticism he is on the point (maybe) of repudiating. Stephen has been dogged by guilt for his dead mother; Bloom by longing for his dead son, the son whose death interfered with his relations with Molly, and thus indirectly left Molly susceptible to the advances of Blazes Boylan. Both men are (at least temporarily) changed. The swing at the mauve lampshade, perhaps (we may infer from the hurt hand) a corresponding swing at Mulligan, these gestures, futile in themselves, mark the possible incipience of a new Stephen. The confidence of the last quarter-hour, after his descent through psychic depths, gives us, for the present, a new Bloom, the Bloom who will ask Molly (738) to bring him tomorrow's breakfast in bed, he who began today by serving her hers. It is too much to suppose that both are forever transformed, though one of the games Joyce is playing involves a parallel to the old-fashioned novel with a happy ending. In life things are not transformed like that overnight, though it was a convention of fiction, once, that they might be, as it is a convention of the pantomime.

Some permanent layer of experience, possible ground for change, has nevertheless, we may surmise, been laid down. This possibility is related, like everything in the book, to Joyce's fundamental presupposition, that lives entail roles. To change one must only (only!) change one's role. As the episode ends, Bloom is *playing* Stephen's father; it is conceivable that he could play that part for some time, though not likely that Stephen will reciprocate. Blazes Boylan, likewise, played Molly's fulfilment, a role Bloom might resume. He is certainly resolved at least at breakfast time, to play the man of the house, as though aware that he has let himself slip into playing the woman. Stephen has been playing the artist, and playing Hamlet, and playing Mulligan's chum; the last of these roles at least he has relinquished, and that will entail a reassessment of the others. He is quite aware that Si Dedalus, albeit 'consubstantial', only plays at being father. As for Molly, she has been playing *artiste*, much as Bloom has played Henry Flower and in the Henry Flower role played at being a gentleman in need of aid with his literary work.

Whatever insights he may have owed to Freud, Joyce was fundamentally unconvinced by Viennese sexual determinism. No one, for him, is locked down in that way. In 'Circe' a nearly accidental psychoanalysis, wholly lacking an analyst, occurs under pressure of unfamiliar surroundings, releasing the day's accumulated strains: the strains moreover of an unusual day, dominated by the knowledge of what is going forward in Eccles street. This occurs in an episode of roles and transformations, prelude perhaps to new roles, or roles newly inflected.

Of their ultimate roles, of course, both are unconscious; Bloom is unaware that he is Ulysses, Stephen that he is Telemachus. And while Stephen has played at being Christ ('I thirst', 50.23), it is Bloom who plays in 'Circe', the Christly role, redeeming, even literally, with money (eleven shillings: not 'one and eightpence too much') the fallen youth in love with Lucifer. The transformation scene is like a resurrection, restoring to the light his lost son Rudy; and details like the tearing of Bloom's coat (584.7)—which recalls the rending of the Saviour's garments—tease us with the supposition that Joyce in planning the episode may have made of the sequential hallucinations a secular Way of the Cross. To imitate Christ, that has long been offered as a role. Bloom, with three religions, yet uncircumcised though twice baptized, plays that role, if he does, without having studied it.

*   *   *

APPENDIX: THE PRINCIPAL FANTASIES

OUTER WORLD	INNER WORLD
429–430 Setting of scene.	
431 Enter Stephen and Lynch.	
434 Enter Bloom.	
437–452	(1) Bloom's recent sexual guilts. Father, Mother, Molly, Mrs Breen.
450–452 Bloom on street. Feeds dog.	
453–474	(2) Bloom's deeper sexual guilt. Mary Driscoll. The trial. The noble ladies.
475–477 Bloom and Zoe (surrenders potato).	
478–499	(3) Bloom as Lord Mayor, Messiah, Martyr.
500–506 In the house. Bloom, Stephen, Lynch, whores.	
506–510	(End of the World.)
510–511 Zoe, Lynch	
512–523	(4) Bloom's grandfather. Sexual knowingness. Stephen as cardinal.
523–525 Lynch, Stephen.	
525–527 Enter Bella Cohen.	
527–554	(5) Bloom's sexual guilt (youth). Change of sex.

OUTER WORLD	INNER WORLD
554–563 Money, fortunes (Bloom regains potato).	
563–569	(6) Bloom as cuckold. Boylan and Molly. Shakespeare.
569–578 Stephen entertains. Dancing.	
579–583	Stephen's hallucination: the mother. Lamp.
583–586 Exeunt Stephen and Bloom.	
586	The hue and cry.
587–598 Stephen, Bloom, Soldiers.	Edward VII.
598–600	Crucifixion Day; Black Mass.
601 Stephen hit. Bloom and Kelleher.	
608–609 Bloom watches Stephen.	(7) The transformation: Stephen into Rudy.

EUMAEUS

Gerald L. Bruns

Of all the chapters in *Ulysses*, 'Eumaeus' seems the most deliberately or strategically placed. Following as it does upon 'Circe',
it appears to carry to its furthest extension that vaguely Keatsian
process whereby dream departs into reality, and so gives us back an
image of such lassitude as no one may be expected to bear. Or, in
relation to 'Ithaca', it may be said to constitute a kind of diminish-
ing world, in whose eventual absence words will find the freedom to
shape themselves in a perfect triumph of art over life. Another way
to put this would be to say that 'Eumaeus' is the most unliterary of
the episodes in *Ulysses,* and without much doubt this is true, but it
is true mainly in the sense in which novels as such seem unliterary
when considered in relation to romance. Thus 'Eumaeus' becomes
what Ortega y Gasset once called 'realistic poetry', whose theme is
the 'collapse of the poetic'—the 'poetic' being, in this instance, a
term in whose shade may be gathered those forces of art and imagination that normally work to set poetry or literature at a firm distance
from ordinary life.[1] In 'Eumaeus' the 'poetic' exists *in potentia,*
and the drama of the episode consists mainly in the ways in which
Joyce works to control this potential—ways, that is to say, in which
what we might take to be the spirit of romance is displaced by the

[1] *Meditaciones del 'Quijote'* (1914), in *Obras Completas,* 2nd ed., Madrid,
1963, I, pp. 381–383.

spirit of ordinary life. It is this spirit of ordinary life—the spirit of Bloom, perhaps—which dominates the episode, but what is extraordinary to observe is how this dominance is originated and maintained.

It is originated and maintained, first of all, by means of language. It is helpful to notice, in this connexion, how far 'Eumaeus' falls outside the commonly accepted tradition of 'realistic' fiction, which paradoxically was concerned to redeem its ordinary content by means of style. In an essay entitled 'The Temptation of (St.) Flaubert', Paul Valéry has explained this paradox as follows:

> Literature . . . which aims at immediate, instantaneous effects, seeks an entirely different 'truth', one that is true for everybody and therefore cannot diverge from the common view of things—from what can be expressed in ordinary language. But the writer's ambition must necessarily be to distinguish himself from the common run, whereas ordinary language is in everybody's mouth and the common view of things is as worthless as the air that everybody breathes. This conflict between the fundamental tenet of Realism —preoccupation with the commonplace—and the will of every writer to turn himself into an exceptional being, a specially endowed personality, drove the realists to an interest in the refinements of style. They created the artistic style. They lavished a care and industry, a subtlety and virtuosity, quite admirable in themselves, on the description of the most ordinary and sometimes the most trivial of objects; but they did so without realizing that in this way they were striving for something which lay outside their principles. . . . In fact, they placed the crudest of characters, who were incapable of taking the slightest interest in colour or enjoying the shapes of things, in settings whose description required a painter's eye, a capacity for feeling which belongs to the sensitive individual who responds to precisely those things that escape the ordinary man. . . . If they spoke, their fatuous remarks and clichés were encased in a highly elaborate style composed of rare terms and studied rhythms whose every word was carefully weighed, betraying its self-regard and its desire to be noticed. Realism ended curiously enough by giving an impression of deliberate artifice.[2]

This passage will help us to speak very precisely about the nature of 'Eumaeus' and its relation to Ulysses as a whole. For the tradition of realism that Valéry describes, with its strange conflicts between the ordinary and the artificial, between 'what can be expressed in

[2] *Masters and Friends*, tr. Martin Turnell, in *The Collected Works of Paul Valéry*, Princeton, N.J., 1968, IX, p. 67.

ordinary language' and what finally is said in 'a highly elaborate style'—this tradition of realism reaches its apotheosis in Joyce. In *Ulysses* the commonplace is repeatedly sublimated by language into an 'artifice of eternity'. But in 'Eumaeus' the sublimation of the ordinary into high art does not take place. What gives this episode its special character is, first, a language which 'is in everybody's mouth', and, second, a 'common view of things' with which this everyday language executes an unexceptionable decorum.

We can amplify this point by examining briefly the narrator of 'Eumaeus'. Early in the episode we read the following:

> *En route*, to his taciturn, and, not to put too fine a point on it, not yet perfectly sober companion, Mr Bloom, who at all events, was in complete possession of his faculties, never more so, in fact disgustingly sober, spoke a word of caution *re* the dangers of night-town, women of ill fame and swell mobsmen, which, barely permissible once in a while, though not as a habitual practice, was of the nature of a regular deathtrap for young fellows of his age particularly if they had acquired drinking habits under the influence of liquor unless you knew a little juijitsu for every contingency as even a fellow on the broad of his back could administer a nasty kick if you didn't look out. (614.29)

This passage continues for another thirty-six lines, and for the most part it is a rendition of Bloom's stream of talk as he guides Stephen from the brothel to the cabman's shelter. The technique of narration here is that of reported speech, specifically the *style indirect libre* developed by La Fontaine and, particularly, Flaubert and brought to perfection by Joyce.[3] What is important to notice, however, is that in *Madame Bovary*, for example, this technique served Flaubert as a means of translating (in Valéry's words) the 'fatuous remarks and clichés' of ordinary characters into 'a highly elaborate style composed of rare terms and studied rhythms'. By reporting Emma Bovary's speech, rather than rendering it directly or merely commenting on her intentions, the narrator was thus in a position to mediate between a woman of elemental sensibility and Flaubert the master stylist. What we observe in the passage quoted above, by contrast, is the heavily formulaic character of the narrator's utterances. Bloom's speech is rendered as a discourse composed of other

[3] For a thorough discussion of the technique of reported speech in Flaubert, see Stephen Ullmann, *Style in the French Novel*, New York, 1964, pp. 94–120.

bits of discourse—*locutions reçues,* to borrow Hugh Kenner's phrase,
through the manifold and indefinite combinations of which the
narrator seeks to tell his story. Of course, *locutions reçues* imply
idées reçues, and, just so, speech in the passage above is formulaic
in its themes as well as in its expressions. The ethical bias, for example, which admonishes against 'the dangers of nighttown, women
of ill fame and swell mobsmen' without absolutely forbidding them,
is situated less in a specific consciousness (the narrator's, Bloom's)
than in the already given world of worn expressions which serves as
the narrator's lexicon.

This is to say, in effect, that the narrator exists as a mind
fabricated out of other minds. The precise sense in which this fact
takes on meaning and interest may be explained in the following
way. J. Hillis Miller, in a brilliant little book entitled *The Form of
Victorian Fiction,* tells us that in certain Victorian novels the narrator is constituted as a kind of 'general consciousness', a 'collective
mind' that is 'embodied in the already existing language of the
tribe'. The assumption at work here, Miller says, is that 'each man
finds himself from his birth surrounded by a transindividual mind,
identical with the words he learns. This mind surrounds him, embraces him permeates him, from the first day of his life to the end'.[4]
Now upon this notion rests the relationship between the narrator
and the protagonist: the narrator in Victorian fiction tends to surround, embrace, and permeate the hero, whom he defines in relation
to himself, as a part is defined in relation to a whole. The narrator
in 'Eumaeus' may be regarded as a rough approximation of this
sort of collectivity, and perhaps here we have a way of specifying
the importance of this narrator. Consider his activity in this passage:

> You frittered away your time, he very sensibly maintained, and
> health and also character besides which the squandermania of the
> thing, fast women of the *demimonde* ran away with a lot of L.s.d.
> into the bargain and the greatest danger of all was who you got
> drunk with though, touching the much vexed question of stimulants,
> he relished a glass of choice old wine in season as both nourishing
> and blood-making and possessing aperient virtues (notably a good
> burgundy which he was a staunch believer in) still never beyond a
> certain point where he invariably drew the line as it simply led to
> trouble all round to say nothing of your being at the tender mercy
> of others practically. (615.17)

[4] Notre Dame, Ind., 1969.

Here we find dramatized Bloom's paternal attitude toward Stephen; specifically, Bloom assumes over Stephen a moral authority that belongs typically to the father's role ('You frittered away your time . . . and health and also character'). It is, what is more, an authority marked by that generalized ethical bias noted above, not only in its warning against bad company ('the greatest danger of all was who you got drunk with'), but particularly in its vapid conjunction of moderation and utility ('touching the much vexed question of stimulants, he relished a glass of choice old wine in season as both nourishing and blood-making'). The point, however, is that this paternal attitude is dramatized indirectly; it is speech reported by the narrator in the narrator's best formulaic manner. And the chief question is: How are we to respond to a paternal attitude that is circulated through a narrator of this sort? The answer is, without much doubt, ironically, but we should be aware that Joyce's irony in 'Eumaeus' is of a special construction. Irony in such a work as Stendhal's *Le Rouge et le noir*, for example, is based on a discontinuity between narrator and protagonist. The narrator in Stendhal's novel shares with his audience a sense of superiority to Julien Sorel and, even more important, a sense of freedom from Julien's situation. But in 'Eumaeus' there is no such discontinuity; or, rather, the discontinuity is of a different order—a discontinuity between narrator and reader. For the narrator in this episode is a figure of impoverished sensibility, a man unable to speak in his own voice but only in the impoverished language of his tribe. Nevertheless, the narrator is all —his impoverished speech remains the medium of Bloom's characterization, with the result that, for example, any authentic feeling that Bloom may be supposed to have for Stephen remains undramatized, deflected into formula, present only by implication as a possibility raised for the action of the episode (as we shall see) eventually to dispel.

We can see how far this point extends by noticing that the narrator speaks not to the reader—not to Joyce's audience—but to an imaginary audience of his peers. For he is manifestly casual in his attitude toward storytelling—casual in a way that reflects the presence of an intimate or at least familiar audience. For example, early in the episode, when Stephen is approached by Corley, the narrator halts his narrative to explain how the young man came to be called Lord John Corley. His father, we are told, had been

Inspector Corley of the G Division, his mother 'a certain Katherine Brophy, daughter of a Louth farmer'; his grandfather had been Patrick Michael Corley, his grandmother Katherine Talbot.

> Rumour had it, though not proved, that she descended from the house of the Lords Talbot de Malahide in whose mansion, really an unquestionably fine residence of its kind and well worth seeing, his mother or aunt or some relative had enjoyed the distinction of being in service in the washkitchen. This, therefore, was the reason why the still comparatively young though dissolute man who now addressed Stephen was spoken of by some with facetious proclivities as Lord John Corley. (616.33)

This is gratuitous information, the matter of a local rather than professional storyteller. Corley's 'genealogy', such as it is, has a local importance that is superior to the story itself. Indeed, it is of such importance that, after resuming his narrative, the narrator halts it once more to make sure that he has his facts straight:

> Taking Stephen on one side he had the customary doleful ditty to tell. . . . He was out of a job and implored of Stephen to tell him where on God's earth he could get something, anything at all to do. No, it was the daughter of the mother in the washkitchen that was fostersister to the heir of the house or else they were connected through the mother in some way, both occurrences happening at the same time if the whole thing wasn't a complete fabrication from start to finish. Anyhow, he was all in. (616.42)

In this passage it is the narrator himself who is dramatized. Suddenly he is temporally situated, no longer an ironic filter, no longer a 'general consciousness' surrounding, embracing, and permeating Bloom or Stephen, but a figure converging momentarily toward personality, an ironic figure in his own right. This suggests that the narrator is a kind of fluid presence, existing as though on a continuum between a general and an individual consciousness, so that at one moment he can become, say, Stephen ('Stephen's feelings got the better of him', 617.32,—how does the narrator know this?), while at another he can present himself as an individual, inviting us (or his own proximate audience) to visit the Malahide mansion ('really an unquestionably fine residence of its kind and well worth seeing'). But however this narrator presents himself, his speech remains constant, for over and against the reader's world Joyce has built up a world of banal locutions within which both narrator and story struggle into being.

There is perhaps little that is unusual in a narrator who is at once himself and others—at once an individual and a general or collective consciousness. But in the case of 'Eumaeus' the narrator is the storyteller as impostor who unfolds his narrative less by becoming his characters than by speaking their parts for them. This sense of a posturing storyteller is strengthened the more by the fact that we have seen these characters, Bloom and Stephen, born of other narrators in previous episodes, and accordingly they tend to have for us an existence that is independent of any storyteller. But most of all there remains the deadly language of 'Eumaeus', by virtue of which all characters are reduced to the common denominator of the narrator himself, and so become less than we feel them to be. In this sense the posturing of the storyteller works to conceal as much as to present the narrative, which means that finally the storyteller is an impostor exposed by his frank inability to bring to life what is essential in his characters.

It is good to dwell upon this notion of imposture, because, as it happens, this is the central theme of 'Eumaeus'—a theme around which a tale of masks and roles is woven. It is formally announced shortly after Bloom and Stephen reach the cabman's shelter, there to encounter two figures, Murphy, the 'redbearded bibulous' sailor (622.11), and the keeper of the shelter, who may or may not be Fitzharris of the infamous Invincibles:

—Sounds are impostures, Stephen said after a pause of some little time. Like names, Cicero, Podmore, Napolean, Mr Goodbody, Jesus, Mr Doyle. Shakespeares were as common as Murphies. What's in a name?

—Yes, to be sure, Mr Bloom unaffectedly concurred. Of course. Our name was changed too, he added, pushing the socalled roll across. . . .

—And what might your name be? (622.40)

The idea that 'Sounds are impostures' adumbrates a basic nominalist formula, according to which a discontinuity is said to prevail between words and things. In the context here the discontinuity is between names and persons, and as the situation develops we are led to wonder, first, whether the keeper of the shelter is really the historical Fitzharris, and, second, whether Murphy is really the romantic figure he purports to be. We are led to suspect, in short, that no real relationship exists between character and role (just as, from the nominalist point of view, no natural relationship exists between thing and name). What is more, we shall see that it is precisely in terms of this suspicion that something like an authentic role (among other, dubious roles) is established for Bloom: namely, the *eiron*, whose business it is to expose the discontinuity between character and role—that is, to expose the impostor and to deflate the romantic.

What takes place first is something like a dramatization of this nominalist position. Murphy, upon learning Stephen's name, asks whether Stephen knows Simon Dedalus, but the Simon that Murphy knows is not Stephen's father but a sharpshooter who 'toured the wide world with Hengler's Royal Circus' (624.11). 'Curious coincidence', Bloom remarks to Stephen (624.13), and, just so, the relationship between person and name is plainly governed by fortune, not nature. In this case, however, the coincidence is pointed, not idle, because of the special delight that Murphy takes in the utterance of names:

> —You must have seen a fair share of the world, the keeper remarked, leaning on the counter.
> —Why, the sailor answered, upon reflection upon it. I've circumnavigated a bit since I first joined on. I was in the Red Sea. I was in China and North America and South America. I seen icebergs plenty, growlers. I was in Stockholm and the Black Sea, the Dardanelles, under Captain Dalton the best bloody man that ever scuttled a ship. I seen Russia. *Gospodi pomilooy.* That's how the Russian prays. (625.20)

This catalogue of place names is plausible enough by itself, which is to say that Murphy could have visited these places, but the fact is that the catalogue exists not by itself but as part of a whole—part of a performance in which Murphy presents himself as a man of rare experience:

> —You seen queer sights, don't be talking, put in a jarvey.
> —Why, the sailor said, shifting his partially chewed plug, I seen queer things too, ups and downs. I seen a crocodile bite the fluke of an anchor same as I chew that quid.
> He took out of his mouth the pulpy quid and, lodging it between his teeth, bit ferociously.
> —Khaan! Like that. And I seen maneaters in Peru that eats corpses and the livers of horses. Look here. Here they are. A friend of mine sent me. (625.29)

What could be more exotic than cannibals, and what, should there
be doubters, could be more telling than a postcard which Murphy
then produces, showing 'a group of savage women in striped loin-
cloths, [squatting], blinking, suckling, frowning, sleeping, amid a
swarm of infants (there must have been quite a score of them)
outside some primitive shanties of osier' (625.42).

Bloom's response to the postcard settles him into his role:

> Mr Bloom, without evincing surprise, unostentatiously turned
> over the card to peruse the partially obliterated address and post-
> mark. It ran as follows: *Tarjeta Postal. Señor A. Boudin, Galeria
> Becche, Santiago, Chile.* There was no message evidently, as he took
> particular notice. Though not an implicit believer in the lurid story
> narrated . . . having detected a discrepancy between his name (as-
> suming he was the person he represented himself to be and not
> sailing under false colours after having boxed the compass on the
> strict q.t. somewhere) and the fictitious addressee of the missive
> which made him nourish some suspicions of our friend's *bona
> fides.* . . . (626.13)

Bloom emerges here as a self-contained and sceptical figure, manifestly the *eiron* who sees directly the discrepancy between name and
person. Murphy is an impostor, a character at play beneath a fabricated identity—a kind of Marlow *manqué.* As though to underscore
this fact, the narrator attributes to him a diversity of names: Sinbad,
Shipahoy, Palgrave Murphy, 'the old tarpaulin', 'the ancient mariner'.
What is interesting, however, is how the deflation of Murphy is
managed. It begins with the momentary fantasy that Murphy's
exotica induce in Bloom: 'Though not an implicit believer in the
lurid story narrated . . . nevertheless it reminded him in a way of
a longcherished plan he meant to one day realise some Wednesday
or Saturday of travelling to London *via* long sea not to say that he
had ever travelled extensively to any great extent but he was at heart
a born adventurer' (626.17). This is Bloom in burlesque of Murphy.
For what distinguishes Bloom's daydream is its utter banality: a
journey from Dublin to London via the long sea (our adventurer
at heart! our Odysseus!). Beyond this, as Bloom's daydream metamorphoses into one of his typical entrepreneurial fantasies—'Also,
without being actually positive, it struck him a great field was to
be opened up in the line of opening up new routes to keep pace
with the times' (627.23)—we encounter what is surely Ortega's
'collapse of the poetic'. Not only has Bloom seen beneath Murphy's

mask and discovered empty space; his own fantasy stands in relation
to Murphy's posturing as the novel stands in relation to romance.
Bloom's is a vision unredeemed by anything like a poetic imagination;
it is a fantasy that, so far from removing him from his commonplace
world, carries him more deeply into it—into its very bourgeois soul.

There is an additional point to be made in this connexion. We
may recall that in the 'Cyclops' episode the personalities that surround Bloom—the citizen, the narrator, even Garryowen, the dog—
are aggressive, hostile. Antagonisms exist in the open, dramatically,
and, like the very language, in a richly amplified form. 'Eumaeus' is
a kind of inversion of 'Cyclops'. Its language is diminished, not amplified, and its antagonisms are underplayed, muted, which is to
say undramatized. Bloom plays *eiron* to Murphy's *alazon*, but such
confrontation as they have passes almost without notice:

> —Have you seen the Rock of Gibraltar? Mr Bloom inquired.
> The sailor grimaced, chewing, in a way that might be read as
> yes, ay, or no.
> —Ah, you've touched there too, Mr Bloom said, Europa point,
> thinking he had, in the hope that the rover might possibly by some
> reminiscences but he failed to do so, simply letting spurt a jet of
> spew into the sawdust, and shook his head with a sort of lazy scorn.
> —What year would that be about? Mr Bloom interpolated.
> Can you recall the boats?
> Our *soi-disant* sailor munched heavily awhile, hungrily, before
> answering.
> —I'm tired of all them rocks in the sea, he said, and boats and
> ships. Salt junk all the time. (629.33)

Here Bloom tries to draw Murphy out into the open. He will later
try to draw Stephen out with about as much success. For Murphy,
'Our *soi-disant* sailor', confronted by Bloom, withdraws from the
role he had been trying to establish a moment before. The point is
not simply that Murphy does not rise to Bloom's bait, but that
Bloom has pricked the man's surface sufficiently to discover, not a
field of rich memories concerning the Rock of Gibraltar, nor even a
spirit (such as appeared everywhere in 'Cyclops') prepared to re-
taliate against Bloom, but 'a sort of lazy scorn'—scorn for Bloom,
no doubt, but curiously enough scorn also for the sea and for the
very way of life that he had just now conjured as part of a romantic
pose. The man of rare experience, under pressure applied by Bloom,
becomes a man wearied to death by the commonplace—by 'all them

rocks in the sea . . . and boats and ships. Salt junk all the time'.
What this suggests, of course, is that irony has already played heavily
with Murphy, that quite like one of Conrad's young men he had
gone to sea in search of the rare experience, and had come away
empty, thus finally settling in a Dublin cabman's shelter, nightly
to defend against the deadly commonplace with anecdotes drawn
from nowhere.

For, indeed, even the mystery to which Murphy had just now
implicitly appealed, the mystery of the sea, is emptied of its romantic
significance. Bloom, failing to get any response from Murphy, falls
to 'woolgathering on the enormous dimensions of the water about
the globe':

> On more than one occasion—a dozen at the lowest—near the
> North Bull at Dollymount he had remarked a superannuated old
> salt, evidently derelict, seated habitually near the not particularly
> redolent sea on the wall, staring quite obliviously at it and it at him,
> dreaming of fresh woods and pastures new as someone somewhere
> sings. And it left him wondering why. Possibly he had tried to find
> out the secret for himself, floundering up and down the antipodes
> and all that sort of thing and over and under—well, not exactly un-
> der, tempting the fates. And the odds were twenty to nil there was
> really no secret about it at all. (630.11)

The image that lodges in Bloom's mind is itself a commonplace:
a man has spent his life pursuing the secret of the sea; having grown
old now, a mere derelict, he simply stares out to sea and wonders
as he has always wondered: What is its meaning? The answer, from
Bloom's point of view, is that 'twenty to nil there was really no
secret about it at all'. The sea simply exists, 'and in the natural course
of things somebody or other had to sail on it and fly in the face of
providence though it merely went to show how people usually con-
trived to load that sort of onus on to the other fellow like the hell idea
and the lottery and insurance . . .' (630.23). The 'secret' of the sea is
a superstition, 'like the hell idea', or a hoax, like 'the lottery and
insurance'; for the sea is a kind of empty space into which expectations are projected but are never to be fulfilled.

In Joyce's Ireland, of course, natural mysteries tend easily to
be displaced by religious mysteries, and these in turn are inevitably
displaced by those diverse and inimitable political mysteries that
make up a kind of national fantasy life. This fantasy life enters

'Eumaeus' chiefly by way of the keeper of the cabman's shelter, who may be a figure out of Irish history—though Bloom, as we might expect, is inclined to doubt it: 'Mr Bloom and Stephen entered the cabman's shelter . . . the former having previously whispered to the latter a few hints anent the keeper of it, said to be the once famous Skin-the-Goat, Fitzharris, the invincible, though he wouldn't vouch for the actual facts, which quite possibly there was not one vestige of truth in' (621.33). As in the case of Murphy, the possible discontinuity here between name and person opens onto a greater discontinuity between what the keeper says and what it is possible (for Bloom) to accept. Thus Fitzharris, on the natural blessedness of Ireland:

> Skin-the-Goat, assuming he was he, evidently with an axe to grind, was airing his grievances in a forcible-feeble philippic anent the natural resources of Ireland, or something of that sort, which he described in his lengthy dissertation as the richest country bar none on the face of God's earth, far and away superior to England, with coal in large quantities, six million pounds' worth of pork exported every year, ten millions between butter and eggs. . . . (640.13)

One way to describe this is to call it Ireland's myth of the Promised Land, as corollaries to which Fitzharris attaches, first, the captivity theme—'and all the riches drained out of it by England levying taxes on the poor people that paid through the nose always, and gobbling up the best meat in the market' (640.20)—and, second, a vision of Ireland's deliverance:

> But a day of reckoning, he stated *crescendo* with no uncertain voice —thoroughly monopolising all the conversation—was in store for mighty England, despite her power of pelf on account of her crimes. There would be a fall and the greatest fall in history. . . . Brummagem England was toppling already and her downfall would be Ireland, her Achilles heel. . . . (640.28)

Skin-the-Goat's political or nationalist faith, like the faith of those ancient Israelites who looked forward to their deliverance, is essentially a faith in history, in the sacred structure of history, according to which all temporal events arrange themselves in patterns of divine justice: 'Brummagem England' must fall, and not fall merely, but enact 'the greatest fall in history', one brought to fulfilment by Ireland, England's enemy and history's hero.

Bloom stands in relation to Fitzharris precisely as he stood

against Murphy. That England 'was toppling already and her down-
fall would be Ireland', is for Bloom so much 'egregious balderdash'
(641.24)—'quite on a par', we are told, 'with the quixotic idea in
certain quarters that in a hundred million years the coal seam of
the sister island would be played out' (641.28). The term 'quixotic'
is exactly to the point here, for in this episode Bloom is a Sancho
Panza surrounded by Quixotes—like the jarvey who, moments later,
insists that Parnell is alive and well somewhere in South Africa: 'One
morning you would open the paper, the cabman affirmed, and read
Return of Parnell. He bet them what they liked. A Dublin fusilier
was in that shelter one night and said he saw him in South Africa.
. . . Dead he wasn't. Simply absconded somewhere. The coffin they
brought over was full of stones. He changed his name to De Wet,
the Boer general' (648.42). In process here is an activity of the kind
that once transformed a Celtic warrior into the legendary King
Arthur; just so, Parnell, dying out of history into legend, can be
expected to return. 'Highly unlikely, of course, there was even a
shadow of truth in the stories' (649.14), Bloom says to himself.

Bloom is, indeed, an ironic but silent chorus to the fantasy at
play in the shelter. His silence is important to mark, because such
silence (like the virtual silence of Stephen) is proper to the nature
of the episode. After all, characters in the shelter seem barely to
interact, or not at all. Perhaps the high point of drama occurs when
Murphy and Fitzharris begin 'to have a few irascible words' (641.18)
over whether an Irishman should serve the British Empire. This
dispute, we are told, 'waxed hotter, both, needless to say, appealing
to the listeners who followed the passage of arms with interest so
long as they didn't indulge in recriminations and come to blows'
(641.18). Not only, however, do the two not come to blows, their
dispute comes to nothing; it is a possibility never actualized. For the
action of the episode is rather more thematic than dramatic. The
interior of the cabman's shelter, wherein Skin-the-Goat and Murphy
presumably harangue one another, is displaced by the interior of
Bloom's mind, wherein the theme of imposture continues to run
its course:

> So the scene between the pair of them, the licensee of the place,
> rumoured to be or have been Fitzharris, the famous invincible,
> and the other, obviously bogus, reminded him forcibly as being on
> all fours with the confidence trick, supposing, that is, it was pre-

arranged, as the lookeron, a student of the human soul, if anything, the others seeing least of the game. And as for the lessee or keeper, who probably wasn't the other person at all, he (Bloom) couldn't help feeling, and most properly, it was better to give people like that the goby. (641.39)

Skin-the-Goat and Murphy are, in short, two of a kind, figures whose every word and motion are to Bloom, 'a student of the human soul', implausible.

We can put the matter here another way: it is the part of Bloom's habit of mind to respond to the implausible (and the romantic) by bringing it nearer his own world, and so to destroy it, or to remake it, not exactly in his own image, but according to his own commonplace view of things. Thus, as we saw, Bloom followed Murphy's exotic anecdotes with his own fantasy of a journey from Dublin to London via the long sea. Similarly does he absorb and transmute into dross the story of Parnell. Of the fantasy that Parnell survives, Bloom considers that Parnell's movements, after all, were always mysterious, which in Bloom's sense means that 'there was absolutely no clue as to his whereabouts which were decidedly of the *Alice, where art thou* order even prior to his starting to go under several aliases such as Fox and Stewart' (649.27), which he did during his affair with Kitty O'Shea. Parnell, that is to say, is figured as the man of masks in a sentimental tale of adultery—that 'historic story', as Bloom recalls it, 'which had aroused extraordinary interest' (650.34):

> First, it was strictly platonic till nature intervened and an attachment sprang up between them, till bit by bit matters came to a climax and the matter became the talk of the town till the staggering blow came as a welcome intelligence to not a few evildisposed however, who were resolved upon encouraging his downfall though the thing was public property all along though not to anything like the sensational extent that it subsequently blossomed into. (650.37)

It is hard to miss the attenuation which this tale of 'extraordinary interest' suffers as it struggles to emerge from the narrator's prose. The point, however, is that it emerges into Bloom's memory, where naturally and inevitably it bumps up against Bloom's own situation, in which he plays cuckold to Boylan's Parnell and Molly's Kitty O'Shea. For as Bloom's meditation upon the tale of Parnell and Kitty unfolds, it becomes inextricably a part of his own self-reflection, and is diminished thereby, the more so as it serves him with a way of dealing with his own particular case.

Much attention has been given to the psychological forces at work in Bloom as his mind toils during the course of the day with the affair of Molly and Boylan. It is doubtless as a defence against this affair that Bloom uses the Parnell story to construct a kind of determinist theory of adultery, thus to place specific episodes of adultery within the governance of a fixed law of nature. For so far as the Parnell story is concerned, 'the simple fact of the case was it was simply a case of the husband not being up to the scratch with nothing in common between them beyond the name and then a real man arriving on the scene, strong to the verge of weakness, falling a victim to her siren charms and forgetting home ties. The usual sequel, to bask in the loved one's smiles' (651.13). Notice that the 'historic story' of Parnell and his paramour is for Bloom neither a romance nor a tale of political intrigue; rather, it takes on meaning for him only as it discloses a common denominator. Whether romantic or mundane, the activity of adultery always proceeds according to a law of the 'simple fact' and 'usual sequel', thus inevitably to pose, in Bloom's formulation, 'The eternal question of the life connubial. . . . Can real love, supposing there happens to be another chap in the case, exist between married folk?' (651.18). The implication appears to be that, in the very nature of things, it cannot. Just so, Bloom sees himself, even as he sees Parnell, as a figure acting a part determined by the ready laws and eternal questions of the triangle; it is by appeal to such laws and questions, with their (Stephen might have said) 'ineluctable modality', that he is defended against cuckoldry—as Parnell (whose memory Bloom treasures) is defended against adultery. For Parnell was, no mistaking it, 'A magnificent specimen of manhood . . . augmented obviously by gifts of a high order' (651.23), and so it follows, quite as a matter of course, that he must have prevailed over 'the usual everyday farewell, my gallant captain kind of an individual' (651.26).

Bloom raises everything to the level of types and kinds, and he does so in order to enforce a dissociation of character from role— a dissociation, for example, of Bloom from cuckold. The story of Parnell and Kitty O'Shea is, in other words, an instance of a type, by virtue of which lover and cuckold lose specificity, become faceless pieces in a design of nature—roles to be acted out in what Bloom

finally judges to be 'the wellknown case of hot passion . . . upsetting the applecart with a vengeance' (652.3). Accordingly, Bloom
deduces that Kitty O'Shea, as the adultress, 'also was Spanish, or
half so, types that wouldn't do things by halves, passionate abandon
of the south, casting every shred of decency to the winds' (652.6).
It is this conclusion which Bloom proposes to Stephen and which,
appropriately enough, he decides to ornament with a photograph of
Molly, an exemplary 'Spanish type' (652.24), the more so as she
happens to be posing, in the photograph, as a Spanish singer—'her
full lips parted, and some perfect teeth, standing near, ostensibly
with gravity, a piano, on the rest of which was *In old Madrid*, a
ballad, pretty in its way, which was then all the vogue' (652.30).
Thus Molly is submerged beneath a role, which she does not exist as
but merely plays, even as it is Molly who is submerged beneath the
carefully appointed theory in Bloom's meditation upon 'man, or
men in the plural', who is (or are) understood to be

> always hanging around on the waiting list about a lady, even sup-
> posing she was the best wife in the world and they got on fairly
> well together for the sake of argument, when [as inevitably even
> this best of wives must] neglecting her duties, she chose to be tired
> of wedded life, and was on for a little flutter in polite debauchery
> to press their attentions on her with improper intent, the upshot
> being that her affections centred on another, the cause of many
> *liaisons* between still attractive married women getting on for fair
> and forty and younger men, no doubt as several famous cases of
> feminine infatuation proved up to the hilt. (655.35)

Indeed, it is necessarily of men and women in the plural that Bloom
thinks—those many impersonations of the one, those 'famous cases'
upon which to predicate the inexorable rule—because to think of
man and woman in the particular, as persons rather than as roles,
is to think of himself and Molly as really they are.

We can pursue this general theme as we turn to take up the
special problem of Bloom's relationship to Stephen. We may say
that, in this context, Bloom is presented as a diversity of roles, hardly
any of which he is able to play adequately or with any meaning. At
the outset he is, by turns, the Good Samaritan (613.3), the *fidus
Achates* out of Vergil (614.22), and, as we have seen, the loving
and sententious father. Commentators on *Ulysses* regularly point to
the association in this episode between Bloom and Christ—'He called

me a jew', Bloom says of the citizen in Barney Kiernan's, 'and in a
heated fashion, offensively. So I, without deviating from plain facts
in the least, told him his God, I mean Christ, was a jew too, and
all his family, like me, though in reality I'm not' (643.1)—but it is
not so regularly pointed out that here Bloom denies his Jewish identity, and appropriately so, for in this episode, at least, Bloom is for
the most part a locus of random identities, identities which circulate
around or near him but do not inhere. 'Ex quibus . . . Christus
or Bloom his name is', Stephen drunkenly remarks, and then adds,
'or, after all, any other, secundum carnem' (643.11): Christ or
Bloom his name is, but any name will do, because names are finally
a matter of indifference. Such indifference is displayed by the Evening Telegraph, which identifies Bloom (who numbered among
Paddy Dignam's mourners) as L. Boom (647.41)—an error that
nettles Bloom and which, for unknown but doubtless mischievous
reasons, the narrator picks up and 'for the nonce' continues to apply
(648.16). The point is, in any case, that Bloom's several possible
selves tend to cancel one another out, that his noble or heroic identities tend to be subverted by his actual behaviour. Thus, if, for
example, at one point he offers bread to Stephen (622.3), and so
seems to adumbrate the figure of the redeemer, at another more
carefully dramatized moment he seems prepared to offer him his
wife.

But Bloom is hardly more pimp than Good Samaritan, because
throughout the episode the motives at work beneath his thinking and
feeling seem to be as nearly unfixed and undefined as his several
identities. The decision to show Stephen the photograph of Molly,
and so to suggest that this 'Spanish type' might play out her role
for the young man, is a spontaneous, improvised one, and in any
event Bloom never allows himself to consider what meaning such a
decision might have in the context of his meditations upon adultery.
So much is clear, at least, from the following:

> The spirit moving him, he would much have liked to follow
> Jack Tar's good example and leave the likeness there for a very few
> minutes to speak for itself on the plea he . . . so that the other
> could drink in the beauty for himself, her stage presence being,
> frankly, a treat in itself which the camera could not at all do
> justice to. But it was scarcely professional etiquette so, though it
> was a warm pleasant sort of a night now yet wonderfully cool for

the season considering, for sunshine after storm. . . . And he did feel a kind of need there and then to follow suit like a kind of inward voice and satisfy a possible need by moving a motion. Nevertheless, he sat tight, just viewing the slightly soiled photo creased by opulent curves, none the worse for wear, however, and looked away thoughtfully with the intention of not further increasing the other's possible embarrassment while gauging her symmetry of heaving *embonpoint*. (653.15)

The ellipses in this passage constitute so many lacunae in Bloom's consciousness—sudden turns of his mind away from those darker spirits he would prefer not to be troubled by. Similarly, the obscurity of the language ('And he did feel a kind of need there and then to follow suit like a kind of inward voice and satisfy a possible need by moving a motion') acts as a kind of defence, a way of submerging beneath a garble of words a plainly sexual impulse. Precisely in this wise does Bloom's mind dance away from cuckoldry:

Suppose she was gone when he? . . . I looked for the lamp which she told me came into his mind but merely as a passing fancy of his because he then recollected the morning littered bed etcetera and the book about Ruby with met him pike hoses (*sic*) in it which must have fell down sufficiently appropriately beside the domestic chamberpot with apologies to Lindley Murray. (653.32)

It is as though Molly drives Bloom to suppress self-consciousness, and thus to disallow any identity for himself. He can hardly, for all of that, elude the name of cuckold; he can only, as we have seen, retreat to a corner of Stoic generality, there to explain away his lot as merely a steadfast theme in the way of the world. Nevertheless, the general import of the episode is reasonably clear: Bloom remains throughout a mainly anonymous figure, identifiable rather paradoxically as the Odyssean Noman who is always at some remove from his possible selves. This fact may take us some way toward explaining why it is that Bloom seeks (frequently and perhaps compulsively) to establish some sort of identity for himself in or through other people, as he does, for example, when he shows the photograph of Molly to Stephen. Molly, in this instance, is no longer simply 'Mrs Bloom'—nor even, we might notice in passing, a 'Spanish type'; she becomes instead 'Mrs Bloom, my wife the *prima donna*, Madam Marion Tweedy' (652.37)—'the accomplished daughter', he shortly adds, 'of Major Brian Tweedy' (652.41). Part of what is happening here, of course, is that Bloom is seeking in the titles 'Madam' and

'Major' something—a magic power, perhaps, which is to say a way
of impressing and thus holding on to Stephen—that the name
'Bloom' doesn't seem to him to have. But he is also, by a process of
association, trying to secure a name for himself. In a roughly similar
way, Bloom delights in recalling (he does so twice) his role in the
'historic *fracas*' (654.21), in which Parnell and his men charged
'into the printing works of the *Insuppressible* or no it was *United
Ireland* (a by no means, by the by, appropriate appellative)' (654.25).
Parnell, as it happened, lost his hat in the melee, but in doing so he
provided Bloom with something approximating a historical identity.
For, 'as a matter of strict history, Bloom was the man who picked
it up in the crush after witnessing the occurrence' (654.42). It is
at once ironic and consistent that Bloom should have entered history
namelessly, as 'the man who' rather than as 'Leopold Bloom', but at
least Parnell (if not history) acknowledged him—'because he turned
round to the donor and thanked him with perfect *aplomb*, saying:
Thank you, sir' (655.9)—and perhaps it is even true that, of such
moments as this, one's self-consciousness is likely to be composed.

We have here one area in which Bloom's relationship to Stephen
may be said to complete a pattern: 'The vicinity of the young man
he certainly relished, educated, *distingué*, and impulsive into the
bargain, far and away the pick of the bunch' (653.39). Bloom is
edified (one is tempted to say, 'identified') by Stephen's presence,
even as he was edified by his brush with Parnell; but more to the
point is that, as Molly (which is to say, 'Madam Marion Tweedy')
serves to impress and perhaps entice Stephen, so Stephen in his turn
will serve Bloom's 'Utopian plans' (658.37):

> Education (the genuine article), literature, journalism, prize titbits,
> up to date billing, hydros and concert tours in English watering
> resorts packed with theatres, turning money away, duets in Italian
> with the accent perfectly true to nature and a quantity of other
> things, no necessity of course to tell the world and his wife from
> the housetops about it and a slice of luck. An opening was all was
> wanted. Because he more than suspected he had his father's voice
> to bank his hopes on which it was quite on the cards he had.
> (658.38)

Bloom here steps briskly from the Good Samaritan role; he seems,
indeed, to avoid the touch of anything figurative or symbolic. If, for
example, he appears to seek Stephen's redemption—that is, to uplift

him from his evidently wasted state—it is because he recognizes in the young man not human but market value. Or, again, if in this episode Bloom may be said to play father to Stephen, it is nevertheless true that he is moved rather to possess than to care for him. For Bloom's angle of vision is such that Stephen appears to him only as a type, not as a person; he is only for Bloom the sum total of so many real or imagined qualities, paramount of which is that 'phenomenally beautiful tenor voice' (663.23), which promises to avail him (and therefore Bloom) 'an *entrée* into fashionable houses in the best residential quarters, of financial magnates in a large way of business and titled people' (663.29). If it appears to us that Bloom is on some sort of quest, we are probably not far wrong: Molly opens the way to Stephen, who in turn opens the way to 'Lady Fingall's Irish industries concert . . . and aristocracy in general' (663.9), at which social level of being Bloom would (he anticipates) at last find himself.

Bloom's 'Utopian plans', in other words, are not Utopian at all but entrepreneurial, the visions of a would-be *parvenu*. What should not be overlooked, moreover, is that the bourgeois magic of Bloom's fantasy carries Stephen from 'a youthful tyro in society's sartorial niceties' (663.37) to a clear burlesque of the salon artist, 'participating in . . . musical and artistic *conversazioni* during the festivities of the Christmas season, for choice, causing a slight flutter in the dovecotes of the fair sex and being made a lot of by ladies out for sensation' (663.40). This is the Stephen, we should remember, who once figured himself as the hero of a romance:

> in his imagination he lived through a long train of adventures, marvellous as those in the book itself, towards the close of which there appeared an image of himself, grown older and sadder, standing in a moonlit garden with Mercedes who had so many years before slighted his love, and with a sadly proud gesture of refusal, saying:
> —Madam, I never eat muscatel grapes. (AP, 63)

And thereby hangs a tale, which is that of Stephen in dwindling progress from a character in a fantasy built up from Dumas to a character in a fantasy by Bloom. We need hardly go much further to point out that Bloom's imagination applies a kind of *coup de grace* to the image of Stephen as the Dedalus, insofar as Bloom pictures for Stephen not merely a life as a local *artiste* but success in the music halls as well, toast of that very world from which the young man had once so eloquently severed himself: 'he had a capital opening to make a name for himself and win a high place in the city's esteem where he could command a stiff figure' (664.22)—a name, public affection, money: Bloom's goals, every one.

Earlier we speculated that beneath Murphy's romantic posturing lay a man wearied to death by the commonplace—that the cabman's shelter constituted for him a final, nether port in which to play out a kind of endgame against a life resolutely unromantic. It was, we saw, largely through the efforts of Bloom, in his role as *eiron*, that this speculation was brought to bear upon Murphy, who proved so unexpectedly vulnerable to Bloom's probings. We may ground Stephen upon a similar speculation, thus to observe that Bloom's relation to Stephen is finally of much the same sort as his relation to Murphy. Bloom's entrepreneurial fantasy is Stephen's endgame; it is the vision of the Dedalus played out once more, this time, however, not in a young man's fervid soul, but upon the bourgeois fields of Bloom's comic fancy, in which 'the angel of mortal youth and beauty, an envoy from the fair courts of life' (AP, 172), is replaced by 'the dovecotes of the fair sex and . . . ladies out for sensation'. Wonderfully appropriate, then, that at the end of the episode Stephen should describe 'Exquisite variations . . . on an air *Youth here has End* by Jans Pieter Sweelinck' (663.12).

Thus the only bond that is established between Bloom and Stephen is utterly commercial and utterly imaginary. The only point of contact between them appears to be a momentary meeting of the eyes when someone in the shelter happens to mention, within earshot of Fitzharris, the Phoenix Park murders: 'At this remark, passed obviously in the spirit of *where ignorance is bliss*, Mr Bloom and Stephen, each in his own particular way, both instinctively exchanged meaning glances, in a religious silence of the strictly *entre nous* variety however, towards where Skin-the-Goat, *alias* the keeper, was drawing spurts of liquid from his boiler affair' (629.11). Unfortunately, this 'religious silence' passes away once more into that profane silence that surrounds and punctuates Bloom's sorry small talk and Stephen's sententious and sometimes disagreeable responses. But, after all, it is this profane silence that is the environment of ordinary life, in which such figures as Bloom and Stephen could hardly be expected to do more than sit and speak at an impasse.

ITHACA

A. Walton Litz

If *Ulysses* is a crucial testing ground for theories of the novel, as it seems to have become, then the 'Ithaca' episode must be a *locus classicus* for every critic interested in the traditions of English and European fiction. Here the extremes of Joyce's art, and of fiction in general, are found in radical form: the tension between symbolism and realism, what Arnold Goldman has called the 'myth/fact paradox',[1] gives the episode its essential life. Joyce once told Frank Budgen that 'Ithaca' was his 'favourite episode', the 'ugly duckling of the book',[2] and his frequent references to the episode in his letters reveal a personal and artistic involvement seldom matched in his work on the other chapters. He was acutely aware that 'Ithaca' culminated his risky 'scorched earth' policy of constantly altering the novel's styles and narrative methods, so that 'the progress of the book is in fact like the progress of some sandblast', each successive episode leaving behind it 'a burnt up field'.[3] He also knew that the reader who had mastered the 'initial style' of the earliest episodes, that subtle blending of interior monologue and distanced description derived from A *Portrait of the Artist*, would prefer it 'much as the wanderer did who longed for the rock of Ithaca'.[4]

[1] Arnold Goldman, *The Joyce Paradox*, London and Evanston, Ill., 1966, p. 105.
[2] Budgen, p. 264.   [3] *Letters*, I, 129.   [4] *Ibid.*

These defensive remarks were made in mid-1919, when Joyce felt compelled to justify the 'musical' techniques of 'Sirens', and they clearly reflect his anxiety at that moment in the composition of *Ulysses* when the life of the novel began to gravitate from external drama to the internal reality of the various styles and artifices. This clearcut shift in artistic aims midway through Joyce's work on *Ulysses* was somewhat masked by the final revisions, when he recast many of the earlier episodes in forms that satisfied his later sense of the novel's design;[5] but he attached so much importance to this transitional moment in the making of the novel that he once thought of writing an '*Entr'acte*' to celebrate the mid-point in the narrative,[6] and on a chart of the episodes sent to John Quinn in September 1920 the first nine episodes (through 'Scylla and Charybdis') are clearly separated from the last nine (beginning with 'Wandering Rocks').[7] Just as the structural centre of *Ulysses* represents a turning point in the motions of Bloom and Stephen, the beginning of their tentative progress toward each other, so it announces a fundamental change in the novel's aesthetic ground-base. From 'Wandering Rocks' and 'Sirens' onward, the 'reality' to be processed into art is both the imitated human action and the rich artistic world already created in the earlier and plainer episodes. Technique tends more and more to become subject matter, and by the time we reach 'Ithaca' the form of the episode is as much the substance as the actual interchanges between Bloom and Stephen.

So both the action and the stylistic development of *Ulysses* reach a climax in 'Ithaca', which Joyce considered 'in reality the end as "Penelope" has no beginning, middle or end'.[8] Although he

---

[5] For discussion of the evolving styles, see Chapter Four of Goldman's *The Joyce Paradox* and Chapter One of my *The Art of James Joyce*, London, 1961. It is interesting to see how the recasting of an earlier episode was often dictated by the form of the later episode then on the stocks. For example, 'Aeolus'—the early episode that underwent the most radical change—was rewritten in 1921 while 'Ithaca' was being drafted, and the inserted newspaper headlines reflect not only the 'history of the language' technique developed in 'Oxen of the Sun' but the chief effect of the question-and-answer method in 'Ithaca', a breaking-down of the narrative into discrete aesthetic units. In a sense, 'Aeolus' slows down the narrative flow of the first half of *Ulysses* and makes the declining pace of the second half less obvious.

[6] *Letters*, I, 149.

[7] *Letters*, I, 145.

[8] *Letters*, I, 172.

had a general sense of the novel's ending from the start of his work on it, and could refer easily to the 'Nostos' (the last three episodes) during the process of composition,[9] Joyce evidently had no clear notion of the local form of 'Ithaca' until 1919–20; yet long before any part of the episode reached paper he had unconsciously rehearsed the role 'Ithaca' was to play in a continuing debate on the aims of English and European fiction. It has often been noted that the two lectures Joyce gave at the Università Popolare of Trieste in 1912 established the twin frontiers of his art and looked forward to *Ulysses*.[10] He chose as his subjects Defoe and Blake, treating them as the ultimate masters of painstaking realism and the universal symbolism of spiritual 'correspondences'. But it has not been noted that the tags Joyce chose for his lectures, *verismo* and *idealismo*, were technical terms in a contemporary critical debate on the validity of the 'realistic' novel.[11] What Joyce did in his lectures was to liberate the terms from literary controversy and use them to describe two complementary methods for universalizing experience. One way toward completeness, as the editors of the Blake lecture remark (*CW*, 214), is through the overwhelming accretion of encyclopaedic detail: Robinson Crusoe is an archetypal figure—Joyce speaks of him as such—because we know him, like Bloom, in all the petty but revealing details of ordinary life. Commenting on Defoe's *The Storm*, Joyce noted that the 'method is simplicity itself'.

> The book opens with an inquiry into the causes of winds, then recapitulates the famous storms in human story, and finally the narrative, like a great snake, begins to crawl slowly through a tangle of letters and reports. . . . The modern reader does a good deal of groaning before he reaches the conclusion, but in the end the object of the chronicler has been achieved. By dint of repetitions, contradictions, details, figures, noises, the storm has come alive, the ruin is visible.[12]

[9] Litz, *The Art of James Joyce*, pp. 3–5.

[10] Harry Levin was the first to discuss the lectures in his *James Joyce: a Critical Introduction*, Norfolk, Conn., 1941, p. 18. The surviving fragment of the Blake lecture is printed in *Critical Writings*, pp. 214–222. For the entire text of the Defoe lecture, see Joseph Prescott, ed., *Daniel Defoe, Buffalo Studies*, I, Buffalo, N.Y., December, 1964.

[11] See, for instance, the use of the terms 'verism' and 'idealism' in the criticism of Hamlin Garland, where the continental debate is given a native American context.

[12] *Daniel Defoe*, pp. 15–16.

This is the technique of much of 'Ithaca', an accumulation of details which has no inherent 'aesthetic' limits but relies on the epic impact of overmastering fact. One can see the method in action in the growth of the notorious question-and-answer on the universal significance of water, where the exchange in the basic manuscript

> What in water did Bloom, carrying water, returning to the range, admire?
>
> Its universality: its equality and constancy to its nature in seeking its own level: its vastness in the ocean of Mercator's projector: its secrecy in springs, exemplified by the well by the hole in the wall at Ashtown gate: its healing virtues: its properties for cleansing, quenching thirst and fire, nourishing plant life: its strength in rigid hydrants: its docility in working millwheels, electric power stations, bleachworks, tanneries, scutchmills: its utility in canals, rivers, if navigable; its fauna and flora: its noxiousness in marshes, pestilential fens, faded flowers, stagnant pools in the waning moon.[13]

finally took this form:

> What in water did Bloom, waterlover, drawer of water, water-carrier returning to the range, admire?
>
> Its universality: its democratic equality and constancy to its nature in seeking its own level: its vastness in the ocean of Mercator's projection: its unplumbed profundity in the Sundam trench of the Pacific exceeding 8,000 fathoms: the restlessness of its waves and surface particles visiting in turn all points of its seaboard: the independence of its units: the variability of states of sea: its hydrostatic quiescence in calm: its hydrokinetic turgidity in neap and spring tides: its subsidence after devastation: its sterility in the circumpolar icecaps, arctic and antarctic: its climatic and commercial significance: its proponderance of 3 to 1 over the dry land of the globe: its indisputable hegemony extending in square leagues over all the region below the subequatorial tropic of Capricorn: the multisecular stability of its primeval basin: its luteofulvous bed: its capacity to dissolve and hold in solution all soluble substances including millions of tons of the most precious metals: its slow erosions of peninsulas and downwardtending promontories: its alluvial deposits: its weight and volume and density: its imperturbability in lagoons and highland tarns: its gradation of colours in the torrid and temperate and frigid zones: its vehicular ramifications in continental lakecontained streams and confluent oceanflowing rivers with their tributaries and transoceanic currents: gulfstream, north

---

[13] Richard E. Madtes, 'Joyce and the Building of *Ithaca*', ELH, XXXI (December 1964), 457–458.

and south equatorial courses: its violence in seaquakes, waterspouts, artesian wells, eruptions, torrents, eddies, freshets, spates, ground-swells, watersheds, waterpartings, geysers, cataracts, whirlpools, mael-stroms, inundations, deluges, cloudbursts: its vast circumterrestrial ahorizontal curve: its secrecy in springs, and latent humidity, re-vealed by rhabdomantic or hygrometric instruments and exempli-fied by the hole in the wall at Ashtown gate, saturation of air, dis-tillation of dew: the simplicity of its composition, two constituent parts of hydrogen with one constituent part of oxygen: its healing virtues: its buoyancy in the waters of the Dead Sea: its persevering penetrativeness in runnels, gullies, inadequate dams, leaks on ship-board: its properties for cleansing, quenching thirst and fire, nour-ishing vegetation: its infallibility as paradigm and paragon: its meta-morphoses as vapour, mist, cloud, rain, sleet, snow, hail: its strength in rigid hydrants: its variety of forms in loughs and bays and gulfs and bights and guts and lagoons and atolls and archipelagos and sounds and fjords and minches and tidal estuaries and arms of sea: its solidity in glaciers, icebergs, icefloes: its docility in working hy-draulic millwheels, turbines, dynamos, electric power stations, bleachworks, tanneries, scutchmills: its utility in canals, rivers, if navigable, floating and graving docks: its potentiality derivable from harnessed tides or watercourses falling from level to level: its sub-marine fauna and flora (anacoustic, photophobe) numerically, if not literally, the inhabitants of the globe: its ubiquity as constitut-ing 90% of the human body: the noxiousness of its effluvia in lacustrine marshes, pestilential fens, faded flowerwater, stagnant pools in the waning moon. (671.26–672.38)

Here the initial passage was enlarged five-fold as it passed through successive typescripts and proofs, while the subject changed from the normal associations of Bloom's inquisitive mind to a conflation of that mind and the novel's 'epic' aims. Like Defoe's encyclopaedic treatment of the storm, Joyce's catalogue finally convinces 'by dint of repetitions, contradictions, details, figures', until it ultimately be-comes the expression of some omniscient mind meditating on the universal virtues of water.

But if the Defoe lecture is filled with Joyce's admiration for a writer who, through accumulated data, can turn fact into myth or archetype, the lecture on Blake reveals his deep affinity with the visionary artist who can divine the universe in a blade of grass, who through symbolic correspondences can make 'each moment shorter than a pulse-beat . . . equivalent in its duration to six thousand years' and can fly 'from the infinitely small to the infinitely large, from a drop of blood to the universe of stars' (CW, 222). Here the debt to Yeats's interpretations of Blake is obvious, and the theory of the epiphany is not far in the background. Like Whitman, Joyce possessed a talent which was both centripetal and centrifugal, tending toward both the symbolic moment and the scrupulous accumulation of 'fact': and these complementary impulses give 'Ithaca' its form and dynamism.

In speaking of the extremes of Joyce's art, it would be pointless to moderate or ignore their obsessive qualities. Both the symbolism and realism of 'Ithaca' have dimensions which are essentially private and disproportionate. Joyce's famous verification of Bloom's entrance into No. 7 Eccles street is a notorious example of a regard for 'realism' that goes far beyond the normal compact between author and reader:

> Is it possible (Joyce wrote to his aunt Josephine) for an ordinary person to climb over the area railings of no 7 Eccles street, either from the path or the steps, lower himself down from the lowest part or the railings till his feet are within 2 feet or 3 of the ground and drop unhurt. I daw it done myself but by a man of rather athletic build. I require this information in detail in order to determine the wording of a paragraph.[14]

In the same way, many of the leading symbols in 'Ithaca' (such as urination) seem to have had more significance for the author than for the reader. Like Henry James's The Sacred Fount, the 'Ithaca' episode relies so heavily on the author's obsessive techniques and themes that they approach self-parody; and although 'Ithaca' is richly comic in its general intent there are times when Joyce, like James, seems unaware of the grotesque effects he is creating. In a sense, 'fact' and the private symbol became substitutes for all those conventional supports of society and art and religion that Joyce had rejected.

These 'obsessive' qualities in 'Ithaca' really lie beyond the reach of conventional criticism, in the realm of psychoanalytic biography or some study of the creative process; they are reminders that most authors need more sanctions and correspondences than they can share with their audience (it is interesting that T. S. Eliot, in his 1956 lecture on 'The Frontiers of Criticism', used J. Livingston Lowes' Road to Xanadu and Joyce's Finnegans Wake to define the 'frontiers'). But we should not let Joyce's personal obsessions obscure

[14] Letters, I, 175.

one central fact: that *Ulysses* is a cross-roads in the history of prose fiction because it both exaggerates and harmonizes certain major tendencies that had marked the novel from its earliest appearances. Emerging in the seventeenth and eighteenth centuries from a convergence of myth (fables, 'Romance', moral tales) and fact (journals, diaries, 'news'), English fiction has always had a paradoxical relation to reality, as the fruitless attempts to separate 'Romance' from 'Novel' testify. If *Ulysses* is to be considered as a novel, rather than an 'anatomy' or some other hybrid form, it must be because the work is true to the fundamental paradox of the genre even while every aspect of the genre is being tested by parody and burlesque.

Perhaps it is a reluctance to accept this essential ambivalence of both the novel-form and *Ulysses* which lies behind the attempts of so many readers to press *Ulysses*—and especially the 'Ithaca' chapter—into some easy equation of 'either/or'. Either Joyce's method is a satire on the naturalistic writer's preoccupation with detail, or it is a humourless exercise in the manner of classic naturalism. Either it is *reductio ad absurdum* of naive nineteenth-century faith in science, or a serious application of scientific theories to human psychology. 'Ithaca' is either a final celebration of Bloom's heroic qualities as Everyman, or a cold revelation of his essential pettiness. Just as the typical reader of *A Portrait of the Artist* finds it difficult to accept the delicate balance of sympathy and irony that marks the novel's close, so the average reader of *Ulysses* seems compelled to indulge in the worst kind of critical bookkeeping, totting up Joyce's ironies and human touches as if some simple formula were really available. But the genius of Joyce and of *Ulysses* lies in the indisputable fact that the form is both epic and ironic, Bloom both heroic and commonplace. The bed of Ulysses is, in its secret construction, known only to Ulysses and Penelope, while the secret of Bloom's bed is a Dublin joke; but when Bloom dismisses Molly's suitors one by one his reason and equanimity are, as Joyce intended, equal in power to the great bow that only Ulysses could draw. At first Joyce had thought of the slaughter of the suitors as 'un-Ulyssean',[15] a bloody act of violence that could not be translated into modern Dublin or reconciled with Bloom's humanism; but finally he came to see that Bloom's equanimity of mind was in its way a comparable achievement. In his attempt 'to transpose the

[15] *Letters*, I, 160.

myth *sub specie temporis nostri*[16] Joyce realized that the contrasts
between the classical world and the modern world would inevitably
be ironic on the level of fact, leading only to mock-heroic effects
where the disparities in setting and action tend to debase the contemporary experience; but he also knew that on the level of symbol, where the fundamentals of human psychology are revealed,
Bloom would prove a worthy counterpart to the hero of Homer's
epic. Any reading of *Ulysses* that aims at doing justice to Joyce's
complex vision must be composed of constant adjustments and
accommodations between myth and fact, and it is in 'Ithaca' that
these adjustments are most difficult to make.

Joyce began work on 'Ithaca' early in 1921, after completing the
drafts of 'Eumaeus', and was still revising the episode on proof in
late January 1922, only a few days before the novel's publication
('Penelope' was actually finished before 'Ithaca' so that Valery
Larbaud could read it while preparing for his famous séance on
7 December 1921). Thus Joyce could write 'Ithaca' with every detail
of the novel's plan and action firmly in mind, and it is not surprising
that the episode fits into the general scheme of *Ulysses* with absolute precision. In the first stages of his work on 'Ithaca' Joyce
went through the usual process of grouping his raw materials on
successive notesheets, listing the themes and motifs and tags of
dialogue which were to be transformed into the episode's characteristic styles.[17] As one might expect, the notesheets are filled with
the cosmic equivalents (such as '$JC = 3\sqrt{God}$') which Joyce referred
to in his well-known letter to Frank Budgen:

> I am writing *Ithaca* in the form of a mathematical catechism.
> All events are resolved into their cosmic, physical, psychical etc.
> equivalents, e.g. Bloom jumping down the area, drawing water from
> the tap, the micturition in the garden, the cone of incense, lighted
> candle and statue so that not only will the reader know everything
> and know it in the baldest coldest way, but Bloom and Stephen

[16] *Letters*, I, 146–147.

[17] For information on the episode's composition, see Richard E. Madtes,
'Joyce and the Building of *Ithaca*', pp. 443–459. This article is a summary of
Madtes's doctoral dissertation, 'A Textual and Critical Study of the "Ithaca" Episode of James Joyce's *Ulysses*', Columbia University, 1961. The *Ulysses* notesheets
in the British Museum have recently been edited by Phillip F. Herring (*Joyce's
'Ulysses' Notesheets in the British Museum*, Charlottesville, Va., 1972). The
entries quoted in this paragraph are, following Herring's enumeration, 5.12,
12.87, and 13.110.

thereby become heavenly bodies, wanderers like the stars at which they gaze.[18]

But mixed with these 'cosmic, physical, psychical etc. equivalents' on the notesheets are the terse phrases in Bloom's natural idiom which trigger the cosmic correspondences. For example, an elaborate attempt to relate Stephen and Bloom to Molly in terms of vectors and tangents is prompted by the colloquial 'fly off at a tangent', while a natural phenomenon jotted down in Bloom's staccatto speech ('See star by day from bottom of gully') is transformed in the text into pseudo-scientific jargon: 'of the infinite lattiginous scintillating uncondensed milky way, discernible by daylight by an observer placed at the lower end of a cylindrical vertical shaft 5000 ft deep sunk from the surface towards the centre of the earth' (698.22). The notesheets provide overwhelming evidence that the 'dry rock pages of Ithaca' [19] are supersaturated with Bloom's humanity, a humanity that is enhanced if anything by the impersonality of the prose. As any viewer of the recent film will remember, 'Ithaca' yielded scenes of far more warmth and feeling than those provided by such 'dramatic' episodes as 'Hades' and 'Nausicaa'. Once again, in the contrast between the apparent coldness of the episode's form and its actual human effects, we are confronted with a paradox to be solved.

It will be best to approach the problems of 'Ithaca' in three stages: (1) an analysis of the catechistical form; (2) a scanning of the episode's scenic progression; and (3) an assessment of the general effect of 'Ithaca' on our experience of the novel. The question-and-answer form is dictated in part by the 'schoolroom' nature of 'Ithaca'; in Joyce's *schema* for the novel the episode is an impersonal counterpart to the personal catechism pursued by Stephen in 'Nestor'.[20] It is customary to think of 'Ithaca' as deriving from the

[18] *Letters*, I, 159–160.

[19] *Letters*, I, 173.

[20] In the elaborate *schema* which Joyce revealed to Stuart Gilbert, the three episodes of the *Nostos* are mirror images of the three episodes in the *Telemachia*, with the characteristic techniques repeated in opposite form. *Nestor* is described as 'Catechism (personal)', while *Ithaca* is 'Catechism (impersonal)'. This symmetry was not evident to Joyce until he had written the last episodes. In the first known *schema*, sent to Carlo Linati in September 1920, the 'Dawn' (*Telemachia*) and 'Midnight' (*Nostos*) have a less exact relationship: *Nestor* is described as '2-person dialogue/ Narration/ Soliloquy', while *Ithaca* is 'Dialogue/ Pacified style/ Fusion'. See the Appendix to Richard Ellmann's *Ulysses on the Liffey* (London and New York, 1972).

form of the Christian catechism and Joyce's early Jesuit training, but the parallels with the catechistical methods of the nineteenth-century schoolroom are equally convincing. Two recent critics have proposed that the form of 'Ithaca' is directly indebted to Richmal Mangnall's *Historical and Miscellaneous Questions*, a textbook of encyclopaedic knowledge which went through over a hundred editions during the nineteenth century and was still in use in Joyce's day. Stephen refers to the book in *A Portrait* (AP, 53), and Robert Graves used it in 1901 at the age of six, although his father thought it out of date.[21] Mangnall's *Questions* is a compendium of undifferentiated 'practical' knowledge, cast in the form of a familiar catechism. Questions that any child might ask are phrased in simple form, while a voice of hectoring authority responds with a surfeit of information and misinformation.

> What are comets?
> Luminous and opaque bodies, whose motions are in different directions, and the orbits they describe very extensive; they have long translucent tails of light turned from the sun: the great swiftness of their motion in the neighbourhood of the sun, is the reason they appear to us for such a short time: and the great length of time they are in appearing again is occasioned by the extent and eccentricity of their orbits or paths in the heavens.
> How many comets are supposed to belong to our solar system: Twenty-one; but we only know. . . .[22]

There can be no doubt that Mangnall's *Questions* was a primary source for Joyce's 'mathematico-astronomico-physico-mechanico-geometrico-chemico sublimation of Bloom and Stephen'.[23] To the modern adult reader it is filled with unconscious humour and grotesque distortions, but to the young Joyce it must have shimmered with the poetic magic of unfamiliar names and mysterious words (such as gnomon and simony). In Stephen's daydream of vindication by the rector he associates himself with 'the great men whose names were in Richmal Magnall's [sic] Questions' (AP, 53). The form of Mangnall's *Questions* would have been easily assimilated into the authoritarian structure of Jesuit education, and it is

[21] Robert Graves, *Good-Bye to All That*, London, 1929, p. 38.
[22] Richmal Mangnall, *Historical and Miscellaneous Questions*, Fifth American edition from the eighty-fourth London edition, New York, 1869, p. 324.
[23] *Letters*, I, 164.

clear from Joyce's early Paris notebook (1903) that he found the catechism a congenial vehicle for his own ideas.

> Question: Why are not excrements, children, and lice works of art?
> Answer: Excrements, children, and lice are human products—human dispositions of sensible matter. The process by which they are produced is natural and nonartistic; their end is not an aesthetic end: therefore they are not works of art. (CW, 146)

As Lynch comments later in A Portrait, such a question has 'the true scholastic stink' (AP, 214), and Joyce himself was certainly aware of the pomposity latent in the form. We may hazard the guess that he chose to cast the most bizarre examples of his aesthetic in catechistical form as a defensive acknowledgment of their potential absurdity. In sum, the catechism must have struck Joyce as a natural and even inevitable form for the climactic episode of Ulysses because it was associated with some of his most profound early experiences, and had proved to be a vehicle for precise intellectual argument which simultaneously allowed scope for exaggeration and self-parody.

The greatest danger inherent in the catechistical form would seem to be monotony. The effectiveness of the catechism in the classroom depends upon a sameness in form and rhythm which—as Wordsworth said of poetic meter—opens the memory and fixes the mind in a receptive mood. But such an effect, useful as it might be for the pedagogue, would be disastrous for the novelist, and Joyce kept the technique flexible in 'Ithaca' by constant shifts in tone, rhetoric, and quality of subject matter. When we think of the 'style' of 'Ithaca' we usually think of those set pieces where Bloom's thoughts and actions are cast in the self-confident language of Victorian science, but in fact many of the answers are simple and direct:

> What did Bloom see on the range?
> On the right (smaller) hob a blue enamelled saucepan: on the left (larger) hob a black iron kettle.
> What did Bloom do at the range?
> He removed the saucepan to the left hob, rose and carried the iron kettle to the sink in order to tap the current by turning the faucet to let it flow. (670.31)

These plain questions-and-answers are then followed by two elaborate exchanges on Dublin's water supply and the universal qualities
of water. The effect is to retard our sense of the action while still
rendering it in sharp detail: it is as if we were viewing Bloom and
Stephen from a great height, against a vast backdrop of general
human action and knowledge, while at the same time standing next
to them and observing every local detail. It is this 'parallax' achieved
by the macrocosmic-microcosmic point-of-view which gives the episode, like Hardy's *Dynasts*, the grandeur and sweep that Joyce certainly intended.

Arnold Goldman remarks that 'the vein of "Ithaca" has been
re-opened in recent French novels. There the entire novel may be
in the style of Joyce's chapter, the programmatic intention of the
artist being to circumvent the metaphysical antinomy of subject and
object by treating everything as an object'.[24] But surely this is just
the opposite of Joyce's intention and achievement. Bloom and
Stephen do indeed 'become heavenly bodies, wanderers like the stars
at which they gaze', but at the same time their subjective lives penetrate every detail of objective description. Alain Robbe-Grillet's
famous description of the *nouveau roman* stands at the opposite
pole from Joyce's method.

> Instead of this universe of 'signification' (psychological, social,
> functional), we must try, then, to construct a world both more
> solid and more immediate. Let it be first of all by their *presence*
> that objects and gestures establish themselves, and let this presence
> continue to prevail over whatever explanatory theory that may try
> to enclose them in a system of references, whether emotional, so-
> ciological, Freudian or metaphysical.
> In this future universe of the novel, gestures and objects will
> be *there* before *something*; and they will still be there afterwards,
> hard, unalterable, eternally present, mocking their own 'meaning',
> that meaning which vainly tries to reduce them to the role of pre-
> carious tools, of a temporary and shameful fabric woven exclusively
> —and deliberately—by the superior human truth expressed in it,
> only to cast out this awkward auxiliary into immediate oblivion and
> darkness.
> Henceforth, on the contrary, objects will gradually lose their
> instability and their secrets, will renounce their pseudo-mystery, that
> suspect interiority which Roland Barthes has called 'the romantic
> heart of things'. No longer will objects be merely the vague re-

[24] Goldman, *The Joyce Paradox*, p. 108.

flection of the hero's vague soul, the image of his torments, the shadow of his desires. Or rather, if objects still afford a momentary prop to human passions, they will do so only provisionally, and will accept the tyranny of significations only in appearance—derisively, one might say—the better to show how alien they remain to man.[25]

The relationship between objects and personality in Joyce's writing would seem to be much more complex than in Robbe-Grillet's. While 'Ithaca' does 'resolve' its human figures into their objective counterparts, at the same time the objective universe is suffused with their personalities. Take the following question-and-answer:

> By what reflections did he, a conscious reactor against the void incertitude, justify to himself his sentiments?
> The preordained frangibility of the hymen, the presupposed intangibility of the thing in itself: the incongruity and disproportion between the selfprolonging tension of the thing proposed to be done and the self abbreviating relaxation of the thing done: the fallaciously inferred debility of the female, the muscularity of the male: the variations of ethical codes: the natural grammatical transition by inversion involving no alteration of sense of an aorist preterite proposition (parsed as masculine subject, monosyllabic onomatopoeic transitive verb with direct feminine object) from the active voice into its correlative aorist preterite proposition (parsed as feminine subject, auxiliary verb and quasimonosyllabic onomatopoeic past participle with complementary masculine agent) in the passive voice: the continued product of seminators by generation: the continual production of semen by distillation: the futility of triumph or protest or vindication: the inanity of extolled virtue: the lethargy of nescient matter: the apathy of the stars. (734.3)

Here the typical movement from microcosm to macrocosm, from the 'frangibility' of the individual hymen to the 'apathy of the stars', is a reflection of Bloom's thought as he strives for equanimity by sinking his own anxieties in the processes of nature. In spite of their pseudo-scientific presentation the 'objects' in this passage are as personal and 'interior' as those in the closing of 'The Dead'. In 'Ithaca' Joyce did not renounce his interest in 'the romantic heart of things', but simply found new means for expressing it.

As Joyce's work on 'Ithaca' neared an end in the autumn of 1921 he told his correspondents that he was putting the episode

[25] Alain Robbe-Grillet, *For a New Novel: Essays on Fiction*, New York, 1965, pp. 21–22.

'in order'.[26] His methods of gathering material had been ideally suited to the making of 'Ithaca', each question-and-answer developing around a phrase or idea and then being fitted into the general design. Clearly he conceived of 'Ithaca' as a series of scenes or tableaux, not unlike the narrative divisions in 'Circe', and on the early typescripts he blocked out these scenes under the titles 'street', 'kitchen', 'garden', 'parlour', 'bedroom'.[27] We may consider the 'narrative' development of 'Ithaca' under these headings, since each scene builds to a revealing climax which forwards our understanding of both Bloom and Stephen.

The scene in the street (666–669) begins with Bloom and Stephen moving in parallel but separate courses. The tone is relaxed, the conversation easy and desultory. Both Stephen and Bloom are 'keyless', the victims of usurpers, poised between thought and action: 'To enter or not to enter. To knock or not to knock' (668.18). But whereas Stephen has fallen under the spell of Hamlet's melancholy and indecision, Bloom—like his Homeric namesake, or the active Hamlet—devises a 'stratagem', and his acrobatic entrance into No. 7 Eccles street is described in ponderous language which simultaneously satirizes the triviality of the event (in its cosmic context) while emphasizing its importance in the context of Bloom's own life.

> Did he fall?
> By his body's known weight of eleven stone and four pounds in avoirdupois measure, as certified by the graduated machine for periodical selfweighing in the premises of Francis Froedman, pharmaceutical chemist of 19 Frederick street, north, on the last feast of the Ascension, to wit, the twelfth day of May of the bissextile year one thousand nine hundred and four of the christian era (jewish era five thousand six hundred and sixtyfour, mohammedan era one thousand three hundred and twentytwo), golden number 5, epact 13, solar cycle 9, dominical letters C B, Roman indication 2, Julian period 6617, MXMIV. (668.28)

The entire 'street' scene establishes Bloom as the focus of our interest, and throws the balance of the narrative toward his competence and resourcefulness. In this episode, by contrast with 'Nestor', Stephen will be more learner than teacher.

---

[26] *Letters*, I, 172, and III, 49.

[27] Peter Spielberg, *James Joyce's Manuscripts and Letters at the University of Buffalo*, Buffalo, N.Y., 1962, V.B.15.a. and V.B.15.b.

Events in the 'kitchen' scene (669–697) explore the sympathetic bonds between Stephen and Bloom, as well as their points of difference, culminating in the 'exodus' from kitchen to garden which brings their relationship into focus through a symbolic tableau not unlike that at the end of 'Circe'.

In what order of precedence, with what attendant ceremony was the exodus from the house of bondage to the wilderness of inhabitation effected?

> Lighted Candle in Stick borne by
> BLOOM.
> Diaconal Hat on Ashplant borne by
> STEPHEN

With what intonation *secreto* of what commemorative psalm?

The 113th, *modus peregrinus: In exitu Israël de Egypto: domus Jacob de populo barbaro.*

What did each do at the door of egress?

Bloom set the candlestick on the floor. Stephen put the hat on his head.

For what creature was the door of egress a door of ingress?

For a cat.

What spectacle confronted them when they, first the host, then the guest, emerged silently, doubly dark, from obscurity by a passage from the rere of the house into the penumbra of the garden?

The heaventree of stars hung with humid nightblue fruit.

(697.33)

Our reading of the symbolic references woven into this scene will determine in large measure our ultimate attitude toward the 'union' of Stephen and Bloom. The echoes from Dante are insistent, and have often been noted.[28] The opening line from the 113th Psalm, 'When Israel went out of Egypt . . . ,' is twice used by Dante as a text to illustrate his fourfold method of allegory (in the *Letter to Can Grande* and the *Convivio*), and it has been suggested that Joyce is covertly instructing us to read 'Ithaca' as a 'polysemous' work, which it certainly is: the literal and the allegorical are never more obvious than in this passage, where each literal detail is packed with

---

[28] See especially William York Tindall, A *Reader's Guide to James Joyce*, London and New York, 1959, pp. 225–226, Mary T. Reynolds, 'Joyce's Planetary Music: His Debt to Dante', *Sewanee Review*, 76 (Summer 1968), 456–458, and Sultan, pp. 391–392.

ceremonial significance. But an elaborate application of Dante's four
'levels' would seem more problematic, and the tag from the 113th
Psalm is best interpreted as a traditional reference to the resurrection
which appears at a crucial turning-point in the *Commedia*.

As Dante and Vergil emerge from Hell at the end of the *Inferno* they are once more able to see the stars (the word upon which
each part of the *Commedia* ends), just as Stephen and Bloom
emerge from the house to confront 'The heaventree of stars hung
with humid nightblue fruit'. A little later, in the first Canto of the
Purgatorio, Cato questions: 'Who hath guided you? or who was a
lamp unto you issuing forth from the deep night that ever maketh
black the infernal vale' (*Purgatorio*, I, 43–45). Similarly, the omniscient voice in 'Ithaca' asks:

> What visible luminous sign attracted Bloom's, who attracted
> Stephen's gaze?
> In the second storey (rere) of his (Bloom's) house the light of
> a paraffin oil lamp with oblique shade projected on a screen of roller
> blind supplied by Frank O'Hara, window blind, curtain pole and
> revolving shutter manufacturer, 16 Aungier street. (702.17)

In the next Canto of the *Purgatorio* Dante and Vergil encounter the
souls about to enter Purgatory, singing the ancient hymn of redemption, '*In exitu Israel de Aegypto*' (*Purgatorio*, II, 46), the
same hymn Stephen chants as he and Bloom leave the kitchen.

The symbolic implications of these accumulated references are
overwhelming: the meeting of Stephen and Bloom has provided a
release from bondage, a release noted through a traditional combination of Hebrew and Christian imagery. The only question is whether
we take these implications as a vehicle for irony, an irony based on
the disparity between the trivial and allegorical levels, or as a
complex statement of psychological potentialities. The critical problem is exactly the same as that produced by the Homeric parallels,
and the same solution suggests itself. On the literal level, bounded by
the twenty hours of the novel's action, Stephen and Bloom are mock-
heroic figures; but on the figurative level they take on heroic and
creative possibilities. Having confined himself to a realistic time-
scheme which made impossible the actual dramatization of that
dynamic growth of personality so characteristic of the conventional
novel, Joyce vested this element in his symbolic structures. To para-
phrase Santayana, *Ulysses* is mock-heroic in immediacy, but heroic

in perspective, and Joyce's delicate balancing of attitudes is nowhere more evident than in this climactic scene. No critical formula of 'either/or' can do it justice. Instead, we must think of Joyce's use of myth in the light of Eliot's 'Tradition and the Individual Talent': a vital interchange between past and present which humanizes the past while it enlarges the present.

As Bloom and Stephen stand in the garden before parting, beneath the lamp of Molly which has been Bloom's guide throughout the day, they urinate together, 'their sides contiguous, their organs of micturition reciprocally rendered invisible by manual circumposition, their gazes, first Bloom's, then Stephen's, elevated to the projected luminous and semi-luminous shadow' (702.35). This is the moment of symbolic union, and the fact that it is richly comic in the manner of Sterne does not detract from its ultimate seriousness. Joyce's identification of micturition with creativity is well known, and although W. Y. Tindall may be overly ingenious in making the identification a major theme in *Chamber Music* (where it is of more interest to the psychoanalyst than the literary critic),[29] the explicit association of urination with creativity in *Finnegans Wake* makes a similar interpretation of this scene in 'Ithaca' more than probable. As Clive Hart has pointed out, the theme of micturition as creation and transubstantiation is established early in *Ulysses* by the Ballad of Joking Jesus (19.8–11),[30] and there can be no doubt that Joyce intended the garden scene in 'Ithaca' to foreshadow a new departure for both Bloom and Stephen. On the literal level they remain divided, each absorbed in his own thoughts; but the 'celestial sign' that they both observe—'a star precipitated . . . towards the zodiacal sign of Leo' (703.24)—reminds us that Stephen's daylong pilgrimage has led toward this encounter with the humane and inquisitive Bloom, whose personality supplies the qualities lacking in his own sterile spirit.

When Bloom and Stephen say farewell the literal narrative leaves them separate once again, with their futures adumbrated but not dramatized, and Bloom turns from the chill of 'proximate dawn' to re-enter the house. Having touched the ultimate reaches of symbol and myth, the episode returns to the level of 'objects' and

[29] W. Y. Tindall, ed., *Chamber Music*, New York, 1954.
[30] Clive Hart, *Structure and Motif in Finnegans Wake*, London and Evanston, Ill., 1962, pp. 206–207.

'things'; and Bloom's exploration of the parlour (705–729) is told in a manner and style that would have delighted Defoe. The catalogues of this section—the furnishings of the room, the contents of the bookshelves, the budget for 16 June 1904—bring the reader back to the irreducible reality of Bloom's life and prepare the way for the next access of myth and symbol at the end of the 'parlour' scene. As Bloom's thoughts drift toward travel and escape (726–727) he is transformed into Everyman and Noman, Elpenor and Ulysses, into a wandering comet whose orbit traces the extremes of his real and potential existences.

> Would the departed never nowhere nohow reappear?
> Ever he would wander, selfcompelled, to the extreme limit of his cometary orbit, beyond the fixed stars and variable suns and telescopic planets, astronomical waifs and strays, to the extreme boundary of space, passing from land to land, among peoples, amid events. Somewhere imperceptibly he would hear and somehow reluctantly, suncompelled, obey the summons of recall. Whence, disappearing from the constellation of the Northern Crown he would somehow reappear reborn above delta in the constellation of Cassiopeia and after incalculable eons of peregrination return an estranged avenger, a wreaker of justice on malefactors, a dark crusader, a sleeper awakened, with financial resources (by supposition) surpassing those of Rothschild or of the silver king. (727.35)

We know from both the Library episode (210.7–11) and an earlier section of 'Ithaca' (700.36–701.3) that a nova in Cassiopeia (whose form is a capital 'W') announced the birth of William Shakespeare, while 'a star (2nd magnitude) of similar origin but lesser brilliancy' had appeared in the Northern Crown to mark the birth of Leopold Bloom. In this passage Bloom disappears in his own personality only to reappear as his mythic counterpart, a Hamlet or Ulysses freed of anxiety and intent upon his mission of revenge. Such transformations become more and more common as the 'parlour' scene wears to a close, and Bloom gradually takes on all the ritual and ceremonial significances of the day that has passed. In fact, one might say that 'Ithaca' progresses by a rhythmic alternation between mythic or 'epiphanic' moments and longer stretches of 'realism' which validate these moments.

Once in the 'bedroom' (730ff) Bloom stretches out on the bed, which still bears the evidence of Boylan's recent occupancy, and meditates on the 'series originating in and repeated to infinity' (731.22) of Molly's lovers. Robert M. Adams has pointed out the bizarre elements in Bloom's catalogue,[31] but at this stage in the episode the criteria of 'realism' seem curiously irrelevant. 'Ithaca' closes on the highest plane of mythopoetic intensity, as Joyce's intentions—so often stated in the letters—are fully realized. The episode has developed through a measured oscillation between the literal and allegorical levels, until at the end the balance is thrown finally and irrevocably to the side of symbolism. The sequence of Bloom's thought—'Envy, jealousy, abnegation, equanimity' (732.14) —sums up the process, as Molly and Bloom are transformed from individual human beings into types and archetypes. It is possible, of course, to see this process as 'something of an evasion',[32] but only if the life of Ulysses is viewed as more surface than symbol. It was Joyce's unique gift that he could turn the substance of ordinary life into something like myth, not only through the use of 'parallels' and allusions but through direct transformation: and the ending of 'Ithaca', like that of 'Anna Livia Plurabelle', would seem to vindicate his method. Most of Ulysses can be understood by the same methods one applies to The Waste Land, where the manipulation of a continuous parallel between contemporaneity and antiquity 'places' the contemporary action, but the ending of 'Ithaca' consists of metamorphosis rather than juxtaposition. As in the conclusion to 'Circe', the model is the transformation scene of a typical pantomime (perhaps the pantomime of Sindbad the Sailor[33]), and we must believe that Molly has merged into her archetype, Gea-Tellus, while Leopold Bloom has become the archetype of all human possibility, 'the manchild in the womb' (737.13). The ironies of the novel still operate on the literal level—Molly is unfulfilled, Bloom unsatisfied—but these are of lesser importance beside the primaeval realities which close the episode. The final questions ('When? Where?') reflect the novel's traditional concerns with time and space, but the answers are a rebuke to such concerns (737.23–28).

When?
Going to a dark bed there was a square round Sinbad the

---

[31] Surface and Symbol, pp. 36–40.
[32] Ibid., p. 42.
[33] Ibid., pp. 76–82.

Sailor roc's auk's egg in the night of the bed of all the auks of the
rocs of Darkinbad the Brightdayler.
　　　Where?

●

In sleep the limits of the rational mind fall away, and Bloom's
desire to solve the problem of 'the quadrature of the circle' (699.20,
718.12–13) is satisfied. At the end of 'Ithaca', which is the end of
Ulysses as novel and fable, Bloom subsides into the mythic world
of the giant roc, where light is born out of darkness, and into the
womb of infinite possibilities. 'La réponse à la dernière demande
est un point', Joyce instructed the printer on his typescript, and
that point contains a double meaning. As a full-stop it marks the
conclusion of Bloom's day, the terminus of the novel's literal action,
but as a spatial object it represents Bloom's total retreat into the
womb of time, from which he shall emerge the next day with all the
fresh potentialities of Everyman. Like the Viconian *ricorso*, the
final moment of 'Ithaca' is both an end and a beginning.

　　　'Ithaca' provides the capstone to our total experience of *Ulysses*.
If the novel ended with this episode our view of the major characters and their motives would remain substantially the same, although
our sense of reality would be somewhat different. 'Penelope' is indeed the 'indispensable countersign to Bloom's passport to eternity',
as Joyce once called it,[34] since it substantiates the novel's promise
of cyclic renewal; but without it we would still have a completed
world to savour and interpret. On Joyce's *schema* for the novel,
'Penelope' alone is assigned no specific time; its materials (Bed, Flesh,
Earth) are essentially timeless. Although its themes are cunningly
orchestrated, the random organization being merely illusion, 'Penelope' does not contribute to the sequence of styles which is one of
our chief interests in *Ulysses*. Instead, the novel subsides into an
appearance of naturalness, and our final impression is that of a voice,
curious, lively, undiscriminating.

　　　'Ithaca', by contrast, has the appearance of extreme artifice, and
has often been taken as the final triumph of Joyce the baroque
elaborator over Joyce the 'novelist'. But such a view rests on the
all-too-common assumption that the 'novelistic' elements in *Ulysses*
must be those of the traditional nineteenth-century novel—the reve-

[34] *Letters*, I, 160.

lation of character through setting, plot, and observed consciousness —and that the devices and correspondences that mark the later chapters must be evaluated as either essential or auxiliary to the novelistic effects.[35] Such a view was put forward in my own earlier work, *The Art of James Joyce*, where many of the artifices found in the last chapters are assigned to the play-instinct or to Joyce's personal need for order while gathering his materials. I still believe that the more recondite correspondences in *Ulysses* were more important to Joyce during the process of composition than they can ever be to us during the process of reading and interpreting, but I have long since abandoned the notion—always a reductive one—that the novelistic elements in *Ulysses* can be separated from the *schema* and claimed as the true line of the work's meaning. What Joyce accomplished in writing *Ulysses* was to shatter the form of the well-made novel and expose its multifarious origins (allegory, 'Romance', history, gossip, 'news'), and then to reconstitute these materials in a variety of experimental forms. The result is a work of art which renders the bourgeois world in all its detail and potentiality, uniting fact and myth in a classic portrayal of Everyman as dispossessed hero. In its radical form 'Ithaca' bypasses the familiar conventions of nineteenth-century fiction and shows us another way in which the novelist's passion for omniscience can be achieved without violating our sense of individual and local reality.

[35] For a discussion of this problem see Peter K. Garrett, *Scene and Symbol from George Eliot to James Joyce*, New Haven, Conn., 1969, pp. 252–271, and Barbara Hardy, 'Form as End and Means in *Ulysses*', *Orbis Litterarum*, XIX (1964), 194–200.

PENELOPE

Fr. Robert Boyle, S.J.

Shakespeare's Cleopatra does not lend herself to easy or absolute judgments. There are, it would seem, as many ways of looking at her as there are lookers, both inside the play and outside, to express what they see—or think they see. She is contradictory and mysterious, yet magnificently convincing and satisfactory. Critical opinion is hopelessly fragmented among those who would condemn and those who would praise her, even among those wiser souls who admit her mysterious inaccessibility to limited human vision. No two people, I would judge, see her quite the same way.

And this is as it should be. If we were able to pluck out the heart of her mystery, she would discourse most eloquent music no doubt, but she would not be an adequate reflection of a complex human animal. Wayne Booth supposes that we should, in looking at a literary character, all see the same thing and all, ideally, react the same way—we should know well whether we should 'swoon or laugh'.[1] But we do not expect such uniformity of response in reality. Mr Booth and I no doubt react in different ways to Elizabeth Taylor, and no doubt make some different judgments about her. And we would do so, I judge, even if we lived with her for years or read a detailed psychiatric report on years of depth therapy. But when such differences in judging another individual exist in critics deal-

[1] *The Rhetoric of Fiction*, Chicago, 1961, p. 329.

ing with a successful literary character, Mr Booth can conclude only that the critics are faulty readers or that the author was uncertain about what he was creating. Mr Booth is, I believe, looking in the wrong direction. The uncertainty may be that of readers faced with an adequate reflection of unfathomable mystery. And this I take to be the glory and rare achievement of our great literary artists, among whom many of us rank Joyce.

Molly Bloom, like Cleopatra and like the Wife of Bath and like Hester Prynne, is not determined to univocal meaning, but enjoys the mystery of autonomy. As humans in reality may choose to love or to hate, so Molly does, and the ultimate reasons for her doing so are not spelled out. They are not clear, even to her. She illustrates the quality which Shakespeare, in Sonnet 116, tells us is inherent in love (and by implication in hate or in selfishness) and which is central to both life and literature:

> If this be error and upon me proved,
> I never writ, nor no man ever loved.

That quality is mystery. Though love is the one necessary guiding star to lead man to his human perfection, to his home port, nevertheless it is a guide 'whose worth's unknown'. The great artist, while intent on holding his 'abcedminded' mirror up to nature and expressing adequately what he sees, manages to express that mystery along with the things he understands. And thus in great literature, as in human reality, ultimate conclusions become impossible, as well as undesirable—except to the literarily unregenerate Shauns of our race. They indeed continue to accuse the artistic and intuitive Shems '. . . of twosome twiminds forenenst gods, hidden and discovered, nay, condemned fool, anarch, egoarch, hiresiarch, you have reared your disunited kingdom on the vacuum of your own most intensely doubtful soul' (FW, 188.14).

Hawthorne understood the mystery involved in creating a convincing and adequate character. In 'The Custom House' he tells of the frigidity of his imagination while he was trying to write in his spare time, and of his stiff and one-dimensional characters, 'snow-images'. But when he could give all his powers to the task, when the light of the moon and of the dying fire mingled in the midnight darkness, then his characters took on a life of their own and became men and women. They could now make, or at least seem to make, their own free choices, determine their own destinies. In such a situation, Hawthorne himself would be unable to tell us with certainty whether Hester was a good or a bad woman, whether the lurid gleam from her tomb was the light of heavenly love emanating from her basic selfless devotion to others or of the selfish flames feeding on her own cannibalistic determination to violate the heart of her man. The artist reflects mysterious reality, not demonstrable geometry.

In reality, 'chaosmos', at least as Christian tradition has seen it, God, analogous to the true literary artist, loves his human creature enough to make it, mysteriously, free. He loves it enough to make it free enough to reject his love if it so chooses, free enough to destroy itself if it will—though of course he desires a return of his love. He wills the good of his creature, and its greatest subjective good is its freedom, which constitutes it an image and likeness of the infinitely free God. When the literary artist creates a totally successful character, he does something at least analogous to this. He reveals to us a creature who will remain, at centre, a mystery. Thus when we are faced with such a one, we will never know for certain whether to laugh or swoon, or to do both or neither. We will simply be able to do what we do with real people, to observe, to judge where we can, to guess where we can't, to respond with sympathy or with laughter or with horror, and, ideally, to be as charitable as possible. Even Judas cannot ultimately be condemned by one of us.

Which of course is not to say that critics, who can to some extent play the role of the objectively judging God in relation to creations made out of ink, may not be forced to condemn a character to literary hell. I myself have in print cheerfully consigned Hester Prynne and Othello to those fictional flames, where with justified pleasure I hear their ink sizzling. But at the same time I am aware that my judgment may be a condemnation of my own lack of perception, of my own psychic hangups, or of my own lack of charity. Critics simply have to take that chance if they choose to be literary gods. But it does seem to me important, before I present my own views of Molly Bloom, that I present them, not as final and definitive judgments, but merely as one interested viewer saying as well as he can what he sees. Many of my views will differ from many of those presented by some of the great Joyce critics,[2] but all views may contribute to illumine various facets of an ultimately mysterious and infinitely varied creature.

Joyce, as I conceive his artistic procedure, approached the matter much as Hawthorne did (or, as I envision it, as Shakespeare or Chaucer or Virginia Woolf did). He did not so much excogitate the character as intuit it. I get uncomfortable with critical studies that approach Joyce's work from those primitive first drafts that have survived, and accept those as the basic truthful and honest intention of the artist. Then all 'additions' are likely to become decorations or difficulties. Rather, those first drafts should be approached as tentative gropings toward an ideal creation, and what follows should not be considered as 'added', but as a closer approach to the desired perfection, an organic development. Thus all critical judgments should be based on the final draft, not on any preparatory one. Those early ones can be enormously helpful, as David Hayman among others has demonstrated, but they should be helpful as tentative stages toward the fully developed text, not as if they were adequate and proper determinants of that text. Thus those who say, for example, that Joyce unnecessarily complicated and muddied the eighth chapter of *Finnegans Wake* by 'adding' hundreds of river names are going at the matter from the wrong end. You will never adequately judge a mature human being by examining him as a week-old embryo, and then deploring the complications of bone, flesh, organs, and mental activity which muddy that happy embryonic simplicity. You can learn much from the embryo, but you are likely to miss the main points about the mature human if you seriously deplore the passing of the embryonic stage.

I wish to look at Molly first, then, not in the light of her development from early texts nor even, at this point, in her development from all the other female characters Joyce had created, but simply in herself as she appears (to me) in the final text. She is a rather ordinary Dublin *Weib*, with a few interesting variations— that is, this is her surface appearance. She was brought up in

---

[2] Phillip Herring, in his perceptive article, 'The Bedsteadfastness of Molly Bloom', *Modern Fiction Studies*, XV, 1 (Spring 1969), 49–61, does an excellent job of lining up the varying judgments about Molly (pp. 57–60). He also indicates, with remarkable acuity, an element often missed by those who wholeheartedly condemn Molly.

Gibraltar, where her father, Major Brian Tweedy, was stationed for something more than seventeen years. He had married Lunita Laredo, or at least had had a daughter by her. Lunita, from the information that Molly received and has remembered, was Spanish and Jewish. She either deserted her family (most likely) or died, and Molly grew up in boarding houses, casually cared for by various women. In the military surroundings, and no doubt with some more than normal attachment to her father, she engaged in her first sexual adventure, at the age of fifteen, with a Lieutenant Mulvey, whose first name she has forgotten. Intercourse was not involved, not, apparently, from moral scruples but because she was in terror of pregnancy. Her not very well-informed 'instruction' in the matter came from 'that old servant Ines' (760.27), and, judging from her often naïve attitudes toward sex, pregnancy, the roles of father and mother in determining the health of the child, and other matters, she has had little instruction since.

She has had few woman friends. In Gibraltar, the slightly older Mrs Hester Stanhope made Molly feel close to another woman. Molly cannot at once remember her first name either (755.17), but she recalls it (756.3).[3] Molly was deeply and unusually moved at parting from her, but was unable to answer her postcard because Hester did not 'put her address right on it' (756.36). Molly speculates that 'she may have noticed her wogger', that is, that she may have observed her husband's interest in young Molly. Hester called her husband Wogger, herself a dog, and Molly doggerina (755.16, 19, 20).[4] She gave Molly novels of romance and mystery, a cut above the works of Paul de Kock. The two women were like cousins. They compared hair, Molly lay in Hester's arms on the night of the

[3] I have profited from discussion about Mrs Stanhope and other matters with my colleagues at Kent State University, Mrs Joan Monahan, who is working on a dissertation dealing with Molly, and Thomas Grayson, who is working on a study of Joyce and Blake.

[4] Thornton refers to the account of Lady Hester in the Encyclopaedia Britannica, 11th ed., 'Stanhope', and states that he can offer no theory on why Joyce chose the name. I can think of two possible reasons. Molly will soon refer to the 'domineering' Mrs Rubio, and the very adjective may have led Joyce to think of other domineering women, among whom Hester Stanhope was outstanding. It is a helpful background to Molly's own Calypso-like domination of Bloom. Further, Joyce may have wished to bolster Molly's remark on women's inherent bitchiness, and thus he names this Hester after a really bitchy woman and has her call herself a dog and Molly doggerina in order to imply not only bitchiness but a further example of the god-dog contrast.

storm, and they playfully fought with the pillow in the morning. Their concern with and arrangement of hair recalls the egocentric woman of *Chamber Music*, No. 24, of whom I will speak later. Apparently Hester was Molly's only close woman friend in Gibraltar. In Dublin Molly was friendly, before her marriage, with the Dillon girls and with Josie Breen (née Powell). Now, it seems, she has no close women friends—at least none who can even momentarily find a significant place in her nocturnal musings.

Molly's thoughts centre in sex. Considering the time, the place, the present activity of her husband, and the recent activity of her lover, this is not surprising. In the eight sentences of this chapter, I suspect that Joyce is using the shape and structure of the figure 8, so frequently repeated, for sexual symbolism, analogous to the familiar treatment of the figure 69. If this is so, and if the 8 symbolizes Molly's genital area, as I think it does, then Bloom, who worships woman particularly in her life-giving and regenerative role, is here ritually approaching the source of human life. Since, as I see it, the black dot at the end of the 'Ithaca' chapter signifies not only darkness but Molly's anus as well, Bloom is at present allowed to approach only the bottom half of the total eight which represents Molly's mesial groove. He does not now have the proper husband's control over Molly's vagina, the upper half of the eight. But, as Stanley Sultan in his superlatively good chapter on Molly points out,[5] Bloom aims, at this point in the book, toward total husbandly control, as his demand for breakfast eggs discloses. I picture them as two, 8-shaped fried eggs, foreshadowing the ones so significantly operative in ritual and eucharistic contexts in the breakfast plans in *Finnegans Wake*. When Bloom achieves his marital goal, if he does, he will then square two circles. At the moment only half of 8, or 4, the square, is his number. In any case, the welter of eights and divisions and multiples of eight throughout the chapter give the effect of eights turning around,[6] revolving, as Joyce's key words and

---

[5] Sultan, pp. 415–450. Sultan's treatment of the 'roc's auk's egg' around which there is a square at the end of the 'Ithaca' chapter (the egg in Bloom's mind, no doubt, because of his request for breakfast eggs), is especially perceptive: 'Thus the egg is called "square-round"': he has squared a circle, the impossible feat mentioned during the chapter as one means he might employ to realize his 'ambition'. Sultan, p. 414.

[6] James Van Dyck Card, in an excellent unpublished thesis, 'A Textual and Critical Study of the "Penelope" Episode of James Joyce's Ulysses', Columbia,

the sentences and rhythms of the chapter revolve, a metaphor for the turning of the earth, the Gea-Tellus of page 737.

This Gea-Tellus is indeed big with wind and fat and female seed, but not with male seed. And until this afternoon, she had permitted no male seed to enter her vagina, it would appear, since 27 November 1893 (736.10). The general jocular tone in various Dublin citizens' references to Molly during the day, it is true, hinted at sexual promiscuity and at sexual appetites too powerful for Poldy's capacity, but those were, after all, mere male gossip, based altogether on conjecture. They expressed admiration for Molly, on the whole, with some measure of appreciation and desire on the part of the speakers. But in no instance do they indicate actual intercourse between Molly and any lover other than Bloom.

The most suggestive of the incidents of sexual adventure, in Molly's thoughts about any of the 25 men on Bloom's list (731.25–36), is her experience with Bartell d'Arcy (745.31–36) on the choir steps. But considering the situation and the clothing conventions at the turn of the century, I cannot conclude that Molly means more than embracing and kissing. 'My brown part' she picks up from the song 'Good-Bye';[7] she repeats this coinage at 780.37. And the fact that she so dramatizes this incident in her mind, thinking that she might show Bloom the very spot, seems to me evidence that Molly's actual sexual experience is indeed limited.

At any rate it is perfectly clear that Bloom's list is made up of men who, in Bloom's experience or conjecture, showed any interest in Molly as a sex object. Some of them he noted looking at her, some he must have judged from her accounts of confession or of experiences, but of none, with the exception of Boylan, can it be said with certainty that he shared Molly's bed. And of most the certainty that they did not is apparent.

Nor does Molly think of actual past intercourse with any men other than Bloom and Boylan. In fact, her reactions to her experience with Boylan and her broodings over past adventures indicate to me, insofar as I am able to judge such matters, a lack of wide sexual experience and certainly a frustration in regard to sexual satisfaction. Her somewhat adolescent musings on the details of geni-

---

1963, indicates that 'Significantly, the Linati chart has the sign of infinity drawn opposite the eighteenth chapter' (p. 107).

[7] Thornton, p. 486.

talia and of coition seem to me expressive, not of excessive experience, which would, I should think, tend to breed boredom with those particular aspects of sexual activity, but of limited experience, which would tend to keep curiosity and appetite active. David Hayman, suggests, as Stanley Sultan so well did before him, that Molly's intercourse with Boylan is her one and only infidelity to Bloom.[8] Hayman bolsters his suggestion with quite profound probings into the psychology of Molly's reactions.

Mr Darcy O'Brien, in an article published in the same volume as Mr Hayman's, states that Molly has had numerous lovers, and cites, as one of his proofs, her statement, 'I never in all my life felt anyone had one the size of that to make you feel full up' (742.10). But this must be interpreted according to the facts themselves. If she had had sexual intercourse with many men, the statement could imply that fact. But she could still reasonably say the words if Bloom and Boylan were the only two men she had actually known in full sexual experience. It is clear that she had felt the genitals of other men, notably Mulvey before her marriage, and somewhat mysteriously Gardner after her marriage, and she is not, it is also clear, without imagination. So I cannot see that the words do really prove Mr O'Brien's contention. Mr Sultan and Mr Hayman and those other critics who take a stand similar to theirs have, to my judgment, much the stronger case.

There is, however, a difficulty—Lieut. Stanley G. Gardner (cf. 746.37; 747.17; 749.1; 762.19–20). Molly has had some kind of passionate affair with him recently. She gave him Mulvey's ring, apparently as he left for the Boer War, so it had to be 1899 or thereafter. She kissed him goodbye and both were passionate—'and I so hot as I never felt' (749.6)—and they had met several times previously. Bloom knows nothing of him, though Molly takes no satisfaction in this thought, as she did in Bloom's ignorance of her experience with Bartell d'Arcy (745.41–42).[9] This might be evidence of a far more serious affair with Gardner. But then, as Sultan also notes, it might not too. The evidence is not conclusive. I judge (as does my friend and colleague Bernard Benstock, with whom I dis-

---

[8] In *Approaches to Ulysses*, ed. by Bernard Benstock and Thomas Staley, Pittsburgh, 1970, pp. 103–136.

[9] Bloom, however, does have d'Arcy on his list, so he may know more than Molly thinks he does.

cussed this matter) that Joyce here deliberately introduces a theme of mystery, faintly analogous to his use of the man in the macintosh, but with far more subtlety, to keep us uncertain about Molly's sexual background. We know more than Bloom, but we do not, possibly, know as much as Molly does. We can speculate, but we cannot reach a definite and certain conclusion. My own speculations lead me to the opinion that with the possible exception of Gardner, Molly had never been unfaithful to Bloom (at least technically, in the sense of intercourse with another man), before her experience with Boylan during the afternoon and evening.[10]

Whatever may be the truth in the matter of her infidelities, Molly makes an odd Earth-Mother on the literal level, since it is not altogether clear that she ever did want a child for its own sake, and there is evidence that at least during the past decade she has taken steps to avoid having another. Still, in his famous sentence on Molly, Joyce calls her 'fertilisable', not 'fertilised'.[11] The capacity is all that is needed for eligibility to the symbolic level; her use of the capacity is her own individual affair. She accepted the first pregnancy, at least in part, I suspect, as a way of committing and, in a way, of trapping the very willing Bloom. The second pregnancy occurred after passionate carelessness occasioned by the sight of the dogs copulating. She says, as she thinks of Rudy's death, 'but I knew well Id never have another' (778.33). This could not very well refer to a knowledge of incapacity, because she thinks 'supposing I risked having another not off him though' (742.31), the 'him' being Boylan. The 'risked' apparently refers, besides to the normal discomfort attending gestation and birth and upbringing, to the chance that the child, like Rudy, would die; Molly goes on to think, 'still if he was married Im sure hed have a fine strong child but I dont know Poldy has more spunk in him' (742.31). She later thinks 'a fine son . . . and I none was he not able to make one it wasnt my fault' (778.27). It is clear that, like Bloom, she does want a son and she feels enough guilt in the matter to deny fault on her part. She is, I am inclined

[10] Sultan interprets Molly's statement in her first sentence, 'anyhow its done now once and for all with all the talk of the world about it people make' (740.36) as clear proof that she has on this day committed adultery for the first time (Sultan, p. 433). I tend at this time to agree with him.

[11] 'Though probably more obscene than any preceding episode it seems to me to be perfectly sane full amoral fertilisable untrustworthy engaging shrewd limited prudent indifferent *Weib*'. Letters, I, 170.

to judge, the source for Bloom's apothegm, on page 96, 'If its healthy its from the mother. If not the man'. That folk-wisdom is of a kind with Molly's information about I.H.S. and I.N.R.I. And of course it helps to give Bloom the profound guilt feeling he has about Rudy's death. But Molly too shares Bloom's feeling that 'we were never the same since' (778.34).

It is not possible, it seems to me now, to determine which of the two, Molly or Poldy, is more responsible for their unsatisfactory sexual relationship.[12] I used to opine that Bloom suffered some psychic impotency, analogous to Odysseus's goring by the boar. But now I doubt that. He does not seem to be impotent, judging from such things as Molly's plan (780.34–42), but he may nevertheless, of course, avoid intercourse for fear of the pain of another death. Still, he does passionately desire a son, and from time to time seems to hope that he might yet beget one.[13] In any case, Bloom is not the sole explanation for the failure of the sexual relationship between him and Molly, nor, as I tend to see the matter now, the principal one.

Molly has in her dealings with Bloom a faint touch of the Mrs Mooney attitude ('The Boarding House'). When she accepts Bloom, or rather, when she chooses and (if the word fits a victim so eager to be enmeshed) traps him on Howth Head, she thinks '. . . and I knew I could always get round him . . .' (782.21). Her dominance might be implied in the seedcake she puts into his mouth, with the seed symbolizing both sperm and the fruit of the Garden of Eden. Further, she thinks (743.12–13) that she could still quite easily turn Bloom's attention from any other woman to herself, if she chose to do so.

Nevertheless, Molly also wants to be dominated. This is partly the reason she accepts the energetic and aggressive Boylan. She both likes and dislikes his crudity and vulgarity, and the fairly late development of an earlier draft, '. . . without even asking permission . . .' (776.26), stresses, in this eighth and last sentence which turns from Boylan toward Mulvey-Bloom, her resentment and disgust; but it implies also her desire to be overcome by a male who

---

[12] Sultan, as I read him, places all the blame on Bloom (cf. especially Sultan, pp. 433 and 442). I cannot agree. Bloom is of course to blame, but Molly is too.

[13] 'I too, last my race. Milly young student. Well, my fault perhaps. No son. Rudy. Too late now. Or if not? If not? If still?' (285.4).

is overpowered by her allure, who cannot wait for formal permission. The attitude is developed by Joyce in *Finnegans Wake* at great length, especially in a passage like the first development of the Quinet sentence, (*FW*, 15.20–22), where 'all bold floras of the field to their shyfaun lovers say only: Cull me ere I wilt to thee!: and, but a little later: Pluck me whilst I blush!' Bloom has failed to cull Molly, in either sense, of choosing her out for his own delight or of calling her before she wilts—she complains '. . . its a wonder Im not an old shrivelled hag before my time' (777.14). And he has failed to pluck her while she blushes. He did that, or thought he did, to his mountain flower on Howth (as Mulvey had attempted to do to his Flower of the Mountain under the Moorish wall), but for more than a decade he has failed. His own guilt over this failure appears in his cry of 'forgive' (541.29). Molly has engineered the failure, but, at the same time as she continues to reject complete intercourse, she resents Bloom's acceptance of her domination, his failure to cull and to pluck.

Molly's present fear of pregnancy, or at least her determination to avoid pregnancy, is quite clear. She makes Boylan withdraw, but at the final encounter, either because she is carried away with passion and pleasure and domination, or, perhaps, because like Bloom she too, at least subconsciously, wants a son, she allows the act to go its full course. On 778.27–28 she indicates that she wants a son, as we have seen, and some fearful guilt that she too, as well as Bloom, might be at fault brings her to denial, 'it wasnt my fault'. But most interesting and puzzling is a further statement a few lines later, 'But I knew well Id never have another'. This cannot mean that she was aware of some physical cause that would make further childbearing impossible, because she has already revealed, as we have seen above, that she might 'risk' having another, though not off Boylan. She wants Bloom's child, if any, though she does fear that he might be for it a principle of death. Possibly Bloom shares her conviction that Boylan would have 'a fine strong child', and this may be a subconscious factor in Bloom's accepting and even arranging Molly's tryst with Boylan (Molly thinks that is why, in 'the way he plots and plans everything out', he sent Milly to Mullingar, 766.16).

Molly's knowing that she'd never have another son must flow from her determination not to go through the horrors of pregnancy, birth, and upbringing again. Hence I judge, as I now see the matter, that Molly has been the dominant force in the unhappy sexual relationship which has existed for so long at 7 Eccles street. That there are signs of a possible change in this relationship emerges from a consideration of Molly's developing attitude in the eight sentences, particularly in the matter of eggs for breakfast (which will be a major theme in *Finnegans Wake*).

Molly has from time to time been criticized for her cold attitude toward her children.[14] She is, in general, somewhat self-centred and unable, apparently, to think of anyone else's good except in some relation to her own. But in this she is not different from most humans, I should judge. And granted this situation, her attitude toward her children appears healthy and even loving.

She is somewhat jealous of Milly. The onset of Milly's 'catamenic hemorrhage' nine months and one day ago brought about some kind of new relationship between the mother and daughter which had further limited both mental and physical intercourse between mother and father (736.16–24). Sultan suggests, and convincingly, that at this point Milly becomes, in the parents' view, an adult, and thus they are no longer bound together by the one tenuous bond which has so far operated—their mutual concern for their child. Molly's thoughts circle around Milly for some three pages (766–768) besides numerous brief glances, and certainly Molly wants the best for her daughter. She blames herself as well as her daughter in the matter of the '2 damn fine cracks across the ear' (768.5), and once again blames Bloom for not dominating and correcting Milly's 'faith' (the dogma involved is that knives should not be crossed, 768.10). Molly grieves over Rudy, and turns her thoughts abruptly from him only because she has so often experienced the despondency and 'glooms' which his death brought. She finds there too, as Bloom had done, one reason for their strained and noncommunicative sexual and emotional relationship. Hence it is clear that she is far from being the unfeeling and selfish woman some have thought her. She is not the ideal mother, as she is not the ideal woman. But she seems to have done the best she could,

---

[14] '. . . Molly's rejection of her live daughter and her dead son point up further the weakness of her maternal instincts and the strength of her self-love'. Erwin R. Steinberg, 'A Book with A Molly in It', *James Joyce Review*, II, 1–2 (Spring-Summer 1958), 58.

granted her limitations, for Milly, and the little woolly jacket is some indication that she would have done the same for Rudy.

In her attitude toward her husband, Molly reveals little that is new to the reader of the previous fourteen chapters. She had seen Bloom as physically attractive, Byronic indeed, as had several other women, Josie in the past, Gertie in the present (though Bloom was careful not to show Gertie his profile; perhaps he thought she might be put off by his semitic nose). Molly sees Bloom as a tireless plotter and planner, endlessly thinking up schemes for the improvement of the universe, as we have seen him doing all day. She sees him as the pimp for Boylan, as indeed in the 'Circe' chapter he was dramatically portrayed. Her thoughts touch only lightly on this aspect of Bloom's motivations, since they are apparently not clear to her. But she intuits Bloom's subconscious desire for her to have an affair with Boylan, and she observes his management of it—the removal of Milly, the statement that he would not be home for dinner, his tension in dealing with Boylan's letter and the time Boylan would arrive, etc. She puts the blame on Bloom if she is an adulteress, and with some justification. As with Bertha in *Exiles*, who resents her husband's complicated motives in leaving her free, Molly judges she would never have been in the situation where this particular adultery, at least, could have been effected if Bloom had not plotted it. And she seems to realize that Bloom wants from it a vicarious sexual experience with her, an exculpation of his guilt over his own failure to dominate her refusal to adequate intercourse, a possible legal son for himself, and perhaps a position for himself as wronged husband ('coronado', 777.9), where domination will become possible for him. At any rate, one or more of these reasons must be operative when she says '. . . no hed never have the courage with a married woman thats why he wants me and Boylan though as for her Denis . . .' (773.13). She is evidently thinking that Bloom would be afraid of the husband, although Denis would be not much threat. But the 'thats why' is then puzzling. Does she mean that Boylan has the necessary courage which Bloom lacks, and Bloom, realizing this, steps aside for Molly's sake and from his own guilt feelings? Or does she mean that Bloom knows that no husband will cause difficulties in this case? Or that Bloom might avoid married women, not only from fear of the husband, but from fear that his son might thus be the legal heir of another man (this is obviously not likely, but not altogether impossible)—and thus would approve of Boylan's affair with Molly in the hope of having a fine healthy legal heir himself? Probably she simply means that Bloom, fearful and guilty himself, approves of the affair because he needs forgiveness from Molly, and having achieved it in her acceptance of a lover, he can assume a more dominant role himself.

Molly contrasts Boylan's crudity not only with Stephen's imagined elegance but with Bloom's real gentility, his insight into what a woman wants, his consideration for a woman's feelings. Gardner indeed could outdo Bloom in some love-play, but this was during the period of Molly's Calypso-like enslavement of Bloom, and, in any case, Bloom has, in the past, satisfied her as no other man has ever done, and he had more spunk in him than has Boylan— i.e., more opportunity for fertility if not more virility. Molly does toy with the notion of a break-up in their marriage, as Bloom also had done, but as her monologue progresses it becomes more and more clear that she will accept Bloom now, as she basically desires to do, on a new level, as a Penelope rather than as a Calypso. She will move from her first Calypso-word in the book, a mumbled 'no', to her final acceptance of the Penelope role in her ecstatic final 'Yes'. The breakfast which Bloom demands and which she finally determines to provide is the most obvious evidence of a new and healthier relationship. As in *Finnegans Wake*, those breakfast eggs may indicate a break with the past and a sunnier future: '. . . iggs for the brekkers . . . sunny side up with care' (*FW*, 12.14). The eggs for breakfast, also symbols of communion at Mass in *Finnegans Wake*, precede the Resurrection, the new beginning. The words of the life-giving letter are 'scribings scrawled on eggs' (*FW*, 615.10). These eggs too may symbolize, as in *Finnegans Wake*, a more perfect communication, a word analogous to the Word announced by Gabriel and uttered by Christ's Church—'oewfs à la Madame Gabrielle de l'Eglise' (*FW*, 184.27).

Molly, narcissistic in many ways, like the women of *Chamber Music* or, on another level, like the sow devouring her farrow, thinks of Stephen as another object she might ingest. She compares him (imagined) to Bloom's little statue of Narcissus, as godlike, a young and desirable lover. In her eighth sentence, she does, like Bloom, briefly consider Stephen in relation to Rudy, thinking of Stephen's not being appreciated as the fine son he is (in her imagination), and implying that if she had a son like him she would appreciate him (778.27–28). But principally, in her seventh sentence, she adds a bit to his age in order to make him more suitable as a lover. She thinks she might find in Stephen the poetry she had mistakenly hoped to find in Bloom, and she dreams of herself as the inspirer of a great poet. She imagines the conversations they might have about Molly herself—'itll be a change the Lord knows to have an intelligent person to talk to about yourself' (775.31)—and sees their two photographs in all the papers (776.18); she will be another 'Mrs Langtry the Jersey Lily the prince of Wales was in love with' (751.27). Her picture of Stephen has little to do with the fearful, brilliant, introspective, ineffectual character we have followed from his babyhood to the early morning urination of 17 June 1904, and it shares, in its romantic gushiness, some touch of Gerty MacDowell's portrait of Bloom. Molly is far more practical about her daydreams, however, and does weave into her rhythmic and flowing thoughts (775.23–31) musical scraps of the songs Bloom remembers her singing before their marriage, while he turned the pages for her (275.23–28).

There is considerable irony for us, the readers of the book, in Molly's aspirations toward drawing the cynical and perceptive Stephen into her orbit. We have seen, in the dying, cliché-ridden language of 'Eumaeus' and in the *rigor mortis* of 'Ithaca', Bloom's pitiful efforts to make intellectual contact with Stephen. We can be well aware that Molly, with her poorly educated mind, her malapropisms, her conventional attitudes, her vulgar tastes, her relatively complacent egocentricity, would fare far worse with Stephen than Bloom has done, especially if she expected him to respond favorably to the bits of poetry she would learn 'off by heart' (776.13). And, of course, if Molly knew or could know Stephen as we know him, she could never cast him in the glamorous roles she dreams up. Joyce wrote to Nora, it is true, of the fame she would enjoy as the lover and inspirer of a great artist,[15] and something of this attitude of his no doubt seeps into Molly's dreams of Stephen, but it is more true, as a number of us students and critics of Joyce's work have yet to learn, that Stephen is not Joyce and that Molly is not Nora.

[15] 'I hope that the day may come when I shall be able to give you the fame of being beside me when I have entered into my Kingdom'. *Letters*, II, 309.

Molly shares with Stephen a fear of thunder, but her reaction to the thunderclap, the same that hits the heart of Stephen as he heard the Father Dolan-like voice from the street (394.32–36), was to ward off the punishment of heaven with a sign of the cross and a Hail Mary (741.34–37). Her religion is much like that of Mrs Kernan in 'Grace', a mixture of poorly digested doctrine and superstition. Her religious instruction can be gauged by her information to Bloom that the I.N.R.I. over the cross (*Jesus Nazarenus Rex Judaeorum*) means Iron Nails Ran In, and that I.H.S., a graphic symbol for 'Jesus' written in Greek capitals, means I Have Suffered. Her faith seems to be based on the common-sense assumption that somebody had to create what exists, and on her version of no atheists in foxholes (782.2–11). Yet she is honest enough to admit that she knows no more about the matter than do the atheists. She considers crossed knives an offence against faith (768.9–12). She shares with Calypso, with Circe, with the woman of *Chamber Music*, No. 24, and with the Temptress of the Villanelle a quality of witchery, of enchantment, that she expressed, for one thing, in her fortune-telling. She shares a name and a birthday with the Blessed Virgin, and like the Mystical Rose, Molly is also a rose, sometimes a white one, symbol of virginity, sometimes a red one, symbol of the blood of martyrdom.[16] The blood in Molly's case is that from the ruptured hymen, the immolation of virginity, and from the menstrual flow, the sign of 'the handmaid of the moon' (47.39), which leads Molly's thoughts around once again to the lily, symbol of the purity of Mary and the name of Edward VII's mistress (770.12).

Molly is connected, too, with the Mass imagery with which *Ulysses* begins and which develops throughout the book.[17] This appears most obviously in her thoughts of Bloom threatening to kneel down, to the danger of his new raincoat, in the wet, if she would not lift her orange petticoat with the sunray pleats (746.30–36). A number of themes coalesce in this particular instance of Bloom's worship of Molly—the golden-haired girl of *Chamber Music*, the sunlight as nymph, the worship of goddesses, water and urine, sacrifice and ritual, the vestments of the Mass.

---

[16] Cf. the treatment of this traditional imagery in Hopkins's 'Rosa Mystica' and in his *Deutschland: The Poems of Gerard Manley Hopkins*, 4th ed., Oxford, 1967, pp. 38–40, 58.

[17] Cf. my article, 'The Priesthoods of Stephen and of Buck', in *Approaches to Ulysses*.

In *Chamber Music*, the youthful Joyce set down several impressions of women which he developed in later characters, including Molly, and brought to a climax in Anna Livia Plurabelle and Issy. The woman of No. 24, with a looking-glass companion like Issy's, foreshadows Molly in her self-centred attention to her hair, and on the selfish witchery which harms her relationship to her lover (the ambiguity of 'negligence' in the last line of No. 24, meaning charming negligent movements and a neglect of her lover, gives the poem considerable depth). Here are the final two stanzas:

> *I pray you, cease to comb out,*
> *Comb out your long hair,*
> *For I have heard of witchery*
> *Under a pretty air,*
>
> *That makes as one thing to the lover*
> *Staying and going hence,*
> *All fair, with many a pretty air*
> *And many a negligence.*

The woman of No. 26 has a divining ear as she listens to threatening rivers rushing forth, and fears the future as Coleridge and Shakespeare, in *The Ancient Mariner* and in *Macbeth*, have taught us to fear the ghosts of the past. Tindall thinks (*CM*, 212) that this lady is 'the first study' for Molly Bloom, as she hears 'that soft choiring of delight' within her chamber and has a horror of the waters from the north; thus Molly listens to her waters and has a horror of the chamber breaking under her. I do think that Tindall reaches very far for his comparison (Molly's waters, for example, surely sound from the south), but I'm less inclined than I used to be to dismiss Tindall's insights concerning the connexions of Joyce's early poems with his mature creations. The 'Goldenhair' of No. 5, the turning from amethyst to deeper blue in No. 2, and above all, the love in light attire of No. 7 furnish themes Joyce develops in *Ulysses* and *Finnegans Wake*. And for Molly lifting her petticoat, as well as for Molly on the chamber-pot (cf. the dainty scented jewelled hand of 551.18, the girls on the Dublin coat of arms, the urinating girls in the park, Issy on the chamber-pot, etc., in *Finnegans Wake*) the narcissistic girl of No. 7 furnishes, according to Tindall's interpretation, an admirable model, as the final stanza demonstrates:

And where the sky's a pale blue cup
Over the laughing land,
My love goes lightly, holding up
Her dress with dainty hand.

In No. 25, the girl is urged

Oread let thy laughter run
Till the irreverent mountain air
Ripple all thy flying hair.

That nymph, combined with the goldenhaired girl, appears in *Ulysses* as sunlight, running toward Mr Bloom as he returns to the scene of his 'sixteen years of black slave labour' (554.3) under Calypso: 'Quick warm sunlight came running from Berkeley Road, swiftly, in slim sandals, along the brightening footpath. Runs, she runs to meet me, a girl with gold hair on the wind' (61.32).

Another nymph, revered by Bloom, who rescued her from 'Photo Bits', kissed her in four places, and with loving pencil shaded her eyes, her bosom, and her shame (546.6–7), watches over his marriage bed. Like the girls of *Chamber Music*, with hair unbound and lightly clad, she descends through incense from her grotto to receive Bloom's adoring prayer (546.11).

Bloom worships woman. As the boy in 'Araby', inspired by Mangan's sister, carried his chalice, and as Stephen raised the chalice to the Temptress of the Villanelle, Bloom has worshipped the 'mesial grooves' of several goddesses during this crucial day and before. He wished to bend in the Museum to examine, and admire, the ample circles of the goddesses; Buck Mulligan gave a perceptive account: 'His pale Galilean eyes were upon her mesial groove. Venus Kallipyge. O, the thunder of those loins. *The god pursuing the maiden hid*' (201.10). Bloom had admired the undergarments of Gerty 'high up above her knee' (366.31), and paid tribute, 'literally worshipping at her shrine' (361.42), with incense in the background. Similarly he had earlier, as he recalls in 'Circe' in a context of the sound of urine in the chamber pot, melodiously expressed in the name, sometimes onomotopoetically altered, of Poulaphouca Waterfall, 'sacrificed to the god of the forest' in masturbation after watching Lotty Clarke rolling downhill, as he had previously watched her, flaxenhaired, at her night toilette through ill-closed curtains (549.16–20). This again recalls *Chamber Music*, and prepares for

Molly's musings on Penrose, Dixon, and the Gibraltar neighbour peeping through the window at her. Bloom had paid tribute also to Mary Driscoll in four places (461.11–12) and offered her emerald garters (460.28). Molly thinks that Mary padded her 'false bottom' to excite him, and she discovered the garters (739.25, 40). Molly's own violet garters, recalled in a context of the strings of chamber music, from Coleridge's dulcimer-playing girl ('Night sky moon, violet, colour of Molly's new garters. Strings. Listen. A girl playing one of these instruments what do you call them: dulcimers', 57.30–32), recall the shifts to the colour of the Blessed Virgin in *Chamber Music*, No. 2, as the girl plays her piano.

> Shy thoughts and grave wide eyes and hands
> That wander as they list—
> The twilight turns to darker blue
> With lights of amethyst.

Another nymph, or siren, uses her garter to make music and tell time for Boylan (266.32–41), and Boylan worships with the sloe gin Molly will smell later (741.24–26). Boylan 'tossed to fat lips his chalice, drankoff his tiny chalice, sucking the last fat violet syrupy drops' (267.1), recalling the priest Bloom watched earlier: 'The priest was rinsing out the chalice: then he tossed off the dregs smartly' (81.37).

Bloom sets up the Black Mass symbolism for his adoration of Molly's rear when he says 'Peccavi! I have paid homage on that living altar where the back changes name' (551.16). Thus his kiss on Molly's anus, like the kiss prescribed for the Black Mass, both expresses the dog-theme ('Dogs at each other behind', 375.9) and suggests the possibility of a return to a previous and life-producing homage on Howth Hill sixteen years before, an aspect of the god-theme.

Joyce's use of urination as an image of creative activity is too well known to need establishing here.[18] Its connexion with the Mass symbolism in *Ulysses* is perhaps not so obvious. Buck Mulligan sets up the theme in two passages in the first chapter. First in Mother Grogan, who makes tea and water, but not, Mrs Cahill hopes, in the one pot (12.31–38). The making of water into wine, as in Mulligan's

---

[18] E.g., William York Tindall, A Reader's Guide to James Joyce, London and New York, 1959, *passim*, and Clive Hart, *Structure and Motif in Finnegans Wake*, London and Evanston, Ill., 1962, pp. 206–208.

song (19.8–11), is linked to Mother Grogan's tea, since Mulligan suggests that those who deny Christ's divinity will be drinking his urine rather than his blood. This recalls Mr Casey's story in the Christmas dinner scene (AP, 28) about Christy 'manufacturing that champagne for those fellows', which is based, I am told, on a story with many variations of a workman mistaking a pail of beer left at the foot of the ladder for a urinal and contributing to its content. I expect this is why Edward the Seventh, in 'Circe', carries *a plasterer's bucket on which is printed:* Défense d'uriner' (590.23). The drinking of urine in relation to sacramental communion Joyce uses in *Finnegans Wake* as he also uses urine in relation to the true artist making the caustic ink by which he will produce the true word that will not pass away (*FW*, 185–186). Buck Mulligan returns to the urination theme, in 'Telemachus', as he describes old Mary Ann's preparation for urinating as 'hising up her petticoats' (13.20–22).

The petticoats keep showing up in religious contexts. Stephen, while he urinates on the strand, sees the weeds 'hising up their petticoats' in religious terms. He quotes St Ambrose, from his Commentary on Romans.[19] Paul is speaking of creation, longing for its deliverance from the slavery imposed by Adam's sin, and Stephen thinks of a weary woman, naked like the Temptress of the Villanelle, vainly drawing a toil of waters (49–50). Later he thinks that his sister, eyes and seaweed hair, will drown him miserable in agenbite, heart and soul (243.27–29). He thus unites urination, the waters of the sea, the activity of the moon, his fear of woman and of involvement, the allure of naked women, and the hising of petticoats.

On the opening page Buck, in yellow dressinggown, ungirdled, pretends to turn wine into blood. In the Black Mass (599.8–30), he wears a petticoat as he elevates the blooddripping host, and this petticoat is hised by Haines Love to reveal the mesial semi-groove with its significant carrot. Molly's petticoat is connected with the Mass (and with Mulligan's two blasphemous elevations) when she recalls thinking of Mulvey 'on the sea all the time after at mass when my petticoat began to slip down at the elevation' (762.13). Thus when Bloom wishes Molly to lift her petticoat, orange like her chamber-pot, gold like Buck's dressinggown, with its sun-rays from the sun like the nymph (with Molly as Earth-Goddess rotating around the sun), and this in the rain, one can perhaps perceive

[19] Thornton, p. 65.

that Bloom is worshipping once again the source of human life.[20] Further, in the Latin passage in which Shem operates as priest of the eternal imagination in *Finnegans Wake*, page 185,[21] Joyce uses 'pluviale' for the priest's outer garment. That meant 'raincoat' for the ancient Romans, as it means cope or chasuble for the current clerical ones. Thus Bloom's possibly ruining his new raincoat by kneeling in the wet, unless the goddess with dainty hand lifts her special petticoat, indicates that Bloom, too (like the cowled Stephen with his Temptress, and blue-tied and blue-socked Boylan with his Siren [or surpliced like a priest with Molly, 'in the half of a shirt they wear to be admired like a priest' 776.27], and petticoated Buck with Mina Purefoy, and blackgarbed Bloom with many of the women he has seen) is in his raincoat a vested priest worshipping at a shrine.[22] In the final pages of the book, therefore, the imagery and symbolism of the opening are recalled, and in this mixture of Mass and petticoat imagery we can see one more preparation for the final mixing of Mulvey and Bloom, her first and last worshippers, in Molly's imagination.

The eight sentences, rolling toward that climactic mixing, fore-shadow the Viconian fours of *Finnegans Wake* and even provide

[20] Joyce's connexions of spinning earth, of sun, of gold (cf. 'Chrysostomos' of 3.28 and 'splendid set of teeth' of 746.30—the gold is transferred from Buck's teeth to Molly's petticoat, but Molly's observing Bloom's teeth parallels Stephen's bitter observation of Buck's), and of petticoats appears in the final lines of a poem Joyce wrote in honour of Molly:

> *May you live, may you love like this gaily spinning*
> *earth of ours,*
> *And every morn a gallous sun awake you to fresh wealth*
> *of gold,*
> *But if I cling like a child to the clouds that are*
> *your petticoats,*
> *O Molly, handsome Molly, sure you won't let me die?*
> Herbert Gorman, *James Joyce*, New York,
> 1939, pp. 282–283.

The passage appears in Ellmann, p. 561, where 'gallous sun' has been trans-mogrified to 'gallous son'.

[21] I discuss this passage in detail in my article, '*Finnegans Wake*, Page 185: an Explication', *JJQ*, IV, 1 (Fall 1966), 3–16.

[22] Sultan, p. 401, says in relation to Bloom's lighting of incense in 'Ithaca': 'None of the many uses of incense in Church ritual with which his action has been associated enlightens it'. Sultan is right and illuminating in his discussion of fumigation, but he is a bit too exclusive in ruling out the connexion with ritual. Bloom will shortly be adoring in the shrine upstairs, as Sultan also notes, p. 446.

an analogue for the arrangement of Book One of *Finnegans Wake*. In the eight chapters of Book One, as I read them, the opening four are predominantly male, the second four predominantly female. In the 'Penelope' chapter, at any rate, the first four sentences are governed principally by the mature Molly, 33 years old. The second group of four is loosely governed by young Molly, 15–18 years old. The first sentence corresponds somewhat with the fifth, the second with the sixth, and so on. To some extent, each sentence is a unit whose ending echoes its beginning.

The first sentence, beginning with the female word 'yes', begins on 738, with a man's upsetting demand upon a woman and ends, on 744, with the possibility of brutal men hanging a woman. It deals largely with Bloom, in the City Arms Hotel, his reaction to seeing Boylan's advances, his questions, his Byronic appearance, his superiority to Breen. The sentence ends with Molly's mixed feelings about Mrs Maybrick, the husband-poisoner.

The second sentence, 744–753, deals mostly with the men Molly has encountered, and winds its repetitious way through their differences—Boylan, Bartell d'Arcy, Bloom, Gardner, Boylan, Griffith, Gardner, Mastiansky, Bloom (Molly not too old, other women, flagellation, Blessed Virgin), and ends with Mr Cuffe's looking at her breasts.

The third short, hectic, and passionate sentence, 753–754, begins with Boylan at her breasts and ends with Boylan in coition with her, with musings on bodies and men, Penrose peeping, and sexual pleasures pantingly mixed together.

The fourth sentence, 754–759, begins with the strength of men and ends with the weakness of women. After opening with Bloom's carelessness, we deal largely with women, mainly Hester Stanhope, the young Molly's Gibraltar friend, with her postcard, and with letters from other women, and we end with Boylan's letter to Molly and her possible response. So, though this sentence does deal at its beginning and ending with the mature Molly, it largely prepares for the next group of four stressing the young Molly, and balances the final sentence with its Gibraltar memories.

The fifth sentence, 759–763, begins with Mulvey, his letter of invitation, the Moorish wall, the first passionate kiss, and ends with Bloom making even the passing of wind difficult. Bloom is foreshadowed in Don Miguel de la Flora; Molly ties up rousing Mulvey with rousing the dog in the hotel, which perhaps provides a background for the associations which led her to such passionate desire when she saw the two dogs copulating in 'the naked street' (778.30); she arranges Mulvey's hat, apparently against his will, with the significant name Calypso on it; she thinks of her mother, Lunita Laredo, of Milly, of giving Mulvey's ring to Gardner, of L.O.S.S., of singers, of Gardner as an Englishman, of singing, of Bloom, and ends, as did the 'Sirens' chapter, combining music and farting.

The sixth sentence, 763–770, begins with winds and ends with waters. Her thoughts return to Gibraltar, her big doll, the mountains, the man peeping; then Bloom's order for eggs bothers her again; a long section on Milly (cf. Bloom's 'Molly. Milly. Same thing watered down', 89.18) follows, then thoughts of Stephen, then menstruation, then adultery, the 'its pouring out of me like the sea' (769.24)—the imagery gets bigger, of mountains and giants and of sea—and ends with Molly on the chamber pot.

The seventh sentence, 770–776, begins with the thoughts of Molly before her marriage to Bloom, meanders on through her first meeting with Bloom, their sixteen years together, the funeral, Stephen on the cards, an affair with Stephen,[23] and ends abruptly with Boylan (or Bloom?) as an impediment to youthful adventure.

The eighth sentence, 776–783, begins with the crudity of Boylan and ends with the desirability of Mulvey-Bloom. In the first sixteen words there are eight negatives dealing with Boylan (possibly, in my theory of Joyce's symbolic use of 8 in this chapter, indicating denial or retraction of the 'permission' he had usurped to control the totality of Molly's genital area); and in the last sixteen words there are four yes's (returning to Bloom at least the possibility of control of the top half of the 8, an extension of his homage on that living altar where the back changes name, 538.16–17). Boylan is like an old rough Lion (Gilbert points out the appropriateness of the capitalized Lion to the Gea-Tellus symbolism); Molly of course is in bed with a milder Leo. Sex, women and desires, romance, Don Poldo on the cards, his breakfast order, women in charge of the world, Stephen, dogs, Rudy, women bitches, Stephen, breakfast—and she determines to get up to get breakfast, a climactic

[23] Sultan, with great insight, demonstrates (pp. 441–444) how thoughts of Stephen lead Molly from Boylan to a return to Bloom.

decision (780.6–7). Her sleepy thoughts roll on through Bloom and
Boylan, Bloom to blame, plan for money, white rose, roses, nature
and God, seedcake on Howth (Bloom, in his sleepy thoughts on
377.6–9, had looked at Howth and thought of that first encounter),
of Mulvey (as Bloom, going to sleep on 382.16–17, also thought
of the young Molly and Mulvey), of Gibraltar. And finally, mixing
together the two most important events in her life, her first kiss
('First kiss does the trick', Bloom thinks at 371.9) under the Moorish Wall and her first coition on Howth Hill, she unites the young
Molly and the mature Molly in her great final acceptance and
affirmation.

A brief comparison of a sampling of balancing elements in the
two groups of sentences may help to demonstrate my theory that
the sentences do correspond in significant ways and to bolster the
general, if shadowy, dominance of the mature Molly in the first
group and of the young Molly in the second:

First Sentence	Fifth Sentence
(a) Bloom's demand.	(a) Mulvey's invitation.
(b) Bloom's slavery to Calypso.	(b) Mulvey's hat (H.M.S. Calypso) straightened by Molly.
(c) Bloom's affairs: ejaculation, lusts, questionings.	(c) Mulvey's kiss: ejaculation, desires, hopes.
(d) Byronic Bloom.	(d) Mythical Don Miguel de la Flora.

Second Sentence	Sixth Sentence
(a) Men desiring women.	(a) Bloom's ordering breakfast (desiring a wife).
(b) Molly not too old.	(b) 15-year-old Milly.
(c) Breasts.	(c) Womb.

Third Sentence	Seventh Sentence
(a) Breasts.	(a) Insides.
(b) Molly attractive to Boylan.	(b) Molly attractive to Bloom at their first meeting.
(c) Bed with Boylan.	(c) Bed with Bloom.
(d) Copulation with Boylan.	(d) Possible copulation with Stephen.

Fourth Sentence	*Eighth Sentence*
(a) Strength of men, Bloom's carelessness.	(a) Crudity of Boylan.
(b) Women (dogs).	(b) Women bitches.
(c) Forced yielding of women.	(c) Willing yielding of women.
(d) Despondent comparison of acceptable young and discarded old women.	(d) Triumphant assertion of the life force in young and in mature woman.[24]

Some five years ago, in an attempt to show the structure of *Ulysses* as analogous to a huge sonata form, I wrote of the 'Penelope' chapter as a great coda, restating the themes of the book in a tonality, in rhythms, in attitudes quite different from those in the main body of the work. I said then: 'In feminine tonality, Molly in random structure states Usurper (the Suitors, with Stephen as a possible, Boylan as actual), History (her own lifetime, much of Bloom, a touch of Stephen), and Reality—a life-in-death attitude of assent to sterile, dog-like sex pleasure'.[25] Molly's 'Yes' I saw as a negative thing, and, indeed, I still do. But even then I was aware that this was not the whole story. I said in my concluding paragraph: 'Nor does Joyce reflect a closed world of evil. He leaves infinite room for the operation of awesome mystery. We see and feel in his characters effects—frustrations, pressures, unhappiness, fears, longings—for which no merely natural explanations are satisfactory'.[26] I was thinking most of all of Molly, with her frustrations and psychic warping occasioned by her mother (I am inclined to think, from Molly's silence on the matter and her somewhat resentful tone about never having a mother, that her mother had deserted husband and daughter), her suppressed grief over her son, her growing and passionate desires for a better life than the one she now has. So I did not even then see Molly as all dog.

But Molly as bitch loomed largest in my mind. Molly shocked me deeply when I first encountered her, and her good qualities were overwhelmed, for me, by many of the bad things Morse and Steinberg stress, plus the offence to the moral codes I myself then

[24] Sultan traces another significant motion through the sentences, from a descending rejection of Bloom through the first four to its 'nadir' (Sultan, p. 436) to a rising acceptance of Bloom through the second four (Sultan, p. 439).

[25] '*Ulysses* as Frustrated Sonata Form', *JJQ*, II, 4 (Summer 1965), 251.

[26] *Ibid.*, p. 254.

stressed too confidently. Further, I reacted against Tindalls' happy-ending views, where charity clearly triumphs and we walk into the sunrise with thunderous triumphant chordal 'yeses' all around us.

But the emphasis has shifted, for me. I am now more favourable to Tindall's (and Sultan's) positive attitude toward Molly's affirmation of life than I have been heretofore. But I can by no means accept that as the whole story (nor, for that matter, can Sultan do so). It is one facet of a great complex whole wherein the forces of evil operate strongly too. The evil in Molly, as well as the evil in her environment, once struck me as dominant. Right now the good in Molly, and the real possible good in her environment (dependent largely on the attitudes, the decisions, the love of not only Molly but of those too with whom she communicates) seem to me dominant.

But I am not settling down in these opinions. Molly is a mystery, as is reality, and I anticipate that in ten years, if I should still be around and *compos*, she may look quite different to me.[27] From my first view of her, she has been fascinating, and she still is, and, I anticipate, will always be—a woman of infinite variety. But I do not expect ever to comprehend her. I am no Theseus, who demanded that reason conquer imagination, that cool reason wipe away the apprehension of strange things with the comprehension of solvable matters—a Shaun! I am content, with Bully Bottom, to realize that I am but an ass when I assay to expound Joyce's wonderful dream. But an ass can sometimes be useful.

When I said above that Joyce was not satisfied with 'merely natural explanations'—no phenomenologist he!—I did not mean to imply that Joyce sought his ultimate solutions in Christian dogma, as, for example, Hopkins does in his 'Heraclitean Fire' sonnet, or that Joyce would take seriously the theosophy of Æ, the mysticism of Yeats, or even the philosophy of Vico. As Ellmann so powerfully

---

[27] I take it, from a consideration of Joyce's famous dream about Molly (cf. Gorman, p. 283n, also in Ellmann, pp. 560–561), that something like this happened to Joyce. As I diffidently interpret this writing on the wall, Joyce was in accord with Bloom in attempting to bring Molly to a decision to bear another son, to institute a new dawn in their relationship. But Molly, in this dream, asserts her autonomy, and her throwing the child's coffin after the retreating Bloom signifies her refusal to cooperate. Joyce's passion, and his conviction that she has misunderstood the chapter in which she exists, merely brings upon him the same rejection as she throws at her creator, her Shem, a sham coffin.

expresses the matter in his comparison of Yeats and Joyce: 'Yeats's mind generated, out of feelings of indignation and pain, images of perfection; Joyce said he preferred the footprint seen on the sand by Robinson Crusoe to the eternal city envisioned by John'.[28] Joyce deals with the human experience in the middle and lower-class citizens of Dublin, and so vividly that he deals with the human race too. But he deals with more than that, since in the human experience there are mystery and chaos and strange inexplicable things. Joyce is no bloodless humanist, like MacLeish in *J.B.* or, on a lower level, like Steinbeck in *Grapes of Wrath.* The blood of mysterious, frightening, inspiring, infinitely alluring and demanding reality flows through his humanism, and makes it live. He makes us see, to apprehend, what it means to be both evil and good, to be drawn and influenced by both hell and heaven. 'Astroglodynamono-logos' is his word for the artist (*FW,* 194.16)—the 'aster' of the heavens, the 'troglodyte' of the bowels of the earth, but dynamically and alone bringing forth the lifegiving *logos,* 'creating at last a conscience in the soul of this wretched race'.[29] Molly takes her place among the great characters of our literature because she escapes cool reason and shows to any mind willing to apprehend without comprehending

> . . . *something of great constancy,*
> *But, howsoever, strange and admirable.*
> *Midsummer Night's Dream,*
> V.i.26–27.

[28] *Eminent Domain,* Oxford, 1967, p. 54.
[29] *Letters,* II, 311.